中华传统美德

Great Virtues in the Chinese Tradition

蔡向升 骆承烈 编著

Compiled by Cai Xiangsheng Luo Chenglie

胡宗锋【英国】罗宾·吉尔班克 译

Translated by Hu Zongfeng Robin Gilbank

群言出版社

QUNYAN PRESS

·北 京·

图书在版编目（CIP）数据

中华传统美德 ： 汉、英 ／ 蔡向升，骆承烈编著 ；
胡宗锋，（英）罗宾·吉尔班克译 . -- 北京 ： 群言出版
社，2025. 3. -- ISBN 978-7-5193-1050-9

Ⅰ . D648

中国国家版本馆 CIP 数据核字第 20250HQ953 号

策划编辑： 李满意
责任编辑： 陈　芳
封面设计： 厚海文化

出版发行： 群言出版社
地　　址： 北京市东城区东厂胡同北巷1号（100006）
网　　址： www.qypublish.com（官网书城）
电子信箱： qunyancbs@126.com
联系电话： 010-65267783　65263836
法律顾问： 北京法政安邦律师事务所
经　　销： 全国新华书店

印　　刷： 西安雁展印务有限公司
版　　次： 2025年3月第1版
印　　次： 2025年3月第1次印刷
开　　本： 710mm×1000mm　1/16
印　　张： 25
字　　数： 368千字
书　　号： ISBN 978-7-5193-1050-9
定　　价： 120.00元

编著者简介

蔡向升，研究员。2006 年任山西大学非遗研究中心研究员，2011—2013 年受聘北京大学历史文化研究所研究员与北京大学地理学专业博士研究生指导老师，2012 年任山西大学杨家将研究所副所长，2016 年任神木市政协文史专员，2017 年创建神木希文书院任院长。2003—2022 年共出版著作 17 部，如《杨家将研究·历史卷》《神木中学文献长编》《中华传统美德》（中文版、中英文版、汉语拼音版）《神木历史地理沿革》《神木历史文化地图》等。

骆承烈，教授。1935 年 5 月生于山东省济宁市，1956 年毕业于山东师范大学历史系。任曲阜师范大学孔子文化学院副院长、儒学史专业硕士生导师，兼任中华传统文化促进会顾问、中国智慧工程研究会学术顾问、孔子文化全球传播委员会专家顾问团副团长。先后获中国广电学会"百家奖"一等奖、中国科技部"发明创新奖"等。

译者简介

胡宗锋，1962年生，陕西凤翔县人。现任中国翻译协会常务理事，陕西省决策咨询委员会委员，陕西省翻译协会主席，陕西斯诺研究中心主任，陕西省汉语国际教育研究会副会长，西京学院外国语学院院长。美国伊里诺依大学高级访问学者。曾任第十一届民建中央文化委员会委员，第十二届西安市政协
委员、西北大学外国语学院院长。担任英美文学、英汉（汉英）翻译理论与实践方向以及MTI硕士生导师，戏剧影视翻译与跨文化研究博士生导师。2024年被中国翻译协会授予"资深翻译家"称号。

罗宾·吉尔班克（Robin Gilbank），1981年生，英国北约克郡人，中世纪英语文学博士（英国阿伯瑞斯特大学）。现为西京学院外国语学院教授、翻译专业硕士导师。出版有英文专著《最美丽的谎言家》《罗宾博士看陕西》《探究中国》等。与人合译的英文作品有贾平凹的《废都》《土门》，叶
广芩作品选《山地故事》，吴克敬作品集《血太阳》，《贾平凹散文选》（汉英），杨争光作品选《老旦是一棵树》，张岂之著作《中国历史文化导论》等。2018年被中国授予"中国改革开放40周年最具影响力的四十位外国专家"，2019年被授予"西安荣誉市民"称号。

目　录

第一章　中华贤母

第二章　正道教子

第三章　诚敬孝亲

第五章　尊师重教

第六章　夫妻和谐

第七章 诚实守信

第八章　清廉俭朴

第九章 卫国利民

第十章 改革创新

CONTENT

Chapter Two:
Teaching Children the Right Way

Chapter Three:
Honoring Parents with Sincerity and Reverence

Chapter Four:
Diligence and Love for Learning

Chapter Five

Respecting Teachers and Emphasising Education

Chapter Six:

Harmonious Marriage

Chapter Seven:
Honesty and Keeping One's Word

Chapter Eight：

Upholding Integrity and Simplicity

Chapter Nine：

Defending the Nation and Benefiting the People

Chapter Ten:
Reform and Innovation

第一章
中华贤母

Chapter One:

Epitomes of Maternal Devotion and Love in China

一、人文始祖（女娲氏）

我国古代传说中，伏羲、女娲结婚，繁衍了人类。又有女娲抟土造人、炼石补天等传说。古时多处建庙祭祀，汉画像石中大量镌刻伏羲、女娲的形象。后世人们称其为"人祖""人文始祖"。传说女娲氏为中华民族第一位贤母。

1. Nüwa: The Cultural Progenitor of Humankind in China

According to ancient Chinese legends, Fuxi and Nüwa, a divine couple in legend of china, united in marriage and gave rise to the human race. Nüwa is also celebrated in folklore for creating humans by molding clay and for repairing the heavens with refined stones. In ancient times, temples were constructed to honor her through sacrificial offerings. Numerous depictions of Fuxi and Nüwa have been discovered engraved in Han Dynasty (206 BC–220 AD) stone friezes. For these contributions, Nüwa is revered as the "Progenitor of Humankind" and the "Cultural Ancestor of Humanity." Legend further portrays her as the first exemplar of maternal devotion and love within the Chinese civilization.

人文始祖赞女娲　抟土造人千古夸
汉画像石形象现　代代繁衍我中华

Nüwa sculpted humanity to found the Chinese nation,
Her handiwork with earth has been praised by every generation.
Her image was set in stone in the Han Dynasty,
Thanks to her China enjoyed its prosperity.

二、黄帝正妻（嫘祖）

《史记·五帝本纪》记轩辕黄帝"娶西陵氏之女，是为嫘祖"。嫘祖为黄帝正妻，生子玄嚣、昌意。黄帝共有子二十五宗，得姓者十四人，繁衍成中华各族人民。黄帝族曾战败过炎帝族、蚩尤族，实际上实现了中华民族大融合。又传说嫘祖养蚕抽丝，作衣裳、定嫁娶，使中华走向文明。

2. Leizu: the Main Wife of the Yellow Emperor

According to *The Annals of the Five Emperors*, the first section of Records of the Grand Historian, the legendary Yellow Emperor "married Leizu, the daughter of the Xiling clan". Leizu was his principal wife, and she gave birth to two sons,Xuanxiao and Changyi. The Yellow Emperor fathered a total of 25 sons, 14 of whom inherited his family name, and their descendants went on to form the various ethnic groups of China. The Yellow Emperor's clan was said to have defeated the Yan Emperor's and Chiyou's clans, symbolizing the great unification of the Chinese nation. According to legend, Leizu also discovered the process of sericulture (silk production), taught the art of weaving silk into garments, and established the rituals of marriage, all of which helped to guide China toward a more civilized society.

黄帝正妻西陵女　文明开启念嫘祖
螽斯衍庆光华夏　衣裳垂拱益千古

As the Yellow Emperor's wife and daughter of Xiling,
Leizu's civilizing touch gave China wings.
She spun silk, creating clothes for the nation,
And her legacy lives in every generation.

三、禹妻涂山（夏启母）

夏禹妻涂山氏，生夏启。贤明仁德、勤劳质朴。夏禹带领大家改堵截为疏导的方式，在外治水九年，尽力劳瘁，三过家门而不入。涂山氏艰苦持家，精心教子，育子成才。禹被推为首领后，启继承禹位，开启我国第一代王朝。

3. Tushan: Wife of Yu the Great and Mother of Qi of the Xia Dynasty

Tushan was the wife of Yu the Great, the legendary founder of the Xia Dynasty (around 2070 BC–1600 BC), and the mother of Qi. Yu was celebrated for his virtue, benevolence, diligence, and simplicity. Under his leadership, the people shifted from merely blocking and diverting river channels to adopting the more effective method of dredging to control floods. Yu devoted nine years to taming the floodwaters, tirelessly working toward this monumental task. Despite passing by his home three times during this period, he never once entered, demonstrating his unwavering commitment to the greater good. Meanwhile, Tushan managed the household with frugality and care, dedicating herself to raising and educating their son Qi. Her efforts eventually shaped Qi into a capable and accomplished leader. After Yu was chosen as the leader of the state, Qi succeeded him and established the Xia Dynasty, the first hereditary dynasty in Chinese history.

> 大禹治水建殊勋　涂山贤淑理家勤
> 教子成才担重任　九州一统利万民

Yu the Great halted the flood's fierce motion,
His wife managed the household with care and devotion.
She nurtured her son to shoulder duties so great,
Uniting the people under a prosperous state.

四、古公贤妻（太姜，季历母）

商朝末年，古公亶父由幽迁至周原。妻太姜端庄和顺，教子有方。古公亶父特别喜爱三子季历的儿子昌，日后成为周文王。长子泰伯、次子仲雍为让王位，离国东行，成为后世吴国的先祖，孔子颂为"至德"。其子季历，遵母教，发展周室，教子成才，成就大业。

4. Tai Jiang: The Virtuous Wife of Gu Gong and Mother of Ji Li

In the final days of the Shang Dynasty (about 1600 BC–1046 BC), Duke Gu Gong Danfu relocated his clan to the Zhou Plain in present-day Shaanxi Province. His wife, Tai Jiang, was known for her dignified, gentle, and harmonious demeanor, and she excelled in raising and educating their sons. Duke Gu Gong held a particular fondness for his grandson Chang, the son of JiLi, who would later become King Wen of the Zhou Dynasty (1046 BC–256 BC). To ensure a smooth succession and avoid contention for the throne, Chang's elder brothers, Tai Bo and Zhong Yong, voluntarily relinquished their claims, leaving their homeland to travel east. There, they laid the foundation for what would later become the State of Wu. Their act of selflessness and virtue earned high praise from Confucius, who honored them as "gentlemen of consummate virtue". Guided by the teachings of his virtuous mother, Ji Li expanded the influence of the Zhou clan and raised his sons to be accomplished leaders, paving the way for the eventual establishment of the Zhou Dynasty.

> 贤母太姜亶父妻　相夫教子光西岐
> 泰伯仲雍至德孝　育儿培孙成大器

Tai Jiang, the wife of Gu Gong, was a virtuous and capable mother,
Supporting her husband and educating her sons with wisdom and care.
Her two eldest sons, praised for their filial piety and virtue,
Carried forward the legacy, securing the dynasty's future anew.

五、胎教育子（姬昌母）

先周季历妻太任，品行端庄，诚挚仁德，行为规范。怀孕时，坐、站、睡、言、行，均循规蹈矩，重视胎教。生子姬昌后，更教其勤政爱民，礼贤下士，团结周边各族，使周的势力大增至"三分天下有其二"，为灭商兴周打下基础。

5. The Mother of Ji Chang: Starting Her Son's Education from Conception

Tai Ren, the wife of Ji Li, the founding father of the Zhou Dynasty (1046BC–256 BC), was renowned for her upright conduct, sincerity, benevolence, and propriety. During her pregnancy, she placed great emphasis on prenatal education,adhering to all the proper rules of behavior—maintaining correct posture when sitting, standing, sleeping, speaking, and acting. After giving birth to Ji Chang, she continued to educate him in diligence, benevolence, and respect for the wise and virtuous. Over time, Ji Chang gained the support of neighboring clans, strengthening the State of Zhou and laying the foundation for the overthrow of the Shang Dynasty and the rise of the Zhou.

太任端庄行规范　始自胎教自律严
良好心态自幼现　仁德文王出岐山

Tai Ren, known for conduct pure and true,
Self-discipline began with her child from the womb too.
From infancy, she instilled virtue with care,
A benevolent king rose from Qishan's air.

六、武王贤母（姬发母）

先周时莘国女子太姒，仁德贤明。丈夫姬昌忙于国事，她生子十人，一人担起家事，教子成才。长子伯邑考随父在羑里被纣王杀害，全忠全孝。次子姬发伐纣兴周，为武王。三子姬旦辅佐武王，制礼作乐，两次东征获胜，屡建功勋。

6. The Virtuous Mother of King Wu of the Zhou Dynasty

Taisi, a noblewoman from the State of Shen before the founding of the Zhou Dynasty, was known for her kindness, wisdom, and virtue. While her husband, Ji Chang, was preoccupied with state affairs, she managed the household and raised ten children, guiding them with care and nurturing them into capable individuals. Her eldest son, Boyi Kao, remained steadfast in his loyalty and filial piety. He accompanied his father during his imprisonment and tragically died at the hands of the tyrannical King Zhou of the Shang Dynasty. Her second son, Ji Fa, later known as King Wu, led the campaign against King Zhou, establishing the foundation for the Zhou Dynasty. Her third son, Ji Dan, assisted King Wu in matters of governance, formulating rituals and music, and achieving victory in two successful campaigns, further strengthening the Zhou cause.

太姒仁德又贤明　恭继祖德忠孝承
武王周公聆母教　灭纣兴周不朽功

Tai Si, virtuous, kind, and wise,
Her ancestors' loyalty shone in her eyes.
Her two brilliant sons, following her lead,
Planted the seeds for a new state to succeed.

七、母教仁德（臧武仲母）

春秋时鲁国大夫臧武仲，曾恃权傲人。其母谆谆教育他修身自省，广交良友。臧武仲听从母教，尊君勤政，交友辅仁，仁德爱民，在国内威信大增。他出使齐国被扣后，在多方支持下鲁军派兵陈于边境，多方设法派人援救，使其安全回国。

7. ZangWuzhong's Mother Teaches Her Son with Benevolence

Zang Wuzhong, a high-ranking official of the State of Lu during the Spring and Autumn Period (770 BC–476 BC), was once proud and arrogant due to his position and power. His mother, however, taught him to cultivate his character through self-reflection and by choosing virtuous companions. Heeding her guidance, Zang showed respect to the king by diligently serving in state affairs, grew in benevolence through friendships with the virtuous, and governed with kindness and care for the people, thereby enhancing his reputation in the state. When he was detained in the State of Qi during a diplomatic mission, Zang's virtues garnered support from many quarters. His home state of Lu, even mobilizing troops to the border of Qi, pressured for his release. Thanks to this widespread support, Zang safely returned to his homeland.

武仲才高交友稀　贤母教诲行仁义
出使被困遭危难　国人搭救抗齐师

Wuzhong, with talent rare, kept his circle small,
His mother taught him virtue, kindness to all.
When detained as an envoy, facing danger and strife,
His fellow countrymen came to his aid, risking their life.

八、母教勤劳（公父文伯母）

春秋时鲁国大夫公父文伯母鲁敬季姜，勤俭知礼，教子有方。一日公父文伯回家，见母纺绩，不悦。其母说："一个人劳动生善心，不劳失善心，生恶心。无论官民，都应劳动，才是正路。"文伯虚心受教，重视生产，勤政爱民，颂声鹊起。

8. The Mother of Gongfu Wenbo Teaches Her Son the Value of Hard Work

Lujing Jijiang, the mother of Gongfu Wenbo, a senior official of the State of Lu during the Spring and Autumn Period (770 BC–476 BC), was a hardworking and frugal woman who raised her son with wisdom and care. One day, when Wenbo returned home from his office, he was displeased to find his mother weaving and spinning. She calmly replied, "Work cultivates kindness in the heart, while idleness breeds wickedness. It is right for all, whether officials or common folk, to keep busy with their hands." Wenbo, humbled by her words, came to understand the importance of labor. He devoted himself to his duties with diligence, showing deep care for the people and earning widespread praise throughout the state.

公父文伯任高官　见母纺绩劝悠闲
母训不劳生邪念　劳动使人趋仁善

Gongfu, a high official of Lu's land,
Saw his mother spinning and could not understand.
She taught him how idleness breeds evil within,
While hard work fosters goodness, keeping the heart free from sin.

九、教子成圣（孔丘母）

孔丘母颜徵在，春秋末期鲁国人。为慕叔梁纥英名，嫁给叔梁纥，生下孔丘。孔丘三岁时孔父去世。孔母为给儿子寻找好的学习环境，携孔丘由家乡鲁源村迁至鲁都阙里，茹苦含辛，辛勤劳作，培养儿子知礼学文，学无常师，广学六艺，终成一代文化伟人。

9. Confucius' Mother Teaches Her Son to Become a Sage

Yan Zhengzai, the mother of Confucius, was from the State of Lu during the late Spring and Autumn Period. Inspired by the renowned reputation of Shu Lianghe, she married him and gave birth to Confucius. Sadly, Confucius lost his father at the age of three. To provide her son with a better educational environment, Yan moved the family from their hometown of Luyuan to Queli, the capital of Lu. Enduring hardships and working tirelessly, she dedicated herself to managing the household and educating her son in the rites and classical teachings. Through her guidance, Confucius learned diligently from various teachers, mastering the Six Arts: rites, music, archery, horsemanship, literature, and mathematics, eventually becoming one of the greatest cultural figures of his time.

叔梁早逝遗孤男　徵在一肩双任担
茹苦含辛育大器　一代至圣出鲁源

Her husband's early death left her a widow with a son,
Zhengzai bore both the home and the child's care, as one.
Through her earnest guidance, a great talent took shape,
And Confucius became history's sage, none could escape.

十、守节护子（楚昭王母）

春秋时期，楚昭王母伯嬴，刚毅循礼。吴军攻下楚都郢后，吴王阖闾入后宫，欲霸占伯嬴。伯嬴保住自身，又护着幼子，义正辞严地责难吴王，说他要建立功业，必须放弃邪念。伯嬴保住幼子昭王之弟，坚持一月，盼来救兵，全忠全节。

10. Preserving Chastity and Protecting a Son

During the Spring and Autumn Period, Bo Ying, the mother of King Zhao of the State of Chu, was known for her resolute character and strict adherence to the rites. When Wu troops captured Ying, the capital of Chu, and King He Lü of Wu broke into the royal palace with the intent to seize her, Bo Ying stood firm. She defended herself and shielded her young son, with unwavering courage. In a stern and dignified manner, she reproached the King of Wu, declaring that if he wished to build a legacy of greatness, he must abandon his vile intentions and show respect for women. Thanks to her determination and wisdom, she was able to protect her son for an entire month, awaiting reinforcements that eventually came to their rescue. Bo Ying's name is remembered in history as a symbol of loyalty, integrity, and maternal devotion.

吴军攻入楚后宫　阖闾仗势霸伯嬴
弱女严责吴王醒　保子保贞人称颂

After the Wu army seized the Chu's domain,
The queen faced the King of Wu's ruthless claim.
With strength and resolve, she made him rethink,
Saving her son and her honor on the brink.

十一、后母爱子（魏国慈母）

战国时，魏相芒卯后妻十分贤惠。她生三子，前妻遗留五子，她同样疼爱，但五子均不理她，她仍然对五个儿子爱护如初。前妻子犯法当死。她日夜奔走相救。魏安釐王念她大义，赦免其子。此后，五子均对她亲附、孝敬。在她培养下，八子成才，均做了大夫。

11. A Kind Stepmother's Love for Her Stepsons

During the Warring States Period, Mangmao, a minister of the State of Wei, remarried a virtuous and loving woman. She bore three sons of her own while caring for the five sons from her husband's first marriage with equal affection. Despite the cold treatment from her stepsons, she continued to love them as her own. When one of them was sentenced to death for breaking the law, she worked tirelessly, day and night, to save him. Touched by her sincerity and righteousness, King Anxi of Wei pardoned the son. From then on, all five stepsons grew close to her, showing her filial piety. Thanks to her nurturing love and guidance, all eight sons—biological and step—became talented and virtuous men, each rising to positions of leadership as ministers of state.

芒卯后妻人称贤　哺育前子排万难
前子犯法倾力救　众子争读《蓼莪篇》

Mangmao's second wife, virtuous and true,
She raised her stepsons, despite all she'd go through.
When one broke the law, she fought to save his name,
Her love inspired all, earning lasting fame.

十二、母教爱卒（子发母）

战国时，楚将子发领兵与秦国作战。回国筹粮时，其母得知楚国将领生活优裕，士兵只食豆粒。战后，子发回国，其母将其拒之门外，并严厉训斥，指出将帅应爱护士卒，方能鼓舞士气作战获胜。子发认错改正，日后善待士卒，士气大振。

12. The Mother of Zifa Teaches Her Son to Care for His Soldiers

During the Warring States Period (475 BC–221 BC), Zifa, a general from the State of Chu, led his troops in battle against the State of Qin. Upon returning to his homeland to gather provisions, Zifa's mother learned that while the generals of Chu lived in comfort, the soldiers were subsisting on little more than beans. After the battle, when Zifa returned victorious, his mother refused to let him into the house and sternly reprimanded him. She reminded him that a true leader must care for his soldiers, for only when the generals show compassion can they inspire the troops and ensure victory in battle. Zifa humbly acknowledged his error and, from that point on, treated his soldiers with greater kindness, greatly improving their morale.

楚将子发驭士兵　兵卒饥困将食丰
贤母怒责子无道　子发改错士卒勇

Zifa, a general of Chu, led his troops to war,
The generals ate their fill, while warriors were left hungry and sore.
His upright mother rebuked him for allowing such discord,
He then corrected his mistake and morale was restored.

十三、责子收金（田稷母）

战国时，齐相田稷曾收取百镒之金，交给母亲保管。田母知儿子三年俸禄不会如此之多，令儿子如实说出原因。田稷承认别人奉送。田母训子不应收不义之财，马上携子带金面见齐王请罪。齐王赦免田稷，对田母倍极敬重。

13. Tian Ji's Mother Rebukes Him for Accepting a Bribe

During the Warring States Period, Tian Ji, the prime minister of the State of Qi, once accepted a bribe worth one hundred ingots of gold and entrusted it to his mother for safekeeping. His mother, knowing that her son's annual salary was far less than that amount, asked him to explain the source of the wealth. Tian Ji admitted that the money was a gift from someone seeking favor. His mother sternly reproached him for accepting ill-gotten gains and immediately took him, along with the bribe, to the King of Qi to confess. The king pardoned Tian Ji and, impressed by his mother's integrity, showed her great respect.

田稷收取贿赂金　田母惊睹倍伤心
携子面君自请罪　齐王盛赞大贤人

After Tian took a bribe, of an extraordinary size,
His mother, shocked, was filled with deep surprise.
She led him to the king to admit his sin,
And the monarch praised her virtue from within.

十四、教子抗暴（王孙贾母）

战国时，齐人王孙贾，多年服事齐闵公。齐相淖齿杀闵公篡位夺权，无人敢抗。王孙贾母教子应扬正气，秉忠义，杀叛贼。王孙贾奉母命，号令百姓袒露右臂，执武器，四百人跟从王孙贾，闯入王宫，刺死淖齿，平定了齐国的内乱。

14. The Mother of Wangsun Jia Teaches Her Son to Fight Against Tyranny

During the Warring States Period, Wangsun Jia of the State of Qi had long served Lord Min. When Nao Chi, the primeminister, assassinated Lord Min and seized power, no one dared to stand against him. However, Wangsun Jia's mother urged him to uphold righteousness and loyalty, teaching him to eliminate traitors. Following her command, Wangsun Jia rallied the people, instructing them to bare their right arms as a symbol of unity. With four hundred followers, he stormed the palace, killed the tyrant Nao Chi, and restored peace to the state of Qi.

王孙贾母识忠义　教子反暴顺民意
振臂一呼齐平叛　铲除淖齿内乱息

Wangsun Jia's mother, with loyalty in her heart,
Taught her son to stand for justice and play his part.
With a call to arms, the people rallied round,
And the tyrant was slain, bringing peace to the ground.

十五、三迁断机（孟轲母）

战国时，邹国人孟母仉氏，丈夫孟激在儿子三岁时去世。为使儿子有好的学习环境，从墓地旁迁到市场旁，又从市场旁迁到子思学宫旁，教子读书。稚子贪玩，学习不用功，孟母又用"断机"的方式，警告儿子学习不可中断。孟子努力攻读，终成大儒。

15. Mencius' Mother Moves House Three Times and Cuts the Loom's Thread

During the Warring States Period, Mencius' mother, Lady Zhang, from the State of Zou, lost her husband when her son, Mencius, was only three years old. In order to create a better environment for her son's education, she moved their home from beside the graveyard to the marketplace, and then again, from the marketplace to the academy of Zi Si, a place where learning and study were easily accessible. As a young child, Mencius was playful and inattentive to his studies. So his mother used a method to teach him the importance of focus. She took scissors and cut the thread of her loom, using this as a lesson to warn him that learning cannot be interrupted. Mencius heeded her words, diligently applying himself to his studies, and eventually became a great scholar, renowned for his wisdom.

> 凫村故里赞三迁　贤母教子光史篇
> 嘎然机断稚童警　千秋母教树懿范

Mencius' mother moved thrice, her wisdom praised,
She shaped her son, his name through history raised.
The snip of the loom, a warning for her son,
This timeless lesson still shines, though ages have run.

十六、自刎励子（王陵母）

秦朝末年，楚汉相争时，沛人王陵跟刘邦南征北战。战争中，王陵母被项羽掳去。项羽叫她劝儿子归降。王陵母知汉王刘邦仁义，项羽惯杀戮。为使儿子坚定跟随刘邦，毅然伏剑自刎，以死教育儿子，坚定了王陵一直扶汉的决心。后来王陵官至汉朝的丞相。

16. Wang Ling's Mother Takes Her Own Life to Inspire Her Son

At the close of the Qin Dynasty, during the Chu-Han struggle for supremacy, Wang Ling, a native of Pei, fought alongside Liu Bang, who would later become the first emperor of the Han Dynasty. During the conflict, Wang Ling's mother was captured by Xiang Yu, the leader of the Chu forces. Xiang Yu ordered her to persuade her son to surrender. Aware of Liu Bang's benevolence and Xiang Yu's cruelty, she took a sword and ended her own life. In doing so, she sent a powerful message to her son, urging him to remain steadfast in his loyalty to Liu Bang. Her sacrifice inspired Wang Ling to continue supporting Liu Bang, and he eventually rose to the position of prime minister in the Han Dynasty.

楚汉之争分项刘　王陵老母辨恩仇
伏剑自刎身教子　辅刘灭项佳话留

Xiang Yu and Liu Bang fought for the throne,
WangLing's aged mother knew both friend and foe.
She took her life with a sword to urge her son,
With courage renewed, the Han Dynasty was won.

十七、教子俭约（刘恒母）

西汉初年，吕后掌权，薄后被贬到代地。她自奉节俭，教子有方。诸大臣诛灭诸吕后，赴代地恭迎薄后之子刘恒即位，即汉文帝。文帝谨遵母教，自奉节俭，轻徭薄赋，使民休养生息。医治好社会上多年战乱造成的创伤，出现了"文景之治"。

17. Liu Heng's Mother Teaches Him Frugality

In the early years of the Western Han Dynasty, Empress Lü held power, while Concubine Bo was exiled to the distant region of Dai. Living simply, she taught her son the value of frugality. After Empress Lü was overthrown, Liu Heng, the son of Concubine Bo, was welcomed back by the ministers and generals, and ascended the throne as Emperor Wen of the Han Dynasty.

Emperor Wen adhered firmly to his mother's teachings, embracing a life of modesty. He implemented reforms to lighten the burdens of the people by reducing taxes and corvée labor, allowing society to recover from the scars of prolonged warfare. His reign marked the beginning of the "Wen-Jing Period", a golden era of peace and prosperity in Chinese history.

> 薄后失宠贬代地　知民甘苦识民意
> 教子为帝倡节俭　汉初兴旺文景治

After Concubine Bo was sent away to Dai,
She saw the people's pain, and knew the reason why.
She taught her son the virtue of frugality,
And he ruled with peace, bringing prosperity.

十八、为子伸冤（张汤母）

汉武帝时，张汤之母教子耿直忠义，张汤恭聆母教，在任御史大夫时，铁面无私，屡建功勋。但此人不会办事，常得罪人，其母知他系为别人陷害被杀。特地丧事从简，以牛车送葬，替子伸冤，惊动了朝野，打动了皇帝，重审此案，为张汤平反，惩治了诬陷之人。

18. Zhang Tang's Mother Seeks Justice for Her Son

During the reign of Emperor Wu of Han, Zhang Tang's mother taught him to uphold principles of honesty, integrity, and loyalty. He listened closely to her teachings and applied them in his life. As the Minister of Justice, Zhang Tang served with great dedication, his conduct marked by strict impartiality and selflessness, earning him many achievements. However, his bluntness and occasional lack of tact made him enemies, and he was eventually framed for a crime. His mother, certain that he had been wronged, believed that his death was the result of a malicious conspiracy. In mourning, she arranged a simple funeral, using a cattle cart to transport his body, and set out to expose the injustice. Her relentless pursuit of justice, combined with her deep grief, captured the attention of both the court and the people. Her efforts moved the emperor, who ordered a reexamination of the case. In the end, Zhang Tang's innocence was upheld, and those who had slandered him were punished for their false accusations.

史载张母教子严　张汤功高却被谗
张母识儿巧申辩　是非分明平子冤

History records that Zhang Tang's mother was steadfast and wise,
Her promising son, unjustly slain, met a tragic demise.
She bravely defended him, despite her grief and pain,
And through her plea, justice for him was regained.

十九、教子仁慈（隽不疑母）

西汉昭帝时，大臣隽不疑母，仁慈贤惠，常教子仁爱待人，刑罚从宽。隽不疑任京兆尹时，每次回家，其母总问他是否善待百姓，每听到为民平反则满心欢喜，否则食旨不甘。隽不疑当政期间，牢记母亲教诲，广施仁德，贤名远播。

19. Juan Buyi's Mother Teaches Him Benevolence

During the reign of Emperor Zhao of the Western Han Dynasty, Juan Buyi, a prominent official, was guided by his virtuous and compassionate mother. She constantly taught him the importance of benevolence and kindness toward others,advocating leniency in the application of punishments. When Juan Buyi was appointed as the governor of the capital, he would always return home to his mother, who would ask whether he had treated the people with kindness. If she learned that her son had righted the wrongs of the people, she was filled with joy. If not, she would refuse to eat and would be filled with sorrow. Juan Buyi took his mother's teachings to heart throughout his governance. His compassionate rule and fair judgments earned him widespread admiration and a reputation for wisdom and integrity.

京兆大尹隽不疑　贤母屡教应仁慈
断狱宽厚慈母笑　执法公允民受益

Juan Buyi, a high official in charge of the state,
Was taught by a mother whose virtues were great.
Her pride swelled as he ruled with justice and grace,
Using the law to uplift the common race.

二十、教子宽厚（严延年母）

西汉下邳人严延年，任河南太守时，其母自东海来，见当地囚犯太多，不肯入府，责备儿子不该滥惩无辜。指出如对民严酷，早晚身受其害，绰号"屠伯"的儿子严延年，不遵母教，自遭杀戮。另四个儿子聆听母教，行仁倡义，均有宦绩。

20. Yan Yannian's Mother Teaches Him to Be Lenient

Yan Yannian, a native of Xiapi in the Western Han Dynasty, served as the governor of Henan. When his mother came to visit him from their hometown, she refused to enter his official residence upon seeing the many prisoners outside. Distressed by the sight, she reproached him for punishing the innocent. She warned that such harshness would inevitably lead to his downfall, as cruelty toward the people would eventually come back to harm him. Despite her wise counsel, Yan Yannian, nicknamed "Butcher" for his brutal methods, ignored his mother's teachings and ultimately met a tragic end. However, his four brothers heeded their mother's advice, embracing benevolence and righteousness in their governance, and achieved great success in their careers.

严母仁德爱百姓　正颜教子恤民情
四子聆教人尊敬　屠伯屠人自丧生

Yan's mother, kind and full of care,
Taught her sons to be gentle, to always be fair.
Four followed her wisdom, earning respect and praise,
But the "Butcher" son defied her, and met his demise in a blaze.

二十一、为子复仇（吕育母）

西汉末年，时值王莽酷政，海曲（今日照）小吏吕育，被县吏冤杀。吕母立志为子复仇，广散家财，联络壮士，奋然起义，自称"将军"，一举攻入阳曲县城，杀死县吏，成为反王莽的第一支农民起义军。

21. Lü Yu's Mother Avenges Her Son

At the close of the Western Han Dynasty, under Wang Mang's brutal rule, Lü Yu, a minor official from Haiqu (modern-day Rizhao), was wrongfully executed by a corrupt county officer. His mother, determined to avenge her son, sold off the family's wealth to raise an army. She rallied warriors and led them in revolt, declaring herself "General". With fierce resolve, she stormed the county seat and killed the official responsible for her son's death. Her uprising became the first peasant rebellion against Wang Mang's oppressive regime.

海曲吕育遭冤死　吕母复仇扬正气
率众反莽诛恶吏　巾帼将军树义旗

After Lü Yu was wronged and slain by a vile foe,
His mother rose to avenge him, the "General" in tow.
With courage she led the people in a bold crusade,
And brought down the tyrant, a banner of justice displayed.

二十二、励子卫国（赵苞母）

东汉人赵苞，奉命到辽西上任时，母亲与妻子被鲜卑人掳去。敌人以释放赵母为条件，要赵苞献城。赵母在阵前正告儿子，国事为重，勿顾私情。鲜卑人残杀了赵母。赵苞坚守阵地，盼来救兵，打退敌人。

22. Zhao Bao's Mother Urges Him to Defend the State

Zhao Bao, an official of the Eastern Han, was sent to serve in Liaoxi. During his mission, his mother and wife were captured by the Xianbei people, who demanded that he surrender the city in exchange for his mother's release. On the battlefield, Zhao's mother admonished him to prioritize the state's affairs over personal ties. She urged him to remain resolute and not sacrifice the public good for the sake of family. Despite her tragic death at the hands of the enemy, Zhao Bao, steadfast in his resolve, held the city until reinforcements arrived and defeated the invaders.

赵母被虏识大义　　以死教子守城池
赵苞忍泪再奋战　　胜敌保城继母志

Zhao Bao's kidnapped mother kept her heart ever true,
And taught her son to guard the city by being tragically slew.
With tearful eyes, Zhao fought on, both fierce and brave,
Her will propelled him to victory, the city to save.

二十三、为子顶罪（孔褒母）

东汉末年，宦官侯览仗势欺人。张俭上书弹劾，遭宦官诬陷，被迫逃亡，由孔褒弟孔融将其留宿家中。侯览得知，下令窝藏张俭者死罪。孔融挺身而出，说人是自己留的。孔褒说张俭是自己的朋友，罪在自己。孔褒母说如果这算犯罪，我来承担。令人敬仰。

23. Kong Bao's Mother Takes Full Responsibility for Her Son's Guilt

At the end of the Eastern Han Dynasty, Hou Lan, a powerful eunuch, abused his authority to bully others. Zhang Jian, a nobleman, wrote a letter of impeachment denouncing him, but was soon framed and forced to flee. Kong Rong, the younger brother of Kong Bao, took Zhang in and sheltered him in his home. When Hou Lan discovered this, he issued an order that anyone harboring Zhang Jian would be sentenced to death. Kong Rong boldly stepped forward, declaring it was he who had hidden the fugitive. Kong Bao, acknowledging that Zhang Jian was his close friend, also took responsibility. Their mother, standing firm in her resolve, declared that if aiding a friend was considered a crime, then she would bear the full guilt herself. Her courage and integrity earned her widespread admiration and respect.

孔融助兄救张俭　孔褒挺身一人担
更有贤母倡正义　一家三口均大贤

Kong Rong assisted Kong Bao to rescue Zhang Jian,
Kong Bao stood out to take the charge of the plan.
Their mother did also their upright deeds endorse,
Hence, the trio was praised for their worthy recourse.

二十四、廉石家宝（陆绩母）

三国时吴人陆绩母教子勤廉。陆绩谨遵母教，一尘不染。当了几年郁林太守，两袖清风卸职回家时，一家人财物不足一船，为怕船轻抵不住风浪，搬块大石压船回家。因财物很少，受陆母夸赞。此石永留，称"廉石"，为陆氏传家之宝。

24. Lu Ji's Mother Cultivates Her Son into an Upright Official

During the Three Kingdoms period, Lu Ji's mother, from the State of Wu, taught her son to be diligent and virtuous. Lu Ji adhered to his mother's teachings with great respect, keeping his integrity untarnished. After serving as the Governor of Yulin for several years, he returned home upon completing his term, leaving office without any ill-gotten gains. When he sailed back, his possessions were so few that they barely filled the boat. To prevent the boat from capsizing in rough waters, he placed a large stone on board for ballast. His mother praised him for fulfilling his duties with honor, having accumulated little wealth. This stone, cherished by the family, came to be known as the "Upright Stone" and became a treasured heirloom of the Lu family.

陆绩母教不贪财　清风为官回家来
一块廉石传家宝　青史讴歌栋梁材

Lu Ji's mother taught him not to crave for gold,
He returned home with wealth untouched, as was foretold.
The upright stone became a heirloom for many a generation.History always hails worthy talents as pillars of the nation.

二十五、退鲊教子（陶侃母）

晋朝鄱阳人陶侃，幼年丧父。陶母对其常教诲，严要求。陶侃曾任管理鱼市交易的小吏，有一次他派人送给母亲一些鲊鱼时，陶母责子不该滥用职权，令其退还。家中请客时，陶母剪发换钱打酒，抽出铺草给客人喂马，陶侃面聆母教，任职节俭奉公，恤民疾苦，为一代良吏。

25. Tao Kan's Mother Instructs Him to Return the Pickled Fish

Tao Kan, a native of Poyang in the Jin Dynasty, lost his father in early childhood. His mother, a wise and strict woman, constantly imparted lessons of integrity and virtue. Once, when Tao Kan served as a minor official in charge of the fish market, he had some pickled fish sent to his mother. However, his mother rebuked him for misusing his position and insisted he return the gift. When entertaining guests at home, Tao's mother would sell her own hair to buy wine and feed their horses with straw taken from her bedding. These actions, though humble, reflected her steadfast values. Tao Kan, ever obedient, took her teachings to heart. He remained frugal and just throughout his career, deeply concerned for the welfare of the people. His reputation as a virtuous and devoted official earned him widespread admiration.

晋朝名臣数陶侃　鲊鱼事小母教严
剪发待客儿受教　大吏终生务勤俭

Tao Kan, a minister of great renown,
The fish affair taught him to never let power drown.
His mother sold her hair to serve the guests with care,
And he became an official ever frugal and fair.

二十六、女中丈夫（司马聃母）

东晋穆帝司马聃母褚氏，二十一岁时丈夫（晋康帝）去世。她受命于危难之时，辅佐一岁的儿子临朝听政达十七年，励精图治、体恤民情，赈济灾荒。为保政治稳定，接受历代教训，不许外戚掌权。人称"女中丈夫"。

26. Sima Dan's Mother Is Praised as a Gentleman among Womenfolk

Lady Chu, mother of Emperor Mu of the Eastern Jin Dynasty, was just 21 when her husband, Emperor Kang, passed away. Despite her young age, she rose to the challenge during a critical time, assisting her one-year-old son in ruling the empire. For 17 years, she guided him through the complexities of state affairs, ensuring the prosperity of the kingdom, alleviating suffering caused by disasters, and addressing the needs of the people. In a bid to maintain political stability, she took lessons from past dynasties and prohibited her family from seizing power. Revered for her wisdom and leadership, she earned the title "A Gentleman Among Women".

晋康之妻褚皇后　临危受命主政务
辅子治国二十载　体恤民情女丈夫

Empress Chu, wife of Kang of Jin,
Took charge when crisis did begin.
For twenty years, she helped her son to reign,
A"gentleman" in a woman's might, caring for the people's pain.

二十七、教孙汉化（拓跋宏祖母）

北魏文成帝后冯氏，鲜卑人。丈夫死后，辅佐儿子拓跋弘、孙子拓跋宏掌管朝政二十多年。其孙在她教育下，自小孝亲爱民，执政后进行以汉化为中心的改制。下诏穿汉服，学汉语，用汉官，改汉姓，与汉族通婚，迁都等。在全国推行全面汉化，促进了中华民族大融合。

27. Tuoba Hong's Grandmother Teaches Him to Embrace Han Culture

Empress Feng, wife of Emperor Wencheng of the Northern Wei, was of Xianbei descent. After the death of her husband, she guided her son and grandson in ruling the state for over two decades. Under her wise instruction, her grandson grew up to be a model of filial piety and benevolence. Upon ascending the throne, he implemented a series of reforms centered on Han cultural integration. His policies included mandating Han clothing, promoting the Chinese language, appointing Han officials, adopting Han surnames, encouraging intermarriage with the Han people, and relocating the capital closer to Han territories. These sweeping reforms helped foster the great cultural and ethnic unity of the Chinese nation.

冯后临朝辅子孙　二十多载掌乾坤
孝文改制促汉化　各族融合中华亲

Empress Feng assisted her son and grandson of late,
For over two decades she handled affairs of state.
Her grandson's reforms promoted ethnic integration,
Like siblings every group now shared the nation.

二十八、责子退米（李畲母）

　　唐朝高邑人李畲，任监察御史时，因多收禄米，李母对其痛责。不但令其如数退还，还令其上报请罪，同时又建议更改官吏历来多收禄米的制度。这一举动，促使朝内多官退还。皇帝得知，也对其表彰，并下令废止官员多收的恶例。

28. Li She's Mother Reproaches Him for Accepting Excess Rice

Li She, a native of Gaoyi in the Tang Dynasty, served as a supervisory censor. During his tenure, he accepted an excessive rice allowance as part of his salary. Upon discovering this, his mother severely reproached him. Not only did she insist that he return the excess rice, but she also instructed him to report his misconduct and seek forgiveness from his superiors. Furthermore, she proposed reforms to address the long-standing practice that allowed officials to receive such excessive allowances. Her actions prompted several other officials in the court to return their surplus rice. When the emperor became aware of the matter, he praised her integrity and issued a decree to abolish the practice of officials receiving excessive rice allowances.

李母惊观禄米多　　怒责李畲特权越
上奏请罪谏更改　　废除陈规百姓悦

Li's mother was shocked by the rice he had gained,
She scolded him harshly for power unchained.
She appealed to the emperor, urging the change,
And the people rejoiced as the laws were rearranged.

二十九、荻书教子（欧阳修母）

北宋庐陵人欧阳修母，夫死家贫，教子以荻草为笔、土地作纸学习。屡以其父为官清廉、勤政爱民之例教子。欧阳修聆听母教，努力攻读，官至参知政事（副宰相），他在执政时勤政爱民，名垂青史。在文学上、书法上也卓有成就。

29. Ouyang Xiu's Mother Teaches Her Son with Reed Pens

Ouyang Xiu's mother, a native of Luling in the Northern Song Dynasty, taught her son with reed pens and the earth as his paper, as the family was poor after the untimely death of her husband. Despite their hardship, she used her husband's example of integrity, diligence, and dedication to public service to inspire her son. Ouyang Xiu, deeply influenced by his mother's teachings, studied diligently. His efforts led him to rise through the ranks to become a councillor, equivalent to a vice chancellor. During his time in office, he governed with care and concern for the people, earning a respected place in history. In addition to his political career, he excelled in literature and calligraphy, leaving behind a legacy of scholarly achievement.

欧母寡居教子勤　以荻作书苦学文
廉洁奉公忠职守　锦绣文章光学林

Ouyang Xiu's mother, a young widow and teacher of worth,
Scratched her sons lessons onto the bare earth.
He grew to be honest, loyal, and just,
His writings admired, as all scholars trust.

三十、辽国女皇（耶律隆绪母）

辽圣宗耶律隆绪母萧太后，小名燕燕，她在丈夫死后辅子辅政27年，平定了内乱。教育儿子学习汉文化，在朝内进行了一些改革，努力开发北疆。与宋军大战后，用以和为贵的精神订立"澶渊之盟"，促进了北方各族之间的经济、文化交流。

30. Yelü Longxu's Mother, the Empress of the Liao State

Empress Dowager Xiao, mother of Yelü Longxu, also known as Emperor Shengzong of the Liao Dynasty, was affectionately called "Swallow" in her youth. After her husband's death, she served as regent for 27 years, guiding her son through a period of civil unrest. She educated him in Han culture and led a series of reforms within the court, while also striving to develop the northern frontier of the Liao state. Following a major conflict with the Song Dynasty, she encouraged her son to sign the Chanyuan Treaty, emphasizing peace and harmony. This pact helped foster economic and cultural exchanges among the various ethnic groups in Northern China.

辽国女皇萧燕燕　教子辅政四十年
经营北疆促发展　宋辽和好万民欢

Of the State of Liao, Xiao was empress,
For two score years she helped her son rule with success.
She strengthened the north, fostering growth and peace,
And with the Song, she made hostilities cease.

三十一、尽忠报国（岳飞母）

南宋汤阴人岳飞，自小受母亲忠君爱民的教诲，早年拜周侗为师，苦练杀敌本领，随时报效国家。其母为激励他，在其背上刺"尽忠报国"四字，令其从军抗金。他组成"岳家军"，在抗金战争中节节胜利。体现尽忠即尽孝，虽未完成宿愿，却为后人崇敬。

31. Yue Fei's Mother Inspires Him to Serve the State with Loyalty

Yue Fei, from Tangyin in the Southern Song Dynasty, was raised by his mother to honor the emperor and care for the people. As a child, he was trained in martial arts by the renowned Zhou Tong, learning combat skills to serve the state in times of need. To inspire him further, his mother had the characters "Serve the country with utmost loyalty" tattooed on his back, urging him to join the military and fight the invading Jin forces. Leading the renowned "Yue Family Army," he secured numerous victories in the Anti-Jin War. His life embodied the deep connection between loyalty to the country and filial duty. Though he did not fulfill all his personal ambitions, he remains an icon of honor and respect for future generations.

岳母刺字誉千古　尽忠报国岳鹏举
率师抗金战功累　遗恨未抵黄龙府

Yue Fei's mother gave her son a famous mark,
A tattoo that echoed loyalty, bold and stark.
He led the charge against the Jin, time and again,
Though victorious, his ultimate goal he could not attain.

三十二、励子远行（徐霞客母）

明朝江阴人徐霞客，出身农家，自幼好学，不去考取功名，惟愿考察祖国的山水。徐母支持儿子，并为他特制"远行帽"，支持他走遍国内各地。直到八十一岁，仍支持儿子外出考察，徐霞客写出《徐霞客游记》，对我国地理学做出了重大贡献。

32. Xu Xiake's Mother Encourages His Journey

Xu Xiake, a native of Jiangyin in the Ming Dynasty, came from a humble farming family. From an early age, he had a deep love for learning. Unlike others who sought to pass the imperial exams, Xu Xiake was driven by a desire to explore the landscapes of his homeland. His mother fully supported his unusual ambition. She even crafted a special "traveling hat" for him, encouraging him to journey across the country. Even at the age of 81, she continued to support her son's travels and fieldwork. Xu Xiake's dedication led to the creation of The Travel Notes of Xu Xiake , a monumental contribution to the study of Chinese geography.

霞客立志频出游　徐母支持儿不愁
锦绣山川多走遍　名著出手光神州

Xu Xiake resolved to venture into every corner of the nation,
And his mother supported his dream without hesitation.
Through mountains and rivers, his travels did span,
His diaries became a geographical gem, admired by man.

三十三、连辅三君（福临母）

清朝初年，福临母孝庄太后，支持丈夫皇太极以及御弟多尔衮入关建立清朝后，帮助儿子福临（即顺治帝）稳定大局，日后又助孙子玄烨（康熙帝）灭鳌拜，平三藩，收台湾，稳西北，使清初内忧外患的局面走向稳定、繁荣的盛世。

33. Fu Lin's Mother Assists Three Emperors in Succession

Empress Dowager Xiaozhuang, mother of Fu Lin, played a pivotal role in the early years of the Qing Dynasty. After supporting her husband, Emperor Huang Taiji, and her brother-in-law, Duoergun, in their conquest of China and the establishment of the Qing Dynasty, she continued to assist her son, Fu Lin, who later became Emperor Shunzhi, in stabilizing the realm. Later, she helped her grandson, Xuanye, who would become the Emperor Kangxi, in his rise to power. She supported his efforts to defeat the powerful general Aobai, quell the rebellion of the Three Feudal Lords, reclaim Taiwan, and stabilize the northwestern borders. Through her guidance and support, the early Qing Dynasty, which had been plagued by internal strife and external challenges, transformed into a period of stability and prosperity.

清初孝庄人知晓　扶子教孙心力焦
排除内忧免外患　换来勃兴康熙朝

The Empress Xiaozhuang was famed in the early Qing Dynasty,
She helped her son and her grandson with ardour and loyalty.
Through tireless efforts, she quelled both internal and external strife,
And brought about an era of peace, prosperity, and life.

三十四、一母三元（颜光敏母）

清朝初年，曲阜颜子后裔、颜伯景妻朱淑人，知书达理，继承其祖颜子好学明礼的家风，在政局混乱的清初，仍教子读书、修德、做人。其子颜光敏、颜光猷、颜光敩，均在康熙年间考中进士，人称"一母三进士"。

34. Yan Guangmin's Mother Cultivates Her Three Sons into Successful Candidates in the Highest Imperial Examinations

In the early Qing Dynasty, Zhu Shuren, the wife of Yan Bojing and a descendant of the esteemed Yan Hui, Confucius ' disciple, was a learned and cultured woman. She inherited her family's deep respect for scholarship and virtue, and, despite the turmoil of the early Qing years, she devoted herself to teaching her sons. She encouraged them to read the classics, cultivate moral character, and uphold propriety in all aspects of life. Her three sons–Yan Guangmin, Yan Guangyou, and Yan Guangxiao—all passed the highest imperial examinations during the reign of Emperor Kangxi, earning the family the distinguished title of "One Mother, Three Scholars".

淑人颜氏志冰清　箪瓢独乐好家风
一母育就三进士　清季文坛树令名

Zhu Shuren, wife of Yan Bojing, wise and refined,
Inherited a love for learning, from her ancestors' mind.
She raised three sons, scholars of great renown,
In the early Qing, her name earned a lasting crown.

三十五、教子清廉（耿庭柏母）

清朝新城人耿鸣世，任都御史，其妻教子甚严，子耿庭柏也官至都御史。庭柏母极重教子勤政爱民，清正廉洁，在寄子书中写道："家内平安报尔知，田园岁入有余资。丝毫不用南中物，好做清官报圣时。"

35. Geng Tingbai's Mother Teaches Her Son to Be Honest and Upright

Geng Mingshi, from Xincheng in the Qing Dynasty, served as an imperial censor. His wife, a strict and diligent teacher, raised their son, Geng Tingbai, to follow in his father's footsteps and also become an imperial censor. She emphasized the importance of diligence in his work, compassion for the people, and above all, honesty and integrity. In a letter to her son, she wrote: "I write to inform you that the family is well and there will be a surplus from the fields this year. There is no need to worry about our sustenance. Instead, focus on being an honest and upright official who contributes to the peace and prosperity of this time."

耿母廉洁勤教子　寄子书含谆谆意
平安温饱勿挂念　好做清官解民急

Geng Tingbai's mother taught her son honesty and diligence.
Her letter to her son was full of hope and patience:
Don't worry, dear son, about food or rest,
Be a fair official, and serve the people best.

三十六、教子励学（蒋士铨母）

清朝江西铅山蒋士铨母，家境贫穷，日夜纺绩，供子读书，十分辛苦，从无怨言。无钱买纸笔，用竹枝作笔，地作纸。听到儿子读书声，百病全消。在她的努力培养下，儿子中了进士，并成为诗文俱佳的文学家、戏剧家。

36. Jiang Shiquan's Mother Teaches Her Son to Devote Himself to His Studies

Jiang Shiquan's mother, from Qianshan in Jiangxi during the Qing Dynasty,came from a poor family. She worked tirelessly at the loom day and night, supporting her son's education without ever complaining. When money was scarce, she made do with bamboo sticks as pens and the bare ground as paper. The moment she heard her son reading, all her worries and ailments seemed to disappear. Under her painstaking cultivation, her son became a successful candidate in the highest imperial examinations and later proved himself as an excellent man of letters and playwright.

蒋母穷苦勤教子　竹枝为笔地作纸
乐闻书声消百病　教子成材母心喜

Poverty was no deterrent to Jiang Shiquan teaching her son,
Bamboo stalks became pens, the ground to write upon.
Every time her son's reading was to be heard, she felt at ease,
On him becoming a writer her joys never did cease.

第二章

正道教子

Chapter Two:

Teaching Children the Right Way

一、铸鼎教子（正考父）

春秋时期宋国的上大夫正考父，连续辅佐过戴公、武公、宣公，曾作《诗经》中的《商颂》。此人为政勤恳，作风清廉，待人谦逊。为教育子孙、端正家风，特令人铸一鼎，上面铭文的意思是：我每次接受任务或提升职务时，都是越来越恭敬。除忠于国事、勤于政事外，鼎上又铸：我用此鼎煮饭和粥，用以充饥，以此保持清廉的作风。他教育的儿子孔父嘉任宋国大司马，曾为宋国屡立战功。

1. Zheng Kaofu Casts a Tripod to Enlighten His Offspring

Zheng Kaofu, a senior minister in the State of Song during the Spring and Autumn Period, served successively under Lords Dai, Wu, and Xuan. He is also credited with composing the *Ode to Shang, found in The Book of Songs*, one of China's earliest collections of poetry. Known for his diligence, integrity, and humility, Zheng was a model official. In an effort to instill proper values in his children and promote a virtuous family tradition, Zheng ordered the casting of a tripod with the following inscription: "Each time I was assigned a new duty or received a promotion, my respect and dedication only grew." Beyond his commitment to the state and diligent governance, he added: "I use this tripod to cook meals and porridge to satisfy my hunger, reminding myself to remain honest and incorruptible." Under his guidance, his son, Kong Fujia, went on to become the Grand Master of the State of Song and earned distinction through numerous military victories.

忠诚谦恭正考父　为教子孙奇招出
鼎铸铭文永示展　家风代代传忠恕

Zheng Kaofu, was for loyalty and humility renowned,
A novel way of educating children he found.
Instructions onto a tripod he had cast,
These family traditions through the ages were passed.

二、周公教子（周公旦）

为灭商兴周立下大功的周公姬旦，建西周国初年两次东征，制礼作乐，分封诸侯时，他被封到东方的鲁国。因在朝内离不开，便派长子伯禽赴鲁就国。临行前教导儿子说："我是文王的儿子，武王的胞弟，不能说地位不高。但我特重礼贤下士，直至'一沐三握发，一饭三吐哺'。"他送给儿子一个金人（童子），背后写上铭文，要求儿子勤谨治国、戒骄戒躁、深藏智慧、后发制人，才能立于不败之地。

2. Duke Zhou Teaches His Son

Duke Zhou, known by his given name Ji Dan, played a crucial role in overthrowing the Shang Dynasty and establishing the Zhou Dynasty. In the early years of the new regime, he led two expeditions eastward, established rituals, and composed music. When the various vassals were appointed to their respective states, he was assigned to govern the State of Lu in the east. However, due to his important duties at the Court, he sent his eldest son, Boqin, to rule Lu in his stead. Before his son left, Duke Zhou gave him this counsel: "As the son of King Wen and the brother of King Wu, I hold an esteemed position, but I place great value on respecting the worthy and the humble. As the saying goes, 'I would shorten my bath and meal to welcome those of virtue'." He gifted his son a golden figurine of a boy, with an inscription on the back urging him to be diligent in governing, avoid arrogance and impulsiveness, and to approach matters with wisdom and patience. By following these principles, his son would remain steadfast and invincible in his rule.

功高盖世数周公　　握发吐哺忑谦恭
三缄其口伯禽戒　　明德勤施万代宗

Duke Zhou's greatness filled the world, a legacy so grand,
With humble deeds, he showed respect across the land.
He warned his son Boqin to be cautious and circumspect,Many generations inherited this code of virtuous respect.

三、诗礼传家（孔鲤）

我国古代著名的思想家、伟大的教育家孔子，一生教出大量有作为的弟子，对子女的教育也很突出。《论语》中记他教儿子孔鲤学诗、学礼。因为"不学诗，无以言"，不学诗不能在大场合中说话。"不学礼，无以立"，不学礼不能在社会上立身、处世、做人。孔鲤虚心听取父亲的教导。为此提问的陈亢深为佩服。"诗"意味着文化的高层次，"礼"意味着守规矩。日后孔子后裔便以"诗礼"作为传世家风。

3. Confucius Passes on His Teachings of Poetry and Rites to His Son

Confucius, the great thinker and educator of ancient China, not only taught countless influential disciples but also placed great emphasis on the education of his own children. In *The Analects*, it is recorded that Confucius taught his son Kong Li the importance of studying poetry and rites. As Confucius stated, "Without learning poetry, one cannot express oneself appropriately in public." Similarly, "Without learning rites, one cannot stand firm in society or navigate social relations." His son, Kong Li, accepted these teachings with humility, internalizing them deeply. The scholar Chen Kang, who explored these teachings in his writings, admired both Confucius ' wisdom and Kong Li's earnestness in following his father's guidance. " Poetry" as Confucius taught, represented the highest cultural achievement, while " rites" signified the importance of upholding rules and maintaining propriety. In the generations that followed, the descendants of Confucius regarded these two principles—poetry and rites—as the core values of their family tradition.

孔子庭训陈亢夸　学诗学礼育英华
圣裔代代遵庭训　千古诗礼传孔家

Confucius taught his son with care, his lessons widely praised,
In poetry and rites, he shaped his mind, with wisdom to be raised.
His descendants cherished these lessons through each age,
For centuries, the legacy of verse and rites did wage.

四、遗子一经（韦贤）

西汉时邹（今山东邹城市）人韦贤，自幼刻苦读书，精通《礼经》《尚书》，是邹鲁一带闻名遐迩的儒学大师。他曾任汉昭帝的老师，宣帝时官至丞相。他经常用儒家的经典教育子孙，叫他们依圣贤的标准立身处世。其子韦玄成以明经入仕，做了七年宰相。他的家风是：读经做人做事，不务虚名，不贪钱财。当时邹鲁一带流行的谚语"遗子黄金百籯，不如教子一经"，便是指韦家而言。

4. Wei Xian Leaves His Children Nothing but the Classics

Wei Xian, a native of Zou (present-day Zoucheng City, Shandong Province) during the Western Han Dynasty, was a dedicated scholar from a young age. He became well-versed in *The Book of Rites* and *The Book of History*, gaining widespread renown as a Confucian scholar throughout the region. Wei Xian served as a teacher to Emperor Zhao of Han and later held the prestigious office of prime minister under Emperor Xuan. He was committed to educating his children in the Confucian classics, urging them to shape their lives and conduct according to the principles of the sages. His son, Wei Xuancheng, an expert in the classics, followed in his father's footsteps, serving as primeminister for seven years. Wei Xian's family motto emphasized the importance of reading the classics: "Study the classics to gain wisdom and guide your actions, without being distracted by fame or fortune."A popular saying in the region reflects his family's values: "Better to leave your children the classics than a hundred chests of gold." This proverb was inspired by the Wei family's long-standing tradition of valuing knowledge above material wealth.

父子丞相汉室奉　乐学孔儒德才增
诗礼教子人称颂　最佳遗产留一经

Father and son both served as premiers in the dynasty of Han,
The Confucian classics taught each self-cultivation as a man.
Folk praised how they took poetry and rites as a touchstone,
The classics are the singular best inheritance alone.

五、不留积蓄（疏广）

汉代兰陵（今山东兰陵）人疏广，在朝内做到太傅。五年后，辞职回家，皇帝念他的功劳，赐给他黄金（赤铜）二十斤，太子又送他黄金五十斤。这在当时是很大的货币数目。他回到家后，经常摆设酒宴，招待族人、亲朋、大量的同乡，花去很多钱。对乡中需要接济的人，慷慨赠送，又花去很多钱。有人劝他置办些田产，留给子孙。他说："我家以前的地由他们耕种，所得已够过日子了。贤而多财，则损其志；愚而多财，则益其过。不多给他们财产，正是疼爱他们。"

5. Shu Guang Leaves No Inheritance for His Children

Shu Guang, a man from Lanling (now in Shandong Province) during the Han Dynasty, served as the Grand Preceptor in the imperial court for five years. Upon resigning from office and preparing to return home, the emperor, recognizing his contributions, rewarded him with twenty pounds of gold (actually scarlet copper). The crown prince also presented him with fifty pounds of gold as a farewell gift. This was a substantial amount of currency at the time. After returning home, Shu Guang frequently hosted banquets and gatherings, entertaining relatives, friends, and many of his fellow townspeople, thus spending much of the money. In addition, he was generous in providing for those in need in his community, which further depleted his funds. Some advised him to buy land or property to leave for his descendants. He responded, "The land our family has been farming is enough to support them if they work hard. A wise man who comes into great wealth may lose his drive, while a fool with too much money will only increase his faults. I show my love for my children by not leaving them a large inheritance."

疏广疏财辞官返　不给子孙留田产
贤者多财损其智　愚者多财惹祸端

Shu Guang, with fortune, returned from his post,
Refused to leave lands, nor wealth to boast.
For wealth, the wise may lose their drive,
While fools with riches only thrive in strife.

六、拒收财物（欧阳地余）

西汉千乘（今山东博兴）人欧阳地余，汉文帝时做到管钱财的少府。他经常告诫儿子们说："我从来不贪财，你们也不要贪财。我将来死后，朝廷会给我很多钱财。你是朝内少府的儿子，更要以清廉著称。只有廉洁，才能干出一番大事业来。"欧阳地余死后，朝廷及少府中一些官员送来很多钱。许多人感念他的功德，也送来不少礼物，他儿子谨遵父嘱，一一婉言谢绝。皇帝听到此事，对他父子大加赞赏与表彰。

6. Ouyang Diyu Refuses Bribes

Ouyang Diyu, a native of Qiansheng (present-day Boxing, Shandong Province), served as the Chancellor in charge of finances during the reign of Emperor Wen of the Western Han Dynasty. He frequently advised his sons: "I have never been greedy for wealth, nor should you be. After my death, the Court will reward me with great sums of money. As the sons of the Chancellor in charge of finances, you must uphold a reputation for honesty and integrity. Only through these virtues can one accomplish great things." After Ouyang Diyu's passing, the Court and his colleagues sent large sums of money and numerous gifts in recognition of his contributions. His sons, honoring their father's wishes, politely declined all offerings. When the emperor learned of this, he praised Ouyang Diyu and his sons highly and rewarded them accordingly.

欧阳地余不贪婪　教育子女亦清廉
拒收钱财遵父教　皇帝赞誉父子贤

Ouyang Diyu never sought to grasp after gold,
Be honest and upright was what his children were told.
After his death, his sons declined all condolences and gold,
The emperor praised both generations of that household.

七、不务私产（范迁）

东汉沛国（今安徽濉溪）人范迁，官做到司徒。此人清廉节俭，对子孙要求也严。当他做渔阳太守时，有宅子数亩，田地一顷。他一点也不要，都送给侄儿。妻子劝他："我们有四个儿子，把你的俸禄省下来，置些产业，留给他们。"范迁回答："我作为国家的大臣，不要整天考虑积累财富，谋取私利。为官应尽忠，应做世人的楷模。"他为官多年，没有留下多少遗产，孩子们都自力更生，学有所成。

7. Fan Qian Never Pursued Private Wealth

Fan Qian, from Pei (modern-day Suixi, Anhui), held the position of Prime Minister during the Eastern Han Dynasty. Known for his integrity and frugality, he held his children to high standards. When serving as the Prefect of Yuyang, he owned a few acres of property and one hectare of land, but he left it all to his nephew, giving nothing to his own children. His wife advised him, "We have four sons. Why not save from your salary and buy some property to leave for them?" Fan Qian replied, "As a minister, I should not focus on accumulating wealth or seeking personal gain. A public official must be loyal to his duties and serve as an example for others." Though he served for many years, Fan Qian left little material inheritance. His children, however, all became self-sufficient and excelled in their studies.

范迁为官多清廉　教子有方均从严
田宅给侄不遗子　儿孙发奋立世间

An honest and decent official by the name of Fan Qian,
Applied strictness when educating his children.
His properties were passed on to a nephew
He encouraged his offspring industry to pursue.

八、父子勤廉（杨震、杨秉）

东汉时华阴（今属陕西）人杨震，深夜拒贿，曾说"天知、地知、你知、我知"，古今闻名。他也以清廉的作风教育儿子。他官职很高，家里却一直粗茶淡饭。孩子们出门无车马，一律步行。一些老友劝他置些田产留给子孙，杨震不接受，还说："我留给子孙的是做一个清官的好名声，让他们高素质地做人做事，这正是一份丰厚的遗产。"果然，其子杨秉官至太尉，清正廉明，被人们称作"酒、色、财三不惑"的好官。

8. Father and Son: Both Diligent and Upright

Yang Zhen, an honest official from Huayin (now part of Shaanxi Province) during the Eastern Han Dynasty, became famous for his integrity. One night, he refused a bribe, famously saying, "Heaven knows, Earth knows, you know, and I know." His reputation for honesty spread far and wide. Yang Zhen also instilled these values in his son. Despite holding a high government position, his household remained simple, living on plain food. His children never rode horses or traveled in carriages; they always walked when going out. When old friends urged him to accumulate property for his children, he refused, saying, "I leave them a legacy of being known as honest officials, so they will uphold good character and conduct. This is the richest inheritance I can give them." True to his father's teachings, his son, Yang Bing, rose to the position of Grand Commandant. Known for his uprightness and wisdom, Yang Bing earned praise as an exemplary official who avoided indulgences in wine, women, and wealth.

人间清廉颂"四知"　　杨震教子亦称奇
不留财富留清名　　　太尉杨秉亦良吏

Yang Zhen famously avoided bribes and corruption,
His educational methods were a model of instruction.
He left them no fortune but instead a good name,
His son followed in his footsteps as officials of fame.

九、千古《女训》（蔡邕）

东汉人蔡邕，字伯喈，是一位饱学的名家，曾有《汉书》等作品。他为了对自己的女儿蔡琰（文姬）进行教育，专门写了一篇《女训》。书中指出："人的心好像人的头脸一样，必须努力修饰它。脸不修饰会沾满灰尘，心不修饰要生邪念。脸不修饰是丑，心不修饰是恶。脸丑尚可，心恶难容于天地之间。"蔡琰谨遵父教，修德攻读，在动乱的年代里颠沛流离到乌桓，二十年后，又返回中原，整理父亲的遗作。

9. *Precepts for Ladies*: An Eternal Masterpiece

Cai Yong, courtesy name Bojie, was a renowned scholar of the Eastern Han Dynasty, known for his vast knowledge and works, including *The Book of Han*. One of his notable writings, *Precepts for Ladies*, was dedicated to his daughter, Cai Yan (courtesy name Wenji), offering her moral guidance. In this work, he wrote: "One's heart, like one's face, must be carefully maintained. If the face is neglected, it will become covered in dust; likewise, if the heart is left unguarded, it will give rise to evil thoughts. An unkempt face is unattractive, but an unkempt heart is a source of wickedness. An unattractive face may be tolerated, but the world cannot bear a corrupt heart." Cai Yan took her father's teachings to heart, diligently studying and cultivating her moral character. During the chaotic times that followed, she was forced to move from place to place. After twenty years, she finally returned to the Central Plains, where she devoted herself to compiling her father's works.

名士蔡邕有心人　为教爱女作《女训》
文姬品高遵父教　才女传世多诗文

Cai Yong, the noted scholar, had great consideration,
He wrote *Precepts for Ladies* for his daughter's cultivation.
His daughter was talented and filial, as per his guidance,
She composed countless poems and prose of influence.

十、丰宴责侄（陆纳）

晋朝吴郡华亭（今苏州）人陆纳，任吏部尚书兼东都卫尉将军时，宰相谢安要到他家拜访。他主张节俭待客，但他侄儿却偷偷准备了一桌丰盛的宴席。事后他训斥侄儿说："你坏了我家节俭清白的名声！"令人将侄儿打了四十棍杖，责令以后要清白节俭做事、做人。

10. Lu Na Rebukes His Nephew for a Lavish Banquet

Lu Na, a man from Huating County in Wu (modern-day Suzhou) during the Jin Dynasty, served as the Minister of Civil Affairs and General of the Eastern Capital. When Xie An, the Prime Minister, came to visit his home, Lu Na, known for his commitment to frugality, expected a modest reception. However, his nephew secretly arranged a lavish banquet to honor the distinguished guest. Afterward, Lu Na was furious. He reprimanded his nephew, saying, "You have ruined our family's reputation for honesty and simplicity!" As punishment, he ordered his nephew to be beaten with forty lashes, insisting that he learn the importance of maintaining a life of integrity and thrift.

高官仍应务勤俭　待客勿用丰盛宴
侄儿不遵遭责打　正道教子家规严

A senior official was still with diligence and frugality blessed,
He refused lavish banquets no matter how lofty was his guest.
His nephew received a beating for not heeding this moral,
He set a good example for teaching children withal.

十一、《家训》示范（颜之推）

南北朝时北齐的颜之推，复圣颜回的后代，原籍琅玡（今山东临沂）。他所著《颜氏家训》十篇，每篇都有对子女的具体要求与训示。其中"教子""治家""勉学"等篇教子的内容更多。书中说：孩子大多是中等智力的人，不经教育，不知好坏。古人重视胎教，生下来更应加强教育，不要急于求成。从婴儿起，就教育他懂仁、义、礼、智、信，慢慢养成习惯。父母的严要求与身体力行，使儿女看到榜样。家中许多子女，都要一视同仁，对谁都不要溺爱。书中也举出一些反面的例子作为教训。此书被历代誉为家训的典范。

11. Yan Zhitui's Family Admonitions

Yan Zhitui, a scholar of the Northern Qi during the Northern and Southern Dynasties, was a descendant of Yan Hui, the most renowned disciple of Confucius. He came from Langya,present-day Linyi in Shandong Province. Yan Zhitui authored *Admonitions* for *the Yan Clan*, a work consisting of ten chapters, each providing specific instructions for his children. Among these chapters were those titled "Teaching Children," "Regulating the Family," and "Encouragement of Learning," which focused heavily on the education of children. In the text, he wrote: "Most children, though of at least average intelligence, must be taught to distinguish between good and evil. The ancients emphasized education beginning from conception, and once born, a child must be nurtured with care, as haste will lead to failure. From infancy, children should be gradually taught the fundamental virtues-benevolence, righteousness, propriety, wisdom, and trust—and cultivate good habits over time. Parents must set strict standards and lead by example, showing their children a model to follow. All children should be treated equally, without favoritism. The book also includes cautionary tales as lessons." This work has been regarded through the ages as a quintessential guide to familial education.

颜裔之推学先贤　《家训》一书光史篇
教子勉学多严峻　瓢家风延千年

Yan Zhitui, followed the example of the sages,
And compiled Admonitions which were passed down through the ages.
He set up strict study standards for his children's ears,
Which sustained his family for thousands of years.

十二、《幼训》教子（王褒）

南北朝时北周的文学家王褒，为教育子女，亲撰《幼训》。内容有：以前大禹不惜美玉，却惜寸阴。一个文人应抓紧读书，一个武人应抓紧时间练武，不要虚度光阴。读书时要保持安静的环境。古人在桌子、手杖、盘盂等器物上都刻有鼓励学习的警语，学子们抬头就能看见。《诗经·大雅·文王之什》里有一首诗说一个人一般有好的开始，却往往不能有好的结局，做人做事干什么都要善始善终。孔子说过：在任何条件下都要坚持学习，一定要记住圣人的名言并付诸实践。

12. Wang Bao's *Admonitions for Teaching Children*

Wang Bao, a renowned scholar of the Northern Zhou during the Northern and Southern Dynasties, wrote *Admonitions for Teaching Children* to guide the education of his children. His teachings included lessons such as: In the past, the great Yu valued time over precious jade, meaning that time should never be wasted. A scholar must seize every opportunity to read, just as a warrior must diligently practice martial arts. He emphasized that reading requires a quiet environment. The ancients inscribed motivational sayings on objects like desks, walking sticks, and plates so that students could see them and be reminded of their importance. In *The Book of Songs*, there is a poem that illustrates how a poor beginning rarely leads to a good end, and that everything worth doing should be done well from start to finish. Confucius also stressed the importance of persistence in learning, regardless of circumstances, and emphasized that the teachings of the sages should always be remembered and put into practice.

王褒《幼训》非宏文　　谆谆教子惜寸阴
善始善终做好事　　　一言一行遵圣箴

Wang Bao's Admonitions were short and concise,
Setting parameters for time management precise.
A good ending should a fine beginning complement,
One's actions should the sage's wisdom implement.

十三、格言教子（房玄龄）

唐初名相房玄龄，临淄（今山东临淄）人，辅佐唐高祖、太宗，居相位十余年，一直勤政清廉，对家人、子弟要求也很严。为使他们不忘规矩，制定下一些具体要求，要子弟们必须遵守。特别要子弟不应恃门第高贵而骄横奢侈。他令人将古今的一些家训集中起来，写到室内屏风上。不仅让子弟们时时观看，还教他们各自抄写一份，带回各自室内，随时阅读。并告诫他们，依此行事可保一生平安无事。要向古人治家有成的人学习，永葆勤恳廉洁的好作风。

13. Fang Xuanling's Admonitions for His Sons

Fang Xuanling, a distinguished statesman from Linzi (modern-day Shandong Province), served as primeminister in the early Tang Dynasty, assisting both Emperor Gaozong and his successor, Taizong. He held the position for over a decade, known for his dedication to governance and his integrity. Fang Xuanling was equally strict with his family and children, setting clear expectations for their behavior. He emphasized that his children should not become arrogant or extravagant due to their family's high status and his own position of power. To instill these values, he instructed an assistant to gather a collection of significant family precepts from both ancient and contemporary sources, which were then inscribed on the screens in his home. He required his children not only to read these mottoes regularly but also to copy them by hand and keep a copy in their own rooms for continuous reflection. Fang Xuanling taught them that adhering to these principles throughout their lives would bring peace and success. He encouraged them to learn from the examples of well-governed families and to maintain a life of diligence, honesty, and integrity.

初唐名相房玄龄　苦心教子书屏风
格言名句时时记　子孙成才家业兴

A renowned prime minister with the surname Fang,
Was attentive to his offspring in the early days of Tang.
Educational mottoes covered every screen in the household,
His children enjoyed prosperity and virtue untold.

十四、拣食训孙（郑澣）

　　唐朝荥阳（今河南荥阳）人郑澣，一生忠于职守，勤俭自律，谦恭下人。他任河南尹时，一个堂兄弟的孙子从农村来，衣冠、言行都不得体，家里人都看不起他，郑澣却十分热情地接待了他，并初步答应在衙门里给他谋个职事的要求。但这个孩子在吃饭时，却将馒头皮全部剥下，扔在地上，郑澣见此奢侈行为，勃然大怒，喝令他马上拣起来，自己全部吃下。吃完后对他严厉地教训了一番，告诉他这么不节俭，不能去衙门任职。于是给他几个钱，打发他回去了。

14. Zheng Han Reprimands His Grandson for Wastefulness

　　Zheng Han, a native of Xingyang (modern-day Xingyang, Henan), lived during the Tang Dynasty. He was known throughout his life for his loyalty to duty, diligence, frugality, and self-discipline, as well as his modest and respectful behavior towards others. While serving as the Governor of Henan, a cousin's grandson visited him from the countryside. The boy's family looked down on him for his inappropriate attire and manners, but Zheng Han welcomed him warmly and was initially willing to help him secure a government post. However, during their meal, the young man removed and discarded the crusts from his steamed buns, throwing them on the floor. Upon witnessing such wasteful behavior, Zheng Han was deeply angered. He ordered the young man to immediately pick up the discarded food and eat it. After the meal, Zheng Han gave him a stern lecture, emphasizing that such extravagance was unacceptable and would prevent him from holding a government position. He gave the boy a small sum of money and sent him back to the countryside.

郑澣谦恭待乡童　热情接待帮谋生
馒头剥皮事虽小　严训此子送回程

To his rustic relative Zheng Han was hospitable and kind,
Ready to support his aspirational mind.
A simple act, just peeling the bread,
But a harsh lesson followed, and his hopes were dead.

十五、谨遵母教（崔玄玮）

唐朝博陵（今河北蠡县）人崔玄玮，官居同平章事、中书令。他做官勤恳清廉，一生牢记母亲的教导。他母亲说："自己虽然有个当大官的儿子，但却不富，这是很好的评价。"她又说："有人当了官，把大量钱财送给自己的父母，许多都是不义之财，和强盗抢来的财物有什么不同。为官应清廉、正直，才对得起你治下的百姓，也对得起你的父母。父母对子女真正的爱，是要他们勤恳工作、遵纪守法、清正廉明。"崔玄玮一生牢记母亲的教导，为官多年。不沾不贪，被人们称作清官。

15. Cui Xuanwei Obeys and Observes His Mother's Teachings

Cui Xuanwei, a native of Boling (modern-day Li County in Hebei Province), was an official during the Tang Dynasty. He held the position of Head of the Secretariat and was known for his hard work, integrity, and dedication to his duties.He was always guided by the teachings of his mother, who once said: "It is a greatthing to have a son in high office, but not to be wealthy—that is truly praiseworthy." She also warned: "Some officials send large sums of ill-gotten money to their parents. This is no different from property stolen by robbers. An official must be honest and upright, as that is the true way to honor both the people and their parents. True parental love lies in encouraging their children to work diligently, abide by the law, and maintain integrity." Cui Xuanwei took these words to heart throughout his life. He remained free from greed and corruption during his time in office, earning a reputation as a just and incorruptible official.

玄玮为官多清廉　得益慈母教诲严
贪官强盗同一物　清正廉明寿百年

Cui Xuanwei was an official upright and decent,
Who benefited from mother's teachings prescient.
Corrupt officials and robbers are one and the same,
But honesty and honor keep a spotless name.

十六、坚守直道（穆宁）

唐朝河内（今河南沁阳）人穆宁，官居太子左庶子、秘书监。他离任归家后，亲自写作《家令》，以此教育自己的子孙。写成后，把子孙们叫到一起，向他们宣读，并令他们每人抄写一份，不断学习、实践。他经常告诉子孙们：一个道德高尚的人，应把事亲、养志当作首要任务。在社会上事事坚守直道。他说："我一生坚守直道，以直道对人、对己、对社会都有好处。如果你们不守直道，早晚会受其害。我死后即使用'三牲''五鼎'祭祀我，我也不承认你们是我的子孙。"

16. Mu Ning Sticks to the Right Path

MuNing, a native of Henei (modern-day Qinyang, Henan), served during the Tang Dynasty in roles such as tutor to the crown prince and curator of the imperial library. After retiring from office and returning home, he wrote *The Order of the Family* as a guide to educate his descendants. Once completed, he gathered his children and grandchildren, read it aloud to them, and instructed each one to copy it for continuous study and practice. MuNing often reminded his family: "A person of high moral standing must prioritize honoring their parents and nurturing their ambitions. In all things, one must adhere to the straight path." He continued, "I have followed the straight path throughout my life, and it has been beneficial both for myself and society. If you stray from this path, harm and misfortune will inevitably follow. Even if, after my death, you offer sacrifices of cattle, sheep, and pigs in my honor, I will not acknowledge you as my descendants if you forsake the straight path."

> 穆宁为官重洁身　亲写《家令》教子孙
> 勤恳务实直道循　为官清廉民欢欣

To honesty and cleanness MuNing adhered,
With *The Order of the Family* his children he reared.
Diligence and sincerity steered him on the course correct,
Eschewing corruption won this official respect.

十七、两清示范（韩休）

唐朝长安（今陕西西安）人韩休，玄宗时官居中书门下平章事（宰相）。他忠于职守、敢于对皇帝犯颜直谏。有人说："韩休为相，皇帝瘦了。"玄宗说："我瘦了，天下肥了。"自身清廉正直的韩休，以自己的行动给儿子韩滉做出榜样。韩滉十分节俭，衣服被褥十年更换一次，宰相府第不设仪仗。当年的门第很小，堂屋没有厢房，也不扩建。为官多年，拉车的五匹马从来没换过，都是死在马棚里。人们对清正廉明的两代宰相赞不绝口。

17. Han Xiu and His Son Set Exemplary Standards as Honest Officials

Han Xiu, a native of Chang'an (present-day Xi'an, Shaanxi), served as prime minister during the reign of Emperor Xuanzong in the Tang Dynasty. Known for his dedication to duty, he was not afraid to speak candidly to the emperor. It was said, " Han Xiu, as primeminister, has made the emperor lose weight due to his frank admonitions." To this, Emperor Xuanzong replied, "Although I may have lost some weight, the world has gained from having such a responsible prime minister." Han Xiu's personal integrity set a strong example for his son, Han Huang. Han Huang was so frugal that he replaced his clothes and bedding only once every ten years and never employed ceremonial attendants at his prime ministerial residence. His house had a modest façade, and he refused to expand it by adding wings or extra rooms. During his many years in office, the same five horses always pulled his carriage, each of them eventually dying in the stable from old age. Both Han Xiu and his son, two prime ministers known for their integrity, were widely praised by the people for their unwavering honesty and uprightness.

韩休忠君敢犯颜　一心为公人清廉
勤恳洁白教韩滉　两代宰相比示范

The dutiful Han Xiu did not fear being frank before the emperor,
He worked wholeheartedly and decently for public welfare.
Diligence and honesty he bequeathed to his son,
As model prime ministers they won praise from everyone.

十八、夫妻教子（贾玭夫妇）

宋初南皮（今河北南皮）人贾玭，任浚县县令时，执政果断严肃，为人仁爱谦恭。他和妻子很重视对子女的教育。他儿子贾黄中，从小聪明伶俐，五岁时就让他端坐识字背书，六岁中童子科，七岁能写文章。夫妻俩在生活上对儿子要求很严格，让他经常吃粗粮，蔬菜，告诉他事业成功方能吃肉。贾黄中在父母的严格教育下，努力攻读，十五岁便中了进士，后来当了累州知州，宋太宗淳化年间官居参知政事。因贾黄中政绩卓著，皇帝亲自接见了他的母亲王氏，夸他教育孩子像孟母一样。

18. Jia Pin and His Wife Work Together to Educate Their Son

Jia Pin, a native of Nanpi (now in Hebei Province), served as an official during the early Song Dynasty. As the county magistrate of Xun, he was known for his decisive and serious governance, while also being compassionate, humble, and diligent. Jia and his wife placed great importance on the education of their children. Their son, Jia Huangzhong, displayed exceptional intelligence from a young age. By the age of five, he was already sitting upright, learning to read and memorize books. At six, he passed the primary level exams, and by seven, he was able to write essays. At home, Jia and his wife were strict with his daily habits. They provided him with a simple diet of coarse grains and vegetables, telling him that he could only enjoy meat once he had achieved success in his career. Thanks to the rigorous education he received from his parents, Jia Huangzhong worked diligently in his studies and passed the imperial examinations at the age of fifteen. He later became the magistrate of Laizhou and was promoted to a high-ranking official position as a counselor during the Chunhua era under Emperor Taizong. Due to his remarkable achievements, the emperor personally summoned Jia Huangzhong's mother, Wang, to praise her for raising her son with the same dedication and wisdom as Mencius' mother.

贾玭夫妇教子严　年幼即令读书篇
教子成材帝赞许　堪比孟母良母范

Both Jia Pin and his wife were strict with their son,
Asking him to read and recite classics from when he was young.
Their guidance earned the emperor'spraise,
Like Mencius' mother, they set high ways.

十九、盲父教子（杨希闵）

宋初冯翊（今陕西大荔）人杨希闵，生下来就双目失明，但很愿学习。自己不能读书，让几个弟弟轮流读给他听。他记忆力特强，无论经书、史书，听过便能记住。他在广泛学习的基础上，勤奋著述，有二十卷文集问世。他有三个儿子，庆幸他们都耳聪目明，杨希闵及时对他们进行教育，叫孩子们珍惜自己优越的条件，努力攻读。写出文章来念给他听，听他提出的意见后进行修改，以古代圣贤之德教育儿子，使他们德才兼备。他的三个儿子都中了进士。

19. Yang Ximin, the Blind Father, Teaches His Sons

Yang Ximin, from Fengyi (now in Dali, Shaanxi), was born blind but had a deep desire to learn. Unable to read himself, he had his younger brothers take turns reading aloud to him. Remarkably, he possessed an excellent memory and could retain everything he heard, whether from classical texts or historical records. Drawing from his vast knowledge, he diligently wrote and published twenty volumes of collected works. Fortunate to have three sons, Yang Ximin was eager to provide them with the best education. He encouraged them to appreciate their own advantages and to work hard in their studies. After they completed their writing, he asked them to read it aloud so he could offer suggestions for improvement. Through his teachings, he instilled in them the virtues of ancient sages, hoping to cultivate both their talents and their moral integrity. As a result, all three sons turned out to be successful candidates in the highest imperial examinations.

盲人希闵学习勤　听书强记学诗文
三子勤奋遵父教　个个成名光仕林

Yang Ximin lost his sight yet was a learner diligent,
As others read literature his ears were intent.
His three sons were uniformly attentive to learning,
All became scholars of wisdom and discerning.

二十、教子成材（向瑀）

北宋开封（今河南开封）的向瑀，曾任五代时北汉的符离县令，此人为人刚毅威严，勤政爱民。夫妇二人对唯一的儿子向敏中从不娇惯，严格要求。从小就要儿子端坐听取教诲，对儿子讲修身、处世、做人的道理，不断向儿子提出修身攻读的具体要求，妻子对儿子的教育也积极配合。向敏中在父母的严要求下，迅速成长，中试后当了朝廷的左仆射，昭文阁大学士。三十多年清廉爱民，百姓们交口称赞他是一位德高望众的好官。

20. Xiang Yu Cultivates His Son's Talent

Xiang Yu, a native of Kaifeng (now in Henan Province) during the Song Dynasty, served as the county magistrate of Fuli in the Northern Han state during the Five Dynasties period. Known for his firmness, resoluteness, and benevolent governance, Xiang was diligent in his duties and deeply cared for the well-being of the people. Both he and his wife were strict with their only son, Xiang Minzhong, never indulging him. From a young age, they required him to sit attentively and listen to their teachings, imparting lessons on self-cultivation, proper conduct in society, and moral values. They constantly set clear expectations for his academic studies and personal development, with his wife fully supporting these efforts. Under the strict guidance of his parents, Xiang Minzhong flourished, both in character and in his pursuit of knowledge. After passing the imperial examinations, he rose to the position of deputy prime minister and Grand Secretary of the Court. For over three decades, he remained honest and devoted in his service, earning the admiration of the people as a wise, respected, and virtuous official.

勤政爱民歌向瑀　敏中立志勤攻读
德高智广喜中试　县令教子成宰辅

Xiang Yu was praised for his benevolence,
His son resolved to be a scholar of eminence.
His talent and virtue ensured success in the examination,
From a servant to the county to prime minister of the nation.

二十一、包公遗训（包拯）

北宋合肥（今安徽合肥）人包拯，字希仁，官至龙图阁直学士，枢密副使，历权知开封府等职。此人为官清廉正直，刚毅果敢，断狱公平，百姓们俗谚"关节不到，有阎罗包老"。他在家对子女一惯严格要求，以身作则。他临死前的遗嘱，实际上就是一篇家训。说："我包姓后世子孙，仕宦有犯赃滥者，不得放归本家。亡殁之后，不得葬入大林。不从吾志，非吾子孙。"这种对子孙生不能入谱，死不能入林的惩罚，在当时应该说是最重的了。

21. Bao Zheng's Final Admonition for His Descendants

Bao Zheng, a native of Hefei (now in Anhui Province) during the Northern Song Dynasty, held the courtesy name Xiren. He rose to the position of Grand Secretary, Vice Director of the Privy Council, and previously served as the Prefect of Kaifeng.Known for his honesty, integrity, and unwavering resolve, Bao was a respected official who made impartial judgments. A common saying among the people went: "If your case isn't fairly judged, report it to Lord Bao, who is as just as the King of Hell." In his personal life, Bao Zheng was equally strict with his children, setting a clear example through his own conduct. His final will, made on his deathbed, served as a powerful family admonition: "Descendants of my clan, take heed: anyone who engages in bribery or abuses their power will be forbidden from entering the family temple or being buried in the ancestral graveyard. Those who disregard my wishes shall no longer be recognized as my descendants." The punishment of being excluded from the family genealogy and ancestral burial site was considered the most severe at the time.

清廉刚毅颂包公　家教育人亦成功
遗嘱谆谆人称赞　代代洁白似冰清

Lord Bao was ever upright and fair,
His family too were educated in a manner rare.
His last will was praised as resolute and precise,
Each later generation should be flawless like ice.

二十二、欧母教子（欧阳修）

北宋著名学者、官居参知政事的欧阳修，字永叔，庐陵（今江西吉安）人。四岁时父亲去世，母亲郑氏对他严格要求，教导他成人。欧阳修在他写的《泷冈阡表》中记述了欧母对他教导的内容："你父亲（欧阳观）为政清廉，又好施舍，死后没留下一间房、一块地。他管法律，判案子，经常秉烛达旦，常为不能赦免的罪人惋惜。他做事从来实实在在，讲究仁爱诚信……孝敬父母不一定要求生活上多丰盛，只要认真听取父母的教诲，天天向好处做就好。"欧阳修谨奉母教，成为居官清廉的一代文豪。

22. Ouyang Xiu's Mother Teaches Him to Follow His Father's Example

Ouyang Xiu, a renowned scholar and prime minister of the Northern Song Dynasty, was a native of Luling (modern-day Ji'an in Jiangxi Province). His courtesy name was Yongshu. He lost his father at the age of four, and his mother, Lady Zheng, took it upon herself to raise him with strict discipline, guiding him toward maturity. In Epitaph for *the Shuanggang Tomb*, Ouyang Xiu recorded his mother's teachings: "Your father, Ouyang Guan, was an honest, upright, and charitable official. After his passing, he left behind neither a house nor land. As a judge, he often worked late into the night, always feeling sympathy for those criminals whose cases he could not pardon. His actions were grounded in principles of integrity, kindness, and honesty... Filial piety does not require providing your parents with lavish comforts, but rather respecting their guidance and striving each day to become a better person." Ouyang Xiu followed his mother's guidance faithfully, becoming both a model of integrity and an esteemed scholar and official.

永叔自幼奉母教　父作榜样亦仿效
不为名利失弘志　政坛大家亦文豪

Ouyang Xiu always followed maternal instruction,
His late father was his template of gentlemanly construction.
Wealth or fame never blindsided his ambition,
To be both a statesman and a scholar of distinction.

二十三、对联添字（苏轼）

宋时眉山（今四川眉山）人苏洵与他的儿子苏轼、苏辙，时称"三苏"，均为当时著名学者。苏轼博通经史，人称青年才俊，自己也说作文如行云流水。他还为自己写了一副对联："识遍天下字，读尽人间书。"苏洵为教育儿子谦虚，在上面各添两字："发愤识遍天下字，立志读尽人间书。"苏轼看后顿感惭愧，此后更加谦虚，学问更大了。

23. Su Xun Educates His Son, Su Shi, by Adding Characters to a Couplet

Su Xun, along with his two sons, Su Shi and Su Zhe, were from Meishan, present-day Sichuan Province. They were collectively known as the "Three Sus" for their esteemed scholarship during the Song Dynasty. Su Shi, well-versed in the classics and history, was regarded as a young prodigy of his time. He often described his writing as flowing as effortlessly as clouds and water. To express his vast knowledge and aspirations, Su Shi wrote a couplet: "I know all the characters under the sun; literary works I've read every last one." In an effort to teach his son humility, Su Xun added two additional characters to the couplet, changing it to: "I strive to know all the characters under the sun; literary works I've set out to read every last one." Upon reading the revised version, Su Shi felt deeply ashamed. From that moment, he became more humble in his approach to learning, dedicating himself to further refining both his knowledge and writing skills.

青年英俊不应狂　怎能写联自夸张
老父分别添两字　谦恭学问才增强

A young talent should not be blown up with pride,
That self-conceited couplet warranted such a chide.
His father added four more words to teach and scold,
Humility is a catalyst to learning, not being bold.

二十四、《教子语》（家颐）

宋人家颐，字养正，眉山（今四川眉山）人。为教育子女，著《教子语》。书中说："教子是人生中的大事，父母对子女不要一切迁就的小慈，父辈应用适当的威严约束孩子，应用礼仪规矩来要求他们。"书中总结教子之法有五条："引导他的性情，开阔他的志向，培养他的才能，鼓励他的气势，纠正他的过失。"总之，德智两者并重，教育他摆正义和利的关系。有钱人家的孩子重点在道德，穷人家的孩子重点在节操。子女的贤与否全在自己努力，但家长也有重要的责任。

24. Jia Yi Writes Words for Children

Jia Yi, a native of Meishan (present-day Sichuan Province) in the Song Dynasty, held the courtesy name Yangzheng. He authored *Words for Children* to provide guidance for future generations. In this book, he writes: "Educating one's children is one of the most important duties in life. Parents should not indulge their children with excessive kindness, but instead, they should discipline them with appropriate authority, insisting that they adhere to proper etiquette and rules." The book outlines five key principles for raising children: "Guide their temperament, expand their ambitions, develop their talents, encourage their energy, and correct their faults." In essence, Jia Yi emphasized a balance between moral integrity and intellectual growth, urging his children to understand the relationship between justice and personal interests. For children from wealthy families, the focus should be on moral character, while for children from poorer backgrounds, integrity should be emphasized. Ultimately, a child's virtues depend on their own efforts, though parents also bear an essential responsibility in their upbringing.

《教子语》教儿曹　五项要求标准高
富贵人家重道义　贫穷之人重节操

Words for Children set forth for the future,
Five high standards, each one a noble feature.
In wealthy homes, moral values should reign,
While in humble ones, integrity must remain.

二十五、严斥劣子（耶律铎鲁斡）

辽国人耶律铎鲁斡，字乙辛隐，曾任南府宰相。此人虽位高权重，却清正廉洁。晚年退职回到乡里时，他儿子普古为古都节度使，派人把他接到府内居住养老。他到后，见住处十分豪华，儿子生活十分奢侈。马上严肃地对儿子说："你到外面为国当官，应千方百计为国家富强、百姓安乐努力。你自己贪图享受，于心何忍？你这么奢侈不对，应马上改正。"过了些日子，儿子不改，他义正辞严地对儿子说："我告诫你多次，你不听。我看不下去，只有马上离开了。"他走后不久，儿子因贪欲太多，被别人杀死了。

25. Yelü Duoluhan Chastises His Wayward Son

Yelü Duoluhan, a native of the Liao Dynasty, bore the courtesy name Yixinyin. He held a senior government position and was known for his integrity despite his high rank. When he retired and returned to his hometown in his later years, his son, Pugu, who served as the military governor of the capital, invited him to live in his luxurious residence. Upon arriving, Yelü Duoluhan was immediately struck by the extravagance of his son's lifestyle. He sternly admonished him: "As an official, your duty is to work relentlessly for the prosperity of the state and the happiness of the people. How can you indulge in such excess? This kind of wastefulness is unacceptable. You must change your ways at once." Despite his father's repeated warnings, Pugu continued to live lavishly. Yelü Duoluhan, now resolute, said to him: "I have advised you multiple times, but you refuse to listen. I cann't tolerate this any longer, and I will leave."Shortly thereafter, his son was killed, his demise brought about by his own greed.

辽国宰相性廉洁　子为高官务豪奢
谆谆教诲终无效　死于贪欲罪应得

The prime minister of Liao was upright and clean in his position,
He warned his son against luxury and extravagant disposition.
He did his best to suggest and correct him in vain,
The boy met a violent comeuppance while still fixated on gain.

二十六、因势利导（胡寅）

南宋崇安（今福建崇安）人胡寅，从小便被伯父胡安国收养。胡寅小时很聪明，学了点文化，但十分顽皮，难以管教。伯父把他关进一间堆满杂木的空房子里，他在屋内用木头刻了一些小人。伯父令人在屋里放进许多书，他越读越有兴趣，读了背诵，背诵后能悟出书中的道理。过了两年，学业大有长进，他伯父请来老师教他，后来又送进太学。不久中了进士甲科，后来当了官。其间被秦桧诬陷后又复了职，他在被贬期间写出《读史管见》《论语详说》等著述及《裴然集》三十卷。

26. Hu Yin is Guided to Become a Devoted Learner

Hu Yin, a native of Chong'an (now in Fujian Province) during the Southern Song Dynasty, was adopted by his uncle, Hu Anguo, at a young age. Though naturally clever and quick to learn, Hu Yin was also mischievous and difficult to discipline. To address this, his uncle confined him to a room filled with logs, hoping to encourage reflection. While locked in the room, Hu Yin began carving small figures from the wood. His uncle then placed books in the room, which sparked Hu Yin's interest. He eagerly devoured the books, memorizing passages and contemplating the lessons they offered. After two years of self-study, Hu Yin showed significant progress in his education. His uncle then hired a tutor, and Hu Yin was later sent to the Imperial College. He soon passed the highest imperial examinations and became an official. Later, after being unjustly slandered and demoted by the corrupt prime minister Qin Hui, Hu Yin was reinstated to his post. During his time in exile, he wrote several influential works, including *On Reading Histories*, *A Detailed Analysis of Confucius' Analects*, and a 30-volume collection of his writings titled Peiran Ji.

性相近来习相远　满屋书卷良习染
勤奋攻读终有效　一代名士歌裴然

Men's natures are similar, but their habits diverge,
A room full of books will help good habits emerge.
Diligent study will always bring its reward,
A renowned scholar, with wisdom stored.

二十七、大儒教子（朱熹）

南宋大儒朱熹，字元晦，婺源（今江西婺源）人，他一生有大量著述，广教弟子，声名卓著，同时也很重视对子女的教育。如《朱子全集》卷八中有篇他写给长子的一封信，其中写着："要早晚多读书，多向老师请教。要敬重别人，不要傲慢放肆；要谦虚谨慎，不要盛气凌人；不要饮酒，免得荒废学业；要交忠厚老实、真言快语的朋友，不要交阿谀奉承、傲慢放荡的朋友。要时时看到别人的长处，随时向别人学习。总之，一定要勤奋谦逊。在家可以学习，出外亦可学习，在外要控制自己，时时奋发有为，方可成功……"

27. Zhu Xi, the Great Confucian Master, Teaches His Son

Zhu Xi, a renowned Confucian scholar from Wuyuan (now in Jiangxi Province), was known for his vast scholarly works and for educating countless disciples throughout his life. Despite his fame and accomplishments, he placed a strong emphasis on his children's education as well. For example, in Volume Eight of *The Complete Works of Zhu Xi*, there is a letter he wrote to his eldest son, which reads: "You should dedicate more time to reading, both day and night, and seek advice from your teachers. Be respectful to others, avoiding arrogance; remain humble and cautious, never acting in an overbearing manner. Refrain from drinking, as it will waste your studies. Choose friends who are sincere, honest, and direct, rather than those who flatter or lead a reckless life. Always recognize the strengths of others and learn from them. In short, be diligent and modest. Whether at home or abroad, continue your studies. Control yourself when interacting with others, and always strive to improve. Only then can you achieve success."

大儒身正教子严　努力攻读学圣贤
勤奋谦逊走正道　子继父业歌薪传

The great master set a strict example for his son,
Through studying hard the sages could integrity be won.
His son followed the proper way with humility and diligence,
Emulating his father's success through deeds of intelligence.

二十八、《放翁家训》（陆游）

南宋大诗人陆游，字放翁，山阴（今浙江绍兴）人，一生诗词著作甚丰，其中还有一篇《放翁家训》，上面说："越是聪明的孩子，越容易变坏，越应严加管束。父母对聪明伶俐的孩子往往放纵、溺爱，还常向别人夸耀，更增长了孩子的傲气。应教育这种孩子谦虚、宽容、厚道、谨慎，加强自身修养，更不要与轻浮及惯于奉承的人交朋友。只有加强道德修养，才能真正成材。历史上多少小时聪明的孩子在吹捧中毁掉，父母悔之晚矣！"

28. Lu You Composes His Own Family Mottoes

Lu You, whose courtesy name was Fangweng, was a great poet from Shanyin(modern-day Shaoxing, Zhejiang Province) during the Southern Song Dynasty. He wrote an extensive body of poetry and prose throughout his life. Among his many works, he also composed a set of his family mottoes, which include the following advice: "The more intelligent a child is, the more susceptible he is to vice, and thus should be disciplined more strictly. Parents often indulge their bright children, praising them to others, which only feeds their pride. It is better to teach them humility, tolerance, kindness, and prudence. They should focus on self-cultivation and avoid associating with shallow or flattering friends. Only by strengthening their moral character can they truly succeed. Throughout history, many clever children have been ruined by excessive praise, and by the time parents realize the damage, it is too late to correct it."

诗词名家陆放翁　一篇训诫诉初衷
聪明孩子勤管教　敦厚谦逊方成功

A noted poet, styled Fangweng, was originally named Lu You,
He crystallised his familial concern in the form of the motto:
A bright child ought to be educated with diligence and discipline;
A honest and modest character will find its flourishing.

二十九、《渭涯家训》（霍韬）

　　明朝人霍韬，字渭先，山阴（今浙江绍兴）人，历任礼部尚书等职。他为了教育子女，专门写了《渭涯家训》，首先要自己的子弟参加农业劳动。只有亲自参加劳动，才知粮食来之不易，还可养成敦厚老实的作风。社会上许多有钱人家境破败，大多是不劳而食造成的。《诗经》中《硕鼠》篇把不劳动的人比作大老鼠，汉代把"孝弟力田"者表彰为社会上的好人。老师也要对学生时时进行是否劳动的考核，以此确定对学生的赏罚。

29. Huo Tao Writes His Family Mottoes

Huo Tao, whose courtesy name was Weixian, was born in Shanyin (now Shaoxing, Zhejiang Province) and served as Secretary to the Ministry of Rites during the Ming Dynasty. In his writings, he emphasized the importance of practical education, particularly urging his children to engage in agricultural labor. He believed that working the land would teach them the value of hard-earned sustenance and help develop a humble and honest character. Huo Tao observed that many wealthy families fell into ruin because they lived in comfort without experiencing the hardships of labor. Drawing on *The Book of Songs*, where those who avoided work are likened to "fat rats", he stressed that true virtue was found in those who worked diligently, especially when combined with filial piety and brotherly affection. Furthermore, he encouraged teachers to regularly assess students' involvement in manual labor,using it as a basis for rewarding or disciplining them.

> 霍韬家训倡务农　敦厚朴实好作风
> 不劳而食为硕鼠　孝弟力田最光荣

Huo Tao's family motto called for work in the field,
Seeing labor as a virtue, a truth that would yield.
Idle men, indulging, were likened to fat rats,
While filial toil in the fields earned the highest of stats.

三十、教子奋发（徐媛）

徐媛，字小淑，明代长洲（今江苏吴县）人，嫁给副史范允临。与丈夫共同筑室居于山下，著《络纬吟》十二卷传世，此书记下一些教子的内容。首先说子女成人后，不要"怯懦无为"，要像雄鹰一样"奋发雄飞"，立志勤学，朝夕无怠。钻研时应聚精会神、深思熟虑、排除杂念。处事要心中有数，又要通情达理，做事应从小处着手，然后扩而大之。一切事情要处理得恰到好处。子女应认真记取父母的箴言，将来才能成为有用之材。

30. Xu Yuan Teaches Her Son to Exert Himself

Xu Yuan, who had the style name Xiaoshu, was from Changzhou in the Ming Dynasty (present-day Wu County in Jiangsu Province). She married Fan Yunlin, the deputy minister. The couple built their own hut and lived at the foot of a mountain. She wrote twelve volumes of *Songs of Principles*, a number of chapters of which are concerned with the education of children. First, it was affirmed that children in their formative years should not be cowardly and lack motivation but instead be vigorous as soaring eagles, resolving themselves to diligently and relentlessly chasing after learning, night and day. One ought to be scrupulous, thoughtful and free from distractions while reading, researching and reflecting. In dealing with issues, one should be well-planned, considerate, and reasonable. One should handle everything with propriety. Children should learn their parents' precepts by heart and strive to be accomplished talents in the future.

徐媛传世《络纬吟》　　夫妻唱和教子孙
应效雄鹰搏万里　　好学修德方成人

Xu Yuan's *Songs of Principles* stands as her lasting fame,
A couple united, in guiding their children to claim.
Children, like eagles, should soar with ambition so high,
For those who cherish learning, success will surely fly.

三十一、庞氏《家训》（庞尚鹏）

明朝人庞尚鹏，字少南，南海（今广东广州）人，曾任福建巡抚等职。此人为官清廉，有鉴于社会上一些弊病，为怕子女染上恶习，特著《家训》，以警后人，上面写："子女要穿布衣，吃蔬食，不要以饮食粗劣、衣不华美为耻。自己能干的事，不要役使别人。半文钱也不应浪费，浪费的人早晚要受惩罚，不浪费的人不会受饥寒。亲朋之间不必过多的馈赠，招待客人只要心诚，不必太丰盛"诸如此类等等。他对子弟们严格要求，自己做出榜样，其子弟一个个被培养成好人。

31. Pang Shangpeng Writes Family Mottoes for His Clan

Pang Shangpeng, styled Shaonan, hailed from Nanhai (modern-day Guangzhou, Guangdong). He served as the Governor of Fujian during the Ming Dynasty. Known for his honesty and integrity, Pang was concerned that his children might fall prey to the vices prevalent in society. To guard against this, he composed a set of *Family Mottoes*, aiming to guide future generations. In these mottoes, he wrote: "My children should wear simple cotton clothes and eat simple meals of vegetables—never shameful of their modest attire and food. Do not ask others to do what you are unwilling to do yourself. Never waste even a single penny, for those who waste will eventually face hardship, while those who save will be spared hunger and cold. Do not overindulge in giving gifts or hosting lavish feasts among friends and relatives.Offer sincere hospitality to guests, not excessive displays." Pang held his children to strict standards, setting an example with his own actions, and as a result, they grew up to be responsible and virtuous individuals.

尚鹏教子写《家训》　教训子孙务勤谨
自力更生成大事　　　勤俭奋发福自临

Pang Shangpeng wrote *Family Mottoes* with his children in mind,
Demanding that posterity uphold him to be diligent and kind.
He believed that self-reliance will prosper great fruits,
Of diligence and hard work blessings will be the shoots.

三十二、《朱子家训》（朱柏庐）

明末清初昆山（今江苏昆山）人朱用纯，字柏庐。一生致力于弘扬儒学，依照程朱学派精神知行并进，特倡主敬学说。康熙初年朝廷征发，固辞不就，在家著书及教育子孙。其《朱子治家格言》简明得体，脍炙人口。此文以传统家庭伦理为指导，从日常起居到家财、家教、家政、持家规戒，以及鼓励子女读书修身等等。文词通俗精练，二百多年来在民间传颂不衰，成为社会上教子理家的重要教材。

32. Zhu Bailu Collects and Popularizes *The Precepts of the Zhu Family*

Zhu Yongchun, styled Bailu, was from Kunshan (now part of Jiang shu) during the late Ming and early Qing Dynasties. He dedicated his life to promoting Confucianism, emphasizing both knowledge and practice in line with the teachings of the Cheng-Zhu school, and advocating respect as a core principle. Early in the reign of Emperor Kangxi, he was called to the Imperial Court but declined, choosing instead to remain in his hometown to write books and educate his children. His work, *The Precepts of the Zhu Family*, is noted for its clear, practical style and quickly gained popularity. Grounded in traditional family ethics, it addresses a wide range of topics, including daily life, family finances, family education, household management, and discipline. It also encourages children to read, study, and cultivate themselves. Due to its simple and concise language, it has been passed down through generations and remains a popular guide for family life and child-rearing, having influenced Chinese households for over two centuries.

《朱子家训》人人夸　　重德循礼立意佳
虽非雄文延百代　　通俗务实传万家

The Precepts of the Zhu Family proved very popular,
Its stress on morality and propriety had influence spectacular.
Its influence has lasted for centuries despite being so concise,
It became a household classic for being pragmatic and precise.

三十三、嘱妻教子（纪昀）

清代前期纪昀,字晓岚,献县(河北献县)人,清初著名学者,文学家,官至协办大学士,加太子太保。有《阅微草堂笔记》等书传世。他常年在外为官,教育子女的重任只好落在妻子身上。在他给妻子的信中说:"一般做母亲的,对子女往往无原则地溺爱,那样会害了子女。对子女应'以其道爱之',他提出对子女教育的原则有'四戒':不准晚起床,不准懒惰,不准奢华,不准骄傲。'四宜':一宜勤学,二宜尊师,三宜爱众,四宜慎食。"要妻子依此教子,将子女培养成人。

33. Ji Yun Entrusts the Task of Educating Children to His Wife

Ji Yun, styled Xiaolan, was from Xian County (now part of Hebei Province). He was a renowned scholar and literary figure in the early Qing Dynasty and held the prestigious position of Grand Secretary with the honorific title of Grand Guardian of the Heir Apparent. His works, including *Notes from the Yuewei Hermitage*, have been passed down through the generations. Due to his official duties that kept him away from home for much of the year, Ji Yun entrusted the responsibility of educating their children to his wife. In a letter to her, he wrote: "It is common for mothers to spoil their children without principle, which ultimately harms them. Parents should love their children without indulging them. Therefore, I propose the 'Four Don'ts' of child education: do not let them sleep in, do not tolerate laziness, do not allow extravagance, and do not permit arrogance. In contrast, the 'Four Dos' are: encourage them to study diligently, respect their teachers, love others, and eat modestly." He urged his wife to follow these principles in raising their children, with the goal of nurturing them into successful and capable adults.

一代文豪重教子　　在外从政嘱贤妻
戒财戒骄有"四戒"　　勤学修德有"四宜"

The noted author attached importance to children's education,
As duty kept him far from home this became his wife's vocation.
The "Four Don'ts" was enshrined as a template for instruction,
Together with the "Four Dos" it formed a manual for self-construction.

三十四、文正训子（曾国藩）

清末名臣曾国藩，字涤生，谥文正，湖南湘乡人。他所著《曾文正公家书》有几百篇教子理家的内容。如他在江西抚州做官时写给次子纪鸿的一封家书中，嘱咐儿子不要羡慕官场，要好好学习，做个读书明理的君子。也要勤俭自恃，习惯于劳作。不要觉得家庭富有而养成奢侈、华丽、懒惰的习惯。社会上无论士农工商只要勤恳节俭，没有不兴旺的，骄奢懒惰没有不衰败的。学习是为了提高自己的品德，年轻时加倍努力，才能达到既定的目的。

34. Zeng Guofan Admonishes His Sons

Zeng Guofan, whose style name was Disheng, was from Xiangxiang in Hunan Province. A prominent official in the late Qing Dynasty, he was posthumously honored with the title Wenzheng. He wrote *The Family Letters of Zeng Guofan*, a collection of hundreds of letters offering advice on education and family values. In one such letter, written to his second son, Zeng Jihong, while he was serving as an official in Fuzhou, Jiangxi Province, Zeng Guofan urged his son to focus on studying and to strive to become a learned and virtuous gentleman, rather than aspiring to acareer in the officialdom. He also emphasized the importance of diligence, frugality, and developing a habit of manual labor. Zeng Guofan warned against the temptation to fall into the bad habits of extravagance, luxury, and laziness, simply because of the family's wealth. He believed that people from all walks of life, whether scholars,farmers, or merchants, could prosper as long as they maintained diligence,earnestness, and frugality. On the other hand, arrogance, luxury, and idleness would inevitably lead to failure. In closing, he encouraged his son to pursue learning as a means of enhancing his character, noting that only through hard work and dedication in youth could one achieve their goals.

文正教子书信勤　修德行仁读诗文
不慕豪华勤磨练　笃学圣贤做完人

With regular family letters Zeng Guofan gave his children guidance,
Advocating morality, reading poetry and practicing benevolence.
The cultivation of virtue was threatened by luxury and glories,
A man could perfect himself by following the sages and their stories.

三十五、示儿节俭（张之洞）

清末名臣，洋务派代表张之洞，字孝达，河北南皮人。曾任总督、巡抚三十余年，直至大学士。他儿子赴日留学，花费甚多。他在信中教育儿子："求学宜先刻苦，不必交友酬应……一方之所销耗，则于学业一途必有所弃，否则用功尚不逮，仍有多大光阴供汝浪费。当稍知稼穑的艰难，尽其求学之本分。非然者，即学成归国，亦必一事能为，民情不知，世事不晓……"

35. Zhang Zhidong Urges His Son to Be Frugal

Zhang Zhidong, whose style name was Xiaoda, was from Nanpi in Hebei Province. A prominent official and a leading figure of the Westernization Movement in the late Qing Dynasty, he held various gubernatorial posts for over three decades before being appointed Grand Secretary. His son, studying abroad in Japan, was spending money recklessly, and Zhang reprimanded him in a letter: "A true scholar should first and foremost dedicate himself to hard study, rather than indulge in socializing or attending banquets. If you waste your time on idle pleasures, your academic efforts will inevitably suffer. However, if you devote yourself to your studies, you will find little temptation in frivolous activities. Remember the hardships of farming, and let them inspire you to remain focused on your primary pursuit— learning. If you return after your studies, yet fail to apply yourself, you will be unfit for real-life challenges, unaware of the struggles of the people or the workings of the world …"

清末名臣张之洞　官高不忘恤民情
儿子留日多浪费　严肃训子倡俭风

Zhang Zhidong, a prominent minister in the later days of Qing,
Never forgot to concern himself with the people's suffering.
On knowing how his son when overseas had been apt to splurge,
A frugal lifestyle he recommended, extravagance to purge.

三十六、贵在践行（钱泳）

清朝书画家钱泳，字梅溪，金匮（今江苏无锡）人。他在《履园丛话》中对年轻人提出"凡事做则会"的观点，认为任何事情你不接触它，不实际去做，就永远不会、不懂，要勇于实践，马上去做。拖拉不做，则贻误终生。为此，他引用本家钱鹤滩的《明日歌》："明日复明日，明日何其多？我生待明日，万事成蹉跎。世人若被明日累，春去秋来老将至。朝看东流水，暮看西日坠，百年明日能几何？请君听我明日歌。"

36. Qian Yong Teaches His Child that Practice Matters

Qian Yong, a Qing Dynasty calligrapher and painter, was born in Jinkui (modern-day Wuxi, Jiangsu Province). In his work *Words Penned in My Garden*, he advises young people with the principle that "everything is learned through doing". He believed that only by engaging with something directly and practically can one truly understand and master it. Therefore, one must be bold enough to put knowledge into practice without delay. Procrastination, he warns, can lead to a lifetime of regret. To emphasize his point, he quotes *The Song of Tomorrow* by his relative, Qian Hetan:

"Tomorrow comes and again comes tomorrow, Tomorrows are like rivers that endlessly flow. If all my things are put off till tomorrow,

My time wasted in delay will breed sorrow.

All mortals are burdened by the weight of tomorrow, As time slips by, they age without knowing.

In the morning, they see the water flowing east,

At dusk, they watch the sun in the west sinking low.

How many tomorrows will you have in your lifetime, Do you know? Please listen to my Song of Tomorrow."

钱泳教子方法多　勿讲空谈实际做
提倡凡事做则会　为此援引《明日歌》

Qian Yong taught his children with wisdom profound,
Emphasizing action, not mere words that confound.
He believed that true learning comes through doing,
And quoted *The Song of Tomorrow* to keep them pursuing.

第三章
诚敬孝亲

Chapter Three:

Honoring Parents with Sincerity and Reverence

一、仁德大孝（虞舜）

舜是我国古代社会有虞氏的首领。他的母亲早死，后母对他不慈，瞎眼的父亲瞽叟糊涂，后母生子象，为侵吞财产，在舜修仓时在下面放火，在舜淘井时在上面投石，多次加害他，舜均安全逃脱。但他对后母、弟弟的加害从不记恨，对父母一直孝敬、顺从。对异母弟一直友好，其孝行远近闻名。尧得知他孝亲爱人，德才兼备，便把管理天下的重任交给他，还把女儿嫁给他。

1. Shun Demonstrates His Supreme Filial Piety with Benevolence and Virtue

Shun was the leader of the Youyu clan in early Chinese society. After hismother passed away at a young age, his stepmother treated him cruelly, while his blind father, who was too confused to recognize the truth, remained unaware of her actions. His stepmother gave birth to a son, Xiang, and in her desire to secure the family inheritance for him, she repeatedly tried to have Shun killed. On one occasion, she had Xiang set the barn roof on fire while Shun was repairing it; on another, she had him drop heavy stones into the well while Shun was working below. Yet, through all these attempts on his life, Shun miraculously escaped harm. Despite this cruel treatment, Shun never harbored resentment toward his stepmother or his half-brother. Instead, he continued to honor and obey his parents with unwavering filial piety. His exemplary behavior, especially his forbearance and kindness toward those who wronged him, became widely known. When Emperor Yao heard of Shun's exceptional virtue, filial piety, and talents, he entrusted him with the governance of the realm and also married his daughters to him.

瞽叟昏聩象害兄　修仓淘井未害成
虞舜大孝闻天下　唐尧重孝禅贤能

Shun's blind father was blind and his half-brother vile,
He narrowly escaped death, through the barn and the well's trial.
His filial piety brought him honor and fame,
And Yao entrusted him with power and acclaim.

二、为孝离家（泰伯、仲雍）

周朝的先人古公亶父居于豳（今陕西邠县一带），有了很大发展。他有三个儿子：泰伯、仲雍、季历。季历的儿子姬昌特别聪慧、仁德，古公很想将地位传给他。泰伯、仲雍深知老父意图，为了完成老父的心愿，以采药为名，离家东去（成为日后吴国的祖先）。后来古公传位给季历，季历传位给姬昌，姬昌即励精图治、日后兴周灭商的周文王。

2. Two Brothers, Taibo and Zhongyong, Leave Home for Filial Piety

Gugong Tanfu, the ancestor of the Zhou Dynasty, originally lived in You, in what is now Bin County, Shaanxi Province. He made significant advancements for his clan and had three sons: Taibo, Zhongyong, and Jili. His youngest son, Jili, had a son named Jichang, who was exceptionally intelligent, virtuous, and benevolent. Seeing these qualities in Jichang, Gugong intended to pass on his position and inheritance to him. Taibo and Zhongyong, knowing their father's wishes, decided to leave home for the east, ostensibly to gather herbs, so that their father's plan could be realized. They eventually became the ancestors of the State of Wu. In time, Gugong passed his legacy to Jili, and Jili, in turn, passed it on to Jichang. Jichang later became Duke Wen of Zhou, and under his leadership, the State of Zhou flourished, eventually overthrowing the Shang Dynasty.

泰伯仲雍二大贤　　为孝老父离家园
季历得传姬昌继　　灭商兴周八百年

Taibo and Zhongyong, two sons of great worth,
Chose to leave their homeland to honor their birth.
They let their younger brother the dynasty take,
And for eight centuries, Zhou flourished in its wake.

三、黄泉见母（郑庄公）

春秋初年的郑庄公，小时候母亲不喜欢他，对其弟共叔却十分偏爱。郑庄公当上国君后，其母强令他违例把共叔封于国都内，后来又支持共叔反叛。郑庄公平定共叔之乱后，得知其母为后台，十分生气，激动地发誓"不到黄泉不与她见面"！数年后，郑庄公孝心未泯，思母心切，在大臣颖考叔的策划下，挖掘地道，在地道中与母亲相见，释怨团圆，满足其孝心。

3. Duke Zhuang of the State of Zheng Reunites with His Mother at the Man-made Yellow Spring

In the early Spring and Autumn Period, Duke Zhuang of the State of Zheng was neglected by his mother during his childhood, while his younger brother, Gongshu, was favored. After Duke Zhuang ascended the throne, his mother insisted on defying tradition by having Gongshu appointed within the capital. Later, she even supported Gongshu's rebellion. After Duke Zhuang quelled the uprising, he was enraged to learn of his mother's treachery. In his anger, he swore that he "would not meet her again until they were together in the Yellow Spring, meaning in the underworld." Years later, despite his anger, his filial piety and deep longing for his mother prevailed. With the advice of his minister Ying Kaoshu, he decided to dig into the earth until he reached the place where Zhuany and his morther to reunite with her there. This act allowed him to reconcile his feelings of resentment, fulfill his filial devotion, and achieve the longed-for reunion with his mother.

共叔为害乱郑国　庄公平叛万民悦
母助反叛酿大过　黄泉得见母子乐

When his younger brother Gongshu rebelled against the state,
Duke Zheng resisted him, causing the masses to celebrate.
His mother's treachery much anguish did bring,
Yet the two were joyfully reunited at the underground spring.

四、鹿乳奉亲（郯子）

春秋时期郯国（今山东郯城）的国君郯子，年少时好学、聪慧仁德，对父母竭诚尽孝。父亲患眼疾，有人说鹿乳可以治愈。他便四处寻找，未成，自己披上鹿皮，假扮小鹿，到深山去接近母鹿寻求母乳。一直未能如愿，却被猎人看见，几乎被射死。猎人感其孝心，送给他一头母鹿，让他汲取鹿乳，治好了父亲的眼疾。

4. Tanzi Serves His Father Deer Milk

Tanzi, the king of the State of Tan during the Spring and Autumn Period (now located in Tancheng, Shandong Province), was a bright and diligent young man known for his intelligence and benevolence. From a young age, he was also deeply filial to his parents, serving them with utmost sincerity. When his father developed an eye disease, it was said that deer milk could cure the ailment. After searching unsuccessfully for the milk, Tanzi took the extraordinary step of disguising himself in the pelt of a young deer. In this guise, he ventured into the deep mountains, hoping to approach a mother deer and obtain her milk. Despite his best efforts, he was unable to fulfill his wish and was nearly shot by a hunter who mistook him for a wild animal.Moved by Tanzi's unwavering filial piety, the hunter spared his life and gave him a doe as a gift. With the deer milk, Tanzi was able to cure his father's eye disease.

幼年郯子孝父尊　为觅鹿乳入山林
翻山越岭难如愿　猎户馈赠全孝心

For an early age Tanzi served his father with filial piety sincere,
He risked his life in the mountains seeking milk from a deer.
His brave but futile search moved a hunter so,
He rewarded his efforts with the gift of a doe.

五、芦衣谏亲（闵损）

闵损，字子骞，春秋末年鲁国武棠（今山东鱼台）人，孔子弟子。他生母死后，父亲又娶后母，生下两个儿子。后母对他不慈、歧视。一次，全家外出，他穿着不保暖的芦花续的芦衣，冻的手拿不住鞭子，父亲责打他时，发现后母给他做的芦衣，气愤的要休后母。闵损跪下苦苦哀求，说："母在一子单，母去三子寒。"父亲饶恕了后母，保住了完整的一家。

5. Min Sun Pleads for His Stepmother with His Reed-Catkin Winter Clothes

Min Sun, whose style name was Ziqian, was from Wutang in the State of Lu (modern-day Yutai, Shandong Province) and was a disciple of Confucius in the late Spring and Autumn Period. After the death of his biological mother, his father remarried, and his stepmother bore two sons. However, his stepmother was unkindand prejudiced toward him. One winter day, the family went out, and Min Sun wore a coat made of reed catkins that his stepmother had made for him. The cold was so intense that he could not hold the whip firmly to drive the cart. Seeing his struggle, his father grew angry and whipped him. Upon realizing that Min Sun's clothes were made of reed catkins, his father, in a fit of rage, decided to divorce his wife. Min Sun, kneeling before his father, begged him with tears: "If my mother stays, I alone will suffer from the cold. But if she leaves, all three of us will be cold." Touched by his filial piety, his father forgave his stepmother, and the family remained intact.

古贤大孝闵子骞　芦衣赶车难御寒
鞭衣父嗔反苦谏　父饶后母家团圆

Min Ziqian practiced filial piety in the days of old,
His garments of reed catkins could not resist the cold.
His father thrashed him on the cart, incriminating his stepmother,
But finally the three relatives were reconciled with each other.

六、恭作《孝经》（曾参）

曾参，春秋末年鲁国南武城（今山东嘉祥）人，与其父曾点同为孔子的弟子。他深悟孔子忠恕一贯之道，是孔子思想的嫡系传人。他在孔子指导下作《孝经》，将孝道提到应有的高度，自己还身体力行，是一名大孝子。他虽家境贫寒，仍然尽力让父母吃好，穿好，平时对父母问寒问暖，关怀备至，为孝养父母，不出外做官。父母死后，泪如涌泉，今曾庙内仍有涌泉井。

6. Zeng Shen Writes The Classic of Filial Piety

Zeng Shen, from Nanwucheng in the State of Lu (modern-day Jiaxiang, Shandong Province), was a disciple of Confucius, along with his father, Zeng Dian.He deeply understood the principles of loyalty and forgiveness as taught by Confucius and was regarded as a direct heir to his master's philosophy. Under Confucius'guidance, Zeng Shen wrote *The Classic of Filial Piety*, elevating the importance of filial devotion to its rightful place in moral thought. Zeng Shen not only taught filial piety but also lived it, earning widespread admiration as a model son. Despite his impoverished circumstances, he did everything in his power to ensure his parents were well-fed, well-dressed, and in good health. He attended to their needs with great care and warmth. To remain by their side, Zeng Shen even declined official positions outside his home,prioritizing his duties to his parents. When they passed away, his grief was so profound that his tears flowed like a fountain. To this day, a well known as "Fountain Spring" is preserved at his temple, symbolizing his enduring filial love.

曾子倡孝重实践　侍奉父母最周全
涌泉井边赞大孝　一部《孝经》万古传

Master Zeng advocated filial piety and practiced what he stated,
He attended to his parents with his care and warmth unabated.
Of his loyalty the fountain is the living testimony,
His *Classic of Filial Piety* has bequeathed a long legacy.

七、高祖孝父（刘邦）

汉高祖刘邦，早年是个狂荡不羁的人，在起义反秦的战争中，对儒生也很不礼貌。但是他称帝后，就重视起儒家思想尤其是儒家的孝道来。他当上皇帝后，每五天按时拜见父母，说："我在外是一国之主，在父母面前却是儿子，应该拜见。"不久，又召集群臣宣布，他父亲是比皇帝还高的"太上皇"，并从此定下汉朝以孝治天下。此后汉朝所有皇帝的谥号前都加一个"孝"字。

7. Liu Bang, the Founding Emperor of the Han Dynasty, Honors His Father with Filial Piety

Liu Bang, the founding emperor of the Han Dynasty, was known for his wild and unruly behavior in his youth, and during his uprising against the Qin Dynasty, he was often dismissive toward Confucian scholars. However, after he ascended the throne, he came to place great importance on Confucian teachings, particularly the virtue of filial piety. As emperor, Liu Bang made it a point to visit and bow before his parents every five days, saying, "Although I am the ruler of the nation, in the presence of my parents, I am still their son, and as such, I must show my respect by bowing to them." Soon after, he gathered his ministers and declared that his father was to be regarded with greater honor than even the emperor himself, and should be referred to as the "Supreme Emperor." This declaration marked the beginning of a policy in the Han Dynasty where the governance of the empire was guided by the principle of filial piety. This tradition continued, and the title of every subsequent Han emperor included the character "filial" to honor their devotion to this core value.

高居帝位亦孝亲　虔诚问候五日勤
太上皇尊高过帝　以孝治国江山稳

Liu Bang, despite an emperor, was filial in many ways,
He visited his parents without fail every five days.
He promoted his father so his privilege exceeded his own,
The Han enshrined filial piety as a virtue of the throne.

八、万石孝顺（石奋）

西汉初年的大臣石奋，河内郡温县（今河南温县）人，早年随刘邦起义，官至太子太傅。他四个儿子：石建、石甲、石乙、石庆，在朝内均做到俸禄二千石的大官，石奋教子有方，儿子们都仁德孝谨。尤其是长子石建，对父母恭敬孝顺，倍极关心，五天一问安，亲自洗涤父母的内衣。他做出的榜样，影响了子孙，有的子孙的孝亲事迹甚至超过了他。

8. Shi Fen Enjoys His Sons' Filial Piety with the Utmost Devotion

Shi Fen, a prominent minister in the early Western Han Dynasty, was from Wen County in Henei Prefecture (modern-day Wenxian, Henan Province). In his youth, he joined Liu Bang's rebellion against the Qin Dynasty and eventually rose to the prestigious position of Mentor to the Crown Prince. Shi Fen had four sons: Shi Jian, Shi Jia, Shi Yi, and Shi Qing, all of whom held high-ranking positions at court, each earning a salary of two thousand bushels of grain. Through his diligent guidance, Shi Fen instilled in his sons the values of benevolence, virtue, filial piety, and discretion. The eldest son, Shi Jian, stood out for his exceptional filial devotion. He treated his parents with the utmost respect and care, visiting them regularly every five days to check on their well-being and personally washing their undergarments. His exemplary behavior became a model for future generations, and some of his descendants even surpassed him in their acts of filial devotion.

父子五人万石君　身荣不忘孝双亲
石建为范孝父母　子孙个个孝道循

Father and son hauled in a salary of over ten thousand loads,
Despite their high official positions, they honoured filial codes.
Shi Jian serving his parents proved a model influential,
His descendants revered their elders with loyalty exceptional.

九、弱女伸冤（缇萦）

西汉时临淄（今山东淄博市临淄区）人淳于意，医术高明，救死扶伤，百姓称颂。但遭恶人陷害后，被押往京城（长安）受刑刑（砍足）。他十五岁的小女儿缇萦历尽艰辛，尾随父亲，远赴京城。千方百计找到了汉文帝，上书哭诉父亲的冤情，皇帝派人调查后，为其父平反。并采纳她的建议，在国内废除了肉刑。

9. Ti Ying, the Fragile Girl, Clears Her Father's Name

Chun Yuyi, a renowned physician from Linzi (modern-day Linzi District, Zibo City, Shandong Province), was celebrated for his exceptional medical skills and his selfless dedication to saving lives and treating the wounded during the Western Han Dynasty. Unfortunately, he was framed by a malicious person and was sentenced to the brutal punishment of having his feet amputated. His youngest daughter, Ti Ying, only fifteen years old, endured great hardship as she followed her father to the imperial capital, Chang'an. After overcoming numerous challenges, she managed to secure an audience with Emperor Wen of Han. With heartfelt and moving words, she pleaded for her father's innocence. Moved by her determination and sincerity, the emperor ordered an investigation into the case, ultimately exonerating her father. Moreover, the emperor heeded Ti Ying's suggestion and abolished corporal punishment throughout the country.

> 弱女缇萦意志坚　远奔京师述父冤
> 冒死上书救老父　废除肉刑惠人间

Ti Ying, the fragile girl wanted justice to prevail,
She sought to clear her father's name by following on his tail.
At the capital she pled his innocence with the bravery of a man,
The emperor was so moved that state torture did he ban.

十、怀念母恩（金日磾）

西汉初年，匈奴浑邪王杀了休屠王降汉，休屠王的儿子翁叔不得已降汉。后被皇帝赐姓金，名日。他认真学习汉朝文化，尤其是《孝经》。他对母亲生前孝敬，死后把母亲画像供于室内，自己每日做过什么好事，犯过什么错，均向母亲的画像汇报。后来成为朝内有名的孝子。

10. Jin Midi Honors His Mother's Memory with Deep Filial Piety

In the early Western Han Dynasty, King Hunye of the Xiongnu killed King Xiutu and surrendered to the Han Dynasty. King Xiutu's son, Wengshu, was forced to submit to the Han as well. The emperor granted him the surname "Jin" and the given name "Ri". Jin Ri devoted himself to studying Han culture, particularly The Classic of Filial Piety. He was deeply filial to his mother during her lifetime and, after her death, displayed her portrait in his home. Each day, he reported to his mother's portrait about the good deeds he had done and the mistakes he had made. Over time, he became renowned in the court as a model of filial piety.

匈奴王子读《孝经》　孝母敬母务力行
慈母虽逝仍孝敬　　供奉画像见真情

The Classic of Filial Piety was devoured by the Hunnish prince,
To his mother he gave service, respect and reverence.
Though she passed, his piety never ceased,
He honored her image, his devotion increased.

十一、卖身葬父（董永）

西汉千乘（今山东博兴）人董永，家境贫寒，少年丧母。为避兵祸，随父流徙到汝南，后又到安陆（今湖北孝感）。为治父病，到处求医买药，陆续变卖掉仅有的一点家产。父亲死后，无钱埋葬，便卖身为奴，给人当佣工换钱葬父。民间传说他在路上遇见仙女，以槐树为媒，与他成亲，并帮助他连夜织锦，得以赎身。

11. Dong Yong Sells Himself into Slavery to Give Father a Decent Burial

Dong Yong was from Qiansheng (now Boxing, Shandong Province) during the Western Han Dynasty. He grew up in a poor family and lost his mother at a young age. To escape the ravages of war, he and his father moved first to Runan, and later to Anlu (present-day Xiaogan, Hubei Province). Determined to cure his father's illness, Dong Yong sought out doctors and remedies, gradually selling off the little family property he had. After his father passed away, Dong Yong was left with no money to bury him. In desperation, he sold himself into slavery, working for a wealthy family in exchange for the funds to give his father a proper burial. According to legend, on his journey, Dong Yong met a fairy, who married him with a great locust tree as a witness. She helped him weave brocade overnight, using the proceeds to buy back his freedom.

董永卖身为葬父　成亲大媒槐荫树
仙女织锦抵身债　孝行感天千古誉

Dong Yong sold himself into bondage his father to bury,
But then wed beneath the locust tree to a girl who was a fairy.
To buy back his freedom she wove the finest brocades,
Thus moving the Heavens and nation for countless decades.

十二、大孝尽忠（赵苞）

东汉甘陵东武城（今河北故城县）人赵苞，字威豪。奉朝廷之命，带母亲、妻子到辽东上任时，母、妻被当时作乱的鲜卑人掠去。贼寇押着他母亲，声言要他献出城池即可放人。其母阵前义正辞严地要求儿子忠于国家，不徇私情。赵苞谨遵母命，眼见母亲被害时，奋力杀敌，取得胜利，保住辽东，全忠全孝。

12. Zhao Bao Manifests Great Filial Piety by Fulfilling His Official Duty

Zhao Bao, styled Weihao, was from Dongwucheng, Ganling (present-day Gu cheng County, Hebei Province) during the Eastern Han Dynasty. Upon the orders of the Imperial Court, he was appointed to an official post in Liaodong, along with his mother and wife. Unfortunately, both were captured by the rebellious Xianbei tribes. The rebels, holding his mother hostage, demanded that Zhao Bao surrender the city in exchange for her release. At the front of the battlefield, his mother sternly urged him to remain loyal to the country, advising him not to be swayed by personal emotions. Seeing her death at the hands of the enemy, Zhao Bao followed her wishes. With great resolve, he fought fiercely and defeated the attackers, ultimately protecting the city and fulfilling both his duty as a government official and his filial duty as a son.

母妻被掠心悲伤　以此换城不应当
大孝为忠男儿志　歼敌慰母青史香

Distressed as he was by his mother and wife's captivity,
He still refused to sacrifice the border city.
Love of the country is piety in its highest degree,
He won immortal fame through defeating the enemy.

十三、行乞孝母（江革）

东汉末年临淄（今山东淄博市临淄区）人江革，年少时丧父，精心奉养老母。当时天下大乱，他背着母亲四处逃难，到处行乞，要点东西给母亲吃，自己经常挨饿。贼寇掳去他母子等很多人，他苦苦哀求，放了他们。待他和母亲艰难地回到家中，以佣工挣钱养活母亲。母亲走不动，自制一辆小车拉着母亲。凡老母所需，无不尽量满足。人们称作"江巨孝"。

13. Jiang Ge Begs for Food to Serve His Mother

JiangGe, from Linzi (now a district of Zibo City, Shandong Province), lived during the late Eastern Han Dynasty. After losing his father at a young age, he devoted himself to caring for and supporting his mother with great devotion. During this chaotic and turbulent period, Jiang Ge carried his mother on his back as they fled from place to place in search of safety. To ensure his mother was fed, he often went hungry himself, begging for food. At one point, they were captured by bandits along with many others. After pleading earnestly for their release, they were set free. Upon their return, Jiang Ge worked as a laborer to earn money and provide for his mother. Since his mother was too frail to walk, he built a small cart to carry her. He did everything in his power to meet her needs, and the people praised him as "Jiang, the great filial son".

行佣供母受煎熬　身被贼掳苦哀告
孝心感人释老母　世间竞传江巨孝

Serving as his mother's carer he bore all on his back,
When seized by thieves he pleaded with the bandit pack.
His filial piety moved the criminals to release his old ma,
For generations his virtue has been praised both near and far.

十四、孝悌尽心（薛包）

东汉时汝南(今河南上蔡)人薛包,谦恭好学,对父母孝敬,远近闻名。其生母病死,后母生子后,怕他分去家产,对他一直存有戒心,挑唆父亲把他赶出家门,他哭着不走,后母把他打走。他在离家不远处结庐居住,每天到家中看望父母、打扫庭院。父母死后,他服丧六年,后来兄弟分家,他要最差的东西。日后其兄弟、子侄破了产,他仍主动帮助。

14. Xue Bao Does His Best to Be a Filial Son and a Fraternal Brother

Xue Bao, from Runan (present-day Shangcai, Henan Province), lived during the Eastern Han Dynasty. Known for his humility, love of learning, and filial devotion, he earned widespread admiration for his respect towards his parents. After his biological mother passed away from illness, his stepmother, fearing that he might claim a larger share of the family inheritance, grew suspicious and hostile toward him. She incited his father to expel him from the household. Despite being driven out and beaten by his stepmother, Xue Bao refused to leave tearfully. He then built a modest hut nearby and continued to visit his parents daily, cleaning their courtyard with dedication. After his parents passed away, he observed a mourning period of six full years. When the family property was divided between him and his stepbrother, he intentionally chose the lesser portion. Later, when his brother and nephews faced financial ruin, Xue Bao willingly offered them help, demonstrating his enduring sense of filial and fraternal duty.

薛包孝亲发内心　后母虽虐仍孝亲
兄弟分家多谦让　照顾子侄仍尽心

Genuine and sincere was Xue Bao's piety,
Being undiminished by his stepmother's tyranny.
When the family property was divided, he drew the short straw.
Seeing his nephews in trouble, he helped them all the more.

十五、孝行感盗（彭修）

东汉时毗陵（今江苏常州）人彭修，十五岁时，父亲带他探亲，路遇强盗，抢去他们的财物。他与父亲拼命反抗，强盗按倒父亲毒打。彭修反抗时，从强盗身上抽出佩刀说："父亲受辱，儿应代替，你们放了我父亲，打我吧，杀了我吧！"强盗们被他的孝心感动，放了他父子，纷纷离去。

15. Peng Xiu's Filial Deeds Move the Bandits

Peng Xiu, from Piling (present-day Changzhou, Jiangsu Province),lived during the Eastern Han Dynasty. At the age of fifteen, he and his father were traveling to visit relatives when they were confronted by bandits who robbed them of their belongings. As the bandits began to beat his father, Peng Xiu fought desperately to protect him. In the heat of the struggle, he managed to seize a sword from one of the bandits and, with great courage, declared: "My father is being humiliated by you. As his son, I should take his place. Please release him. I place myself at your mercy—beat me, or kill me, but spare my father!" Moved by his filial piety, the bandits were so touched that they released both father and son, and left without further harm.

> 幼年彭修知孝亲　　途遇强盗尽力拼
> 为救父亲愿身替　　强盗感动即放人

Peng Xiu, although young, knew true fidelity,
He struggled hard against the bandits' brutality.
He would lay down his life his father to rescue,
Moved by his filial deed, the robbers released the two.

十六、杀鸡奉母（茅容）

茅容，字季伟，东汉陈留（今河南开封）人。这位四十多岁的农民，与大家一起在田野耕作。忽然天降大雨，许多人避雨时天南地北地乱谈，茅容却独自一人坐在一旁。当时朝内名家郭林宗也在那里，问他在想什么？茅容说，在想家里的房子是不是漏雨？老母在大雨时是否淋着？郭林宗感到此人不俗。茅容留郭到家中住宿。第二天一早，郭见茅杀鸡做菜，以为是招待自己的。但茅容将鸡炖好，直接送给老母食用，却用一般菜蔬招待郭。郭林宗对这位孝子的行为一再赞扬。

16. Mao Rong Kills a Chicken to Serve His Mother

Mao Rong, whose courtesy name was Jiwei, was a native of Chenliu(present-day Kaifeng, Henan Province) in the Eastern Han Dynasty. At over forty years of age, he worked as a farmer alongside others in the fields. One day, a sudden downpour forced everyone to take shelter. While many of the others engaged in idle chatter, Mao Rong sat alone, deep in thought. By chance, Guo Linzong, a prominent minister at the imperial court, was also seeking shelter there. Guo asked him what he was thinking. Mao replied that he was worried whether his house would leak in the storm and whether his elderly mother was getting soaked in the rain inside. Impressed by Mao's devotion, Guo invited him to his home. The next morning, Guo saw Mao slaughtering a chicken and assumed it was for his guest. However, once the chicken was stewed, Mao served it to his mother, reserving only common vegetables and simple dishes for Guo. Moved by this gesture, Guo Linzong praised Mao's filial devotion, calling him an exemplary son.

陈留质朴一农夫　日夜孝母历寒暑
贵客临门虽礼敬　杀鸡美食奉老母

Mao Rong, a simple countryside peasant,
Strove daily to make his mother's life easy and pleasant.
Although he treated honoured guests with due protocol,
He killed and cooked the chicken only for mama's bowl.

十七、整父遗作（蔡文姬）

三国时人蔡琰（文姬）是东汉大学者蔡邕的女儿。她父亲撰写的《后汉书》等作品尚未完成，便因社会动乱终止，不久死去。她被掳到乌桓，生活了十二年后，生下两个孩子。为了弘扬文化，曹操派人请她归来。她忍着别夫弃子之痛，毅然返回中原，整理父亲的遗作，并写出脍炙人口的《胡笳十八拍》。

17. Cai Wenji Collects Her Father's Works After His Death

Cai Yan, also known as Wenji, was a prominent figure during the Three Kingdoms period. She was the daughter of Cai Yong, a distinguished scholar of the Eastern Han Dynasty. Her father had begun compiling works such as *The Book of the Later Han*, but his efforts were interrupted by social unrest, and he passed away before completing them. Cai Wenji was later captured and taken to the Wuhuan tribe, where she lived for twelve years and gave birth to two children. In an effort to preserve and promote cultural heritage, the warlord Cao Cao sent an envoy to invite her back to the Central Plains. Despite the profound anguish of leaving behind her husband and children, she resolutely returned to the heart of China. She devoted herself to organizing and completing her father's unfinished works, and also composed the renowned *Eighteen Notes of the Nomad Flute*, a heartfelt and evocative piece that remains celebrated to this day.

才女文姬去乌桓　　远离家乡十二年
为弘文化承父志　　毅然南归著鸿篇

The talented Wenji was captured by tribes on the wild border,
For fully a dozen years she missed her hometown with its order.
To promote and enact her father's last testament,
She returned to the Central Plains full of literary intent.

十八、怀橘遗亲（陆绩）

三国时，吴（今江苏苏州）人陆绩，博学多识，以孝亲著称。在他六岁时，到九江去见当时的大权贵袁术。袁术对这个少年十分赞赏，拿出橘子来叫他吃。陆绩临离开前向袁术行礼时，怀中的橘子掉到地上。袁术诧异地对他说："你来我家做客，为什么还把橘子拿走呢？"陆绩跪下回答说："请大人原谅！我母亲爱吃橘子，但在市面上买不到这么好的，我拿回去给母亲吃。"袁术听了非常惊奇地说："这个少年将来必成大器。"

18. Lu Ji Hides Oranges to Take Them Back for His Mother

During the Three Kingdoms period, Lu Ji, a native of the Wu state (present-day Suzhou, Jiangsu), was known for his extensive learning and his filial piety. When he was just six years old, he visited Yuan Shu, a powerful figure of the time. Impressed by the boy's talents, Yuan Shu offered him some oranges. As Lu Ji bowed to take his leave, the oranges he had hidden in his clothes fell to the ground. Surprised, Yuan Shu asked, "Why, as a guest in my home, are you taking the fruit with you?" Lu Ji kneeled and replied, "Please forgive me, my lord. My mother is very fond of oranges, and these are far better than any I can find in the market. I wanted to bring them back for her." Yuan Shu was astounded by the boy's response and said, "This young man will surely achieve great things in the future."

六岁陆绩做客人　已食甜橘想母亲
怀橘遗亲传佳话　年小一样有孝心

Lu Ji, though aged only six years, visited a house of fine repute,
His thoughts turned to his mother when served with choicest fruit.
He purloined some oranges to give her a treat,
This green youth displayed filial love complete.

十九、舍命卫母（司马芝）

　　三国时河内郡温（今河南温县）人司马芝，早年时和母亲一起到荆州避乱，在鲁阳山上遇见贼寇。很多人只顾自己的性命，拼命逃跑，只有司马芝坐在那里守护老母。贼寇把刀搁到他脖子上要杀他时，他大声说："我在这里守护着母亲，你们杀了我，谁管她老人家！"贼寇们相互说："这是个孝子，杀孝子是不应该的。"于是放了他，司马芝努力攻读，学业有成，后来在荆州当了太守，对百姓仍然施行仁德。

19. Sima Zhi Risks His Life to Protect His Mother

Sima Zhi, a native of Wen County in Henei Prefecture (now in Henan Province), lived during the Three Kingdoms period. In his youth, during a time of widespread turmoil, he and his mother fled to Jingzhou to seek refuge. On their journey, they were ambushed by bandits in Luyang Mountain. As panic spread and other travelers fled for their lives, Sima Zhi remained resolutely by his mother's side, determined to protect her. When the bandits approached and pressed a blade to his neck, Sima Zhi boldly declared, "I remain here to protect my mother. If you kill me, who will look after her?" The bandits, moved by his filial piety, exchanged glances and one of them said, "This is a dutiful son. It is wrong to harm such a son." They then released him. Sima Zhi continued his studies diligently and eventually became the Prefect of Jingzhou, where he governed with benevolence and compassion toward the people.

　　　　荆州避难入深山　　寇至众人皆逃散
　　　　司马芝却护老母　　感动贼寇即放还

Sima Zhi took refuge in the deep mountains of Jingzhou,
His companions all fled at the sight of the bandit foe.
But he protected his mother by refusing to flee,
Moved by his filial deed, the bandits set them free.

二十、幼女搬兵（荀灌）

晋朝人荀灌是襄阳太守荀崧的女儿，从小便知孝敬父母、贤淑知礼。她不爱读书，却跟父亲学了一身好武艺。有一年，杜曾叛乱，将襄阳团团围住。城内兵少粮缺，外面不知信息。荀崧心急如焚，上下均无计可施。荀灌向父亲提出突出重围对外报信，几次才得允许。她率领几十名勇士突围出去，搬来救兵，解救襄阳之危，全忠全孝，荣载史册。

20. Xun Guan, a Young Girl Brings Back Relief Troops to the City

Xun Guan, the daughter of Xun Song, the Prefect of Xiangyang during the Jin Dynasty, was known for her filial piety, respect for her parents, and virtuous character from a young age. Though she was not particularly fond of reading, she had diligently learned martial arts from her father. One year, Du Zeng led a rebellion and besieged Xiangyang. Inside the city, there was a dire shortage of both soldiers and supplies,and the outside world was unaware of their predicament. As the city's guardian, Xun Song was consumed with worry, but neither he nor his officers could find a solution. Xun Guan, however, proposed a daring plan to break through the siege and send a message for help. After much persuasion, her father reluctantly agreed. She then led a group of brave warriors in a bold mission, breaking through the enemy lines and returning with reinforcements. Her actions saved Xiangyang and its people from disaster. Her courage, loyalty, and filial piety were immortalized in history.

习武少女荀灌娘　为救危城勇担当
率兵突围解父难　全忠全孝救襄阳

Xun Guan, a girl well-versed in martial arts,
Stood up for the people with her band of brave hearts.
To aid her father she broke the line of the enemy,
Her loyal and filial deed finally saved the city.

二十一、母命廉清（陶侃）

晋朝浔阳（今江西浔阳）人陶侃，字士行。早年丧父，家庭贫苦，在母亲淇氏的教育、培养下，好学不倦。他当县吏管渔业时，派人给母亲送了几条大鱼，母亲认为他占了公家的便宜，把他训了一顿。他谨遵母命，为官清廉、正直。为了不忘母亲的教诲，磨练意志，每天将一百块坏在室里室外搬来搬去。日后做到太尉，一直勤奋、廉洁、节俭，对其部下嗜酒赌博者，严令责打，并将酒器博具投于江口。督令造船时，竹头木屑均令留下，日后务尽其用。

21. Tao Kan Follows His Mother's Instructions to Be an Honest Official

Tao Kan, a native of Xunyang (present-day Jiangxi Province) during the Jin Dynasty, was given the courtesy name Shixing. He lost his father at an early age, and despite the poverty of his family, he was an eager learner, thanks to the education and guidance of his mother, Lady Qi. While serving as a county clerk responsible for fish busness, Tao Kan sent his mother a few large fish. In response, she scolded him for taking advantage of his public office. Deeply respecting her principles, Tao Kan took her lesson to heart and committed himself to being an honest and upright official. To further remind himself of her teachings and strengthen his will, he made it a daily habit to move one hundred bricks, both inside and outside his home. Later, when he rose to the rank of Tai wei (a high-ranking military officer), Tao Kan continued to lead with diligence, integrity, and frugality. He reprimanded subordinates who indulged in drinking and gambling, insisting that their drinking vessels and gambling tools be thrown into the river. When overseeing shipbuilding, he ordered that even the smallest scraps, such as bamboo tips and sawdust, be saved for future use. His foresight and careful management proved to be both practical and beneficial.

晋人陶侃廉洁称　母训无时不怠松
县吏太尉有权势　官大官小身正清

Tan Kan, an official of Jin, true honesty savoured,
His mother's teaching he took to heart and always favoured.
Power is bestowed on many a great and small politician,
He was ever upright and decent whatever his position.

二十二、孝悌光里（王祥）

晋朝人王祥，字休征，琅玡（今山东临沂）人。性至孝，其母早死，后母偏袒自己的儿子王览。令王祥干重活，吃孬饭，他毫无怨言，对父母一贯孝敬。后母病中要吃鲜鱼，天寒地冻时，他到河中，破冰求鲤，感动了后母。王祥与王览兄友弟恭，远近闻名，人们将他们住的地方称"孝悌里"。至今仍存。

22. Wang Xiang Enlightens the Neighbourhood as a Filial Son and Fraternal Brother

Wang Xiang, with the courtesy name Xiuzheng, was a native of Langya (present-day Linyi, Shandong Province) during the Jin Dynasty. He was profoundly filial by nature. After the early death of his biological mother, his stepmother showed clear favoritism toward her own son, Wang Lan, forcing Wang Xiang to do the hardest chores and endure poor meals. Despite these hardships, Wang Xiang never uttered a word of complaint and continued to show respect and devotion to both his father and stepmother. When his stepmother fell ill and craved fresh fish during the bitterly cold winter, Wang Xiang broke the ice on the river and caught carp for her, an act that deeply touched her. Wang Xiang and his half-brother Wang Lan became renowned for their exemplary fraternal bond, with Wang Xiang as the elder brother and Wang Lan as the respectful younger one. The people of the area referred to their neighborhood as the "Filial and Fraternal Village", a place that continues to be remembered to this day.

孝悌里中颂王祥　破冰求鲤美名扬
深情厚意感后母　王览仿效敬兄长

In Filial and Fraternal Village Wang Xiang was a model son,
Him breaking ice to capture carp the broadest praise won.
His affectionate concern melted his cold stepmother,
Setting a new precedent for his spoiled younger brother.

二十三、辞征孝祖（李密）

晋朝人李密，阳武（今四川彭山）人。父早亡，母改嫁，自小在祖母抚养下成人。长大后努力攻读，成为当时著名的学者。祖母生病时，衣不解带，饮食、汤药必先尝后进。因他学问、道德均高，晋泰始初年，皇帝三次征诏他为太子洗马。李密以祖母年高，不肯受命，写下《陈情表》。其祖母死后，他才出来做官。其《陈情表》情真意切，千古传诵，李密孝敬祖母的事迹也传颂千年。

23. Li Mi Declines Royal Offers to Serve as an Official in Order to Care for His Grandmother

Li Mi, a native of Yangwu (present-day Pengshan, Sichuan Province) during he Jin Dynasty, lost his father at an early age. After his mother remarried, he was raised by his grandmother. Through his diligent studies, he became a renowned scholar.Whenever his grandmother fell ill, Li Mi would remain by her side day and night,personally ensuring she received her meals, water, and medicinal soups. Due to his scholarly achievements and virtuous character, the emperor of the Jin Dynasty summoned him three times, offering him the prestigious position of Tutor to the Crown Prince. However, Li Mi declined these high honors, citing his grandmother's advanced age and his filial duty to care for her. In his letter of refusal, known as *My Sincere Apology*, Li Mi eloquently expressed his dedication to his grandmother, a letter that became famous and has been read for centuries. He only agreed to take on an official post after her passing. His deep filial devotion was praised and his story has been celebrated throughout Chinese history.

朝廷三征不应诏　祖母老迈需照料
婉言字字皆孝义　千古名篇《陈情表》

Three times he declined an offer from royalty,
Preferring to serve his grandmother with unbending loyalty.
Full of polite sentiments was his letter of rejection,
Now hailed as an age-old exemplar of filial affection.

二十四、替父从军（花木兰）

北朝乐府词中有一首《木兰辞》，记述了木兰从军的故事。木兰姓花，父亲名弧，是当时被编入军籍的一名老兵。敌人打到边疆时，其父本该应征入伍，但年老体衰，难以从军。十分孝敬他的女儿木兰提出女扮男装，替父从军。从军后在外作战、戍边十二年，屡立战功。班师回朝时，向皇帝表示不要任何赏赐、官职，只求回家孝敬父母。此时人们才知她是一位巾帼英雄。

24. Hua Mulan, a Filial Daughter, Joins the Army in Her Father's Place

The Ballad of Mulan, a narrative poem from the Northern Dynasties, tells the story of Mulan's decision to take her father's place in the military. Mulan's family name was Hua, and her father, Hua Hu, was a veteran soldier enlisted in the army. When enemy forces invaded the borders, her father was called to serve, but due to his old age and frailty, he was unable to fight. Out of filial devotion, Mulan offered to disguise herself as a man and take her father's place in the army. She fought bravely on the battlefield and defended the borders for twelve years, achieving numerous victories. When the army returned victorious, Mulan met with the emperor, where she declined all rewards and official positions, requesting only to return home and care for her parents. It was only then that her true identity as a heroic daughter in disguise was revealed.

好个木兰艺超群　女扮男装勇从军
行孝代父去征战　班师回朝孝双亲

In martial arts Mulan had skill magnificent,
Disguised as a man she entered the family regiment.
Fighting in place of her father so dear,
She returned in triumph to honor them near.

二十五、代父受刑（吉翂）

南北朝时梁朝人吉翂，字彦霄，冯翊莲勺（今陕西大荔）人。世代居于襄阳。十五岁时，任吴兴原乡令的父亲遭人陷害，被捉去治罪。他到处哭述父亲的冤情。父亲被判罪后，他提出代父受刑，甚至代父受死。在对他行刑时，他面对酷刑毫无惧色，很多官员惊讶，皇帝也被他感动。派人重审此案，为之昭雪，最后赦了他父亲，也释放了小吉翂。

25. Ji Ji Takes the Punishment in Place of His Father

Ji Ji, courtesy name Yanxiao, was from Lianshao, Fengyi (present-day Dali,Shaanxi Province) in the Liang Dynasty, during the period of the Southern and Northern Dynasties. His family had lived in Xiangyang for generations. At the age of fifteen, his father, the county magistrate of Yuanxiang in Wuxing, was falsely accused and arrested. Ji Ji tirelessly pleaded his father's innocence. After his father was convicted, Ji Ji offered to take the punishment in his place, even volunteering to face the death penalty. When the execution was carried out, he bravely endured the harsh torture without fear. His courageous resolve astonished many officials and deeply moved the emperor. In response, the emperor ordered a re-investigation of the case, which ultimately cleared his father's name. Ji Ji's father was pardoned, and Ji Ji himself was released.

小小吉翂年十五　代父受刑不怕苦
感动上司重审案　赦父免刑传千古

Ji Ji, a lad of fifteen would rather.
Receive the cruel punishment meant for his father.
His filial piety ministers and the emperor celebrated,
Through re-investigation his father was exonerated.

二十六、舍身护婆（卢氏）

唐朝范阳（今北京大兴区）郑义宗的妻子卢氏，自小恭顺、仁德、读书明理，出嫁后对公婆十分孝顺，关怀备至。一天夜里，丈夫外出，一伙强盗闯进家中抢劫，逼令拿出钱财。卢氏用身体护住婆婆，强盗对她多次毒打，几乎打死，仍然护住婆婆不放。事后有人问及此事，她说："这是我应该做的。婆婆如果死了，我岂能独生？"

26. Lady Lu Protects Her Mother-in-law at the Risk of Her Own Life

Lady Lu, the wife of Zheng Yizong, a native of Fanyang (present-day Daxing District, Beijing) during the Tang Dynasty, was known for her gentle nature, kindness, and wisdom. These qualities were nurtured by her diligent studies from a young age, and after marriage, she proved to be extremely filial and considerate toward her parents-in-law. One night, when her husband was away, a gang of robbers broke into their home and demanded the family's wealth. Lady Lu courageously shielded her mother-in-law with her own body. The robbers brutally beat her, nearly to the point of death, but she refused to let go of her mother-in-law. After the incident, when asked about her actions, she simply replied, "This is what a dutiful daughter-in-law should do. If my mother-in-law had died, how could I possibly live on?"

卢氏孝行人堪钦　强盗入室护婆身
人问如何不怕死　孝亲敬老仁义心

Lady Lu's filial deeds won the widest of favour,
During the burglary, she was her mother-in-law's saviour.
When someone asked why she did not fear death,
She replied: "Filial piety should command our every breath."

二十七、弃官寻母（朱寿昌）

宋朝天长（今安徽盱眙）人朱寿昌，父亲做官时娶妾生下他。七岁时父亲将母亲遗弃，母子一别五十年。后来朱寿昌当了阆中县令，时时想念母亲，到处打听却无结果。在他五十七岁那年，决心弃官寻母，他走遍南北各地，经历千难万苦，终于在陕州一个姓党的家中找到早已改嫁三十多年的母亲及两个弟弟。他毅然说服母亲带三人回家，不去做官，奉养父母。

27. Zhu Shouchang Relinquishes His Office to Search for His Mother

Zhu Shouchang was a native of Tianchang (present-day Xuyi, Anhui Province) during the Song Dynasty. He was the son of a concubine, born while his father was in office. When Zhu was just seven years old, his father abandoned his mother, and the two were separated for fifty years. Later, when Zhu became the county magistrate of Langzhong, he often thought of his long-lost mother and made many unsuccessful attempts to inquire about her whereabouts. At the age of fifty-seven, he resolved to give up his official position and search for her. He traveled throughout the country,enduring many hardships, and eventually discovered that his mother had remarried into the Dang family in Shanzhou more than thirty years ago, and had two sons. With great determination, Zhu persuaded his mother to return with him and his two younger brothers, vowing to care for them and live a life of filial devotion without seeking further official titles.

阆中县令朱寿昌　自幼失怙常悲伤
弃官寻母历艰苦　母子团聚夙愿偿

Zhu Shouchang, the county magistrate of Langzhong,
Felt sad at being parted from his mother for so long.
He gave up his office and withstood every peril,
Their eventual reunion did his cherished wish fulfil.

二十八、孝亲报国（岳飞）

　　岳飞，字鹏举，南宋时汤阴（今河南汤阴）人。幼年家贫，父亲早死，事母至孝。早年拜周侗为师，学得一身武艺。金兵南下，朝廷募兵，岳飞认为父死母老，应亲自奉养母亲。岳母却教育他孝为小忠、忠是大孝，男儿应以大局为重，亲手在他背上刺"精忠报国"四字。岳飞遵母命，从军抗金。他所率领的"岳家军"能征惯战，取得很多抗金的战绩。但在朝内投降派的诬陷下惨死，宏愿未遂。数十年后冤案昭雪。

28. Filial Piety and Loyalty to the Nation

　　Yue Fei, whose style name was Pengju, was from Tangyin (present-day Tangyin, Henan Province) in the Southern Song Dynasty. Born into a poor family, he lost his father at an early age and was extremely dutiful and respectful to his mother. In his youth, he studied martial arts under Zhou Tong, a renowned master, who taught him the skills of combat. When the Jin army invaded and the government began recruiting soldiers, Yue Fei initially considered staying home to care for his elderly mother, as his father had passed away early. However, his mother advised him that filial piety was a smaller form of loyalty, and the greater duty of a man was to serve his country. She urged him to think of the nation's well-being above personal obligations. To emphasize her point, she had four characters tattooed onto his back, reading "Serve the Country Loyally", hoping to inspire him. Yue Fei followed his mother's guidance and joined the army to fight against the Jin invaders. He led the renowned "Yue Family Army", which became famous for its victories and played a crucial role in the resistance. Unfortunately, he was later falsely accused and framed by members of the appeasement faction in the imperial court, leading to his tragic death in prison before he could achieve his dream of restoring the lost territories of the Song Dynasty. Decades later, his name was cleared, and his wrongful death was posthumously avenged.

名将岳飞出汤阴　背上刺字慈母训
能征善战传千古　精忠报国立功勋

From Tangyin came Yue Fei, loyal and bold,
His mother's wise words in his heart took hold.
For triumph in battles his troop went down in history,
He did his utmost to preserve and protect this country.

二十九、孝亲杀虎（石明三）

石明三是元朝时的一名猎户，居于山中，终日打猎为生，以此奉养老母。有一天，外出打猎回来，他找不到母亲，发现母亲已入虎口，家中还有三只小虎。他愤怒地杀死三小虎后，一只母虎冲进屋中，他几斧把母虎砍死，又赶来一只公虎。此时他虽然已经力尽，但为了给母亲报仇，又奋力砍死公虎。邻居们听到声音赶到，才发现老虎头上有他的斧子。连杀五虎，为母报仇的石明三，累死在老虎身边。

29. Shi Mingsan Slaughters Tigers to Avenge His Mother

Shi Mingsan, a huntsman in the Yuan Dynasty, lived in the mountains. He spent his days hunting to make a living, using the proceeds to care for his elderly mother.One day, after returning home from hunting, he found that his mother was missing.Upon searching, he discovered that she had fallen victim to a tiger. At home, he found three tiger cubs, which he immediately killed in a fit of rage. As he was dealing with the cubs, a tigress charged into the house. With no hesitation, he struck her down with his axe. Then, a male tiger appeared. Although he was exhausted from the earlier struggle, the thought of avenging his mother gave him the strength to fight on, and he managed to kill the male tiger as well. His neighbors, alarmed by the commotion,arrived at the scene only to find his axe embedded in the male tiger's head. Having slain five tigers in succession to avenge his mother, Shi Mingsan collapsed from exhaustion and died beside the beasts he had killed.

好个明三石猎户　为母报仇杀五虎
斧头累举解仇恨　一片孝心勇捐躯

Shi Mingsan, the hunter, could great prowess display,
When avenging his mother five tigers did he slay.
By lifting his axe in fury, he paid back what was owed in blood,
He sacrificed himself heroically so filial values stood.

三十、思母归国（鞠祥）

明朝永乐年间，永平（今河北昌黎）人鞠祥，父亲为金山百户时，倭寇犯境，将十四岁的鞠祥掠去。倭王见他聪明伶俐，将他改名元贵，给他娶了妻子，授予官职。但他一直没忘记自己是中国人，时时想念自己的母亲。宣德时随倭国使臣到明朝，想留下来，未被批准。后经不断努力，变卖财产，辞去官职，回到故乡，与失散二十多年的母亲团聚。

30. Ju Xiang Returns to His Motherland Because of His Yearning for His Mother

Ju Xiang, from Yongping (present-day Changli, Hebei Province), lived during the reign of the Ming Dynasty's Emperor Yongle. At the age of fourteen, while accompanying his father, a minor military officer, he was captured by invading Japanese pirates. The pirate leader, impressed by the boy's intelligence and quick wit, renamed him Yuangui, arranged for his marriage, and bestowed an official position upon him. However, Ju Xiang never forgot his identity as a Chinese and never ceased to long for his homeland and his mother. During the reign of Emperor Xuande, he accompanied a Japanese diplomatic mission to China. He applied to stay in the country but was initially refused. Undeterred, he tirelessly worked toward his goal, selling off his property and resigning from his official position in Japan. Finally, after two decades of separation, he was able to return to his hometown in China and reunite with his mother.

> 鞠祥早年被倭掳　心向故国思老母
> 冲破万难归华夏　多年失散终团聚

The young Ju Xiang was captured by a Japanese privateer,
He always remembered his native land and his mother so dear.
At last he set foot again in China after every tribulation,
The family reunion ended decades of separation.

三十一、打虎救母（谢定柱）

明朝初年，广昌（今山西大同）的一个农家孩子谢定柱，十二岁那年，家里耕牛走失。母子几人寻找耕牛，走入山中，遇见一只老虎向母亲、弟弟扑去。他奋不顾身地拾起大树枝猛击猛虎，老虎惊悸地逃走。接着又转了回来，他又搬起一块石头，猛击虎头，将老虎砸死，救了母亲和弟弟。永乐十二年，皇帝下诏对他们的孝行予以表彰。

31. Xie Dingzhu Fights Against and Kills a Tiger to Save His Mother

In the early Ming Dynasty, Xie Dingzhu, a twelve-year-old boy from a farming family in Guangchang (present-day Datong, Shanxi Province), faced a grave challenge when his family's oxen went missing. While searching for the animals in the mountains, he and his mother, along with his younger brother, encountered a tiger. As the beast lunged toward his mother and brother, Xie Dingzhu bravely grabbed a large tree branch and struck the tiger fiercely, putting his own life at risk. Alarmed, the tiger fled momentarily. However, it quickly returned, and Xie Dingzhu, with no other option, picked up a large rock and struck the tiger on the head with all his might. The tiger was killed, and Xie Dingzhu successfully saved his mother and brother. In the twelfth year of the Yongle Emperor's reign, the emperor issued a decree to commend and reward his extraordinary filial act.

冲龄少年谢定柱　孤胆打虎效丈夫
临危更见孝母心　皇帝旌表青史书

Xie Dingzhu, a young lad from the country,
Killed the fierce tiger with gall aplenty.
Crisis made his filial love plain to see,
And won the approval of imperial decree.

三十二、愿代父死（周琬）

明朝初年，江宁人周琬的父亲为滁州牧，犯了罪，按律当死。十六岁的周琬挺身而出，向皇帝请求自己代父去死。皇帝认为是别人教唆或指使，不一定是真心，遂下令斩首。周琬得知，面不改色。皇帝不杀他，把他的父亲也轻判为戍边。周琬又向皇帝上奏说："戍边与斩首都是一个死。眼看着父亲死去，儿子何颜偷生，还是请皇帝斩了我，免去父亲的罪吧。"皇帝下诏把他绑缚市曹问斩，周琬也不害怕，皇帝看到这个少年的诚意，下令赦免了他，并且为之亲题御匾："孝子周琬"。

32. Zhou Wan Offers to Take the Death Penalty in Place of His Father

In the early Ming Dynasty, Zhou Wan's father, the Prefect of Chuzhou, committed a crime punishable by death. When Zhou Wan, just sixteen years old, learned of his father's fate, he courageously stood up and pleaded with the emperor to allow him to die in his father's place. The emperor, suspecting that Zhou Wan's plea might have been coerced or influenced by others, ordered the sentence to be carried out. Upon hearing that the emperor had sanctioned his beheading, Zhou Wan remained unshaken, his expression unchanged. Later, when the emperor commuted his father's death sentence to exile at the border, Zhou Wan once again approached the emperor. He said: "It makes no difference to my father whether he is sentenced to death or sent into exile. As a son, how could I live without shame, knowing that my father is suffering while I am spared? I beg Your Majesty to execute me instead, so that my father may be pardoned." The emperor, moved by Zhou Wan's steadfast resolve, ordered that the young man be bound and taken to the market to be beheaded. Yet Zhou Wan remained fearless. His sincerity finally won the emperor's favor, and both Zhou Wan and his father were pardoned. The emperor personally wrote an inscription in his honor, declaring: "Zhou Wan, a Dutiful Son."

少年周琬有孝心　愿代父死报父恩
酷刑加身不畏惧　帝题御赞世人钦

Zhou Wan, a lad overflowing with filial piety,
Was prepared to assume his father's death penalty.
He stood fearless in the face of tortuous abomination,
The emperor rewarded him with a glorious citation.

三十三、以身示孝（陆陇其）

清朝学者陆陇其，平湖（今浙江嘉兴）人。在他任灵寿知县时，一老年妇女带一个少年告儿子不孝，他见此子不像坏人，询问以后便对其母说："你回去，我惩罚他。"他把此子留下在自家当书童。陆陇其平时对母亲生活照料无微不至，母病日夜照应，母训俯首恭听，以自己的行动教育了书童。半年后，书童跪下认错，检讨自己不该对母亲不孝。陆陇其将其子交给老人。日后这个少年也成为一名孝子。

33. Lu Longqi Practices and Demonstrates Filial Piety in Person

Lu Longqi, a scholar from Pinghu (present-day Jiaxing, Zhejiang Province) during the Qing Dynasty, was serving as the county magistrate of Lingshou when an elderly woman brought her son before him, accusing him of being unfilial. After questioning the boy, Lu Longqi felt he was not a bad person and decided to act wisely. He told the woman, "You may return home, and I will punish your son myself." Lu Longqi then took the boy into his own household as a study assistant. He personally demonstrated filial piety by providing meticulous care for his mother, attending to her every need. When she fell ill, he tended to her day and night, and when she gave instructions, he listened attentively and respectfully. Through these actions, he taught the young boy the true meaning of filial piety. Six months later, the boy, moved by Lu Longqi's example, knelt before him and confessed his wrongdoings. He reflected on his past unfilial behavior and vowed to change. Lu Longqi then sent the boy back home, and from that point forward, he became as dutiful and respectful to his own mother as his benefactor had been to his.

灵寿县令陆陇其　不孝少年罚作役
孝敬老母身作范　耳濡目染教稚子

Lu Longqi, the county magistrate,
Took the unfilial lad home to berate.
By serving his mother, he set a bright example,
Teaching his children with love, his wisdom ample.

三十四、积钱葬母（哑乞）

清朝时，昆明有母子两个乞丐，母亲有病，儿子是哑人，母子住在一座破庙里。哑子对母亲特别孝敬：要来干的给母亲吃，自己吃稀的。要来的饭食不多，给母亲吃，自己则挨饿。天冷抱着母亲以自身的温度给母亲取暖。要到铜钱，不断扔到庙旁一座枯井里。其母死后，他指着枯井"哇哇"叫，有人知道里面有东西，挖出不少铜钱，以此埋葬他母亲，完成他的孝心。

34. The Mute Beggar Collects Money to Give His Mother a Decent Burial

In Kunming during the Qing Dynasty, there lived a beggar mother and her mute son, residing in a dilapidated temple. The mute son was exceptionally filial to his mother. Whenever he begged for food, he would give her the best portions, leaving only scraps for himself. When the food was scarce, he would give it all to her and go hungry himself. On cold winter nights, he would embrace her, using his own body to provide warmth. Whenever he managed to collect copper coins, he would throw them into a dry well beside the temple. After his mother passed away, the mute son pointed to the well and made loud gestures, signaling to passersby that there was something of value inside. The people dug into the well and found the coins he had collected over time. These funds were then used to give his mother a proper burial, fulfilling his deep filial duty.

昆明哑孝美名传　瞻养老母费万难
井中储钱为母葬　不孝子孙应汗颜

The mute beggar in Kunming, being famously a dutiful son,
Was praised for giving his mother every meal and scrap he won.
He hid the funds for her send-off down a deep well,
An act of love that should serve to shame those not so filial.

三十五、异国寻母（沈仁业）

清朝时江苏吴县（今苏州）人沈仁业，是他父亲到越南经商时娶一女子时所生。他八岁时随父归家，母亲留在越南。他长大后，一直想念母亲，父亲死后，思母之心更切，决定出国寻母。他请人绘了父亲的图像带在身上，到越南寻母。几经曲折到了越南，找到母亲。回来的路上，遇到台风，他一直抱着母亲。终于在好心人帮助下，办了入境的文书，将母亲接回家中。

35. Shen Renye Searches for His Mother in a Foreign Land

Shen Renye, from Wu County in Jiangsu Province (present-day Suzhou), lived during the Qing Dynasty. While conducting business in Vietnam, his father married a local woman and had a son，was Shen Renye. At the age of eight, Shen Renye returned with his father to China,leaving his mother behind in Vietnam. As he grew older, he missed his mother deeply, and after his father's death, his longing for her intensified. Determined to find her, he arranged for a portrait of his father to be painted and set off for Vietnam to search for his mother. After numerous difficulties and obstacles, he finally located her in Vietnam. On the return journey to China, they were caught in a typhoon, and Shen Renye held his mother tightly to protect and comfort her. With the assistance of kind-hearted strangers, he was able to complete the necessary paperwork to bring his mother back to China, where they were reunited at last.

为寻生母赴越南　　跋山涉水历万难
孝子终有好人助　　异国寻母终团圆

Looking for his mother to Vietnam did he trail,
High mountains and seas posed many a travail.
Kindhearted persons did his plight understand,
They were finally reunited in that far-flung foreign land.

三十六、四子争孝（吴姓）

清朝崇明（今江苏崇明）吴姓夫妇，家贫，无法养活四个儿子，无奈将他们卖给别人家为奴。孩子们长大以后，个个赎身后攻读、谋生，各自娶妻成家生子。兄弟四人对父母当年因贫穷卖子十分理解，人人都想尽孝。他们商定后，对父母轮流抚养，到谁家时均好酒好饭招待父母，各自给老人零钱，还经常教育下一代。老人愉快、长寿百年，在当地传为佳话。

36. The Four Sons of the Wu Family Vie to Serve Their Parents

In the Qing Dynasty, a poor couple from the Wu family in Chongming (present-day Jiangsu Province) were unable to support their four sons and, out of necessity, sold them into servitude. When the sons grew up, each of them bought back their freedom, pursued education, and made a living. All four later married, had children, and started families of their own. They fully understood the reasons behind their parents' decision to sell them due to poverty, and each son was determined to care for his elderly parents. The brothers agreed to take turns caring for their parents, ensuring that the couple always had good food and drink, as well as providing them with pocket money. They also took the opportunity to teach their own children about filial piety. Thanks to their devoted care, the parents lived happily and enjoyed a long life, becoming the subject of a local legend admired for generations.

江南吴姓孝子家　四子争孝人人夸
衣食相比家家好　寿翁百岁乐无涯

The four dutiful sons of the family Wu,
In filial service tried each other to outdo.
To offer the finest food and clothes did they compete,
Their parents' old age with every comfort was replete.

第四章

勤奋好学

Chapter Four:

Diligence and Love for Learning

一、韦编三绝（孔丘）

　　孔子幼时即善于学习，曾"陈俎豆，设礼容"，学习古代的礼仪。少年时"入太庙，每事问"，进入太庙学习实际知识。成年后向郯子学官，向苌弘学乐，向师襄学琴。带领弟子远赴洛邑，一面到国都学习传统的礼仪，一面向老子当面求教。在周游列国的十四年中，到处实地观察，认真学习。他学《易》时，竟至"韦编三绝"（指编联竹简的皮绳断了多次，可见读书勤奋）。他不仅学古籍文献，还学社会上的各种知识，成为我国古代最好学，最会学，最学习有成的人。

1. The Leather Straps of His Books Broke Many Times

Confucius was an avid learner from a young age. As a child, he would "prepare ritual offerings and practice ceremonies", immersing himself in the study of ancient rites. In his youth, he "entered the Imperial Ancestral Temple and asked questions about the rituals", seeking to understand these traditions in practice. As an adult, he studied governance under Tanzi, music with Changhong, and the art of playing the guqin (a stringed instrument) from Shixiang. He also led his disciples to Luoyang to study the traditional rites and sought guidance from Laozi himself. During his fourteen years of travel across various states, Confucius was relentless in his pursuit of knowledge, observing and learning from real-world experiences. His dedication to studying *The I Ching* was so intense that the leather thongs used to bind the bamboo slips broke three times, a testament to his perseverance and diligence.Confucius didn't just study ancient texts; he also sought knowledge from all aspects of society, becoming one of the most learned and accomplished scholars of ancient China.

韦编三绝学《易》勤　　深奥哲理书中寻

假我数年无大过　　　　夫子好学诲后人

Confucius's diligence at studying *The I Ching* caused the leather straps to break,
He grasped the philosophy in the book without error or mistake.
He declared "I shall never blunder even if I've few years left to live",
His studiousness was for generations a legacy worthy to give.

二、学子楷模（颜回）

孔子最得意的弟子颜回，一名颜渊，鲁国（今山东曲阜）人，名列孔门"四科"中德行之首。他穷的用竹筒子吃饭，用水瓢喝水，住到一个穷陋的巷子里。因为经常得到孔子的教诲，以此为乐。他经常向老师发问，老师回答后认真思考、发挥，"闻一知十"。他努力学习，修德行仁。治国主张仁政德治，孔子说"仁"的德行在他身上停留的时间最长。被人们称作孔门弟子中的楷模。

2. A Model for Students

Yan Hui, also known as Yan Yuan, was one of Confucius's most beloved disciples. He came from the State of Lu (present-day Qufu, Shandong Province) and was renowned for his exceptional virtue, ranking first among the four pillars of Confucian education: virtue, speech, governance, and literature. Living in extreme poverty, he ate from a bamboo tube and drank from a ladle, residing in a humble and rundown alley. Despite these hardships, he found great joy in receiving Confucius's teachings. Yan Hui often asked thoughtful questions, and after receiving answers, he would ponder deeply and expand on them, demonstrating a remarkable ability to learn quickly—what Confucius described as "hearing one thing and understanding ten." He devoted himself to learning, cultivating virtue, and practicing benevolence.

Advocating for a government based on benevolence and moral governance, Confucius remarked that the virtue of benevolence remained with Yan Hui longer than with anyone else. Yan Hui was thus regarded as the model disciple among all of Confucius's followers.

> 箪瓢陋巷学中乐　修德行仁自超越
> 勤学好问深领会　三千学子一楷模

Yan Hui ate with bamboo utensils in a shabby lane,
Peerless virtue and benevolence he strove hard to maintain.
He was diligent in studies and concentrated his best,
Among the students of Confucius he was a model to the rest.

三、活学实用（公明宣）

　　孔子的弟子曾参，继承孔子的学说，又不停地向弟子传授。有个叫公明宣的弟子，向曾子学了三年，一直没动简册。曾子很奇怪地问他为什么？聪慧老实的公明宣说："我在不停地学习，我见您在家对父母恪尽孝道，对师祖孔子的学说认真发扬。对客人恭敬、礼貌，对学生关怀备至，又严格要求。这些好品德我都牢记在心，并力求实行。"这番话使曾子豁然开朗说："你会学啊。"

3. Learning with a Practical and Lively Mindset

Zeng Shen, a disciple of Confucius, inherited his master's teachings and passed them on to his own students. One of his students, Gongming Xuan, studied under Zeng for three years without ever touching the bamboo slips on which his teachings were written. Curious, Zeng asked him why. Gongming Xuan, being both wise and sincere, replied: "I have been learning continuously. I observe how you fulfill your filial duties to your parents, how you diligently promote the teachings of our late Master Confucius, how you treat guests with respect and courtesy, and how you balance strictness with care in your teaching. I have kept these virtues in mind and made a conscious effort to practice them." Hearing this, Zeng was struck with understanding and exclaimed, "You truly know how to learn."

好学求实公明宣　三年就学未动简
曾师不解问何故　观察言行学实践

Gongming Xuan was studious and practical too,
For three years he followed his teacher not touching the bamboo.
Zeng Shen was curious and asked the reason why,
In truth he wanted to observe and await his time to try.

四、亚圣好学（孟轲）

孟子三岁丧父，孟母"三迁"之后又用断机之喻，教育儿子学习不能中断。孟轲聆受良母教诲，一改陋习努力学习，拜孔子之孙孔伋的弟子为师，学到孔学真传。在"争于力气"的战国时期，孟子以说理、争辩的方式捍卫了儒家思想，对孔子的仁政德治思想，多有发挥。成为儒家思想的重要继承人，被后世尊为"亚圣"。

4. The Second Sage's Pursuit of Wisdom

Mencius lost his father when he was only three years old, and his family had to move three times. His mother used these relocations to impart an important lesson on him: that learning should never be interrupted. To illustrate this, she cut the leading thread of her loom, halting her weaving and showing the boy how an unfinished task was like neglecting one's studies. Mencius heeded his mother's wise guidance, overcoming his bad habits and dedicating himself to his studies. He sought out a disciple of Kong Ji, the grandson of Confucius, to learn the true teachings of Confucianism. During the Warring States Period, a time dominated by power struggles, Mencius defended Confucian thought through reason and debate. He passionately upheld Confucius's principles of benevolence and virtuous governance, becoming a prominent figure in the transmission of Confucianism. Revered as "the Second Sage", he is considered one of the most important successors of Confucius.

子思宫前歌三迁　嘎然机断警稚顽
崇孔深解多创意　战国乱世成大贤

Mencius thrice sang a song before the home of his late mother,
The shuttle taught him a lesson more profound than any other.
He cherished Confucius's teachings and developed his philosophy,
That sage and man of virtue lived through days of calamity.

五、刺股奋学（苏秦）

战国时洛阳人苏秦，字季子。早年学了些本领，外出游说，在秦国一年多，未见秦王一面，只好狼狈回家。妻子、嫂子都不理他。他深知自己学问不大，才到处受冷遇。于是又坐下来努力攻读，日夜学习，揣摩天下大势。晚上学习困乏，便用木锥猛刺大腿，清醒后再学。通过刻苦学习，学业大有长进，再到各国成功游说，同时挂齐、楚、燕、韩、赵、魏六国相印，成为当时有名的纵横家。

5. Pricking Himself to Stay Awake and Study Hard

Su Qin, courtesy name Jizi, was from Luoyang during the Warring States Period. As a young man, he learned various skills and ventured out to pursue a career as a political envoy. He spent over a year in the State of Qin, but despite his efforts,he never had the chance to meet the king, and eventually, he returned home in disappointment. His wife and sister-in-law, disappointed by his failure, refused to speak to him. Su Qin recognized that his lack of knowledge and success had caused this cold reception. Determined to improve, he resolved to study relentlessly, dedicating both day and night to his education and attempting to understand the larger geopolitical landscape. When fatigue set in during his late-night study sessions, he would prick his thigh with a wooden awl to stay awake and continue learning.Through relentless perseverance, Su Qin made significant progress in his studies. He then set out once again to seek positions in various states, this time with great success. He was appointed as an adviser to six states—Qi, Chu, Yan, Han, Zhao, and Wei—earning recognition as one of the most influential diplomats of his time.

季子自幼立宏愿　锋芒初试出世艰
刺股奋学悟大势　六国拜相喜荣迁

Jizi had aspirations from a tender age,
Facing setbacks the first time didn't blunt his courage.
He pricked his thigh to stay awake while studying intently,
As the Prime Minister of Six States he served consequently.

六、奋作《史记》（司马迁）

司马迁，西汉时夏阳（今陕西韩城）人。父亲司马谈是朝中的"太史令"，想修古史未成，临终前要儿子完成自己修史的遗愿。司马迁在父亲的嘱托下，为完成使命，认真阅读各种文献，又南游江淮，上会稽，探禹穴，窥九嶷，浮沅湘，北涉汶泗、齐鲁，孔子讲学之邦，过梁楚以归，实地调查获得许多资料。但不久遭李陵之祸，身受腐刑。在十分艰难、屈辱的情势下，发愤写出一部"究天人之际，通古今之变，成一家之言"的史学名著《史记》。

6. Endeavoring to Complete *the Records of the Grand Historian*

Sima Qian was from Xiayang (modern-day Hancheng, Shaanxi) during the Western Han Dynasty. His father, Sima Tan, served as the Imperial Astronomer and had started compiling a history of ancient times, but he was unable to complete it before his death. On his deathbed, Sima Tan entrusted his son with the task of finishing this monumental work. Driven by a deep sense of duty and determination, Sima Qian set out to fulfill his father's wish. He diligently studied a wide array of historical texts and traveled extensively—south to the Yangtze and Huai rivers,Kuaiji, and even to sites like the tomb of Yu the Great and the Jiuyi Mountains. He also ventured north to the regions where Confucius had taught, crossing through the states of Qi and Lu, and returning home after passing through Liang and Chu. These extensive travels allowed him to gather a wealth of material through direct research. However, Sima Qian soon found himself in political trouble after defending General Li Ling, who had been accused of betraying the Han by surrendering to the Xiongnu. As punishment, Sima Qian was subjected to castration. Despite the harsh and humiliating circumstances, he persevered and completed his magnum opus, *the Records of the Grand Historian*, which is praised for "navigating the boundaries between heaven and man, connecting the changes of the past and present, and creating a unique school of thought".

巍然史星太史公　承传父志继家风
名著穷究天人际　史载古今变幻中

The Grand Historian shone like a star most brilliant,
He assumed his father's torch and became a scholar diligent.
His famous work explored the boundary between nature and mankind,
Thereby gauging the changes in history with logic refined.

七、负薪读书（朱买臣）

西汉时吴（今江苏苏州）人朱买臣，字翁子。年轻时家贫，靠上山砍柴担到市场上卖柴为生。但他喜欢读书，在担柴的路上背诵古籍。他妻子不理解，常对他冷潮热讽，竟至离异再嫁。朱买臣不受家庭影响，继续攻读。他善词赋，尤精《楚辞》。因他德才兼备，汉武帝任命他为会稽太守，日后又出使西南夷，为国立功。后来官至主爵都尉、丞相长史。

7. Reading While Carrying Firewood

ZhuMaichen, from Wu Prefecture (present-day Suzhou, Jiangsu Province) during the Western Han Dynasty, had the courtesy name Wengzi. In his youth, he was very poor, earning a living by cutting firewood in the mountains and selling it at the market. Despite his hardships, he loved reading and would recite ancient texts while carrying firewood on his journeys. His wife, unable to understand his passion for learning, frequently criticized him and eventually divorced him. Undeterred by his personal misfortunes, Zhu Maichen continued his studies. He excelled in writing verse, particularly in the style of *The Songs of Chu*. Due to his talents and virtuous character, Emperor Wu of the Han Dynasty appointed him as the Prefect of Kuaiji. Later, he was sent on a diplomatic mission to Southwest China, where he achieved significant success for the empire. Eventually, he rose to the positions of Commandant of Titles and Secretary General to the Prime Minister.

负薪苦读学习勤　妻不理解抱怨贫
学就宏文善词赋　出使西南立功勋

Zhu Maichen was showed care in reading while carrying kindling,
His wife complained about their poverty, of him she had no inkling.
Finally he became a great scholar adept at prose and verse,
He quested to Southwest China and performed exploits diverse.

八、凿壁借光（匡衡）

西汉时承县（今山东邹城）人匡衡，字稚圭。家里几代务农，无一人识字。匡衡见别人知书明理，非常羡慕。但因家贫，为保吃穿，整日担柴卖柴维持生活。为了读书，他设法向邻居家借书读，白天抽空读一点，晚上买不起灯油，见墙上有一小洞，借邻舍之光夜读。由于勤学苦读，成为一位很有学问的人，能给各地学者解答多种问题。汉元帝时做到丞相，封乐安侯。

8. Borrowing Light from a Neighbour

Kuang Heng was from Cheng County (present-day Zoucheng, Shandong Province) during the Western Han Dynasty. His courtesy name was Zhigui. Coming from a family of farmers with no one able to read or write, Kuang Heng greatly admired those who were learned and rational. Due to his family's poverty, he had to make a living by cutting and selling firewood. Despite his financial struggles, he was determined to learn. He borrowed books from his neighbors and studied during the day whenever he could spare the time. At night, unable to afford oil for a lamp, he discovered a small hole in the wall that allowed him to borrow light from the neighbor's home. His tireless dedication to learning eventually made him a scholar of considerable renown, capable of resolving complex issues for other learned individuals. In recognition of his achievements, he was appointed Prime Minister and was granted the title of Marquis of Le'an during the reign of Emperor Yuan of Han.

农家子弟酷爱学　挑担挣钱维生活
凿壁借光成佳话　学富五车居相国

A peasant's son, with books he was keen,
But to earn his living, he carried wood between.
He borrowed light from a neighbor, a tale widely told,
And rose to Prime Minister, with wisdom bold.

九、悬梁苦读（孙敬）

汉朝信都（今河北冀县）人孙敬，字文宝。自幼好学，家贫无力买简帛，只好向别人借书阅读。读后要还，难以记录和复习，他便采集一些较粗的柳条，把字写在上面，编到一起，日夜攻读。夜里读书困乏，便用绳一头系到梁上，一头系到自己的头发上。瞌睡时一低头头发因拉扯而痛，驱逐困意。后来成为一位饱学之士。诗人李商隐曾赞颂过他"悬梁曾苦学"的精神。

9. Tying One's Hair to the Beam to Stay Awake While Reading

Sun Jing was from Xindu (now Ji County, Hebei Province) during the Han Dynasty. His courtesy name was Wenbao. A dedicated student from a young age,Sun's poor family could not afford the bamboo slips and silk used for writing, so he had to borrow books from others. Since these books were temporary loans, he found it difficult to take notes and review the material. To solve this problem, he collected rough willow branches, wrote on them, and bound them together to create his own makeshift books. When he became tired at night, he would tie one end of a rope to a ceiling beam and the other to his hair to keep himself awake. If he began to doze off, the pain of his scalp being tugged would jolt him back to attention. Through his tireless efforts, Sun Jing became a scholar of great learning. The famous poet Li Shangyin later praised his perseverance, calling it the spirit of "studying hard by tying his hair to the beam".

柳编简册苦就学　日夜攻读永不辍
学海茫茫欣然赴　悬梁勤读苦中乐

Sun Jing studied hard by binding books out of willow,
Never did he even let his head rest upon the pillow.
Navigating seas of knowledge was all he dared to dream,
He pleasured himself in study with his hair tied to the beam.

十、西汉大儒（董仲舒）

西汉广川（今河北景县）人董仲舒，少年时刻苦学习《春秋》，景帝时当了博士。后托病辞官，设帐教学，及时努力攻读。他认为人生短暂，学问却如大海，只有精神专一才能达到理想的彼岸。他学习时"三年不窥园"。后被汉武帝重用，成为继孔孟之后的一代大儒。

10. A Great Confucian in the Western Han Dynasty

Dong Zhongshu was from Guangchuan (now Jing County, Hebei Province) during the Western Han Dynasty. As a young man, he devoted himself to studying *The Spring and Autumn Annals*, and during the reign of Emperor Jing of Han, he became a Court scholar. Later, he resigned from his official post, citing illness, and set up his own school, where he continued to intensify his studies. Dong believed that life was short, but knowledge was as vast as the ocean. Only through complete focus could one reach the distant shore of ideal wisdom. He was so dedicated to his learning that he "did not step into the garden for three years". Eventually, he was appointed to a prominent position by Emperor Wu of Han, becoming a leading Confucian scholar in the tradition of Confucius and Mencius.

西汉大儒董仲舒　勤学深思多著述
武帝重用兴炎汉　罢黜百家尊儒术

Dong Zhongshu was a great Confucian scholar of the Western Han,
Studious, adroit and prolific was this especially wise man.
The Emperor Wu promoted him to revise his dynasty,
He railed against the One Hundred Schools, upholding Confucius only.

十一、奋著《汉书》（班固）

东汉安陵（今陕西咸阳）人班固，字孟坚，是大学者班彪之子。九岁能背《诗经》《尚书》，并能写出文章。年长后，熟读百家之书，无不穷究问底。为学更多知识，遍访名师，博览群籍。汉明帝得知后，令他任典校秘书。他继承父志，积二十年之功，著成《汉书》，在史字界开创断代史新体。不久，白虎观会后作《白虎通义》，成为东汉时期崇儒的法典。

11. Exerting One's Self to Write *The History of the Han Dynasty*

Ban Gu, the son of the renowned scholar Ban Biao, was from Anling (now Xianyang, Shaanxi Province) during the Eastern Han Dynasty. His courtesy name was Mengjian. By the age of nine, he was already able to recite *the Book of Songs* and *the Classic of History*, and could write essays. As he grew older, he read extensively across the teachings of the Hundred Schools of Thought, dedicating himself to thoroughly understanding each subject. Eager to acquire more knowledge, he sought out famous teachers and read a wide range of classical works. Upon hearing of his scholarly pursuits, Emperor Ming of Han appointed him as the Classics Proofreading Secretary. Following in his father's footsteps, Ban Gu spent twenty years completing *The History of the Han Dynasty*, a groundbreaking work that established a new genre of dynastic history. Shortly thereafter, he wrote *The White Tiger Chronicles* after the White Tiger Pass Forum convened by the emperor, which became an authoritative text upholding Confucianism during the Eastern Han period.

兰台令史班孟坚　　博览群籍著宏篇
《汉书》初创断代史　《白虎通义》儒法典

Ban Mengjian, head of the Lantai Bureau's reign,
With classical works, he crafted a literary gain.
His History of the Han established a lasting line,
And *The White Tiger Chronicles* enriched Confucius' design.

十二、隔帘听讲（承宫）

东汉时姑幕（今山东诸城）人承宫，字少子。小时家穷，给人家放猪谋生。每当他赶着猪路过学舍时，见同龄的孩子读书，羡慕得直掉眼泪。一天，他在学舍门前经过，听老师徐子盛讲课，便在篱笆墙外旁听。发现猪到处乱窜，赶回来再听。一天，正听得入神，头上重重地挨了一棍，原来被主人发现，尾随到此。不但打他，还叫他赔猪。老师徐子盛好言劝说主人，猪钱不要让他赔了，徐还收下这个好学的学生，从此承宫努力攻读，后来当了博士，官至侍中祭酒。

12. Listening to Lectures from behind the Curtain

Cheng Gong, whose courtesy name was Shaozi, was from Gumu (now Zhucheng, Shandong Province) during the Eastern Han Dynasty. Born into a poor family, he made a living tending pigs. Every time he passed by the school while driving his herd, he would shed tears, envious of his peers who were able to study. One day, as he passed by, he was drawn in by the sound of a lecture being given by the teacher Xu Zisheng. He stopped by the fence and listened in. While trying to round up his pigs, he would return to the lecture whenever he could. One day, while engrossed in the lecture, he was struck on the head with a heavy blow—it turned out that his master had followed him. Not only did the master scold him, but he also demanded compensation for the pigs that had run astray. Teacher Xu Zisheng kindly mediated, convincing the master to forgo the compensation for the pigs, and even accepted Cheng Gong as a student. From that point on, Cheng Gong dedicated himself to his studies, eventually becoming a Court academician and later being appointed Privy Libation Counsellor.

少年承宫放猪人　舍外旁听学入神
猪跑主责师器重　荣任祭酒光学林

Young Cheng Gong, a swineherd by trade,
But in lectures, his keen mind was laid.
His master rebuked, yet his teacher was kind,
As Privy Libation Counselor he set an example refined.

十三、市肆借读（王充）

东汉上虞（今浙江上虞）人王充，字仲任。自小失去父亲，长大后进入京师的太学，拜班彪为师。他自小酷爱学习，家里无书，向邻居家借。几家邻居的书都看完了，便到市场上的书肆中去看书。有时一看一天，直到天黑被店主人撵走。他看书十分专心，许多古籍都能背下来。日子长了，对诸子百家、各个学派的学说都领会、精通，在此基础上，阐发自己的观点，写出我国两千年前充满唯物主义思想的名著——《论衡》。

13. Reading Books at the Market

Wang Chong, whose courtesy name was Zhongren, was from Shangyu (now Shangyu District, Zhejiang Province). Losing his father in childhood, he later entered the imperial academy in the capital and studied under Ban Biao. A passionate learner from childhood, he had no books at home, so he borrowed them from his neighbors. After finishing the books from his neighbors, he would go to the market stalls to read. Sometimes, he would spend the entire day at the stall, only to be chased away by the owner at nightfall. Wang was deeply focused on his studies, and he could memorize and recite much of the classical literature. Over time, he became well-versed in the teachings of the various schools of thought. Based on this foundation, he expounded his own ideas and wrote the famous work *On Balance*, a classic full of materialist philosophy from two thousand years ago.

王充失怙入太学　埋首书海自得乐
独辟蹊径舒高论　名著《论衡》新意多

Wang Chong lost his father young but that was no catastrophe,
He studied tirelessly and entered the imperial academy.
He forged new paths with theories profound,
On Balance remains his work renowned.

十四、德学并进（徐庶）

三国时颍川（今河南禹县）人徐庶，字元直。年轻时仗义任侠，精通剑术，曾因替人报仇杀了人，被判死罪。幸朋友搭救，得以幸免，逃脱在外。从此他觉悟过来，痛改前非，决心读书求取学问。开始时，学友都对他疏远，他却卑躬谦逊，求得大家谅解，认真听取老师教诲，学业大进。与诸葛亮友善，欲辅刘备，曹操强占他母亲，徐母自缢告诉他不辅曹操。徐庶在曹营多年，未献一策。

14. Making Progress in Virtue and Knowledge

Xu Shu, courtesy name Yuanzhi, was from Yingchuan (now Yu County in Henan Province) during the Three Kingdoms Period. In his youth, he was righteous and chivalrous, skilled in swordsmanship. He was once sentenced to death for killing a man in vengeance. Fortunately, a friend intervened, and he managed to escape. This experience led to a turning point in his life—he repented deeply for his past actions and resolved to pursue education and knowledge. At first, his classmates distanced themselves from him, but he humbled himself and sought their forgiveness. Gradually, he won their understanding and devoted himself wholeheartedly to his studies, making significant progress. Xu Shu was on friendly terms with Zhuge Liang and initially hoped to support Liu Bei. However, when Cao Cao captured his mother as a hostage, she chose to end her own life rather than swear allegiance to him. Heeding his mother's wishes, Xu Shu refused to offer any counsel to Cao Cao for many years.

徐庶早年忒轻狂　杀人罹罪逃外乡
痛改前非学文化　见识高远德行强

Xu Shu, in youth, was reckless and wild,
Accused of murder, he fled, exiled.
Thoroughly repentant he embarked on a course of study,
His foresight and vision transmitted virtue to everybody.

十五、映雪读书（孙康）

晋朝京兆（今河南洛阳）人孙康，从小聪慧明敏，但家境贫寒，白天读书，晚上点不起灯油，冬天便趁下雪时发出的亮光读书。先在门内，后在室外，但因为室外太冷，他穿上厚衣再读书。这样还冷，他一面走动一面读书背书。如此坚持苦学，学业大进。他为了多读书，不饮酒，不下棋，不参加宴会，性情孤高不俗，很少与人交往。日后官至御史大夫，尽责尽力，为官清廉，不谋私利，被世人称道。

15. Reading by the Reflection of the Snow

Sun Kang was from Jingzhao (now Luoyang City in Henan Province). He was exceptionally bright from an early age, but his family was poor and could not afford a lamp for him to study at night. During the day, he read whenever he had the chance, and in winter, he relied on the reflected light from the snow to continue his studies.Initially, he read indoors, but when it became too cold, he moved outside, layering himself in warm clothing. Even this did not suffice, so he walked around while reciting to keep warm. His persistence paid off, and his academic progress was remarkable. He was known for his austere lifestyle, rarely socializing with others. He avoided drinking, playing chess, and attending banquets, focusing entirely on his studies. His solitary and elevated character made him stand apart from others. Later, he was appointed Grand Secretary, where he served with integrity, remaining upright and avoiding personal gain. His honesty and dedication earned him widespread respect and admiration.

瑞雪丰年万民欢　洒落大地益农田
映雪读书成佳话　铸就一代博学官

People were gladdened with the dusting of seasonal snow,
The fields would now be nourished, helping next year's crops to grow.
How torch-less Sun Kang used that glistening white
Shows that a pauper can rise when knowledgeable and bright.

十六、发誓攻读（皇甫谧）

晋朝安定朝那人皇甫谧，自小过继给堂叔父，二十多岁前叔父不管他，整日沉溺于游乐之中。叔母任氏教育他说："当年孔子、孟子勤学成名，你并不笨，却整日贪玩，是我们对你教育不够。"说毕痛哭。皇甫谧深受感动，决定洗心革面，立志读书。几年后，得了中风症，仍手不释卷。有时读起书来忘记吃饭、睡觉。郡府推荐他为"孝廉""贤良方正"，均不应召，却潜心著述，写出《历代帝王世纪》《高士传》等著作。

16. Swearing to Work Hard at Studying

Huangfu Mi was from Zhao na, Anding Prefecture. As a child, he was adopted by his uncle, who was lenient and allowed him to indulge in recreation and leisure. One day, his aunt scolded him, saying, "Confucius and Mencius became famous through their diligent study. You are not stupid, but you waste your time playing. This is because we have failed to educate you properly." She spoke these words with tears. Deeply moved by her admonition, Huangfu Mi resolved to reform himself and dedicate himself to study. A few years later, he suffered a stroke, but even then, he continued to read tirelessly, often forgetting meals and sleep. His dedication to learning became well-known, and the government praised him for his "filial devotion and personal integrity" as well as his "upright and worthy character". Despite these accolades, he declined all official appointments. Instead, he focused on writing, producing works such as *Biographies of the Emperors of Past Dynasties* and *Biographies of the Elites*.

浪荡少年皇甫谧　婶母教育改前非
日夜攻读不释卷　著述多部创奇迹

Huangfu Mi, in youth, was wild and wayward,
But with his aunt's guidance, his past was altered.
He read day and night, a scholar so bright,
His works became legends, a miraculous sight.

十七、洛阳纸贵（左思）

　　晋朝临淄（今山东临淄）人左思，字太冲，父亲左雍曾任殿中侍御史。左思自小就喜欢读书、做文章，也喜爱书法、弹琴等。父亲批评他爱好太多，读书太少，从此他努力攻读，发誓超过父亲。他虽语言迟钝，但却肯于动脑，极赋文采。先用一年的时间写成《齐都赋》，连获好评。不久，迁到洛阳后，又广泛搜集资料，用了十年的工夫，写成《三都赋》。此作一发表，京师大震。许多富豪之家、达官贵人竞相传抄，以致出现"洛阳纸贵"。

17. The Price of Paper Rises in Luoyang City

　　Zuo Si was from Linzi (now Linzi City, Shandong Province) during the Jin Dynasty. His courtesy name was Taichong. His father, Zuo Yong, had once served as Assistant to the Imperial Censor. As a child, Zuo Si was passionate about reading, writing essays, calligraphy, and playing the lyre. However, his father criticized him for having too many interests and not enough focus on his studies. From that point onward, Zuo Si became determined to apply himself more rigorously to his studies and vowed to surpass his father's achievements. Though his speech was slow and deliberate, Zuo Si's sharp intellect and literary talent were evident. In just one year,he completed his *Ode to the Capital of the State of Qi*, which was met with widespread acclaim. After relocating to Luoyang, he spent ten years meticulously gathering materials and refining his work, eventually completing *the Ode to the Three Capitals*. When this work was published, it caused a sensation in the capital. So many rich families as well as high officials and noble lords vied for copies of the essay, resulting in the price of paper in Luoyang City being hiked up.

聪慧左思爱好多　严父教诲集中学
多项作品富文采　洛阳纸贵惊四座

Young Zuo Si was clever, with interests vast,
His father urged him to focus, and study steadfast.
His works, rich in style, with flair did abound,
In Luoyang, paper's price soared all around.

十八、囊萤夜读（车胤）

晋朝南平（今湖北公安）人车胤，字武子。其祖会稽太守车浚，为官清廉，荒年时将家财救济穷人，到车胤时家境已穷。但车胤谨遵父、祖之教，酷爱学习。夏日晚上买不起灯油，便到郊外捉来一些萤火虫，放进缝好的纱袋内，借它们的光亮读书。过几天袋内萤火虫死去，再去捉。如此日夜攻读，学业大进，义理兼通。当时文人聚会时，总爱听他引经据典，解释疑团，当时竟有"无车不乐"的说法。日后他官至征西长史、护国将军、吏部尚书。

18. Putting Fireflies in a Bag as a Lantern for Night Reading

Che Yin, courtesy name Wuzi, was from Nanping (now Gong'an County in Hubei Province) during the Jin Dynasty. His grandfather, Che Jun, had served as the Prefect of Kuaiji and was known for his integrity. During times of hardship, he used his family wealth to help the poor. By the time Che Yin came of age, his family had fallen into poverty. Despite this, Che Yin adhered to the teachings of his father and grandfather, dedicating himself to his studies. During the summer, when he could not afford oil for a lamp, he would go out into the fields to catch fireflies and place them in a small gauze bag to use their light for reading. When the fireflies died after a few days, he would catch more. His determination to read day and night led to great progress in his studies, and he became well-versed in both the classics and the deeper meanings of texts. At literary gatherings, intellectuals often sought him out for his insightful explanations, citing ancient works and classics. It was said that there could be "no fun without Mr. Che". Later, Che Yin served in several high-ranking positions, including Secretary General for Subduing the West, Lord Protector General, and Minister of Personnel.

小小萤虫时闪光　微光伴就读书郎
车胤囊萤成佳话　学富五车国栋梁

Little fireflies glimmered all through the night,
Young scholars took them as their reading light.
How he bagged fireflies was a story celebrated,
He became a pillar of the state, a scholar widely feted.

十九、炼丹著述（葛洪）

东晋句容（今江苏句容）人葛洪，字稚川。自幼酷爱学习。家贫，买不起纸笔，上山砍柴卖了挣钱供学习用。夜里读书、抄书、复习、背诵。为了安心学习，他不喝酒，不赌钱，不下棋，排除各种嗜好，多读书，明义理。后来平定石冰之乱，被封为伏波将军，辞官谢客，到处寻书阅读，著《抱朴子》等书。他曾到南方做句漏令，在那里得到丹砂。晚年隐居罗浮山，进行冶炼，成为我国古代进行化学实验的第一人。

19. Writing Books on Alchemy

Ge Hong, courtesy name Zhichuan, was from Jurong (now Jurong City in Jiangsu Province) during the Eastern Jin Dynasty. He was passionate about learning from a young age. However, born into a poor family, he could not afford paper or writing tools, so he chopped firewood and sold it to earn money for his studies. At night, he would read, transcribe, review, and memorize books. To focus on his studies, he refrained from drinking, gambling, and playing chess. He eliminated all distractions and dedicated himself solely to reading in order to deepen his understanding of principles and concepts. Later, after helping quell the Rebellion of Shi Bing, he was appointed General for Quenching Waves. He eventually resigned from the military and withdrew from social life, devoting himself to seeking books from all corners. During this time, he wrote *Baopuzi: The Book of Embracing Simplicity*. After serving as magistrate of Julou County in the south, he obtained cinnabar. In his later years, he retreated to Mount Luofu, where he practiced alchemy, becoming the first person in Chinese history to conduct chemistry experiments.

文武兼备葛稚川　博览群书著鸿篇
潜居深山丹砂炼　实验功成光科坛

Ge Hong was equipped with swordsmanship and learning,
He produced great works with scholarship discerning.
He secluded himself in the deep mountains to pursue alchemy,
His successful experiments illuminated the scientific community.

二十、映月读书（江泌）

南北朝时，南齐考城（今河南卫辉）人江泌，字士清。少年时家中贫寒，一家人以卖木屐为生。但他热爱学习，夜里买不起灯油，便借着月光来读。月光倾斜，看不清了，他便沿着梯子爬到屋顶上借光再读。他母亲早亡，对父亲极尽孝心，在地方上十分有名，人称"江巨孝。"年长后，父亲也去世，为怀念父母，不吃父母当年爱吃的鲥鱼、菜心。努力学习，学问日增，后被南康王请去做其子琳的侍读。

20. Reading by the Moonlight

Jiang Mi, courtesy name Shiqing, was from Kaocheng (now Weihui City in Henan Province) in the Southern Qi Dynasty, during the period of the Northern and Southern Dynasties. Born into a poor family, they made a living by selling wooden clogs. Despite their poverty, Jiang Mi had a deep love for learning. Unable to afford a lamp, he would read by the moonlight. When the moonlight became too faint, he would climb a ladder to the roof to catch the light and continue his studies. Jiang Mi lost his mother at an early age but was profoundly dutiful to his father, earning a reputation for filial piety in his community. He became well-known as "Jiang the Ultra-Filial Son". After his father's passing, in remembrance of his parents, Jiang Mi refrained from eating trout and cabbage hearts, both of which had been their favorite foods. His dedication to learning never wavered, and he steadily expanded his knowledge. Eventually, he was invited by King Nankang to serve as a tutor to his son, Lin.

孝子江泌喜诗文　巧借月光阅读勤
读书明理恪尽孝　学高德增示后人

Jiang Mi, the filial son, read poems and essays with delight,
He devoured books voraciously beneath the moonlight.
Filial and dedicated he shone with propriety,
Later generations have been nourished by his wisdom and fidelity.

二十一、抄书勤读（王筠）

南北朝时梁人王筠，字元礼，琅琊（今山东临沂）人。七岁能写文章，长大后学习更努力。他学习的特点是抄书。从十三岁起，儒家经典、其他诸子百家的书均抄写一遍。每借到一本书后，爱不释手，马上抄下来再归还，这样便记得牢，于是学问越来越大，著作越来越多。他在晚年自编文集，有《洗马》《中书》等集 100 卷。各书均以职官分类，眉目清晰，引经据典，文词华丽，体现了当时的时代特点。

21. Transcribing for Reading

Wang Yun, courtesy name Yuanli, was from Langya (now Linyi City in Shandong Province) and lived during the Liang Dynasty, a period of the Northern and Southern Dynasties. He was able to compose essays by the age of seven and continued to dedicate himself to studying as he grew older. A distinctive feature of his learning was his habit of transcribing texts. Starting at the age of thirteen, he meticulously copied the Confucian classics and works from the other schools of thought. Whenever he borrowed a book, he would become so fond of it that he could not resist transcribing it before returning it to its owner. This method helped him better retain the material, and as his knowledge deepened, so did his collection of works. In his later years, Wang Yun compiled his own anthologies, including *The Crown Prince's Herald* and *The Royal Book Collection*, totaling 100 volumes. These works were carefully organized by topic and title, with clear indexing and elegant citations from classical texts. They reflected the intellectual and literary style of his era, showcasing his scholarship and the characteristics of the time.

南朝王筠读书勤　爱书手抄记忆深
常抄牢记学问大　广泛著作可等身

Wang Yun pored over books at the time of the Southern Dynasty,
Transcribing them longhand gave him greater certainty.
Writing out and memorising caused his learning to mushroom,
Many volumes of his own made his reputation bloom.

二十二、遇难仍学（沈约）

南北朝时梁人沈约，武康（今浙江德清）人，字休之。父亲沈璞官临淮南太守，被奸人杀害。十三岁的沈约遭此大难后，悄悄逃走。不久遇到大赦，才得以幸免。逃亡在外时，无亲无故无财产，只得一面劳作，一面苦学，学起来经常夜以继日。母亲怕他累坏，常熄灭灯火，逼他休息。他却在黑暗中背诵白天学的内容。因坚持学习，学识渊博，曾著《晋书》《南齐书》《齐纪》《梁武纪》及文集百卷。其《四声谱》在研究我国声律学中也是一大创见。

22. Continuing to Learn in the Midst of Misfortune

Shen Yue, courtesy name Xiuzhi, was from Wukang (now Deqing City in Zhejiang Province) and lived during the Liang Dynasty in the period of the Southern and Northern Dynasties. His father, Shen Pu, had served as the Prefect of Huainan but was tragically murdered by a villain. At the tender age of thirteen, Shen Yue was forced to flee following this catastrophe. Not long after, an imperial amnesty spared his life, allowing him to escape by sheer luck. During his time in exile, Shen Yue was destitute and without family support. He had to work to make a living, but he never abandoned his studies. Often studying late into the night, his mother, concerned for his health, would extinguish his lamp to force him to rest. Yet even in the darkness, he would continue reciting what he had learned during the day. His perseverance in learning paid off, and his scholarship became vast and profound. Shen Yue authored over one hundred volumes, including *The History of the Jin Dynasty*, *The History of the Southern Qi*, *The Chronicles of Qi*, *The Chronicles of Liang and Wu* etc. His work *Four Tones* was a milestone in the history of the study of rhythm in China.

家难未损鸿鹄志　一朝赦免学更勤
夜以继日苦研读　多部史著贻后人

Family calamities did not dampen his ambition,
He could study ever harder thanks to imperial manumission.
Day and night he applied himself with the utmost concentration,
His history books providing a boon to every generation.

二十三、主攻算学（信都芳）

南北朝时北齐河间（今河北河间）人信都芳，自幼爱读各种书，他对古籍经典不感兴趣，却喜欢日常中计算的学问。他认为算术（数学）中有巧妙的构思，变化无穷。每当他聚精会神地思考算术问题时，便会忘了一切。有一次在路上考虑问题时，掉进坑里。他常对人说："古人发明算术，十分巧妙。这门学问既精微，又实用，我每次进入它的奥妙之处，连打雷都听不见。"由于他专心研究算学，日后撰了一些勾股方面的文章，成为古代一位数学家。

23. Working on Mathematics

Xin Dufang was from Hejian Prefecture (now Hejian City in Hebei Province) and lived during the Northern and Southern Dynasties. From a young age, he had a passion for reading, though he was not particularly interested in ancient classics.Instead, he preferred the study of mathematics, particularly in its everyday applications. To him, mathematics was a field full of intricate ideas and endless possibilities. When he became deeply absorbed in solving mathematical problems, he would lose awareness of everything else. On one occasion, while pondering a problem as he walked, he fell into a pit without noticing. He often told others, "The ancient sages invented mathematics in a wonderfully ingenious way. It is a subject both subtle and practical. Once I immerse myself in its mysteries, I am so absorbed that I cannot even hear the sound of thunder." His intense focus on mathematics led him to write several essays on the Pythagorean theorem, earning him a place as one of the great mathematicians of ancient China.

不喜经典信都芳　偏爱勾股和积商
废寝忘食学术数　方便实用利梓桑

Xin Dufang was not fond of classical rhetoric,
Preferring Pythagoras and advanced arithmetic.
He skipped meals and sleep to study everything mathematical,
He boosted his hometown with concepts most practical.

二十四、挂角读书（李密）

李密，隋朝京兆长安（今陕西西安）人，字玄邃。少时好读书，曾任隋炀帝的宿卫，整日站岗，无暇读书，便辞去职务，专心读书，从书中学到知识，找到乐趣。有一次，他骑着牛路过缑山，牛角上挂着《汉书》。他一面骑牛前行，一面读书，被隋朝的大臣杨素看见，认为这是一位奇才，令儿子杨玄感与他结交，二人成为挚友。不久，杨玄感起兵反隋，因没用李密的计谋而失败。后来他率领农民起义军与翟让等一起据洛口（瓦岗寨）起兵反隋，称魏公。隋亡后，辅佐唐王。唐朝建立后，拜光禄卿。

24. Reading on the Back of an Ox

Li Mi, whose courtesy name was Xuansui, was from Chang'an in Jingzhao Prefecture (now Xi'an City, Shaanxi Province) during the Sui Dynasty. He developed a passion for reading at a young age. Later, when he served as a guard to Emperor Yang of the Sui Dynasty, he found the demands of sentry duty left him no time for study. Determined to pursue his love for books, he resigned from his post and devoted himself entirely to reading, finding both knowledge and enjoyment in his studies. On one occasion, as he rode an ox past Mount Gou, he fastened *The History of the Han Dynasty* to the ox's horns and read while riding. His unusual sight caught the attention of Yang Su, a high-ranking minister. Impressed by his intellect, Yang Su regarded Li Mi as a prodigy and arranged for his son, Yang Xuanggan, to befriend him. Not long after, Yang Xuangan led a failed rebellion, partly because he ignored Li Mi's advice. Later, Li Mi joined forces with Zhai Rang and led a peasant uprising against the Sui Dynasty. They seized Luokou (Wa'gang Zhai), and Li Mi was granted the title Duke Wei. Following the fall of the Sui Dynasty, he became an advisor to Li Shimin, the future Tang Emperor. After the Tang Dynasty was established, Li Mi was appointed Minister of the Imperial Household.

坚辞公职为阅读　牛角悠悠挂《汉书》
勤学博得大人赞　灭隋兴唐功勋殊

Li Mi wanted only to read, resigning his post resolutely,
Even when riding an ox he studied *The History Han Dynasty*.
A minister praised his spirit most studious,
Helping the Tang defeat the Sui made Li illustrious.

二十五、撰写二史（李延寿）

唐朝相州（今河南安阳）人李延寿，自幼爱好学习。其父李大师经常向他讲宋、齐、梁、陈、北齐、北周及隋朝各代的优劣。那时战乱不已，国家不统一，南方称北方为"索虏"，北方称南方为"岛夷"，各国的史书都是本国详，别国略。为改变这一情况，他遵父命，要写两部南北综合的史书。积多年之功，仿《春秋》的形式，写出《南史》《北史》共 180 篇，献给唐太宗，深得皇帝嘉许，对我国史学做出了贡献。

25. Writing Two History Books

Li Yanshou was from Xiangzhou (now Anyang City, Henan Province) in the Tang Dynasty. He was passionate about learning from an early age. His father, Li Dashi, often shared insights on the strengths and weaknesses of various dynasties,including the Song, Qi, Liang, Chen, Northern Qi, Northern Zhou, and Sui. During this tumultuous period, the country was divided, with the southern states referring to the north as "pig-tailed tribesmen" and the northerners calling the southerners "barbarians." Each state's history focused in detail on its own achievements, while glossing over or neglecting the history of others. To address this imbalance, Li Yanshou, following his father's guidance, set out to write two comprehensive histories—one for the Southern Dynasties and one for the Northern Dynasties. After years of diligent work, he completed *The History of the Southern Dynasties* and *The History of the Northern Dynasties*, modeled after the style of *The Spring and Autumn Annals*. He presented these works to Emperor Taizong of Tang, who praised them highly, recognizing Li Yanshou's significant contribution to the field of Chinese historical scholarship.

南北朝时战不休　　　各国史记互为仇
《南史》《北史》综合现　编年体成又《春秋》

During the Southern and Northern Wars, strife would never end,
Each state's history wrote of its foe, a bitter trend.
The Southern History and Northern Annals emerged side by side,
Both in Chronicle style, like *Spring and Autumn Annals* did abide.

二十六、铁杵磨针（李白）

唐朝大诗人李白，字太白，蜀地昌明（今四川绵阳）人。一生写出了许多脍炙人口的诗作，但他小时候却凭着聪颖过人，经常玩耍嬉戏，学习时一遇困难便退缩。有一次游玩时，在河边见一位老妇人，拿一根铁杵在石头上磨。李白惊奇地问她做什么？她说："我把它磨成一根绣花针。"李白说："这怎么可能呢？"老人郑重地对他说："年轻人，只要功夫深，铁杵磨出绣花针。"李白知道老人在设法教育他，从此奋发学习，坚持不懈，学问天天提高，日后写诗作文时都能做到妙语联珠，成为被人们称作"诗仙"的大诗人。

26. Grinding an Iron Pestle into a Needle

Li Bai, the great poet of the Tang Dynasty, whose courtesy name was Tai Bai, was from Changming (now Mianyang City in Sichuan Province). He composed many widely loved and often-quoted poems throughout his life. However, as a child, he was naturally gifted but often spent his time playing and relying on his wits. He would easily shy away when faced with difficulties. One day, while wandering near a river, he saw an elderly woman grinding an iron pestle against a stone. Surprised, Li Bai asked what she was doing. The woman replied, "I am grinding this iron pestle into a needle." Li Bai skeptically questioned, "How could that be possible?" The woman, speaking seriously, answered, "Young man, with persistence and effort, even an iron pestle can be ground into a needle." Li Bai understood that the woman was trying to impart a lesson. Inspired, he redoubled his efforts in learning, persisting without giving up. As a result, his knowledge and skill grew day by day. In time, Li Bai became known for his poetic brilliance, and his eloquent verses earned him the title of the "Immortal of Poetry".

只要功夫下得深　铁杵能磨绣花针
老妇懿行寓深意　造就一代大诗人

Only if one is willing to tolerate hassle,
Can a needle be ground from an iron pestle.
The old crone provided an example profound,
A great poet emerged with his·feet set on the ground.

二十七、郑虔三绝（郑虔）

唐朝荥阳（今河南荥阳）人郑虔，字弱齐。自小努力攻读诗书，又爱写字、画画，有了一些名望。曾以私撰国史之罪被贬十年。归来后，唐玄宗任其为广文馆博士，他仍醉心于书画。他为官清廉，家无积蓄，买不起纸。一天，发现慈恩寺内数间房中贮有一些干枯的柿叶，便经常拿来写字、作画。水平日益提高，他将一幅诗书画送给唐玄宗后，皇帝拍案叫绝，当即在画之尾部题"郑虔三绝"，并特置广文馆，诏授其为首位博士，史称"名士""高士"，时号郑广文。

27. Zheng Qian's Three Artistic Skills

Zheng Qian, whose courtesy name was Ruoqi, hailed from Xingyang (now Xingyang City in Henan Province) during the Tang Dynasty. From a young age, he dedicated himself to the study of poetry and literature, and also developed a passion for calligraphy and painting, earning a notable reputation for his artistic skills. However, he was once exiled for privately writing a history of the state. After his return, Emperor Xuanzong of Tang appointed him as an academician at the Guangwen School, affiliated with the Imperial College. Despite his official duties, Zheng remained deeply engrossed in his love for calligraphy and painting. He was known for his integrity as an official but had little money, and thus could not afford paper. One day, he discovered dried persimmon leaves stored in several rooms of the Ci'en Temple. He began using them to practice writing and painting, and his skills continued to improve. Eventually, Zheng presented a set of poems, calligraphy, and paintings to Emperor Xuanzong, who struck by their excellence, slapped the table in admiration. At the bottom of the work, the emperor inscribed, "Zheng Qian's Three Artistic Skills". He then established the Guangwen School, naming Zheng as the first imperial academician. From that point on, Zheng Qian was honored as "Mr. Zheng Guangwen" and became celebrated as a "gentleman" and a "genius".

痴迷书画创新意　贬抑十年不减志
柿叶片片练书画　郑虔三绝惊当世

Zheng Qian was engrossed with calligraphy and art,
A decade of banishment didn't kill the ambition in his heart.
Dried persimmon leaves became his practice material,
His three artistic skills were judged sensational.

二十八、铁砚磨穿（桑维翰）

五代时后晋开封人桑维翰，字国侨。努力攻读后，参加朝廷的科举，考中进士。主考官认为他成绩虽好，但桑同丧音，录取不吉利，便取消了他的资格。别人劝他别再走科举的路子了，他认为这个主考官无理，下一个主考官不一定无理。他创作出《日出扶桑赋》，表达自己自强不息的心态。又造了一个铁砚，明确表示："等我把铁砚磨穿，便不考了。"从此，更加奋发地学习，终于又考中进士，实现了自己的理想。后来官至中书令、枢密使。

28. Wearing Away the Inkstick

Sang Weihan, whose courtesy name was Guoqiao, was from Kaifeng in the Later Jin Dynasty during the Five Dynasties period. After diligently pursuing his studies, he sat for the imperial examination and was recognized as a successful scholar. However, the chief examiner, while acknowledging his impressive results, disqualified him because his surname, "Sang" sounded like the word for "death" in Chinese, and he feared it would bring bad luck. Despite this, Sang Weihan refused to be discouraged. Others advised him to abandon his pursuit of the imperial exams, but he believed that the next examiner might not share the same irrational bias. To demonstrate his resolve, he composed the *"Ode to the Sun Rising Above the East"*, a work that reflected his determination and resilience. Sang Weihan then fashioned an inkstick from iron and declared, "I will not give up my studies for this exam until I have worn this inkstick away." With renewed vigor, he dedicated himself even more fervently to his studies, ultimately passing the examination and fulfilling his aspirations. Later, he was appointed to prestigious positions, including Chancellor (Zhongshuling) and Military Affairs Commissioner.

考官低劣人才埋　维翰不屈从头来
铁砚磨穿述壮志　龙门荣登凭真才

The chief examiner unfairly dismissed a true talent,
But Sang Weihan proved himself utterly resilient.
With an iron inkstick, he swore to grind away,
And through tireless effort, he rose to win the day.

二十九、与民忧乐（范仲淹）

北宋时吴（今江苏苏州）人范仲淹，字希文。两岁时父亲去世，随母改嫁到朱家。生活虽然贫穷，但自小就有远大的志向。长大知道自己的身世后，告别母亲，恢复范姓，到应天府依靠亲戚读书。刻苦学习，日夜不懈，有时候吃不上饭仍坚持学习。考中进士，当上广德军司理参军后，把母亲接回赡养。他官至兵部尚书、参知政事，在平定西夏时立有战功，在西北威信很高。尤其乐善好施，置义田给族人。其"先天下之忧而忧，后天下之乐而乐"的名句更永垂千古。

29. Sharing Joys and Sorrows with the People

Fan Zhongyan, whose courtesy name was Xiwen, was from Wu (now Suzhou, Jiangsu Province) during the Northern Song Dynasty. He lost his father when he was only two years old and, after his mother remarried, took on the surname Zhu. Despite growing up in poverty, he harbored ambitious goals from a young age. Upon learning the truth of his origins in adolescence, he bade farewell to his mother, reclaimed his birth surname of Fan, and went to Yingtian Prefecture to live with relatives while pursuing his studies. He worked tirelessly, studying day and night, sometimes sacrificing meals to continue his learning. After passing the imperial examination and becoming a jinshi (successful candidate), he began his official career as a low-ranking official in charge of prisons and criminal affairs in Guangde. In a gesture of filial piety, Fan Zhongyan later brought his mother to live with him. He eventually rose to high-ranking positions, including Minister of War and Vice Chancellor. His military achievements, particularly in the campaign against the Western Xia, earned him a distinguished reputation, especially in the northwest. Known for his generosity and public-mindedness, he purchased land to provide for his clansmen. His famous phrase, "Be the first to worry about the troubles of the people, and the last to enjoy their joys", has become a lasting symbol of his commitment to public service and his compassion for the people.

贫儿异姓有大志　日夜不懈勤学习
文治武功垂千古　忧乐天下识民意

The poor boy with a different family name still had ambitions in his sight,
So he ploughed through his studies each and every day and night.
His political and military feats went down in history,
He shouldered the will of the people with concern exemplary.

三十、纸贵慎书（米芾）

北宋襄阳（今朝北襄阳）人米芾，又称米颠。少年时爱好书法，练了好久一直练不好。一天村里来了一位书法家，他急忙跑去求教。书法家叫他练习写帖，先向古人学，又说只能买自己的纸。纸并不多，却要五两纹银。米芾家里很穷，为了练字，母亲卖了自己的首饰，买下书法家的纸。米芾小心、认真地在这些纸上摹帖。过了些日子，书法家来到村里，见到他写的字，夸奖很好，并告诉他因为纸贵，所以才会写的认真，能出成绩，希望日后再认真练习。临走前把五两银子退给米芾。米芾把这五两银子永置案头，教育自己勤学苦练，终成一代名家。

30. Writing with Caution on Expensive Paper

Mi Fu, also known as Midian, was from Xiangyang (now Xiangyang City in Hubei Province) during the Northern Song Dynasty. As a child, he was passionate about calligraphy, but despite relentless practice, he struggled to perfect his skills. One day, a calligrapher visited his village, and Mi Fu eagerly sought his guidance. The master advised him to study the works of ancient calligraphers and told him that he should buy his own paper, which cost five taels of silver. Mi Fu's family was poor, but his mother, seeing his determination, sold her jewelry to buy the paper for him. Mi Fu then carefully and conscientiously practiced his calligraphy on the precious sheets. A few days later, the calligrapher returned to the village. Upon seeing Mi Fu's work, he praised him and explained that the boy's carefulness was likely due to the high cost of the paper. He encouraged Mi Fu to continue practicing with even greater perseverance. Before leaving, the calligrapher returned the five taels of silver to Mi Fu, who placed the money on his desk as a reminder. This experience fueled Mi Fu's dedication, and he went on to become a master of calligraphy.

米芾书画百代传　少时苦练不畏难
认真全赖纸金贵　良师巧诲育大贤

Mi Fu's calligraphy and paintings are the stuff of lore,
But his childhood was beset with trials, much hardship he bore.
He was mindful of how the paper was so expensive,
The master taught him excellence through first being apprehensive.

三十一、老而奋学（苏洵）

宋朝四川眉山人苏洵，字明允。年少时不知学习，二十七岁时才在别人的启发下努力读书。曾参加一次科举，未考上，他决心不走仕途，写文章时也不走别人的老路。他广泛学习，通六经百家之说，下笔顷刻数万言。宋仁宗嘉佑年间，与二子苏轼、苏辙同至京师，欧阳修将其作品介绍给士人，引起轰动。宰相韩琦奏于朝后，被授予秘书校书郎。其父子三人在文坛上均有盛名，他被人称作"老苏"或"苏老泉"。

31. Rising to Study in Old Age

Su Xun, whose courtesy name was Mingyun, was from Meishan in Sichuan Province during the Song Dynasty. In his youth, he was unaware of the importance of learning. It wasn't until he was twenty-seven that he was inspired by others to begin studying diligently. He once took the imperial examination but failed, after which he resolved not to pursue a career in government and to forge his own path in writing, rather than following traditional methods. Su Xun became an avid learner, studying widely and mastering the Hundred Schools of Thought. His knowledge was vast, and he could quickly compose essays of ten thousand words. During the Jiayou era of Emperor Renzong's reign, he traveled to the capital with his two sons, Su Shi and Su Zhe. When Ouyang Xiu introduced his works to the scholarly community, they created a sensation. The PrimeMinister, Han Qi, reported Su Xun's achievements to the emperor, who then appointed him as an Official Collator. Su Xun and his sons became highly respected figures in the literary world, and Su Xun was affectionately known as "Old Su" or "Su Laoquan".

三苏之首苏老泉　少不读书贪游玩
中年奋发学未晚　老当益壮光文坛

Sulaoquan was the head of the Su clan,
Play rather than books occupied him as a young man.
Yet in his later years, he found the scholar's way,
And amazed the literary world with his wisdom's sway.

三十二、议政著书（王应麟）

南宋庆元（今浙江宁波）人王应麟，字伯厚。他九岁通六经，理宗淳祐年间中进士，殿试时因成绩优秀为首选。他不满当时官场的人沽名钓誉，不懂典章制度，不了解国情民情的情形。针对这些问题，他自己努力学习，研究学问。任礼部尚书时，经常议论朝政，正确分析形势，教育群僚。他一生有二十余种著作。其《困学纪闻》《玉海》等在学术研究上贡献很大，他所编的《三字经》这本以通俗语言写成的古代百科全书，流传近千年。

32. Writing Books and Commenting on State Affairs

Wang Yinglin, whose courtesy name was Bohou, was from Qingyuan (now Ningbo City in Zhejiang Province) during the Southern Song Dynasty. He mastered the Six Classics by the age of nine and passed the imperial examination with distinction during the Chunyou era of Emperor Lizong's reign, ranking first in the palace examination. Dissatisfied with the state of the government, where officials often sought fame without understanding the law, national conditions, or the people's concerns, Wang Yinglin dedicated himself to studying these issues deeply. As the Minister of Rites, he frequently discussed state affairs, offering insightful analyses of current situations and educating his fellow officials. Wang wrote over twenty works in various fields, with his *Study Assiduously the Classics* and *The Jade Ocean* making significant contributions to academic research. His *Three Character Primer*, a simple yet encyclopedic work written in accessible language, has endured for centuries.

殿试龙首王应麟　　不事花招真学问
一生等身多著述　　《三字经》成传古今

Wang Yinglin took first place in the palace examination,
A triumph of memory over inspiration.
In due course, he had many books to his name,
The Three Character Primer ensured him lasting fame.

三十三、嘉言善行（脱脱）

元末蒙古人脱脱，至元中累迁御史大夫，官至中枢右丞相。曾主持修撰《辽史》《金史》《宋史》。他早年向老师吴直方学习时，不只重视书本上的知识，也重视实践中的知识和行为。他向老师请教时说："您每天要我端端正正地坐着读书，不如叫我牢记一些古人的嘉言善行，我照着他们的样子去做才好呢。"既重理论又重实践的脱脱，作为一位少数民族学者，能以主编三部正史，正是他向老师活学活用的成果。

33. Good Words and Acts of Kindness

Tuotuo, a Mongolian from the late Yuan Dynasty, served as Assistant Grand Secretary and later as the Senior Prime Minister. He was responsible for compiling *The History of the Liao Dynasty*, *History of the Jin Dynasty*, and *History of the Song Dynasty*. In his youth, Tuotuo studied under his teacher, Wu Zhifang, who emphasized not only book learning but also practical knowledge and conduct. Tuotuo once said to his teacher: "Instead of asking me to sit still and read, why not have me memorize the good words and virtuous actions of the ancients? It would be better to follow their example." A scholar from an ethnic minority background, Tuotuo valued both theory and practice. His ability to oversee the compilation of three major historical works was a direct result of his application of his teacher's teachings and his creative use of what he had learned.

历来学问重实践　只认书卷慎空言
脱脱务实作榜样　嘉言善行德为先

Learning should be put into practice without fail,
Reading to furnish shallow talk is truly of no avail.
Tuotuo was pragmatic and set a fine example,
Virtue brought forth words and deeds more than ample.

三十四、庙灯夜读（王冕）

明朝诸暨（今浙江诸暨）人王冕，幼年时父亲因病去世，靠母亲做点针线活，他给人家放牛来维持生活。但他爱学习，善于观察生活。白天一面放牛，一面看书，晚上买不起灯油，苦于无法学习。一天他路过一座寺庙，见庙内供佛的屋里日夜亮着灯，便征得僧人同意后每晚到庙内学习。主人给他的零用钱，他都买了书。后来努力学习，知识越来越丰富，对事物观察越来越细致。他特别羡慕梅花的傲骨精神，后来成一位善于吟咏画梅花的诗人及画家。

34. Reading by the Temple Lamps

Wang Mian, from Zhuji (now Zhuji City in Zhejiang Province) during the Ming Dynasty, lost his father at an early age. He supported himself by herding cattle for others, while his mother sewed. Despite their financial struggles, Wang Mian was passionate about learning and had a keen eye for observing life. By day, he would read while herding the oxen. However, at night, his family could not afford oil for a lamp, making it difficult for him to continue studying once darkness fell. One day, while passing by a temple, he noticed that the lamps in the Buddha's shrine were burning both day and night. With the permission of the monks, he began to study there every evening. He also used all the pocket money given to him by his employer to buy books. Through his diligent efforts, Wang Mian grew increasingly learned and became more observant of the world around him. He developed a particular admiration for the resilient spirit of plum blossoms, which later inspired him to become both a poet and a painter, renowned for his depictions and verses celebrating these flowers.

王冕丧父家又贫　好学不倦学古人
寺内借光夜夜读　梅花傲骨见精神

Wang Mian lost his father and lived on the edge,
He craved the ancient way of truth and knowledge.
Night and day the temple was his reading room.
His works bore the bouquet of the plum in bloom.

三十五、首倡维新（康有为）

康有为，字广厦，清朝末年广东南海人。出身书香世家。父亲康赞修在他五岁时便教背唐诗，老师琴凤仪教他读"四书"和《孝经》。十岁丧父后，祖父对他精心教育。十三岁随祖父到广州，通过社学考试。但他不满足于中国传统的学问，到香港游历不久后，了解了西方文明，努力学习西方的学问，接受进化论等观点，与我国古代治国安邦的理论相结合，形成了一套变法维新的思想体系，促进了我国近代史上的维新变法运动。

35. The First Advocate of Reform

Kang Youwei whose courtesy name was Guangsha, was from Nanhai in Guangdong Province in the Qing Dynasty. He was born into a scholar-gentry family. His father, Kang Zanxiu, taught him the poems of the Tang Dynasty when he was five years old and his teacher, Qin Fengyi, taught him The Four Books and *The Piety Scripture*. Unfortunately he lost his father at the age often, and his grandfather tookover the task of teaching him. He followed his grandfather to Guangzhou and passedthe imperial examination at the county level. But he was discontent with traditional Chinese studies and so learned about Western civilisation after touring Hong Kong.Then he worked hard at understanding Western learning and accepted the theory ofevolution, combining it with the traditional Chinese ideology of governance of state affairs. He formed the ideological system of political reform which facilitated theCampaign for Constitutional Reform and Modernisation.

自幼博学又多闻　穷则思变多改进
百日维新载青史　近代觉醒先行人

Kang Youwei was very learned and well-informed from an early age,
He knew that change came from adversity stoking one's courage.
The One Hundred Days of Reform marked a historical watershed,
His outlook was ahead of his times, a visionary head.

三十六、变革先锋（梁启超）

清末广东新会（今广东江门市）人梁启超，字卓如，号任公。六岁时读完"四书""五经"，又跟父亲学中国历史。八九岁时能写千言的八股文章，十一岁考中秀才，人称"神童"。十三岁在学海堂读经、史、子、集，十七岁去广州万木草堂，向康有为学了许多新观点，接受了一整套变法改良的学问，开始走向维新变法的道路。他创办《中外纪闻》，以新观点宣传资本主义思想，对封建势力进行猛烈地抨击，成为戊戌变法中卓越的宣传家、理论家，中国近代史上变法维新的二号人物。

36. A Pioneer of Reform

Liang Qichao, whose courtesy name was Zhuoru and styled himself Rengong, was from Xinhui (now Jiangmen City in Guangdong Province) in the late Qing Dynasty. At the age of six, he completed his study of the Four Books and the Five Classics, and began learning Chinese history under the tutelage of his father. By the age of eight or nine, he was able to write an Eight-Legged Essay of thousands of characters and passed the county-level imperial examination, earning the title of "child prodigy". At thirteen,Liang Qichao studied a wide range of subjects, including Confucian classics, historical records, philosophy, and other writings at Xuehaitang. At seventeen, he moved to Guangzhou's Wanmu Caotang, where he was greatly influenced by Kang Youwei's new ideas on political reform. Embracing these revolutionary concepts, he began to advocate for constitutional reform and modernization. Liang Qichao later founded the periodical News From Home and Abroad, where he promoted capitalist ideas and launched fierce critiques against feudal forces. As a leading publicist and theorist during the 1898 Reform Movement, he became one of the most prominent figures advocating for political change in modern China, second only to Kang Youwei in importance.

近世才子梁启超　中学深厚赶新潮
追随南海报国志　维新勇将青史标

Liang Qichao is remembered as a modern Chinese seer,
In him traditional knowledge combined with many a new idea.
He followed Kang Youwei to render service sincere,
His attempts to reform the nation made him a brave pioneer.

第五章

尊师重教

Chapter Five

Respecting Teachers and Emphasising Education

一、渭水访贤（周文王）

商朝末年，西方的周族兴起，到姬昌（周文王）时，已"三分天下有其二"。那时商纣王暴虐无道，姬昌想取而代之，但缺一位驰骋天下、总揽全局的帅才。听人说渭水之滨有一贤才，他便轻车简从来到渭水边，见一老人在垂钓，二人交谈一番，姬昌大获教益，当即拜他为师。此人姓姜名尚，姬昌尊他为"师尚父"。姬昌请到老师后，授以军权。不久姜尚率军灭纣兴周成功。

1. Searching for Talents along the River Wei

In the late Shang Dynasty, the Zhou clan rose to prominence in western China. By the time of Ji Chang (King Wen of Zhou), the Zhou had already gained control over "two-thirds of the land under heaven." At that time, King Zhou of Shang ruled with tyranny, and Ji Chang had long desired to replace him. However, he lacked a capable commander who could oversee the vast campaign and unite the efforts of the Zhou. Hearing of a wise talent living along the banks of the Wei River, Ji Chang made his way there with a simple cart and a few retainers. He found an old man fishing by the river, and after a conversation, Ji Chang was deeply impressed by the man's wisdom. He immediately invited him to be his teacher. The man, named Jiang Shang, was respectfully referred to by Ji Chang as "Master Shang Father". After bringing him into his service, Ji Chang entrusted Jiang Shang with military command. Soon after, Jiang Shang led the Zhou army to victory, overthrowing the Shang Dynasty and establishing the Zhou.

仁德文王解民悬　谦恭礼让访大贤
渭水喜逢师尚父　周室基业八百年

A benevolent and virtuous saviour was King Wen,
He showed great modesty when visiting talented men.
By the Wei River, he met his learned guide,
And laid the Zhou's foundation, lasting far and wide.

二、子路心服（仲由）

　　春秋末年下（今山东泗水）人仲由，字子路。出身贫苦，性格豪爽，身材魁梧。当他和孔子初见时，对孔子讲文习礼的主张很不理解，甚至"欲陵暴孔子"。经孔子向他讲清道理后，对老师心悦诚服。日后一直跟随孔子，后来成为孔门"四科"中"政事"科的代表。孔子说自己如果不得意到海外去，跟随去的只有仲由。

2. Accepting Confucius' Teachings Wholeheartedly

　　Zhong You, whose courtesy name was Zilu, was from Bian (modern-day Sishui, Shandong) and lived during the late Spring and Autumn period. He was strong in build and generous in character. When he first met Confucius, he struggled to understand the teacher's emphasis on studying literature and practicing rites, even entertaining the idea of challenging him. However, after Confucius explained his reasoning, Zilu became genuinely convinced by his teachings. From that point on, Zilu devoted himself to following Confucius and became a key representative of the "Political Affairs" school, one of the four major fields taught by Confucius. Confucius once remarked with emotion that if he were ever to be exiled overseas due to his teachings falling out of favor, Zilu would be the only disciple to accompany him.

<blockquote>
豪爽刚直仲子路　　未识德才只识武
夫子高论谆谆诲　　弟子心悦又诚服
</blockquote>

Zhong You, bold and straightforward in his ways,
Knew only strength, not virtues to appraise.
Yet Confucius' wisdom, gentle and profound,
Taught him to grow, with virtue unbound.

三、子贡尊师（端木赐）

端木赐（子贡）是孔门"四科"中"言语"科的代表，他不但以仁德修身，能言善辩，也对老师特别尊重。他把孔子比作天上的太阳、月亮，谁也超不过。把老师比作天，谁也上不去。说老师的学问是高数仞的宫墙，任何人也不得其门而入。有人妄图贬低孔子，他坚决予以反驳。在周游列国等活动中，更以自己的实际行动体现对老师的支持与敬重。

3. Respecting His Teacher Confucius

Zigong, whose real name was Duanmu Ci, was a leading disciple in the "Language" field, one of the four key areas emphasized by Confucius. He not only cultivated himself through benevolence and virtue, excelling as an orator, but also showed profound respect for his teacher. He likened Confucius to the sun and the moon—unrivaled and incomparable—and to the sky, a realm beyond reach. He described Confucius' knowledge as a palace with towering walls, accessible only to those who could find the door. When others tried to undermine Confucius, Zigong firmly defended him, refuting such attacks with conviction. Throughout Confucius' travels to various states, Zigong demonstrated his unwavering support and deep respect for his teacher through both words and actions.

子贡尊师伴终身　恭奉师严护道尊
师如上天日月照　宫墙数仞人难进

Zi Gong admired and accompanied Confucius his whole life long,
Worshipping him and defending his doctrines against the wrong.
He regarded his teacher as the sun and the moon in the sky,
Like a royal palace few could easily reach so high.

四、驱车拜师（孟尝君）

孔门弟子，七十二贤之一的任不齐，晚年在齐国讲学。齐相孟尝君（田文）慕名，要向他学习，派人到任不齐处去请。任不齐答应，但迟迟不去。过了些日子，有人告诉孟尝君：拜师应自己去，哪能叫老师来？孟尝君大悟，马上派出车辆，备好礼品，自己亲自前去拜师。任不齐向他讲述儒家的仁德及中庸学说，孟尝君便成为儒家的再传弟子。

4. Driving a Cart to Invite His Teacher

Ren Buqi, a disciple of Confucius and one of the seventy-two worthies of the Confucian school, spent his later years lecturing in the State of Qi. Lord Mengchang, the PrimeMinister of Qi, greatly admired Ren's reputation and decided to learn from him. He sent a messenger to invite Ren, who accepted but delayed in his response. After some time, someone advised Lord Mengchang that a disciple should invite his teacher in person, not through a third party. Realizing his mistake, Lord Mengchang immediately arranged a cart and prepared gifts, setting off to personally invite Ren Buqi. Once they met, Ren Buqi imparted the Confucian teachings on benevolence, morality, and the doctrine of the "Golden Mean". As a result, Lord Mengchang became a devoted follower of Confucianism.

广泛交友孟尝君　师尊不比门客身
驱车拜师多恭敬　愿学仁德入儒门

Lord Mengchang mixed among a wide social section,
And held his teacher dearer than his guests in affection.
He drove a cart and invited his teacher in person,
Willing to learn integrity through this great lesson.

五、稷下尊师（齐威王）

稷下在春秋战国时期齐国都城临淄的稷门一带。齐威王时首创学宫，齐宣王继其祖业，予以扩充，招纳天下贤士近千人，任其各抒己见，议论政局。学宫中汇集了儒、道、墨、法、兵、农等百家之学，著名的有孟轲、荀况、田骈、慎到、淳于髡等人，齐王对他们十分尊崇，其中七十七人被授予"上大夫"之职。此学宫历时一百五十年，促进了百家争鸣的开展和先秦时期学术思想的繁荣。

5. Showing Respect to Teachers at Jixia

Jixia was located in Jimen, near the capital of the State of Qi, Linzi, during the Spring and Autumn and Warring States periods. King Wei of Qi was the first to establish an academy at Jixia, which was later expanded by his successor, King Xuan. This academy attracted over a thousand scholars and intellectuals from all over the world, giving them the opportunity to voice their opinions and engage in discussions about politics. The academy became a melting pot for a wide range of philosophical schools, including Confucianism, Taoism, Mohism, Legalism, Militarism, Agriculture, and more. Among the notable scholars who gathered there were Mencius, Xunzi, Tian Ping, Shen Dao, and Chun Yuwan. The Kings of Qi held them in high regard, appointing seventy-seven of them to the prestigious title of "Upper Minister." The academy continued for one and a half centuries, playing a key role in fostering intellectual debate and contributing to the flourishing of scholarly thought in the Pre-Qin era.

> 百年稷下聚贤俊　各抒己见发高论
> 舞台展示百家志　争辩褒贬学风新

Jixia attracted worthies and talents for over a hundred years,
Each could tell one's mind and views with attentive ears.
A platform created for showing different schools of thought,
An academic atmosphere for debate was sought.

六、躬读古籍（晁错）

西汉初年，百废待兴，汉文帝为弘扬传统文化，下令整理古籍。听说济南有位九十多岁的老人伏生，能将《尚书》全部背下来，便派晁错前去。晁错带着许多礼物，拜见伏生时，没摆官架子，进门便跪下拜师，请他将《尚书》背诵下来，自己愿当弟子学习。伏生应允后，他一面口授，晁错在他孙女的帮助下一面记录，直到把《尚书》全部记录下来，传给后人这部重要的儒家经典。

6. Researching the Ancient Classics with Diligence and Devotion

In the early Western Han Dynasty, after years of turmoil, society was in dire need of revival. Emperor Wen ordered the collection and preservation of ancient classics to promote and restore traditional culture. Upon hearing that Fu Sheng, a scholar over ninety years old living in Jinan, could recite the entire *Classic of History*, the Emperor sent Chao Cuo to learn from him. When Chao Cuo arrived, he brought many gifts and, instead of adopting an official's air, he knelt down to show respect and humbly requested Fu Sheng to teach him. Chao Cuo pleaded to learn *The Classic of History* from memory and became Fu Sheng's disciple. Once Fu Sheng agreed, Chao Cuo, with the help of Fu Sheng's granddaughter, transcribed everything he was taught. This resulted in the complete recording of *The Classic of History*, ensuring that this important Confucian text was passed down to future generations.

古传《尚书》一经典　秦皇焚毁万民怨
晁错拜师亲聆教　　伏生口授古籍传

The Classic of History is a priceless heritage,
Burnt by the first emperor of Qin in a fit of rage.
Zhao Cuo learned the complete version from his teacher Fu,
Who dictated from memory so others its lessons knew.

七、文明治蜀（文翁）

西汉时舒（今安徽庐江）人文翁，博学多才，汉景帝时为蜀郡太守。他上任后，见蜀郡偏僻、闭塞，于是从郡县中抽出一些人，把他们送到京师学习，学成归蜀后，对他们大胆重用。又在蜀郡各地修学馆，蜀地便形成了重文教的好风气。汉武帝下令全国仿效蜀地兴建学校。蜀地百姓对兴学重教的文翁特别感恩，为他建造祠堂，一年四季对他祭拜。

7. Governing Sichuan with Civility

Wen Weng, a native of Shishu (present-day Lujiang in Anhui Province) during the Western Han Dynasty, was known for his vast knowledge and diverse talents. He served as the Governor of Shu Prefecture (modern-day Sichuan Province) during the reign of Emperor Jing. Upon assuming office, Wen Weng realized that the region was isolated and underdeveloped. To remedy this, he selected promising individuals from local counties and sent them to the capital to pursue further education. After their return and successful completion of their studies, he appointed them to important positions and gave them significant responsibilities. Additionally, Wen Weng established academies throughout Shu Prefecture, fostering an environment that greatly valued education and intellectual growth. As a result, Emperor Wu of the Han Dynasty issued an imperial decree to encourage other regions to emulate Shu and build schools. The people of Shu, deeply grateful for Wen Weng's efforts to promote education, built a temple in his honor, where they paid tribute and made offerings throughout the year.

文翁治蜀多政绩　广育人才好风气
兴文重教全国效　百姓感恩四时祭

Wen Weng governed Sichuan with accomplishment.
Cultivating talents in a conducive environment.
Culture and education were promoted with magnitude,
The grateful masses worshipped him with gratitude.

八、下拜贤师（暴胜之）

西汉人隽不疑，精通《春秋》，德才兼备，曾任渤海郡的文学掾。汉武帝派暴胜之到各地巡视时，暴慕其名，亲自登门拜访。隽不疑穿着全套武将的官服，与暴胜之见面后当面训斥："一个人要想求学问，不要摆官架子。当官应给百姓实惠，才算成功。"暴胜之虚心接受了他的教诲。二人谈到深夜，暴胜之尊隽不疑为师，并推荐隽不疑为青州刺史。

8. Learning from one's Teacher with Modesty

Juan Buyi, a renowned scholar of the Western Han Dynasty, was well-versed in *The Spring and Autumn Annals* and was celebrated for both his virtue and talent. He had served as a literary compiler in Bohai. When Emperor Wu of Han sent Bao Shengzhi on an inspection tour, Bao, impressed by Juan's reputation, personally visited him. Juan Buyi, dressed in full military attire, met Bao and, without hesitation, admonished him: "If you truly wish to pursue knowledge, you must shed the airs of an official. A true official is one who benefits the people, and that is the mark of success." Bao Shengzhi humbly accepted Juan's advice. The two conversed late into the night, and Bao, deeply impressed by his wisdom, respected Juan Buyi as his teacher. He later recommended him to the Emperor as the Governor of Qing Prefecture.

胜之位高尊大贤　屈己求教解疑团
举荐不疑重德治　识才荐才美政坛

Bao Shengzhi in his high position respected the worthy scholars,
Solving his puzzles by seeking a teacher via different collars.
Recommending people according to their virtues sound,
His fame was praised by the people all around.

九、狱中拜师（黄霸）

黄霸，字次公，汉朝阳夏（今河南太康）人。在他任丞相长史时，下属主管长信少府的夏侯胜犯了大罪，他因知情不报，也关进监狱。他平时知夏侯胜学识渊博，便拜夏侯胜为师，学习《尚书》。夏认真教，黄认真学，有时二人讨论。三年后，黄霸出狱，学业大进。日后官至丞相，封建成侯。

9. Learning from One's Teacher in Prison

Huang Ba, whose courtesy name was Ci Gong, was a native of Yangxia (present-day Taikang, Henan) in the Han Dynasty. While serving as the chief secretary to the Prime Minister, his subordinate Xia Housheng, who was responsible for managing the Longxin Treasury, committed a serious crime. Huang Ba was imprisoned for failing to report the wrongdoing. During their time together, Huang Ba recognized Xia Housheng's deep knowledge and, despite his position as a subordinate, chose to learn from him. Huang Ba earnestly studied *The Classic of History* under Xia's tutelage, and the two engaged in frequent discussions. After three years in prison, Huang Ba was released, having made significant progress in his studies. Later, he rose to the position of Prime Minister and was granted the title of Marquis.

黄霸好学精益精　　狱中拜师夏侯胜
恭学《尚书》勤领会　　好学精神人称颂

Huang Ba was a devoted learner who sought a greater horizon,
He insisted on learning from his subordinate in prison.
Studying *The Classic of History* with diligence and reverence.
His devotion to learning was praised on all conference.

十、云敞葬师（云敞）

西汉平陵人云敞，早年拜同县人吴章为师。吴章专修《尚书》，学问渊博，在朝为博士。因为反对王莽倒行逆施，被腰斩弃市。吴章当年的一千多弟子纷纷躲避，有人甚至改换门庭。而当时在朝内任大司徒掾的云敞，却不怕丢官和迫害，毅然为老师收尸埋葬，尽弟子之责，深受世人敬佩。

10. Yun Chang Buries His Teacher

Yun Chang, a native of Pingling in the Western Han Dynasty, became a disciple of Wu Zhang, a fellow townsman, in his youth. Wu Zhang, a master of *The Classic of History*, was renowned for his profound knowledge and was appointed as a scholar in the imperial court. However, after he opposed Wang Mang's usurpation of the throne, Wu Zhang was executed and his body was publicly displayed. In the wake of his death, over a thousand of Wu Zhang's students fled, and some even renounced their teacher. Yet Yun Chang, who held the position of High Minister in the court at the time, was undeterred by the fear of losing his office or facing persecution. Out of filial duty to his teacher, he courageously collected and buried Wu Zhang's body. His actions earned him deep respect and admiration from the people.

吴章反莽遭危难　无耻弟子鸟兽散
独有云敞师恩恋　为师送终人称赞

For opposing Wang Mang's rule Wu Zhang was executed,
His disciples all scattered like he was a leper they refuted.
Only Yun Chang repaid his teacher's dedication,
He buried Wu and won nationwide admiration.

十一、力求封师（钟兴）

东汉汝阳人钟兴，年幼时跟少府丁恭学《春秋》。丁恭将钟兴推荐给皇帝，被封为郎中，不久又升为中郎将。皇帝又因钟兴教育太子有功，要把他晋升为关内侯。钟兴说："我的学问是老师给的，应该封我的老师。"皇帝封了丁恭，又要封钟兴。钟兴说："老师已被封，就不要封弟子了。"他坚决推辞对自己的封赠。

11. Insisting on Rewarding His Teacher with Honours

Zhong Xing, a native of Ruyang during the Eastern Han Dynasty, studied *The Spring and Autumn Annals* under Ding Gong, a scholar at the palace of the Crown Prince. Ding Gong later recommended Zhong Xing to the Emperor, who appointed him as a minister and soon promoted him to general. When the Emperor, recognizing Zhong Xing's success in educating the Crown Prince, intended to further elevate him to the rank of a lord, Zhong Xing respectfully declined the honor, stating, "All my learning was granted by my teacher, so it is my teacher who should be rewarded." The Emperor agreed to Zhong's request,promoting Ding Gong to a higher position.However, when the Emperor sought to bestow further honors upon Zhong Xing, Zhong humbly replied, "Since my teacher has already been rewarded,I, the disciple, need nothing more." In this way, he firmly declined any personal honors or rewards.

钟兴拜师学贵勤　春秋大义铭在心
功高被封中郎将　坚辞封爵让师尊

Zhong Xing learned from his teacher in diligence,
Engraving the classics in his mind with brilliance.
Tremendous contributions won him a high position,
He declined personal honours with a student's submission.

十二、为师鸣冤（杨政）

东汉京兆人杨政，拜代郡人范升为师，获益良多，他对老师也特别尊敬。范升被人诬告入监，杨政得知后，来不及穿上衣，抱起范升的幼子，躲到路旁，等皇帝驾到，为老师鸣冤。卫士们用箭射他，用戟刺他，他胸前流着血，仍继续说理哀求。后来皇帝派人了解是一冤案，放了范升。

12. Yang Zheng Affirms His Teacher's Innocence

Yang Zheng, a native of Jingzhao in the Eastern Han Dynasty, studied under Fan Sheng, a scholar from the Dai Commandery. He greatly benefited from his teacher's guidance and held him in the highest regard. When Yang Zheng learned that Fan Sheng had been falsely accused and imprisoned, he rushed out in such haste that he did not even have time to properly dress. Carrying Fan Sheng's young son in his arms, he hid by the roadside, waiting for the Emperor to pass by, intending to clear his teacher's name. The royal guards, seeing him, shot arrows at him and stabbed him with spears. Despite the blood streaming from his chest, Yang Zheng persisted in his pleas, calmly defending his teacher's innocence. Moved by his unwavering determination, the Emperor ordered an investigation and, discovering the falsehood of the charges, released Fan Sheng.

> 杨政恩师被收监　救师拦驾苦鸣冤
> 箭射戟刺均不怕　师冤平反苦亦甘

Yang Zheng's teacher was thrown into jail,
He stopped the emperor and claiming his teacher's hail.
Unafraid and unmoved by arrows and spears,
Helping his wronged teacher with attentive ears.

十三、礼葬恩师（廉范）

东汉杜陵（今陕西长安东北）人廉范，字叔度。家中世代高官，曾祖廉褒做到右将军，祖父廉丹当过大司马，他也官至云中太守。他出身贵胄，却拜博士薛汉为师。后来薛汉因楚王谋反的事被杀。薛的弟子、亲朋好友纷纷躲避，廉范却亲赴刑场收尸并埋葬。显宗皇帝训斥他时，他说："薛汉有罪当杀，但他是我的老师是事实。于公我不对，于私我没错。"皇帝得知他是赵国廉颇、朝内廉褒、廉丹的后人，便饶了他。

13. Burying One's Revered Teacher with Proper Rites

Lian Fan, whose courtesy name was Shudu, was a native of Duling (present-day northeastern Chang'an in Shaanxi Province) during the Eastern Han Dynasty. His family had a long-standing tradition of high-ranking officials: his great-grandfather Lian Bao served as a commanding general, his grandfather Lian Dan was a prominent minister, and Lian Fan himself rose to the rank of governor. Despite his noble lineage, he chose to study under Xue Wen, a scholar who was later executed due to his involvement in a conspiracy with the rebellious King of Chu. When Xue Wen's other disciples, friends, and relatives fled in fear, Lian Fan did not hesitate. He went to the execution ground, personally retrieved his teacher's body, and buried it with the appropriate rites. When Emperor Xianzong rebuked him for this, Lian Fan responded: "Xue Wen was condemned to death by law due to his crimes, but he was my teacher, and that is an undeniable truth. Legally, I have committed a wrong; personally, however, I acted in accordance with my respect and affection for him." Upon learning that Lian Fan was a descendant of the loyal general Lian Po and the esteemed officials Lian Bao and Lian Dan, the Emperor pardoned him.

虽为贵胄拜师尊　一日为师百日恩
师虽遭难仍礼敬　可赞一片弟子心

Despite his noble birth, Lian Fan respected his teacher,
One day an instructor and then forever a great preacher.
Showing respect even though he was in trouble,
As a disciple whose deed was praised as noble.

十四、后宫之师（班昭）

东汉扶风安陆人班彪之女班昭，字惠班。自幼聪慧明敏，博学多才，长大后嫁给曹世叔。丈夫逝世后，她不停地攻读古籍。不久，被汉和帝召入后宫，令皇后、贵人拜其为师，称曹大家（音姑）。班昭作《女诫》七章，以各种礼仪、品德教育后宫诸人，被尊为女中良师。其兄班固著《汉书》未成而死。班昭又奉诏继续将书编成。

14. A Lady Teacher for the Concubines in the Royal Palace

Ban Zhao, whose courtesy name was Huiban, was the daughter of Ban Biao, a native of Anlu in Fufeng during the Eastern Han Dynasty. She was a remarkably intelligent and perceptive child, and as she grew, she further expanded her knowledge through extensive reading. She married Cao Shishu, but after his death, she dedicated herself to studying the ancient classics. Not long after, Emperor He summoned her to the royal palace, where she became the teacher to the Empress and the concubines,earning the honorary title of Madame Master Cao. Ban Zhao wrote *Admonitions for Ladies*, a work consisting of seven chapters that offered guidance on proper conduct, etiquette, and virtues for the women of the royal palace. She became renowned as an exceptional teacher for women. When her elder brother, Ban Gu, passed away before completing his monumental work, *The History of the Han Dynasty*, Ban Zhao was appointed by the Emperor to finish the task, continuing her family's scholarly legacy.

女中魁元曹大姑　　后宫良师古史殊
七章《女诫》明礼仪　继兄大任完《汉书》

Ban Zhao was a champion bluestocking,
A teacher for palace ladies was in principle shocking.
Admonitions for Ladies contains the rites for women to read,
Her brother's *History of the Han Dynasty* she completed.

十五、互教互学（杜林等）

东汉茂陵（今陕西兴平）人杜林，少年时酷爱学习，家中的书已读了很多，还去拜同郡擅长文采的张竦为师，学问日增，人称"通儒"。他做了侍御史，又去拜擅长古文经学的郑兴、卫宏为师，二人却认他为老师。三人相互切磋，均获教益。杜林临终前把多年来珍藏的古文《尚书》交给郑兴、卫宏，二人不负所托，将此书传了下来。

15. Friends Teach and Learn from Each Other

Du Lin, a native of Maoling (present-day Xingping, Shaanxi) in the Eastern Han Dynasty, developed a passion for learning from an early age. He read extensively at home and also sought out Zhang Song, a local scholar renowned for his expertise in the classics and poetry, to be his teacher. Through his diligent study, Du Lin's knowledge grew, and he earned the reputation of being a "comprehensive scholar". After Du Lin became a minister under the Emperor, he sought to further his learning by studying under two masters of the ancient classics, Zheng Xing and Wei Hong. However, in an unexpected turn, both of these scholars regarded him as their teacher. The three of them exchanged insights and benefited from one another's knowledge. On his deathbed, Du Lin entrusted his treasured collection of *The Classic of History* to Zheng Xing and Wei Hong. True to their word, the two scholars upheld his trust and passed this important work down to future generations.

杜林学高再求知　恭拜张竦为良师
郑兴卫宏师亦友　互教互学均获益

A well-acknowledged scholar still pursued his learning,
Treating his teacher with respect and great yearning.
Zheng Xing and Wei Hong were both his friends and teachers,
They benefited from each other as mutual preachers.

十六、逃婚续学（戴封）

东汉人戴封，济北刚（今山东兖州一带）人，十五岁到国家的学署太常学习，拜鄾县县令东海郡的申君为师。申君告诉他不要认定一个老师，应广泛再学习。申君死后，他远赴东海送葬。回家后父母命他不再学习，在家结婚。戴封难违父命，拜天地后，当晚离家赴京，再度拜师学习。其学问越来越大，日后做了中山相，拜太常正卿。

16. Pursuing Learning as a Runaway Groom

Dai Feng, a native of Gang County, Jibei Prefecture (present-day Yanzhou, Shandong) in the Eastern Han Dynasty, began his studies at the state academy at the age of fifteen. He became a disciple of Shen Jun, the Magistrate of Mao County in Donghai. Shen Jun advised him not to limit himself to a single teacher, but to seek knowledge from various sources. After Shen Jun passed away, Dai Feng traveled all the way to the Eastern Sea to attend his teacher's funeral as a final tribute. Upon returning home, his parents insisted that he stop his studies and marry. Although he reluctantly complied with their wishes and went through with the wedding ceremony, that very night, Dai Feng secretly left his home and journeyed to the capital to resume his studies. His thirst for learning led him to accumulate great knowledge. In time, he was appointed Minister of the Central Mountain and later became Minister of Rites.

戴封拜师增学问　师殁送葬祭师魂
洞房花烛未留恋　再度拜师学习勤

Dai Feng studied under his teacher to enhance his learning.
He attended his teacher's funeral in earnest mourning.
Even the wedding could not distract his attention,
He stuck to his diligent learning without mention.

十七、力报师恩（王成）

东汉后期，李固被梁冀冤杀后，梁冀又派人追杀李固的三个儿子。其长子李基、次子李兹被捕后，在狱中死去。十三岁的三子李燮逃到嫁往远处的姐姐文姬家。文姬找到李固当年的弟子王成。王成感念师恩，带着李燮逃往徐州。让李燮改名，在一家酒店当雇工，自己以占卜为掩护，帮助李燮攻读，十几年后梁冀被杀，李燮出山。王成去世后，李燮对他依礼埋葬，每逢节日，都以上宾之礼祭祀。

17. Repaying One's Teacher's Cultivation

In the late Eastern Han Dynasty, Li Gu was wrongfully executed by Liang Ji, who also sent assassins to kill Li Gu's three sons. Li Gu's eldest son, Li Ji, and second son, Li Zi, were both captured and died in prison. The youngest son, Li Xie,only thirteen years old at the time, narrowly escaped and sought refuge with his older sister, Wenji, who had married and moved far away. Wenji turned to Wang Cheng,one of Li Gu's former disciples, to ask for his help. Deeply grateful for the teachings of his former master, Wang Cheng took Li Xie to Xuzhou. There, Wang Cheng changed the boy's name and arranged for him to work in a restaurant. Meanwhile,Wang Cheng, disguised as a fortune-teller, continued to tutor Li Xie in secret. Over a decade later, Liang Ji was killed, and Li Xie was able to step into public life. After Wang Cheng's death, Li Xie buried him with full rites and continued to honor him by offering sacrifices during festivals, treating him as an esteemed guest even after death.

王成大义报师恩　隐藏师子费苦心
谆谆教诲为再起　奸相倒台师冤伸

Wang Cheng, with gratitude, repaid his teacher's grace,
Hiding the fugitive son in a secret place.
He raised him with patience, with hope for the days ahead,
And when the villain fell, his teacher's name was cleared and spread.

十八、勇除三害（周处）

晋朝义兴阳羡（今江苏宜兴）人周处，父母早亡，缺乏教养。仗着体力过人，经常横行乡里。在他扰民时，一位老人向他说当地有"三害"：一是南山的白额虎，一是长桥的蛟龙，一是他——横行乡里的周处。周处听后很受震动。马上去南山打死猛虎，到长桥斩除蛟龙，自己也洗心革面，誓做好人。到吴地拜大学者陆云为师，回来一改旧貌，学问大增。官至御史中丞、平西将军。

18. Vanquishing the Three Scourges through Valour

Zhou Chu, a native of Yangxian in Yixing (present-day Yixing in Jiangsu Province), lived during the Jin Dynasty. After losing both parents at a young age, he was deprived of education and proper guidance. Relying on his exceptional physical strength, Zhou often bullied the local townsfolk. As his reputation as a troublemaker spread, an elderly man told him that the region suffered from three scourges: a fierce tiger with a white forehead that lived in the southern mountain, a dangerous dragon beneath the longbridge, and the notorious town bully, Zhou Chu himself. The words struck Zhou deeply, and he was profoundly moved by the realization. He immediately ventured to the southern mountain, killed the tiger, and then traveled to the long bridge where he slew the dragon. With these feats accomplished, he resolved to change his ways and live as an upright person. Zhou Chu traveled to the Wu region to study under the great scholar Lu Yun. Upon returning to his hometown, his transformation amazed the locals, who were astonished by his newfound humility and learning. Eventually, Zhou Chu was appointed as a judicial official and later as a general tasked with pacifying uprisings in the western regions.

> 晋人周处行不检　老人教诲警愚顽
> 知过必改除三害　修德行仁效前贤

Zhou Chu revelled in many a misdeed,
Yet the old man's advice he was willing to heed.
Aware of the faults he expelled three disasters,
Cultivating his virtues he followed former masters.

十九、尊师成名（范缜）

南北朝时的范缜，字子真，南阳舞阴人，二十岁以前跟学者刘瓛学习。当时和他一起学习的有许多富人家的阔少，大家都有车有马，讲吃讲穿。而范缜却一直穿着草鞋和粗布衣裳。老师对这一刻苦学习、不讲吃穿的穷学生特别钟爱，在他二十岁时亲自给他行加冠礼。他在老师的精心教育下，范缜日后当上宜都太守、晋安太守、国子博士等官。其《神灭论》更是我国古代宣扬无神论的一部名著。

19. Distinguishing Himself as a Respectful Student

Fan Zhen, courtesy name Zizhen, was a native of Wuyin in Nanyang during the Southern and Northern Dynasties. Before the age of twenty, he studied under the renowned scholar Liu Huan. His classmates were mostly young lords from wealthy families, accustomed to riding in carriages and enjoying luxurious food and clothing. In contrast, Fan Zhen adhered to a simple and modest lifestyle, wearing straw sandals and coarse clothing. Liu Huan greatly admired Fan Zhen's diligent and humble nature, especially his focus on study despite his impoverished background. When Fan Zhen turned twenty, Liu Huan personally conducted his coming-of-age ceremony. Under his teacher's careful guidance, Fan Zhen went on to hold important official positions, including governor of various prefectures and a scholar in the Imperial Academy. Fan Zhen's most notable work, *The Death of Gods*, became an influential text in ancient Chinese atheism.

芒履布衣学子吟　不美豪华读书勤
乐学好问多创意　千古名著《神灭论》

A young scholar wearing straw sandals and clothes plain,
Devoted to reading and without a cosseted brain.
Fond of learning and thinking with creative inspiration,
The Death of Gods was hailed by future generations.

二十、好学日进（卢思道）

隋朝范阳（今河北涿州市）人卢思道，自小勤奋好学。十六岁时，中山县的刘松把给别人写的碑文给他看，很多地方卢思道看不懂，深知自己的学识浅薄，便努力攻读。除了把自己关到屋里博览群籍外，又拜河间大儒邢子才为师，过了几年，拿出自己的文章给刘松看，刘松反而看不懂了。卢思道并不满足，又设法拜当时的名家魏收为师，从他那里借到许多文学、史学、哲学等方面珍贵的书籍阅读。日后成为著名的诗人，隋时官至散骑侍郎。

20. Being Fond of Learning and Making Progress EveryDay

Lu Sidao, a native of Fanyang (present-day Zhuozhou, Hebei Province), lived during the Sui Dynasty. From an early age, he had a strong passion for learning. At the age of sixteen, he read an epitaph written by Liu Song, a scholar from Zhongshan County. He found many parts of the text difficult to understand, and this realization of his own limited knowledge motivated him to study harder. In addition to dedicating himself to reading a wide range of texts in his study, he sought out the guidance of Xing Zicai, a great Confucian scholar from Hejian. After several years, he showed Liu Song his own writings, only for Liu Song to find them incomprehensible. Still unsatisfied, Lu Sidao sought out another renowned scholar, Wei Shou, as his mentor. From Wei, he borrowed many valuable books on literature, history, and philosophy, further expanding his intellectual horizons. Through his relentless dedication, Lu Sidao became a distinguished poet and held a high official position in the Sui Dynasty.

多方拜师学习勤　学感不足方日进
文史哲经广泛读　成就一代大诗人

A diligent learner would seek his teachers from many a field,
An eagerness in learning would never make him yield.
Extensively read in Classics, history, philosophy and literature,
A great poet of his generation was formed through nurture.

二十一、太子名师（李百药）

唐朝初年，安平人李百药，学识渊博，曾受命撰写二十四史之一的《北齐书》，他也是一位名师。唐太宗为了对儿子进行良好的教育，封李百药为右庶子，让他教育太子。他作了一篇《赞道赋》，以古人优秀的品德作榜样，教育太子。唐太宗得知，十分高兴，夸奖他不负重托，奖给他绸缎五百匹。

21. A Renowned Teacher of the Crown Prince

In the early Tang Dynasty, Li Baiyao, a native of Anping, was known for his profound learning and vast knowledge. He was appointed by the Emperor to compile *The History of the Northern Qi*, one of the Twenty-Four Histories. In addition to his historical work, Li Baiyao was also a distinguished educator. Emperor Taizong, eager to provide his son with an excellent education, appointed Li Baiyao as a teacher for the Crown Prince. To guide the prince, Li wrote *The Ode of Morals*, encouraging the young prince to emulate the exemplary virtues of ancient sages. When Emperor Taizong learned of Li's efforts, he was greatly pleased and praised him for fulfilling his responsibilities with distinction, rewarding him with five hundred bolts of fine satin.

一代名师李百药　教诲太子费心血
颂德倡仁《赞道赋》　太宗首肯奖励多

Li Baiyao was an excellent teacher of his generation,
Taught the Crown Prince heart and soul with inspiration.
The Ode of Morals he composed and advocated,
Winning the Emperor's praise and thanks for being so dedicated.

二十二、力作拜师（李贺）

唐朝福昌人李贺，自幼喜读书、写诗。十八岁时，到洛阳去拜韩愈为师。韩愈正在室内休息，侍者报一个穿戴整齐的年轻人求见，韩愈不见。过了半天，又来报那个青年一直站到门前不走，韩愈也未在意。又一会，侍者拿来这个年青人的诗作，韩愈一见大惊，连呼"才子，才子"，马上叫他进来。李贺恭敬地拜韩愈为师，在韩愈的指点下，李贺进步很大，成为唐朝一位著名的诗人。

22. Winning a Teacher's Favour with His Own Poems

Li He, a native of Fuchang in the Tang Dynasty, developed a love for reading and writing poetry from a young age. At the age of eighteen, he traveled to Luoyang to seek out HanYu as his teacher. At that time, HanYu was resting in his study when a servant informed him that a young man, neatly dressed, was requesting an audience. Han Yu refused to meet him. After some time, the servant reported that the young man had been waiting at the door without leaving. Still, Han Yu paid him no attention. Eventually, the servant brought in a collection of the young man's poems, and upon reading them, HanYu was astonished. He exclaimed, "A genius! A genius!" and immediately summoned the young man inside. Li He respectfully bowed and acknowledged Han Yu as his teacher. Under Han Yu's guidance, Li He made significant progress in his poetry and became one of the most renowned poets of the Tang Dynasty.

千里拜师亲求教　名家识才多开导
才子锦上添花絮　又一诗人出唐朝

Li He called on his teacher from a thousand miles away,
HanYu recognised his genius and offered guidance without delay.
The talented young man was offered new wings,
As striking a poet as one dynasty brings.

二十三、心领神会（颜真卿）

唐朝大书法家颜真卿，自小酷爱书法。为进一步提高，拜书法名家张旭为师。张旭教给他一些古人的字帖和自己的书法作品，叫他认真临摹。急于学成的颜真卿请老师告诉他写字的诀窍。张旭说："写字没有现成的诀窍，只有对名家的作品认真摹写，仔细揣摩，悟出其中的道理，才能真正提高。"颜真卿照此来做，取得了成功。为此他专门写了一篇记述跟老师张旭学习的文章，用以表达对老师的感激之情。

23. Understanding through Insight

Yan Zhenqing, a great calligrapher of the Tang Dynasty, had a passion for calligraphy from a young age. In order to refine his skills further, he sought out Zhang Xu, a renowned calligrapher, to be his teacher. Zhang Xu provided Yan with several specimens of calligraphy bypast masters, as well as his own works. He instructed Yan to carefully copy these examples and practice with dedication. Eager to master the art, Yan Zhenqing asked his teacher for any secret techniques that could help him improve. Zhang Xu responded: "There are no shortcuts to mastering this art. Only through diligent imitation, thoughtful reflection, and by truly understanding the works of the great calligraphers can you make genuine progress." Yan Zhenqing followed this advice and ultimately succeeded. Later, he wrote an essay recounting how he learned from Zhang Xu, as a way to express his deep gratitude to his teacher..

学习贵在自用心　心领神会方传神
名师张旭慎教诲　又一书圣出颜门

Study resides entirely in personal effort,
True understanding comes from mind of a sort.
Master Zhang Xu gave guidance with a genuine heart,
Another calligraphic sage head and shoulders apart.

二十四、舍外高徒（戚同文）

戚同文，字文约，宋代楚丘（今山东曹县）人。幼时家贫，听说同乡杨悫学识渊博，品德高尚，正招收弟子讲《礼记》时，他天天在舍外听讲，每天背诵一卷。杨发现后很惊奇，收他为弟子。不到一年，便将"五经"全部学完。当时天下很乱，他不愿出仕，只知研究学问。后来老师在官场死后，他对老师礼葬，并照顾老师全家。他写过好多诗，留有《孟诸集》等。

24. An Outstanding Disciple outside the Hall

Qi Tongwen, courtesy name Wenyue, was a native of Chuqiu (present-day Cao County in Shandong Province) during the Song Dynasty. Born into a poor family, he learned that his fellow townsman, Yang Que, a scholar of great learning, virtue, and integrity, was enrolling students to study *The Book of Rites*. Qi, eager to learn, stood outside Yang's house and listened attentively to his teachings. Every day, he memorized one chapter of the text. Impressed by his diligence and devotion, Yang Que took him as a disciple. In less than a year, Qi had mastered all of the Five Classics. Despite the social turmoil of the time, Qi declined offers to take up official posts, preferring to dedicate himself entirely to academic pursuits at home. After his teacher passed away while in office, Qi gave him a proper burial according to the rites and took care of his teacher's family. Qi wrote numerous poems and left behind a literary legacy, including his *Collected Works of the Disciples of Mencius*.

舍外高徒戚同文　家境虽穷学习勤
杨悫喜得好弟子　同文终生报师恩

Qi Tongwen became an outstanding disciple listening outside the hall,
Stuck to diligent reading despite his family being poor all in all.
Yang Que was lucky to encounter and enroll such a talent,
Qi Tongwen repaid his teacher's favour with a lifelong present.

二十五、帝王尊师（赵匡胤）

宋太祖赵匡胤出生在一个武官家庭。七岁时，进了辛文悦的塾馆，勤奋好学，对老师十分尊敬。他发现老师家里穷，常瞒着大人给老师送东西。他当上皇帝后，特地把辛文悦请到朝中。见面时不要辛行君臣之礼，自己却跪下行弟子之礼。他又到处设儒馆，请来很多有学问的人研讨和传授学问，使整个宋朝文化空前发达，知识分子备受尊敬。

25. An Emperor Respects His Teacher

Zhao Kuangyin, the founding emperor of the Song Dynasty, was born into a military family. At the age of seven, he enrolled in the private academy of Xin Wenyue, where he showed great diligence in his studies and deep respect for his teacher. Observing that his teacher was poor, Zhao would secretly send him gifts,keeping this act between himself and his teacher. After ascending to the throne, Zhao Kuangyin invited Xin Wenyue to the imperial court. When they met, Zhao did not expect his teacher to honor him as the emperor, but instead, he knelt and paid his respects as a humble disciple. Moreover, Zhao Kuangyin established Confucian academies throughout the empire, inviting learned scholars to teach and spread knowledge. This fostered an environment of intellectual growth and respect for scholars, leading to an unprecedented flourishing of culture and education during the Song Dynasty.

帝王师长孰最尊　文化本为国之根
尊师重文数宋代　开启良风赵匡胤

Emperors and teachers, which are dearer?
A nation should be rooted in cultures superior.
The Song Dynasty focused on respecting teachers and cultures,
Zhao Kuangyin was the creator of the fashion and nurtures.

二十六、程门立雪（杨时、游酢）

北宋人程颢，是当时全国著名的大儒。儒生杨时、游酢二人学问也不差，但他们还要向学问更大的人学习。一年冬天，二人冒雪去拜望程颢。走到门前，见程颢正在室内闭目养神，为不打扰先生，便在门外等候。程颢睁眼一看，站到外面的两个人身上已布满白雪，忙请二人进屋，把雪掸掉，交谈学术。后人把"程门立雪"当作尊师的代称。

26. Standing Respectfully in His Teacher's Yard in the Snow

Cheng Hao, a renowned Confucian scholar of the Northern Song Dynasty, was widely respected across the country for his profound learning. Yang Shi and You Zuo, both highly accomplished scholars in their own right, still sought to learn from even greater minds. One winter, they braved a snowstorm to visit Cheng H ao. As they approached his house, they saw that Cheng was sitting inside with his eyes closed in meditation. Not wanting to disturb him, they waited quietly outside. When Cheng Hao finally opened his eyes, he was surprised to find that the two scholars had been standing in the snow for such a long time that they were covered in a thick layer of it. He immediately invited them inside, brushed the snow off their clothes, and they engaged in a discussion on academic matters. The story of "standing in snow in front of Cheng's door" became a symbol of profound respect and reverence for one's teacher, and is often used to represent the highest form of respect in the teacher-student relationship.

> 杨游踏雪访大贤　程门立雪佳话传
> 尊师正是尊学问　历代竞赞师尊严

By braving the storm Yang Shi and You Zuo visited the great scholar,
Standing in the snow out of respect was widely known and popular.
To respect one's teacher is to acknowledge his learning,
People have always praised their mentors with words discerning.

二十七、一贯尊师（陆佃）

北宋时期，山阴人陆佃，家贫苦学，幼年映月读书，长大后在王安石门下学习经书。王安石执政时，曾任国子监直讲。因和老师政见不同，王安石在政治上一直对他很冷淡。哲宗登基后，清洗王派势力，许多王的弟子纷纷改换门庭，陆佃说自己和老师虽然政见不同，但仍然是老师的学生。王安石死后，他到灵前痛哭、祭拜。日后任江宁知府时，又常到王安石墓上祭奠。

27. Invariably Respectful to One's Teacher

Lu Dian, a native of Shanyin during the Northern Song Dynasty, was a dedicated and hardworking scholar despite coming from a poor family. As a child, he often studied under the moonlight, and as an adult, he continued his studies under the guidance of the renowned scholar Wang Anshi. When Wang Anshi rose to the position of Prime Minister, Lu served as the principal lecturer at the Imperial Academy. However, due to their differing political views, Wang remained indifferent toward him, and their relationship grew distant. After the ascension of Emperor Zhezong, the new ruler purged the influence of Wang Anshi and his followers. While many of Wang's disciples abandoned him, Lu Dian chose to honor his teacher,disregarding their political differences, and continued to acknowledge Wang Anshi as his teacher. When Wang Anshi passed away, Lu was deeply moved, weeping at his teacher's bier and paying his respects. Later, when Lu became the Governor of Jiangning, he frequently visited Wang Anshi's tomb to offer sacrifices.

陆佃拜师学经书　尊师焉能计荣辱
门庭若市尊师道　门可罗雀亦归附

Lu Dian acknowledged his teacher and studied classics,
Respecting him regardless of honour or shame in tactics.
He kept his teacher's doctrines when his threshold was cramped,
Showed his unswerving loyalty when others decamped.

二十八、终生尊师（王野）

南宋金华人王野，在潭州任职。他听说真德秀很有学问，便去拜他为师。在请真德秀到自己官府当幕僚时，对真亦执弟子礼。后来王野升任端明殿大学士，对真仍以师礼相待。当他得知真德秀是朱熹的弟子时，日后凡是遇到朱熹的门人弟子，王野一律送去贺礼。在他当建宁知府时，创建了建安书院，院中设朱熹和真德秀的牌位，每年按时祭祀。

28. Maintaining Lifelong Respect for one's Teacher

Wang Ye, a native of Jinhua during the Southern Song Dynasty, held an official post in Tan Prefecture. Upon hearing of Zhen Dexiu's scholarship, Wang Ye visited him and acknowledged him as his teacher. This respect continued even when Zhen served as an advisor in Wang's office. Later, when Wang was promoted to an academician in the royal court, he still treated Zhen with the same reverence as his teacher. When Wang learned that Zhen Dexiu was a disciple of Zhu Xi, the eminent Confucian scholar, he made it a point to send gifts and greetings to any of Zhu Xi's disciples. After Wang became the Governor of Jianning, he established the Jian'an Academy, where he set up tablets in honor of both Zhu Xi and his teacher Zhen Dexiu. Each year, he organized ceremonies to offer sacrifices and pay homage to them.

师道尊严胜官爵　位高尊师颂王野
礼贤尊敬真德秀　朱门弟子尽欢悦

A teacher's dignity outweighs official ranks on earth,
People praise Wang Ye who cared not about noble birth.
Zhen Dexiu was a man with true virtue and benevolence
His disciples were all delighted to share his brilliance.

二十九、千里吊师（汪应辰）

南宋玉山（今江西玉山）人汪应辰，考中进士第一名，朝廷授予他镇东军签判的职务。他听说张九成学问大，便拜到张名下，向他学习。不久，张九成坐罪被贬谪，许多亲友与之断绝关系，汪应辰却照样与他来往。张九成的父亲去世，别人对他父子在舆论上大加攻击时，汪应辰却远道一千多里前去吊唁，以尽弟子之情。

29. Paying Homage to One's Teacher from a Thousand Miles Away

Wang Yingchen, born in Yushan, Jiangxi Province, ranked first in the imperial examinations and was appointed to a clerical position in the military. Upon learning of Zhang Jiucheng's great scholarship, Wang sought him out as a teacher and learned from him. Later, Zhang Jiucheng was exiled to a remote region due to a political misfortune, and many of his friends and relatives severed ties with him. However, Wang Yingchen remained steadfast in his loyalty and continued his association with Zhang. When Zhang's father passed away and others criticized the elder Zhang and his son, Wang Yingchen, as a devoted disciple, traveled over a thousand miles to pay his respects, demonstrating his deep filial piety and unwavering respect for his teacher.

应辰科举中头名　屈驾拜师学问增
师遭贬谪仍尊重　千里吊唁情意浓

Wang Yingchen won the laurels in the imperial examination,
Yet still sought out a teacher to enhance his cultivation.
His teacher's demotion and exile did not diminish his respect,
For he made sure the deceased father's memory was saved from neglect.

三十、继志修史（萧永祺）

金元时代的萧永祺，字景纯，少时好学，通晓契丹文字。广宁知府耶律固奉皇帝之命翻译《辽史》，将萧永祺召到门下，把自己所有的学问都传授给他。耶律固逝世后，萧永祺带领耶律固的弟子们为师送葬，并决定完成老师的未竟之业。经过几年的努力，将《辽史》修成献给皇帝。后世因修《辽史》时以高官脱脱为首，故署名脱脱修，实为耶律固师生修撰。

30. Compiling a Historical Record

During the Jin and Yuan Dynasties, Xiao Yongqi, whose courtesy name was Jingchun, was a dedicated scholar from a young age, mastering the Khitan language. Yelü Gu, the magistrate of Guangning, was tasked by the Emperor to translate *The History of Liao*. He summoned Xiao Yongqi to become his disciple, imparting all his knowledge to him. After Yelü Gu passed away, Xiao Yongqi and his fellow disciples escorted their teacher to his final resting place and vowed to complete his unfinished work. After years of diligent effort, they successfully finished *The History of Liao* and presented it to the Emperor. Although the later generations attributed the compilation to Tuotuo, the high-ranking official in charge of the project, the actual authorship lay with Yelü Gu and his disciples.

永祺拜师学契文　耶律倾囊诲后人
谨遵师命完夙愿　《辽史》问世光史林

Xiao Yongqi studied the Khitan language,
Yelü Gu shared all his learning with homage.
The disciple fulfilled his teacher's unfinished dream
Completing *The History of Liao* with great esteem.

三十一、尊师重文（阔阔）

元朝蔑里吉氏部族的阔阔，是忽必烈最信任的内史和参谋。忽必烈听说王鹗学识渊博，派人把他请来，令阔阔拜他为师，向他询问治国之道。不久，阔阔出使外地，王鹗走了，阔阔回来得知，放声大哭，几天没吃饭。忽必烈得知，又派人把王鹗请来，阔阔继续向他学习，对他优礼备至。王鹗指出阔阔的缺点，阔阔马上改正。在王鹗的教育下，阔阔为忽必烈做了许多好事。

31. Respecting Teachers and Emphasising Scholarly Learning

Kuo Kuo, a member of the Mieli Ji clan, was one of the most trusted advisers and counselors to Emperor Kublai Khan. When the Emperor heard of Wang E's vast knowledge and cultured nature, he summoned Wang and ordered Kuo Kuo to acknowledge him as his teacher, seeking guidance on matters of governance. Not   long after, Kuo Kuo was sent on a diplomatic mission, during which time Wang E departed. Upon Kuo Kuo's return, he was deeply saddened by the loss of his teacher, weeping and losing his appetite for several days. When Emperor Kublai khan learned of this, he promptly summoned Wang E back, allowing Kuo Kuo the chance to continue his studies under Wang's tutelage, treating him with great respect. Whenever Wang E pointed out Kuo Kuo's flaws, the diligent pupil immediately corrected them. Under Wang E's instruction, Kuo Kuo went on to accomplish many virtuous deeds on behalf of the Emperor.

元蒙称帝用汉人　阔阔拜师礼仪真
牧歌声声始汉化　王鹗治国建殊勋

The Mongolian emperor respected Han scholars,
Kuo Kuo treated his teacher with courteous manner.
Pastoral songs started to display a touch of Han culture,
All this is owed to Wang E's governance and nurture.

三十二、尊师为父（袁宗道等）

明朝湖北公安的袁宗道、袁宏道、袁中道三人，同时考中进士后，设宴款待家乡父老，特别请他们三人历届的老师坐上席。却忘了袁中道的一位启蒙老师刘福锦。刘派人给他们送了一封信，上面只写"高塔入云有一层"七个字，三人马上发现自家的失误，三人马上回信续诗："孔明不能自通神。一日为师终生为父，谨请先生谅晚生。"老师见信后，怒气全消。

32. Respecting One's Teachers as One's Father

The Yuan brothers—YuanZongdao,YuanHongdao,andYuanZhongdao—were from Gong'an District in Hubei Province. After excelling in the imperial examinations, they held a grand banquet to celebrate their success and honor their fellow townspeople, with their teachers seated at the highest place of honor. However, in the bustle of the preparations, they accidentally overlooked Liu Fujin, the teacher who had first enlightened Yuan Zhongdao. Disappointed by this neglect, Teacher Liu sent them a letter, containing a single line of poetry: "A soaring high tower must have its first storey." Upon reading this, the brothers immediately recognized their mistake and sent a heartfelt reply, adding three more lines to the poem to express their apology: "Kong Ming could not self-study his way to glory. Once a teacher, always a fatherly figure. Your highness, please forgive your students' oversight." When Teacher Liu received their reply, his anger dissipated.

袁氏喜摆谢师宴　蒙师不满传一笺
一日为师终生父　弟子悔过师释嫌

The Yuan brothers held a thanksgiving banquet with delight,
But were cursed by a former teacher they neglected to invite.
The brothers acknowledged the teacher as their lifelong parent.
Their sincere apologies smoothed the displeasure apparent.

三十三、敬拜幼师（董沄）

明朝人董沄，擅长诗句。六十四岁在会稽山上游玩时，听人说有位大学者王守仁在设坛讲学，便去听讲。因晚去室内已无位置，便坐在屋檐下听得入了迷，别人离去，他还坐在那里。王守仁发现这位老人，把他请进屋内，董沄要拜王守仁为师，比董小十几岁的王守仁不答应，但董执意行了拜师礼。董沄向王守仁学习后，思想与学业都提升了新的境界。

33. Showing Earnest Respect to One's Younger Teacher

DongYun, a scholar from the Ming Dynasty, was well-versed in poetry. At the age of sixty-four, while touring Mount Kuaiji, he heard that the renowned scholar Wang Shouren was giving a lecture there. Eager to learn, he decided to attend. Arriving late, he found the room full, so he sat under the eaves outside, listening attentively to the lecture. Even after the other attendees left, he remained seated, absorbed in the teachings. Wang Shouren, noticing the elderly man, invited him inside for further discussion. Despite being a dozen years older than Wang, Dong Yun insisted on paying his respects and acknowledging Wang as his teacher. After studying under Wang Shouren, Dong Yun experienced a profound intellectual and personal transformation, reaching new heights in both his thinking and academic pursuits.

守仁学高光儒林　董沄受教铭在心
年长拜师传佳话　学问何能年龄分

Mr. Wang Shouren was a scholars' scholar,
The Elder Dong Yun attended his lecture so popular.
A junior teacher and a senior student is a tale well known,
How could academic studies be concerned with one's age shown.

三十四、入狱探师（史可法）

明朝末年，任左金都御史的左光斗，被魏忠贤陷害，关进大牢。其弟子史可法为营救老师，多方奔走无效，只得花五十两银子买通狱卒，化装成工匠到狱中探望老师。左光斗感激弟子的心意，为了保住国家栋梁，一面假装对他责打，一面教育他不要作无谓牺牲，留下性命为国家效力。史可法明白老师的深意，日后奋力抗清，成为扬州抗清名垂千古的英雄。

34. Visiting One's Wronged Teacher in Prison

In the late Ming Dynasty, Zuo Guangdou, an upright official, was framed and imprisoned by Wei Zhongxian, a corrupt eunuch who had gained control of the court. Shi Kefa, a devoted disciple of Zuo, made every effort to secure his teacher's release, but all attempts were in vain. In the end, Shi resorted to bribing the prison guards with 50 taels of silver and disguised himself as a craftsman to visit Zuo in prison. Zuo, deeply moved by his disciple's loyalty, was reluctant to put Shi at risk. He pretended to scold and beat him in front of the guards, all the while advising him not to sacrifice himself in vain. Instead, Zuo urged him to preserve his life for the greater good of the country. Understanding his teacher's deeper intentions, Shi Kefa went on to become a heroic figure, fiercely resisting the Qing invasion and leaving a lasting legacy in Yangzhou.

恩师忠诚被诬陷　弟子冒险勇探监
留得青山反奸佞　扬州十日青史鲜

An upright teacher was wronged and put into prison,
His disciple risked his life by visiting the gaol with no reason.
Green mountains remain fresh for those who are righteous and fair,
His sacrifices should be memorable and for evermore rare.

三十五、名医拜师（叶天士）

清朝康熙年间，苏州人叶天士，是当地祖传三代的名医。一位外地商人来看病，经过诊断，他认为此人病已很重，表示已无法治疗。此人又找到当地一位老僧，老僧给他开了药，过了一年病情好转。叶天士为了继续提高，改名换姓到庙中甘拜老僧为师。老僧诊病时认真观察学习，收获很大。日后老僧得知实情后，便将自己的医术及秘方全部传给了他。

35. A Noted Herbalist Learns More from His Teacher

During the reign of Emperor Kangxi in the Qing Dynasty, Ye Tianshi, a renowned herbalist from Suzhou, was the third-generation practitioner in his family. One day, a merchant from outside the area came to see him for a diagnosis. After examining the merchant, Ye concluded that the illness was too advanced to be treated. The merchant then sought out a local elderly monk, who prescribed a remedy, and within a year, the merchant's condition improved significantly. Determined to further enhance his medical knowledge, Ye adopted a pseudonym and went to the temple to learn from the monk. He carefully observed the monk's methods of diagnosing and prescribing treatment, gaining invaluable insight. When the monk eventually passed away, Ye, now well-versed in his techniques, inherited the monk's medical knowledge and secret remedies.

为求医术精益精　天士屈身事老僧
各行均有名人在　谦逊恭敬学自增

In order to perfect his medical learning,
Dr. Ye served the senior monk with hands discerning.
There are great masters in life's every field,
Modesty will progress and relief yield.

三十六、尊师送米（林纾）

清朝末年闽县人林纾，年少时在家乡跟一位老先生学习。老师生了病，他去探望，见老师穷的无米下锅，便回到家中，趁父母不在，用袜子装了两袋米送给老师，老师知他是未经父母允许下干的事，教育他做事要讲诚信，叫他马上送回家去。其父母得知后，同意用米袋装上米送给老师。林纾对老师一贯尊敬，日后成为一位大文学家，仍念念不忘恩师。

36. Sending Rice to One's Elderly Teacher

Lin Shu, a native of Min County in Guangdong Province, lived during the late Qing Dynasty. As a young man, he studied under the guidance of an elderly scholar in his hometown. One day, when he visited his ailing teacher, he found that the teacher had run out of rice. Feeling distressed, Lin hurried home and, seeing that his parents were away, secretly stuffed two bags of rice into his socks and took them to his teacher. The teacher, realizing that Lin had acted without his parents' consent, gently reminded him of the importance of honesty and instructed him to return the rice immediately. Once Lin's parents were informed of the situation, they agreed to send the rice in proper bags to the teacher. Lin Shu always held his teacher in high regard, and even after he became a renowned literary scholar, he never forgot the kindness and lessons of his teacher.

> 林纾送米报师恩　少年行为须诚信
> 谆谆师诲勤教训　仁爱忠诚遵人伦

Lin repaid his teacher with rice,
He learned how to be honest and nice.
With his teacher's edicts echoing in his mind,
He always adhered to virtues kind.

第六章

夫妻和谐

Chapter Six:

Harmonious Marriage

一、卫姬谏君（卫姬）

春秋"五霸"之首的齐桓公，国势强大后便霸道起来。他令诸侯们来朝贺，卫国国君没来，他发了火，要讨伐卫国。卫君的女儿得知后，素衣简装拜见桓公，指出他骄横霸道的毛病及由此可能导致的恶果。桓公听后十分感动，次日上朝时怒气全消，还立卫姬为夫人、管仲为"仲父"，令他们分管宫内外。在他们的帮助下，继续发展了霸业。

1. A Princess Advises a Duke

After the State of Qi grew strong during the Spring and Autumn Period, its ruler, Duke Huan,the leader of the Five Hegemons, became increasingly domineering. On one occasion, he summoned the other princes to congratulate him on his achievements, but when King Wei failed to appear, he became enraged and planned a military campaign against Wei. Upon hearing this, the daughter of King Wei, dressed simply in plain clothes, visited Duke Huan and courageously pointed out his arrogance and overbearing attitude, warning of the potential disastrous consequences. Moved by her words, Duke Huan's anger dissipated. The following day, when he attended court, he honored her by making her his concubine, and appointed his primeminister, Guan Zhong, as a "fatherly figure". Both were entrusted with managing affairs both within the palace and beyond. With their guidance, Duke Huan's hegemony flourished.

齐桓初霸忒强势　讨伐卫侯逞不义
卫姬婉言述利害　桓公省悟改前非

Duke Huan of Qi was overbearing in the early days of his hegemony,
Plotting an unjust campaign against the King of Wei.
The Princess of Wei admonished him tactfully,
Then Duke Huan realised his error and behaved pacifically.

二、结发老妻（晏婴）

春秋后期的齐相晏婴，治国有方，生活简朴。一天，田无宇到他家，见一妇人，头发班白，面貌丑陋，穿麻布衣服，在家中进出。便问晏婴："这是何人？"晏婴说："是我结发的妻子。" 田无宇惊奇地说："您地位这么高，怎么还有这样的老妻呢？"晏婴回答："见色而忘义，处富贵而失伦，谓之逆道。"他还说无论如何不能做逆道的事。讥笑别人的田无宇无地自容。

2. The Aged First Wife

During the late Spring and Autumn Period, Yan Ying, the prime minister of the State of Qi, governed wisely and lived a simple life. One day, Tian Wuyu visited his home and saw an elderly woman with grey hair, wearing plain linen clothes, moving about the house. Curious, he asked Yan Ying, "Who is this woman?" Yan Ying replied, "She is my first wife." Surprised, Tian Wuyu asked, "Given your high position, how is it that you still have such an aged wife?" Yan Ying answered, "To surround oneself with beauty at the expense of righteousness, and to indulge in licentiousness despite wealth and power, is to act against the Way." He further stated that one should never commit immoral acts. Tian Wuyu, who had been mocking others, was left deeply ashamed.

古人廉洁数晏婴　居简行俭遍颂声
结发老妻频爱护　庸夫闻之无地容

Yan Ying was known as a saintly official in Qi and thereabouts,
People praised his humble carriage, escort and house.
Though wizened and decrepit he adored his first spouse,
The vulgar man who taunted him was made to feel a louse.

三、贤妻劝谦（御者妻）

　　齐国晏婴准备出行，御者之妻在门外，见丈夫得意洋洋的样子，顿生忧虑。丈夫回家后她说："人家晏子高不过六尺，身为国相，却一直谦恭礼让，待人宽厚，治国有方。你身高八尺，不过是他的车夫，为什么趾高气扬？"车夫接受了意见，从此勤奋敬业，谦虚有礼。晏子见车夫变了样，十分奇怪，当得知是他妻子劝导的结果后，认为此人能听善言，勇于改正，是一贤才。把他推荐给齐景公，当了大夫。对他妻子也赐给"命妇"的称号。

3. A Virtuous Wife Admonishes Her Husband

　　As Yan Ying, the primeminister of the State of Qi, was preparing to depart, the wife of his coachman noticed her husband's smug and proud demeanor, which caused her to worry. When her husband returned home, she said, "Yan Ying may be short, but as the primeminister, he is humble, courteous, and generous, governing the state effectively. You, on the other hand, are tall and strong, yet as his coachman, why do you act so arrogantly?" The coachman took her words to heart and began to change his attitude, becoming diligent, modest, and respectful. Yan Ying was surprised to see the transformation in the coachman. When he learned that it was his wife who had given him this valuable counsel, Yan Ying considered the coachman to be a virtuous person, one who was capable of self-reflection and improvement. He recommended him to Duke Jing of Qi, who appointed him as a counselor. The coachman's wife was also honored with the title of "Lady of the Household".

车夫之妻见识远　　仁厚视人敢荐言

丈夫改过晏子赞　　知过必改学圣贤

The coachman's wife possessed foresight,
And was unafraid of being forthright.
Her husband's conversion roused Yan Ying's delight,
He overcame vice to become a sage upright.

四、祭夫倾城（杞梁妻）

春秋时期，齐庄公与莒国作战时，齐国人杞梁战死。庄公领兵回国时，要在路上对杞梁吊唁。杞梁妻说丈夫为国捐躯，应回国正式吊唁，庄公依此而行。杞梁夫妻平时相亲相爱，相濡以沫，丈夫忽然死去，妻子十分悲痛。她每天到城墙下对着丈夫的墓哭泣，感动了许多人。十天后，城墙倒塌，她为了追随丈夫，也跳入淄水而死。此事日后演绎为孟姜女哭长城的故事。

4. A City Wall Collapses Due to a Wife's Mourning for Her Husband

During the Spring and Autumn Period, Duke Zhuang of the State of Qi fought a war against the State of Ju. A soldier named Qi Liang from Qi was killed in the battle. As Duke Zhuang was returning to Qi, he planned to hold a memorial ceremony for Qi Liang along the way. However, Qi Liang's wife suggested that, since her husband had died serving the country, the memorial should be held back in Qi. The Duke accepted her advice. While Qi Liang was alive, he and his wife had shared a deep love and mutual respect. His sudden death left her heartbroken. Every day, she went to the foot of the city wall, weeping by her husband's grave, and her mourning moved many onlookers. Ten days later, the city wall collapsed, and in her grief, she threw herself into the River Zishui, hoping to reunite with her husband's spirit. This tragic story later evolved into the legend of Lady Meng Jiang, whose tears were said to have caused the Great Wall to collapse.

齐莒之战殇杞梁　国祭亡人妻哀伤
城墙竟被爱哭倒　留贻后人话孟姜

Qi Liang lost his life in the war between Ju and Qi,
The state funeral stoked his wife's grief immeasurably.
The city wall came tumbling down as she wept pitiably,
The tale of Lady Meng Jiang derives from this story.

五、为夫伸冤（弓匠妻）

春秋时晋国有个有名的制弓工匠，晋平公要他制出一只能穿透三层铠甲的硬弓。他苦心钻研，三年造成，交给国君。晋平公拉弓射箭时，连一层铠甲也未穿透。顿时大怒，要杀弓匠。弓匠的妻子晋见国君说："我丈夫多次改进技术，精心制作。您说弓不好，可否找找别的原因？"晋平公向别人请教了拉弓的方法后，仍用此弓，居然穿透七层铠甲，马上赦免了她的丈夫。

5. A Wife Asks Forgiveness for Her Husband's Sin

During the Spring and Autumn Period, there was a renowned bowmaker in the State of Jin. Duke Ping of Jin ordered him to craft a bow strong enough to pierce through three layers of armor. The bowmaker dedicated himself to the task, spending three years perfecting the bow before presenting it to the Duke. However, when Duke Ping tried the bow, the arrow failed to penetrate even a single layer of armor. Enraged, the Duke ordered the bowmaker's execution. The bowmaker's wife, hearing of the Duke's fury, asked for an audience. She said, "My husband has labored tirelessly to perfect this bow, and he believed it was flawless. Since Your Highness deems it inadequate, might I suggest you reconsider the situation more carefully?" After consulting others on the proper technique for drawing the bow, Duke Ping tried again. This time, the arrow pierced through seven layers of armor, prompting him to immediately pardon the bowmaker.

能工巧匠造良弓　偏遇昏庸晋平公
匠妻代夫巧争辩　识货方可显奇能

A skilled craftsman of ancient Jin hewed a peerless bow,
Unfortunately its recipient was a doltish fellow.
His wife's quick tongue helped Duke Ping's temper to mellow,
And finally he was redeemed by a single nifty arrow.

六、乡音认妻（百里奚）

春秋时虞国人百里奚，年轻时家境贫寒，但夫妻恩爱。他努力攻读后，要外出干事业，其妻子杀了一只鸡，用门闩当柴烧，吃后为他送行。百里奚先去齐、周，未被录用，又到虞国、晋国，后来竟沦落为奴隶身份，成为陪嫁的媵人。识才的秦穆公用五张羊皮把他换回秦国，授以国政。他执政七年，便使秦国独霸西戎。他妻子却流落街头，洗衣、干杂活为生。当她得知丈夫信息后，便到其府上吟唱家乡的俚曲。百里奚听后，下堂认妻，夫妻团圆。

6. A Wife is Recognized by the Chant of her Hometown

In the Spring and Autumn Period, Baili Xi from the State of Yu was born into poverty, yet he and his wife shared a deep bond of affection. He devoted himself to study and sought to make a name for himself. As he prepared to leave in pursuit of greater opportunities, his wife killed a chicken to prepare a farewell meal. Lacking firewood, she burned a bolt from the door to cook. Baili Xi first went to the States of Qi and Zhou but found no employment. He then traveled to the States of Yu and Jin, but his efforts were in vain, and he eventually sank into the status of a slave, presented as a concubine's gift. Recognizing his talent, Duke Mu of Qin bought Baili Xi for five goat hides and appointed him to govern the state. After seven years in office, the State of Qin emerged as the dominant power over the Western tribes. Meanwhile, his wife had fallen into poverty, making a living by washing clothes and performing menial tasks. Upon learning of her husband's situation, she went to his residence and began singing a folk song from their hometown. Hearing the familiar tune, Baili Xi rushed out from the main hall, and the couple was joyously reunited.

历经磨难百里奚　　位高未忘结发妻
一曲乡音故人醒　　老夫老妻终生依

Baili Xi endured countless tests and strife,
But in his heart he never forgot his beloved first wife.
A chant from their hometown roused his memory,
And the old couple was restored to blissful matrimony.

七、荐王纳贤（樊姬）

春秋时期，楚庄王的夫人樊姬贤明仁德。庄王即位后，经常外出打猎，樊姬多次劝阻不听，她以不食猎来禽兽之肉向丈夫讲保护动物的道理。庄王改正，勤于国事。一天，庄王回宫很晚，问起原因，说："与贤人交谈，不知疲倦。"一问"贤人"是虞丘子。樊姬说："虞丘子执政十一年，楚国毫无起色，怎能为贤人。"楚王将此话告诉虞丘子，虞丘子十分惭愧，后亲自推荐孙叔敖给楚王。经过三年，楚国便国富军强。庄王对能言敢谏的樊姬更敬重了。

7. The Queen Advises the King to Seek Out Sages

During the later Spring and Autumn Period, Fanji, the wife of King Zhuang of Chu, was known for her wisdom and benevolence. After her husband ascended to the throne, he frequently went hunting, a habit that Fanji tried repeatedly to dissuade him from, though without success. To make her point, she stopped eating the meat of the game, hoping to convey the importance of protecting animals. Eventually, King Zhuang gave up his hunting pursuits and became more dedicated to state affairs. One evening, King Zhuang returned to the palace late. When Fanji inquired about the reason, he replied, "I was talking with a sage and did not feel tired in the least."Curious, Fanji asked who this "sage" was, and he revealed it was Yu Qiuzi. Fanji responded, "Yu Qiuzi has held the position of prime minister for eleven years, yet our state has stagnated during this time. How can he truly be called a sage?" King Zhuang, reflecting on her words, relayed them to Yu Qiuzi, who felt deeply ashamed. In response, Yu Qiuzi recommended Sun Shu'ao as a capable candidate. Three years later, the State of Chu had flourished and its military forces were strengthened. King Zhuang's respect for Fanji grew even more, for she was not only eloquent but also courageous in offering sound advice.

一鸣惊人楚庄王　兴国必先用贤良
樊姬识贤王纳谏　孙叔敖出楚国强

With one bold act, King Zhuang of Chu stunned the land,
He knew that wisdom was the key to a nation's grand.
His queen's wise counsel led him to choose with care,
Sun Shu'ao, the savior, made Chu's strength rare.

八、恶疾不弃（宋女）

春秋时，宋国一个女子嫁到蔡国。成亲后，发现丈夫有恶疾。当时婚嫁比较自由，许多人（包括她母亲）都劝她改嫁别人。她说："我和他结亲，命运就连到一起。生病不是他的罪过，我不能弃他而走。"当她得知新鲜的车前草能治丈夫的病时，不怕气味难闻，到处寻找。采摘来之后，回家浸泡以后给丈夫治病。日久天长，把丈夫的病治好了，两人继续过幸福的生活。

8. A Wife Remains Devoted to Her Husband Despite His Disease

During the Spring and Autumn Period, a woman from the State of Song married a man from the State of Cai. After their marriage, she discovered that her husband suffered from a serious illness. In those times, marriage was often entered into or dissolved with relative ease, and many—including her mother—urged her to leave him and marry someone else. However, she replied, "When I married him, our fates became intertwined. His illness is not his fault, and I cannot abandon him." When she learned that fresh plantain could be used to treat her husband's condition, she overcame her aversion to its unpleasant smell and set out to find the herb. After gathering it, she made a medicinal infusion and treated her husband. Over time, his illness was cured, and the couple continued to live a happy life together.

夫妻结发一条心　荣辱兴衰不可分
夫患恶疾妻不弃　人间真爱见精神

The married pair's hearts were bound for all eternity,
They were to be inseparable in prosperity or adversity.
The wife did not leave her husband in spite of his malady,
Their union stands as a model of loving matrimony.

九、誓死忠贞（息君夫人）

春秋时，中原的息国被楚国灭掉，息国国君被罚作守城门的苦役。息君夫人貌美，楚王要把她纳入后宫为妃。但息君夫人不肯享荣华富贵，不愿和息君分离。有一天，楚王外出游玩，她乘机逃到城门口找到息君，要一起逃走。但周围全是楚军，逃不出去。息君夫人说："这辈子我们已不能在一起了，死后见吧！"说毕，自杀了。息君见夫人如此钟情，也同时自尽。楚王对他们忠贞于爱情的精神深受感动，依诸侯之礼将他们埋葬。

9. Swearing Loyalty with One's Life

During the Spring and Autumn Period, the State of Xi, located in central China, was destroyed by the State of Chu. The ruler of Xi was sentenced to the humiliating task of guarding the city gates. His wife, a woman of great beauty, caught the eye of the King of Chu, who sought to take her as a concubine. However, she refused to live in luxury and separation from her husband. One day, when the King of Chu went on an excursion, she seized the opportunity to escape and made her way to the city gates to find her husband, hoping to flee together. But the area was surrounded by Chu's troops, and the chance of escape was slim. In that moment, the wife of the ruler of Xi said, "In this life, we cannot be together, but I will meet you in the afterlife." With these words, she took her own life. Witnessing her devotion, the ruler of Xi also committed suicide. The King of Chu, deeply moved by their unwavering loyalty and love, ordered that they be buried together with the honors reserved for nobles.

> 好个春秋息夫人　荣华不忘夫遭窘
> 生前不能再团聚　双双殉情感楚君

> What a great woman was the consort of the State of Xi,
> She craved her husband's lowliness and rejected royalty.
> Suicide was the answer to being parted in this mortal life,
> The King of Chu was awestruck by the loyalty of this wife.

十、劝夫勤政（周南妻）

春秋时期周王室中有个叫周南的大夫，夫妻恩爱。妻子十分贤明，一直支持他的工作。经常劝他勤于王事，服务百姓。周王任命周南治洪水，妻子多次向他捎信，要他不怕困难，勤于公事。过了预定时间周南还没回来，妻子怕他想家，又捎信要他善始善终，尽职尽力，不要怕别人指责，做好工作就是为父母、家庭争光。周南在妻子的理解与鼓励下，做了许多对国家、对百姓有益的工作。

10. A Wife Admonishes Her Husband to Be Diligent in Official Affairs

During the Spring and Autumn Period, there was a royal official named Zhou Nan, who was deeply devoted to his wife, and they shared a strong, loving relationship. His wife was wise and supportive, frequently advising him to dedicate himself to the king's affairs and to serve the people diligently. When the King of Zhou appointed Zhou Nan to manage flood control, his wife sent him several messages, urging him not to be deterred by difficulties and to remain focused on his official duties. When the agreed-upon time passed and Zhou Nan had not yet returned, his wife, concerned that he might be feeling homesick, sent another message reminding him to stay committed and finish his work, no matter the criticism from others. Fulfilling his responsibilities, she said, would bring honor to his family. Encouraged and supported by his wife's understanding, Zhou Nan was able to accomplish many tasks that benefited both the state and the people.

天下难得周南妻　多次劝夫勤国事
为国为民忠勤守　大情大爱显鸿志

It is hard to find a woman like the wife of Zhou Nan,
Prepared to admonish her spouse to be a worthy statesman.
Zhou Nan committed himself to the people and the land,
Their great love for him matched his ambition grand.

十一、断机警夫（乐羊子妻）

春秋时中山国的乐羊子，外出求学，其妻在家勤于纺绩，供他读书。乐羊子读了几年，很想家，便辍学回来。其妻持刀走到织机前说："这丝是由无数蚕茧抽出来的，放到织机上，一寸一寸地织，日积月累，才能织成绸缎。今天我若一刀砍断，便前功尽弃了。你学习也是这样。要想学有所成，决不应半途而废。" 乐羊子听后倍受感动，很快返回继续学习，后来成为魏国一位名将。

11. Cutting the Silk to Admonish Her Husband

During the Spring and Autumn Period, Yueyang Zi, a scholar from the State of Zhongshan, left home to further his studies. While he was away, his wife supported him by spinning and weaving at home. After several years, Yueyang Zi began to miss home and decided to abandon his education and return. Upon hearing of his decision, his wife took a knife and approached the loom, saying: "This silk is made from countless cocoons, carefully drawn and woven, inch by inch, over time, until it becomes a fine fabric. If I were to cut it now, all the previous effort would be wasted. The same is true for your studies. If you wish to succeed, you must not give up halfway." Yueyang Zi was deeply moved by his wife's words and quickly returned to continue his studies. Later, he became a renowned general in the State of Wei.

世传贤良乐羊妻　劝夫勤学示断机
乐羊敬重贤内助　奋发就学创佳绩

Yueyang Zi's wife's virtue became world-renowned,
Threatening to cut the unfinished silk was a gesture most profound.
He came to respect his better half because of this admonishment,
It drove him on a path of study towards greater achievement.

十二、丑女正妃（钟离春）

战国时期，齐国无盐的钟离春，黄发稀疏，两眼凹陷，仰鼻露孔，驼背凸胸，皮肤漆黑，面貌特丑，四十多岁还没嫁人，但此女熟读古籍，才华横溢。有一天，她去见齐宣王，许多人对她嗤之以鼻，齐宣王却好奇地召见她。无盐女向齐王讲出了许多高明的治国方案，齐王听得入了迷，对她敬佩不已。为了留她在宫中，随时聆听教诲，打破常规，将她立为正妃。在她的帮助下，齐国日益强大起来。

12. An Ugly Woman Becomes an Official Concubine

During the Warring States Period, Zhong Lichun, a woman from Wuyan in the State of Qi, had sparse, graying hair, sunken eyes, flaring nostrils, a hunched back,and an unattractive appearance. Her skin was dark, and by the time she was in her forties, she had still never married. Despite her looks, she was well-versed in the classics and possessed remarkable intelligence. One day, she went to see King Xuan of Qi. While many people mocked her appearance, the king, intrigued, decided to meet with her. Zhong Lichun shared several insightful strategies for governing the state, and the king, captivated by her wisdom, grew to admire her greatly. Eager to keep her in the palace and benefit from her guidance, King Xuan broke with tradition and made her his official concubine. With her counsel, the State of Qi grew stronger and more prosperous.

奇丑莫过无盐女　识高善辩超文武
治国大计宣王用　齐国中兴胜往古

No one surpassed the Wuyan lady in ugliness,
Yet her wisdom and speech were beyond all fairness.
King Xuan sought her counsel on matters of state,
And under her guidance, Qi thrived in its fate.

十三、琴音永爱（卓文君、司马相如）

西汉年间，四川临邛富翁卓王孙，有个女儿卓文君，丈夫死后住在娘家。卓王孙慕成都才子司马相如之名，请他到家饮酒，与卓文君一见钟情。相如弹琴时奏了一曲《凤求凰》，文君会意，两人相互爱慕，连夜离家奔往成都，琴瑟和鸣。因相如家贫，二人又回临邛开了一间小酒馆，文君当垆卖酒，卓王孙以此为耻。经人劝说，卓王孙给他们一些财物，二人复归成都。相如潜心攻读，作《上林赋》等，被汉武帝赏识。后又被派出通西南夷有功，拜孝文圜令。

13. The Sound of the Lyre is a Token of Love

During the Western Han Dynasty, there was a wealthy man named Zhuo Wangsun in Linqiong, Sichuan. He had a daughter named Zhuo Wenjun, who returned to her parental home after the death of her husband. Admiring the talents of the Chengdu scholar Sima Xiangru, Zhuo Wangsun invited him to his home for a drink. At first sight, Sima Xiangru fell in love with Zhuo Wenjun. While playing the tune *The Phoenix Seeks the Mate* on the lyre, Sima Xiangru subtly expressed his feelings, and Zhuo Wenjun, understanding the gesture, reciprocated his affection. That very night, they eloped to Chengdu, their hearts in harmony like the strings of a lyre. However, due to Sima Xiangru's humble background, the couple returned to Linqiong and opened a small tavern. Zhuo Wenjun sold wine, a situation that brought shame to her wealthy father. Persuaded by others, Zhuo Wangsun provided them with some money to save face, and they returned to Chengdu. There, Sima Xiangru devoted himself to study and composed works such as *The Ode to the Royal Garden*, which earned the admiration of Emperor Wu of Han. He later served as an envoy to the southwestern regions and was appointed to oversee the royal gardens.

相如一曲《凤求凰》　　文君心仪识才郎
当炉卖酒显风雅　　《上林赋》成惊汉皇

At the sound of *The Phoenix seeks the Mate*,
Ms Zhuo fell for bookish Sima on their first date.
She retained her elegance even when serving liquor to men,
Eventually the Emperor was taken by *Ode to the Royal Garden*.

十四、不弃糟糠（宋弘）

东汉初年长安人宋弘，官至大司空，被封为宣平侯。那时光武帝的姐姐湖阳公主的丈夫已死，湖阳公主盛赞宋弘，想嫁给他。光武帝召见宋弘时，湖阳公主在屏风后偷听。皇帝对宋弘说："一个人富裕了应换朋友，地位高了应换妻子。"宋弘（此时已有妻）却说："我听说贫贱时交的朋友，富贵时不能忘；穷困时娶的结发妻，富贵时更不能抛弃。"湖阳公主听后打消了嫁宋弘的念头。

14. Refusing to Abandon a Wife Who Has Shared Hardships

In the early years of the Eastern Han Dynasty, Song Hong, a native of Chang'an, served as the Minister of Works and was bestowed the title of Marquis of Xuanping. At that time, Princess Huyang, the elder sister of Emperor Guangwu of Han, had recently lost her husband. She admired Song Hong greatly and wished to marry him. When the Emperor summoned Song Hong for an audience, Princess Huyang secretly listened from behind a screen. Emperor Guangwu advised Song Hong, saying, "When a man becomes wealthy, he should change his friends, and when he rises to a high position, he should change his wife." To this, Song Hong (He had his wife in that time) responded, "I have heard that one should never forget the friends made in poverty, and when one gains wealth, they should not abandon them. Likewise, one should never forsake their first wife, no matter how high their status may rise." Upon hearing this, Princess Huyang gave up her intention of marrying him.

皇姑位高皇帝劝　休妻再娶结新欢
好个宋弘婉言退　富贵不忘结发缘

The Emperor and his sister were of the same view,
On bettering his lot a man needed to take a wife brand new.
Song Hong could not stomach this proposal,
To love or to reject? That's not at our disposal.

十五、举案齐眉（孟光）

东汉时，平陵富家女孟光，长的又黑又丑，三十多岁还未出嫁。儒生梁鸿，家中贫寒，放猪自给，但却博览群籍，傲骨亮节。孟光羡其才华，自愿嫁给他。初嫁时，梳洗打粉，穿上华丽的衣服，戴上高档的首饰，梁鸿七天不理他。后来孟光布衣淡装，在家洗衣做饭，梁鸿与其和好。二人互敬互爱，情深意笃。孟光每当做出饭来，依礼将食盘高举过眉，梁鸿恭敬地接受。后人便把"举案齐眉"当作夫妻恩爱的代称了。

15. Lifting the Tray to Eyebrow Level as a Token of Respect

Meng Guang, from a wealthy family in Pingling during the Eastern Han Dynasty, was dark-complexioned and plain in appearance. By her thirties, she was still unmarried. Liang Hong, a Confucian scholar from a poor family who raised pigs for a living, was known for his extensive reading and noble character. Despite his humble background, Meng Guang admired his intellect and voluntarily chose to marry him. After their marriage, she initially dressed in fine clothes, applied makeup, and wore jewelry, but Liang Hong ignored her for seven days. Eventually, Meng Guang adopted a simpler lifestyle, focusing on cooking and household chores. This change led to Liang Hong reconciling with her. Their relationship flourished, marked by mutual respect and deep affection. Every time Meng Guang prepared a meal, she would lift the serving tray to eyebrow level, a gesture of respect, and Liang Hong would accept it with equal reverence. This act became a symbol of their loving and respectful marriage, and later generations used the phrase "lifting the tray to eyebrow level" to describe couples with such mutual affection.

昔日梁鸿娶孟光　夫才妻丑又何妨
识才知心相濡沫　举案齐眉千古扬

Liang Hong married Meng Guang in the ancient past,
A talented man with an ugly wife - a formula to last.
Mutual understanding bound tightly the pair,
The legend of lifting the tray spread far and near.

十六、布衣同心（鲍宣）

东汉时渤海高城人鲍宣，学习刻苦，品德高尚，但家境贫寒。老师对他特别钟爱，要把女儿嫁给他。出嫁时，女方陪嫁了很多财物及一些仆人，鲍宣对此不满。妻子少君说："我嫁给你是我父和我爱你有才，我一切听你的。" 鲍宣提出把大量的东西送走，仆人送还。少君遵照丈夫的意见，将陪嫁的一切均退回去，回来换上平民穿的衣服，二人乘着百姓常用的鹿车回家。少君拜见婆母后，和百姓一样地挑水做饭。夫妻情投意合，相爱终生。

16. Cotton Clothes Betoken Mutual Love

Bao Xuan, from Gaocheng near the Bohai Sea during the Eastern Han Dynasty, came from a humble background. Despite his family's poverty, he was a diligent scholar and exemplified great virtue. His teacher was so impressed with his character and intellect that he offered his daughter's hand in marriage to Bao. On their wedding day, the bride brought with her a substantial dowry, including much wealth and several servants. This, however, displeased Bao Xuan. In response, his new wife, Shaojun, said, "I am marrying you because both my father and I admire your talent,and I will follow your wishes in everything." Bao Xuan suggested they return most of the dowry and send the servants back. Shaojun, in full agreement with her husband's wishes, returned everything and exchanged her fine attire for simple, common clothes. The couple then traveled home in a modest cart, the kind typically used by ordinary people. After paying a formal visit to her mother-in-law, Shaojun set to work fetching water and cooking meals, just like any other humble housewife. The couple shared a deep bond, loving and supporting each other throughout their lives.

富女下嫁穷鲍宣　锦衣厚衾心不安
财物送还心平静　夫妻恩爱鱼水欢

Poor Bao Xuan married a rich lady in something of a hurry,
He found himself discomforted by the size of her dowry.
Returning the gifts restored his state of mind,
The couple shared a life together with joy unconfined.

十七、一门忠烈（诸葛亮）

三国时蜀汉丞相诸葛亮，智多谋广。襄阳人黄承彦有女，据说很丑，但自幼随父攻读诗书，才华出众。翩翩少年的诸葛亮到黄府求婚，不怕别人讥笑，结了婚。二人恩爱相伴，从无二心。黄氏不但治家规整，教子有方，还经常帮助诸葛亮出谋划策。诸葛亮对蜀主鞠躬尽瘁，他们的儿子诸葛瞻、孙子诸葛尚在蜀汉后期的战斗中，均英勇战死，一门忠烈。

17. A Loyal and Faithful Family

During the Three Kingdoms period, Zhuge Liang, the prime minister of the Shu State, was known for his wisdom and strategic acumen. Huang Chengyan, a man from Xiangyang, had a daughter who was said to be strikingly unattractive. However, from a young age, she had followed her father's example and diligently studied the Classic of Poetry, demonstrating exceptional talent. The young and handsome Zhuge Liang, undeterred by the potential mockery of others, visited the Huang household to propose marriage. The couple's love for one another remained unwavering and sincere. Huang not only managed the household with great skill but was also an exemplary mother. She frequently assisted Zhuge Liang in devising strategies and plans. Zhuge Liang dedicated himself wholeheartedly to his monarch, and his loyalty extended through generations. His son, Zhuge Zhan, and his grandson, Zhuge Shang, both bravely sacrificed their lives in battle for the Shu State, cementing their family's legacy as one of unyielding loyalty and patriotism.

潇洒多情诸葛亮　偏娶丑女作妻房
共献智谋终生爱　鞠躬尽瘁多贤良

Zhuge Liang was handsome and charming,
Yet his chosen bride's looks were less than disarming.
The loving couple were well-matched in wit and virtue,
And their progeny laid down their lives for Shu.

十八、共传古籍（韦宋氏）

晋朝韦逞的母亲宋氏，出嫁前已熟知古籍。嫁到韦家后，夫妻二人和睦恩爱，经常一起研讨《周礼》。并告诉儿子："《周礼》是周公亲自制订的经典制诰，记载着古代的典章制度。现在天下大乱，此书不可失传。"不久，他家在战乱中迁到山东，宋氏和丈夫又推着装载《周礼》的车到了冀州。他们白天打柴，晚上教育儿子。后来韦逞学习有成，做了前秦的太常，宋氏献出《周礼》，皇帝派一百二十人学习，使此古籍得以流传。

18. Passing on the Ancient Book

Before her marriage to Wei Cheng, Madam Song was already well-versed in the Chinese Classics. After their marriage, the couple lived in harmony and often studied *The Rites of Zhou* together. She told her son: " *The Rites of Zhou* was personally compiled by the Duke of Zhou, documenting ancient systems and rites. In these times of chaos, it is of utmost importance that this book is preserved and not allowed to fade into obscurity." Soon, war forced the family to relocate to Shandong. The couple pushed a cart carrying *The Rites of Zhou* to Jizhou Prefecture. By day, they gathered firewood; by night, they continued to educate their son. Eventually, Wei Cheng became an accomplished scholar and was appointed as the Minister of Ceremonies under the Former Qin. Madam Song then presented *The Rites of Zhou* to the emperor, who ordered 120 men to study the text, ensuring that this ancient work would be passed down for generations.

韦逞父母鱼水依　历尽艰险传《周礼》
教子成材多奉献　古籍传世民受益

Wei Cheng's parents were filled with affection,
Through hardships and danger *The Rites of Zhou* had their protection.
They educated their son to serve the state,
And the classics once more had the chance to circulate.

十九、真爱化蝶（梁山伯、祝英台）

晋时会稽（今浙江绍兴）人梁山伯曾为鄞县令。相传与上虞女子祝英台同学相爱。英台先归，山伯去祝家求亲，知英台父母已将其许配马家，回家病死，葬于清道山下。马氏娶英台时，英台跃入墓中，双双化蝶飞去。山东济宁曾有明时专载二人的碑刻。此故事已与南方四地共获世界非物质文化遗产。

19. The Butterfly Lovers

During the Jin Dynasty, in Kuaiji (modern-day Shaoxing, Zhejiang Province), there lived a man named Liang Shanbo, who once served as the magistrate of Yin County. According to legend, he fell in love with his classmate, Zhu Yingtai, from Shangyu Prefecture. After graduation, Zhu Yingtai returned home, and Liang Shanbo went to propose marriage to her family. However, Zhu Yingtai's parents had already arranged her betrothal to a member of the Ma family. Heartbroken, Liang Shanbo returned home and died. He was buried at the foot of Mount Qingdao. On the day of Zhu Yingtai's wedding to the Ma family's son, as the bridal procession passed Liang Shanbo's grave, Zhu Yingtai threw herself into the tomb, and the two lovers were transformed into butterflies, flying away together. A monument commemorating their love was erected during the Ming Dynasty in Jining, Shandong Province. The story, together with four related sites in southern China, has been recognized as part of the world's intangible cultural heritage.

梁山伯与祝英台　心心相印两无猜
此生不能成眷属　化蝶双双永相爱

Liang Shanbo and Zhu Yingtai,
Hearts united that would not die.
Denied matrimony during mortal life,
As butterflies they eloped as husband and wife.

二十、夫妻孝母（徐孝克）

南北朝梁朝郯人徐孝克，妻臧氏，夫妻二人情深意笃，虽家境贫寒，却相亲相爱，共同孝敬老母。侯景作乱时，他们的生活更加困难，但仍对老母十分孝敬。不久妻子被侯景的一个将领掳去，徐孝克到处去找。找到妻子后，二人仍回家孝敬老母。徐孝克后来当国子祭酒时，每次宴会，总在襟中掖一点好饭菜，皇帝知道他是为了回家孝敬老母，每次宴会后叫他带一点回家，交给妻子热后奉给老母吃。

20. A Couple Who Are Filial to Their Old Mother

During the Southern and Northern Dynasties, there was a man named Xu Xiaoke from Tan, within the Liang Dynasty. His wife, from the Zang family, and he shared a deep and unwavering affection for each other. Despite their humble circumstances, their bond remained strong, and they both showed great filial piety toward his elderly mother. When the rebellion of Hou Jing broke out, their lives became even more difficult, but their devotion to the old woman did not falter. Soon after, Xu Xiaoke's wife was captured by one of Hou Jing's generals. After a long and exhausting search, Xu Xiaoke finally found her and brought her back. The couple then returned home to continue caring for his mother. Later, Xu Xiaoke was appointed as the head of the Imperial Academy's kitchens. At every banquet, he would discreetly tuck some food into his pocket. When the Emperor learned of this, he approved and insisted that Xu Xiaoke be allowed to take a portion of the feast home for his mother. He would have his wife warm the food, which she then served to the elderly matriarch, providing her with the sustenance she needed.

夫妻恩爱情义笃　双双诚心孝老母
战火离乱不改志　母心欢畅儿心舒

The loving couple was affectionate and kind,
Their mother's welfare was at the forefront of their mind.
This did not alter even under the shadow of war,
The mother was content and he as dutiful as before.

二十一、破镜重圆（徐德言、乐昌公主）

南北朝时期，南朝陈太子舍人徐德言与乐昌公主成婚。隋灭陈后，二人被迫分离前，徐德言对妻子说不忘旧情，乐昌公主更表示忠于爱情的决心。二人将一面镜子摔破，一人一半，约定明年正月十五京中见面。陈亡后，乐昌公主被隋重臣杨素掳去，藏进府中。一年后，徐到京都，见一老者拿着半个镜子叫卖，实为乐昌公主派人寻找丈夫。徐拿出半个镜子交给老人，转交乐昌后，她为此终日悲泣。杨素得知此事，派人将徐德言接进府中，将公主归还。

21. A Broken Mirror is Pieced Back Together

During the Southern and Northern Dynasties, Xu Deyan, a secretary to the Crown Prince of the Chen Dynasty, married Princess Lechang. After the fall of the Chen Dynasty, the couple was forced to separate. Before they parted, Xu Deyan promised his wife that he would never forget their love, and Princess Lechang vowed to remain faithful to him. The two broke a mirror in half, each keeping one part, and agreed to meet in the capital on the 15th day of January in the following year. After the fall of the Chen Dynasty, Princess Lechang was captured and taken to the mansion of Yang Su, a powerful minister of the Sui Dynasty. One year later, Xu Deyan traveled to the capital and saw an elderly man trying to sell half of a broken mirror. In truth, the old man had been sent by Princess Lechang to find her husband. Xu took out his half of the mirror and gave it to the man. Upon receiving the other half, Princess Lechang wept bitterly for days. When Yang Su learned of the reunion, he summoned Xu Deyan to his mansion, where he was reunited with his wife, Princess Lechang.

乐昌爱恋徐德言　以镜为介立誓愿
虽遭离乱苦寻找　当年破镜又重圆

Lechang loved Xu with a heart so true,
They swore an oath, then broke a mirror in two.
Through war and hardship, they searched with care,
A shattered mirror mended—proof Xu was there.

二十二、太宗贤助（长孙皇后）

唐太宗是我国历史上有作为的一位君主，人们多肯定他那时的"贞观之治"。除了有一批能干的文武大臣外，他还有一位贤明的长孙皇后。此人恪遵礼法，相夫教子，作《女则》十卷，在治国方面也常助丈夫。有一次魏征憨谏太宗，使皇帝难堪，唐太宗回宫后，发了火，说："要杀这个乡巴佬。" 长孙皇后却对皇帝祝贺说："因为皇帝圣明，才有这样能言憨谏的大臣。" 这番话扭转了皇帝对魏征的看法。日后唐太宗采纳了魏征提出的许多好建议，出现贞观盛世。

22. Emperor Taizong of Tang Enjoys a Wise and Supportive Consort

Emperor Taizong of Tang is one of the most accomplished monarchs in Chinese history, renowned for his effective governance during the "Zhenguan Era", which is often regarded as a golden age in the Tang Dynasty. In addition to a group of capable civil and military officials, Taizong was also supported by his wise and virtuous consort, Empress Zhangsun. She was a model of propriety, adhering to the rules of etiquette, educating their children, and offering invaluable assistance in state affairs. Empress Zhangsun was also the author of a ten-volume work entitled *The Code of a Woman*, which offered guidance on the conduct of women in society. On one occasion, the blunt advisor Wei Zheng, in his straightforward manner, embarrassed the emperor with a bold suggestion. After returning to the palace, Taizong, furious, exclaimed, "I will have this country bumpkin executed!" However, Empress Zhangsun, ever wise and composed, responded by saying, "Your Majesty's wisdom is what enables such a forthright minister to speak so candidly." Her words prompted the emperor to rethink his stance on Wei Zheng. From that moment on, Emperor Taizong came to appreciate Wei Zheng's honest counsel, and their collaboration played a key role in the flourishing of the Zhenguan Era.

唐初国兴赖明君　明君治国赖铮臣
魏征憨谏太宗怒　长孙祝贺消帝嗔

The Tang Dynasty rose on the back of wise Taizong,
Though he relied on blunt ministers to drive affairs along.
Wei Zheng embarrassed him by being too direct,
But the Empress reassured that his counsel was correct.

二十三、拒当驸马（尉迟恭）

唐初大将尉迟恭，作战勇敢，为人忠厚正直，深得皇帝喜爱。皇帝要把女儿嫁给他。能娶公主为妻，当上驸马，是许多人梦寐以求的事，尉迟恭却对皇帝委婉地说：“属下已有妻子，虽其貌不扬，却是我贫贱之交，跟我患难多年。我还知道古人有‘富贵不另娶’的美德，我不能抛弃妻子另娶。” 唐太宗为他这一番衷恳的至理名言所折服，不但放弃了嫁女的动议，还对他加以奖赏。

23. Refusing to Be the Emperor's Son-in-Law

At the beginning of the Tang Dynasty, General Yuchi Gong was not only brave in battle but also known for his loyalty and integrity, qualities that earned him the Emperor's deep admiration. The Emperor, impressed by his valor and virtue, decided to offer him the hand of one of his daughters in marriage. Many would have eagerly accepted the opportunity to become a royal son-in-law, but Yuchi Gong declined with great tact, saying: "Your Majesty, I already have a wife. Though she may not be striking in appearance, she has stood by me through many hardships. I have always understood that in ancient times, the virtue of remaining loyal to one's wife, regardless of changing circumstances, was greatly valued. I cannot abandon her for the sake of a marriage to your daughter." The Emperor Taizong, moved by Yuchi Gong's sincerity and principled stance, not only respected his decision but also rewarded him for his unwavering loyalty.

帝家驸马最光采　富贵荣华滚滚来
敬德婉拒帝王意　糟糠之妻终生爱

To be the Emperor's son-in-law, nothing could be more glorious,
Wealth and fortune would come to him who was victorious.
Yuchi Gong declined his monarch's generous will,
For his present wife had seen him through good and ill.

二十四、不攀权贵（王义方）

唐朝初年，涟水人王义方，举明经后，被任命为晋王府参军直宏文馆的职衔。开国名臣魏征看他德才兼备，要把侄女嫁给他。他却认为这样有高攀的嫌疑，婉言谢绝了。魏征死后，有人又提起这门亲事，他概然应允，娶了此女。有人问他为什么不给魏征留点面子？他说："我尊重魏大人，不是以当他侄女女婿的形式尊重他。今天我娶了他侄女，正是为了报答知己。" 成亲后二人鱼水和谐，白头到老。

24. Not Marrying for Social Position

In the early years of the Tang Dynasty, Wang Yifang from Lishui passed the imperial examinations and was appointed as the Military Commissar to the King of Jin. Wei Zheng, a founding minister of the dynasty, recognized Wang's talent and virtue and sought to arrange a marriage between him and his niece. However, Wang declined, fearing that such a match might be seen as an attempt to climb the social ladder. After Wei Zheng's death, the marriage proposal was raised again, and this time, Wang accepted. When asked why he had not given face to Wei Zheng earlier, Wang explained: "I respected Minister Wei, but not in the capacity of a future relative. I am marrying his niece now to honor the friendship and trust we shared." The couple lived in harmony and affection, growing old together.

权贵在位婚未允　名臣殁后喜成亲
结亲不应攀权贵　挚爱烈火炼真金

Wang refused to marry a serving magnate's niece,
The uncle's death brought him a form of release.
Marriage should not be founded on social gain,
The fire of true love can melt a gold chain.

二十五、慕德嫁女（韦诜）

唐朝人韦诜，女儿要出嫁，到处寻访道德高尚的人。一天，韦诜在楼上见对面邻居在花园里埋东西，得知那人叫裴宽。一打听，裴宽为官从来不收礼。有人送来一大块鹿肉，放下就走了。他既无处退，又不愿收，就把他埋掉。韦诜听后，很佩服这个小官，决定把女儿嫁给他。结亲时，裴宽穿着青色的衣服，又瘦又高，其貌不扬，宾客们多不理解，韦诜却说这是理想的乘龙快婿。夫妻一生恩爱，家庭和睦。一尘不染的裴宽，日后做到户部尚书。

25. Marrying One's Daughter to a Virtuous Gentlemen

During the Tang Dynasty, Wei Shen was seeking a man of high moral character to marry his daughter. One day, while upstairs, he noticed his neighbor across the street burying something in his garden. Upon inquiry, Wei learned that the man was Pei Kuan, a government official known for refusing bribes. Someone had left a large piece of venison at his door, but Pei Kuan, unable to return it and unwilling to accept it, simply buried it in the ground. Wei Shen was deeply impressed by this integrity and decided to marry his daughter to Pei Kuan. On the wedding day, Pei Kuan appeared in plain black clothes, tall but thin, and unremarkable in appearance. Many of the guests were puzzled, but Wei Shen insisted that he was the perfect match. The couple lived in love and harmony throughout their lives. Pei Kuan, whose reputation remained untarnished, eventually rose to the position of Minister of Revenue.

> 有女嫁给尚德人　　何惧官小与家贫
> 裴宽清廉韦诜敬　　乘龙快婿跳龙门

Marrying his daughter to a person of morality,
Wei Shen overlooked his low rank and lack of property.
Instead he admired Pei Kuan's virtue unbending,
The bright son-in-law could rise by never once offending.

二十六、入藏和蕃（文成公主）

公元6世纪，我国西南部吐蕃（今西藏）族首领松赞干布统一了青藏高原。为了和唐朝友好，希望与唐朝的宗室联姻。唐太宗派他侄女（任城王李道宗之女）文成公主与松赞干布结婚。文成公主入藏时，带去许多蔬菜种子及一些工匠。在当地教给吐蕃人冶炼金属，制造农具，纺纱织布，制作陶器，还有碾米，酿酒，造纸等工艺。二人结婚后，相互尊重，生活和洽。文成公主在大昭寺前栽的柳树，当地叫"唐柳""公主柳"。每当四月十五公主的生日，当地还年年庆祝呢。

26. Travelling to Tibet to Unite Two Peoples Through Matrimony

In the 6th century AD, Songtsan Gambo, the leader of the Tubo tribe in southwestern China (modern-day Tibet), unified the Qinghai-Tibet Plateau. Seeking to establish peaceful relations with the Tang Dynasty, he proposed a marriage alliance with the Tang royal family. Emperor Taizong sent his niece, Princess Wencheng (the daughter of Li Daozong, King of Ren Cheng), to wed Songtsan Gambo. Upon entering Tibet, Princess Wencheng brought with her a variety of vegetable seeds and several craftsmen. She taught the Tibetan people various skills, including metalsmelting for agricultural tools, spinning and weaving, pottery making, rice milling, winemaking, and papermaking. After their marriage, Princess Wencheng and Songtsan Gambo lived in mutual respect and harmony. The willows she planted in front of the Jokhang Temple became known as "Tang Willows" or "Princess Willows". Each year, on April 15th, the locals celebrate her birthday in her honor.

唐蕃联合喜成婚　文成入藏汉蕃亲
公主远撒文化种　中华文明喜添锦

The Tang and Tubo were bound through a wedding,
So Han people and Tibetans became kin.
The princess planted the seeds of culture,
Expanding Chinese civilisation for the future.

二十七、共研金石（赵明诚、李清照）

宋朝诸城人赵明诚，工诗文，好古籍，曾任湖州知州。其妻李清照，号易安居士，系宋朝名臣李格非之女。温文尔雅，亦聪颖过人。二人成亲后，琴瑟和鸣。赵明诚酷爱研究金石，李清照与丈夫密切配合，夫妻二人夜以继日地对夏、商、周以来的各种青铜器及汉唐以来的各种刻石精心辨识研究之后，编成《金石录》，南宋绍兴年间，李清照向皇帝奏上，受到宋高宗高度赞扬，此书成为历代研究考古学的权威之作。

27. A Couple Studying Epigraphy Together

Zhao Mingcheng, born in Zhucheng during the Song Dynasty, was skilled in poetry and had a deep passion for ancient texts. He served as the governor of Huzhou Prefecture. His wife, Li Qingzhao, who took the literary name Yian Jushi, was the daughter of the renowned minister Li Gefei. She was elegant, gentle, and exceptionally intelligent. After their marriage, the couple lived in harmony. Zhao Mingcheng was particularly fascinated with the study of epigraphy, and Li Qingzhao worked closely with him, dedicating themselves to the meticulous research of bronzes from the Xia, Shang, and Zhou dynasties, as well as engraved stones from the Han and Tang periods. Together, they compiled their findings into *The Golden Stone Records* during the Shaoxing period of the Southern Song Dynasty. Li Qingzhao presented the work to Emperor Gaozong of Song, who praised it highly. This book became an authoritative reference for archaeological studies in subsequent generations.

明诚清照两才人　　　共研金石爱更深
《金石录》成垂青史　　夫妻贡献光史林

Zhao Mingcheng and Li Qingzhao were two talents in Song,
Their common interest kept their love ever young.
Perennial was the influence of *The Golden Stone Records*,
It helped future historians reap ever greater rewards.

二十八、失明不负（刘庭式）

宋朝齐州人刘庭式，自幼家贫，发愤苦读，与同乡一女子相恋。虽未经订婚手续，二人却心心相印，暗自许婚。当他考中进士的大好消息传来时，贫穷的女方却因眼疾未愈瞎了眼。有人劝他悔婚另娶，他却毅然与瞎眼女子成了亲。成亲后，夫妻和睦，感情笃厚，生下几个儿女。当他的好友苏轼问及此事时，他说："我们相爱大半生，都出自真心。我爱她，不是因为美色，而是心仪。那种只爱美色的人，色衰爱弛，和那些嫖客与妓女的关系有什么不同？"

28. Not Rejecting a Fiancée Who Goes Blind

Liu Tingshi, a native of Qizhou in the Song Dynasty, grew up in poverty and channeled his determination into his studies. He eventually fell in love with a local girl. Although they never had a formal engagement, they shared a deep bond and privately pledged to marry. Just as Liu received the news of his success in the imperial examinations, the girl was tragically struck blind by an illness. Despite being advised to break the engagement and marry someone else, Liu resolutely chose to stay true to his commitment. After they married, they lived in harmony and trust, and she bore several children. When Liu's close friend, Su Shi, asked him about this, he replied: "We've loved each other for nearly half a lifetime, and it's been genuine from the heart. I love her not for her beauty, but for the person she is. Those who love only beauty will grow distant when it fades with time. How is that any different from the relationship between a client and a prostitute?"

新科进士刘庭式　女盲亦娶见大义
内心相爱是真爱　君子有情远势利

Liu Tingshi, an imperial scholar newly crowned,
Married his blind fiancée, love profound.
The heartfelt feelings betokened true love and passion,
A gentleman should stay faithful in the face of snobbish fashion.

二十九、同抗金兵（韩世忠、梁红玉）

宋朝延安人韩世忠，忠勇弘毅，在南宋初年平寇抗金中，屡建功勋。宋高宗手书"忠勇"二字相赐。其妻梁红玉，貌美贤淑，不但与丈夫恩爱同心，在保国抗金上也见解一致。她用各种方法支持丈夫，对丈夫的事业予以配合。如韩世忠在镇守楚州时，与士卒同力役，亲织锦以为屋，很受军士们的拥戴，助长了士气。在宋金黄天荡战役中，宋军以八千之众抗击十万金兵时，梁红玉亲冒矢石。擂鼓助阵，宋军士气大震，大败金帅兀术。

29. A Couple Fights Together Against the Jin Army

Han Shizhong, born in Yan'an during the early years of the Song Dynasty, was known for his loyalty, bravery, and resilience. He achieved great victories in the fight against the Jin Dynasty, earning the admiration of the Emperor Gaozong, who personally wrote the words "Loyalty and Bravery" to honor him. His wife, Liang Hongyu, was not only beautiful and virtuous but also fully aligned with her husband's convictions, both in their mutual affection and their shared commitment to resisting the Jin Dynasty and protecting the country. She supported him in many ways, actively participating in his military endeavors. For instance, while Han Shizhong was stationed in Chu Prefecture, she worked alongside the soldiers, personally weaving brocade to make tents, earning the respect of the troops and boosting their morale. During the Battle of Huangtiandang, when 8,000 Song soldiers faced 100,000 Jin soldiers, Liang Hongyu bravely exposed herself to arrows and flying stones. She beat the war drum to rally the soldiers, inspiring them to fight fiercely. Ultimately, the Song forces emerged victorious, even defeating the Jin commander, Wuzhu.

金山战鼓响咚咚　击鼓助战抗金兵
世忠喜配梁红玉　共保宋室利苍生

The sound of drums echoed over Jin Mountain,
The troops of Song were roused by this loud pounding.
Han Shizhong and Liang Hongyu were perfect soul mates,
They protected royal and commoner alike through dire straits.

三十、买妾义还（袁升）

宋朝人袁升，做了一个小官，家境比较富裕。夫妻恩爱三十年，均已近五十岁，却无儿无女，妻子准备了一些钱，叫丈夫买个小妾，以接续香火。丈夫虽不愿去，妻子一再催促，只好到临安买来一个年轻女子。此女虽身着华丽服饰，却头扎麻绳，一脸愁容。仔细盘问原来是蜀地一位清白知县的女儿卖身葬父，袁升不要聘礼放了她，回家还是和结发妻共同生活。两人相亲相爱，心情舒畅，第二年生了儿子。儿子长大后，做到临安府尹、参知政事。

30. Returning a Concubine After She Has Been Bought

Yuan Sheng, a minor official during the Song Dynasty, came from a fairly prosperous family. He and his wife had been happily married for thirty years, both nearing fifty, but were childless. In hopes of continuing their family line, the wife set aside some money and urged her husband to take a concubine. Although reluctant, Yuan Sheng eventually agreed after persistent requests from his wife. He traveled to Lin'an and purchased a young woman. She was dressed in fine clothes, but her expression was sorrowful, and her hair was bound with a hemp cord. Upon questioning, Yuan Sheng learned that she was the daughter of a virtuous magistrate in Sichuan, who had sold herself to raise money for her father's burial. Moved by her story, Yuan Sheng returned her to her freedom, insisting that he would not take the dowry. He then continued to live happily with his wife. Their mutual affection remained strong, and the following year they were blessed with a son. When the son grew up, he went on to serve as Vice Mayor of Lin'an and later as an Assistant Administrator.

袁升妻老本无怨　劝买小妾续香烟
义还孝女仁慈尽　仍谐老妻鱼水欢

Yuan Sheng's wife was old though he could not fault her,
She asked him to find a concubine to bear a son or daughter,
He showed kindness by releasing the filial lass,
The old couple still shared their life and whatever came to pass.

三十一、虽穷亦娶（黄龟年）

宋朝福州永福人黄龟年，做中书舍人兼给事中时，永福主簿李朝旌见他聪明老实，德才兼备，要把女儿嫁给他，他答应了这门亲事。不久黄龟年中了进士，李朝旌却因病去世，家境自然败落。有人劝他娶妻应门当户对。现在两家太悬殊，应取消这门亲事。黄龟年却说："不要因为人家老人死了，家里穷了，就毁弃前盟，辜负人家。如果嫌贫爱富，我还能在世上做人吗？" 于是娶了李朝旌的女儿。夫妻相爱一生，传为佳话。

31. Poor Family Fortunes Are No Deterrent to Marriage

In the Song Dynasty, Huang Guinian, a native of Yongfu in Fuzhou, was serving as a secretary when his superior, Li Chaojing, recognized his intelligence, honesty, and moral character. Li, admiring these qualities, arranged for his daughter to marry Huang, and he accepted the proposal. Not long after, Huang passed the imperial examinations. However, Li Chaojing soon passed away, and his family fell into financial hardship. Some advised Huang to seek a wife of similar status, noting the significant disparity in wealth between the two families. They suggested he cancel the engagement. Huang, however, replied: "The death of her father and the decline of her family are no reason to break our promise. If I abandon her now for being poor and seek out wealth instead, how could I continue to live with myself?" Therefore, he married Li Chaojing's daughter. The couple remained deeply in love throughout their lives, and their story became a celebrated example of devotion.

> 龟年李女爱在先　人间沉浮若天渊
> 不耻门当户又对　毅娶贫女重诺言

Huang Guinian was betrothed to the daughter of Li,
But the vicissitudes of life blighted her family.
He cared not for her humble station,
Married her still, fulfilling his vow's foundation.

三十二、患难相依（耶律奴、萧氏）

辽国大臣耶律奴之妻萧氏，是当朝公主的女儿。她出嫁时，没摆排场，十分朴素，对公婆孝敬，夫妻相敬如宾。后来，耶律奴获罪被流放。其外公（皇帝）、母亲（公主）都劝她离婚，她说："遇到患难而离异的人，与禽兽何异？"她毅然跟随丈夫流放，在艰苦情况下亲自操持家务，对丈夫关怀备至。在度过艰难的岁月中夫妻生活虽苦犹乐。

32. Sharing Weal and Woe

The wife of Yelü Nu, a minister of the Liao Dynasty, was a princess. When she married, she deliberately avoided any extravagant displays and chose a simple,modest wedding. She was respectful and dutiful toward her mother-in-law, and she and her husband treated each other with the utmost courtesy. Later, when Yelü Nu was exiled for a crime, her grandfather, the Emperor, and her mother, the Princess Royal, urged her to divorce him. She replied resolutely: "If I abandon him in his time of trouble, what would be the difference between me and a beast?" Unwavering in her loyalty, she followed him into exile. Despite the hardships, she cared for him deeply and managed the household with dedication. Even in the face of adversity, their love and devotion remained strong, and they lived happily together.

当朝公主亦朴素　敬夫理家孝婆母
夫遭危难更呵护　患难更显情爱笃

The princess led a simple life without glamour,
Treating her husband and mother-in-law with honour.
In times of trial, her care did not sway,
Through hardship, her love grew stronger each day.

三十三、大脚皇后（马皇后）

出身贫苦的朱元璋，早年参加郭子兴领导的反元起义军。因其作战勇敢，胸怀大志，郭子兴把养女马氏嫁给他。马氏随他到处作战，相夫教子，殚精竭虑。朱元璋当上皇帝后，虽位高权重，但对"大脚"的马皇后却一直尊重，两人恩爱如常。马氏常向朱提出些治国、爱民的建议，要丈夫不忘根本，重视农业。多年后民间还有一幅画，画的是立春那天，朱元璋扶耧、马皇后播种的形象呢。

33. The Large-footed Empress

Zhu Yuanzhang, born into poverty, joined the anti-Yuan rebellion led by Guo Zixing in his early years. Recognizing his bravery and ambition, Guo Zixing arranged for his adopted daughter, Ma, to marry him. Ma accompanied him throughout his military campaigns, supporting him and raising their children with great devotion. After Zhu became emperor, despite his high status and power, he always held the "large-footed" Empress Ma in deep respect, and their relationship remained affectionate and harmonious. She often offered counsel on statecraft, urging him to prioritize agriculture and never forget his humble beginnings. Many years later, a popular image circulated among the people, depicting Zhu Yuanzhang plowing the field while Empress Ma sowed seeds on the first day of spring.

明初皇帝朱元璋　称帝仍旧敬妻房
大脚皇后识民意　重农爱民乐梓桑

Emperor Zhu founded the dynasty of Ming,
As monarch he respected his wife more than anything.
The Large-footed Empress understood the public sentiment,
And she cared about the people and agricultural furtherment.

三十四、恩爱孝亲（潘周岱）

清朝安徽泾县人潘周岱，是个普通的竹工。在贫穷的生活中，夫妻恩爱，相互体贴，共同照顾父母。二人平时节衣缩食，却经常做些好饭菜给父母吃。二人还经常用各种方式，使老人快乐。父亲受了伤，二人更照顾得无微不至，夜间轮流照顾，无怨无悔。母亲生病时，要用泉水熬药，妻子支持丈夫夜里来回八十里取来泉水，给婆婆煎药喂药。他父亲常对人说："我们的儿子、媳妇都很孝顺，我们虽穷，但却比那些富裕之家过得还舒坦。"

34. An Affectionate Couple Shows Filial Piety Towards Their Parents

Pan Zhoudai, a bamboo craftsman from Jing County, Anhui, lived in the Qing Dynasty. Despite their modest means, Pan and his wife shared a deep love for each other and a strong commitment to caring for their parents. Though they practiced frugality in their daily lives, they often went out of their way to prepare delicious meals for their elders. When Pan's father was injured, the couple took turns caring for him through the night, always without complaint. When his mother fell ill and the medicinal herbs required boiling in spring water, his wife supported him by accompanying him on the 80-mile round trip to fetch the water. Over time, Pan's father often told others, "Our son and daughter-in-law are truly dutiful. Though we are poor, we live more comfortably than many wealthy families."

孝亲古为仁之本　尽孝何能贵贱分
难得夫妻共尽孝　居家和谐乐天伦

Filial piety lies at the root of benevolence,
Duty is necessary, no matter one's importance.
Seeing husband and wife being filial together is rare,
A harmonious family warrants the greatest care.

第七章

诚实守信

Chapter Seven:

Honesty and Keeping One's Word

一、一笑倾国（周幽王）

西周最后一个天子周幽王，是个爱好声色歌舞的昏君。他用重金从褒地买来一个名叫褒姒的美女，十分宠幸。但褒姒却不肯笑。据传说，幽王用了许多办法她也不笑，便想起点烽火的事。原来周天子与诸侯约定，国家有难，点起烽火，诸侯前来救驾。这次点起烽火，各路诸侯急速前来救驾时，原来只是周幽王为博得褒姒一笑。诸侯们对天子这一失信的行为十分不满。不久，犬戎打来，再点烽火，谁也不再来救驾，西周灭亡了。正是"一笑倾国"。

1. One Laugh Destroys a Kingdom

King You of Zhou, the last ruler of the Western Zhou Dynasty, was a foolish king who indulged in pleasure, particularly in singing and dancing. He purchased a beautiful woman named Bao Si from the Bao region, showering her with attention. However, Bao Si refused to smile. Aaording to legend, despite King You's numerous attempts to make her laugh, she remained indifferent. In frustration, he decided to light the beacons,which were a signal for vassals to come to the king's aid in times of danger. When the beacons were lit, the vassals hastened to his rescue, only to find that it was a prank designed solely to make Bao Si smile. Furious at the king's deceit, the vassals lost all trust in him. Soon after, the Quan Rong, a nomadic tribe, attacked the kingdom. When the beacons were lit again, none of the vassals responded. The Western Zhou Dynasty ultimately fell, and the phrase "one laugh destroys a kingdom" became a cautionary tale.

幽王荒淫误邦国　　亵渎诚信燃烽火
失信为博褒姒笑　　一笑竟能灭国祚

King You's dissipation led the Zhou astray,
Beacons were not built to be lit for comical display.
His attempt to make Bao Si grin sealed his fate,
Proving that even one laugh can destroy a whole state.

二、守信送鼎（柳下惠）

春秋初年鲁国身为士师（法官）的柳下惠，忠厚诚信，在国内外威信很高。有一次，齐国要打鲁国，扬言鲁国如献出国内的重器岑鼎，便不攻打。鲁僖公不愿给，又不能不给，便有人建议拿一个假的顶替。齐国前来的使臣不放心，提出柳下惠说是真的才要。鲁君叫柳下惠把假的说成真的，他却不撒谎，坚持把真的给齐国。齐君收到真岑鼎，见人家诚信，自己也不得不讲诚信，放弃了打鲁国的主张。一个真岑鼎避免了一场战争。

2. Keeping One's Word and Delivering the Cauldron

In the early Spring and Autumn Period, Liu Xiahui, a judge in the State of Lu, was known for his honesty and integrity, earning widespread respect both at home and abroad. On one occasion, the State of Qi threatened to attack Lu unless it surrendered the national treasure, the "Cauldron of Cen". Duke Xi of Lu was reluctant to part with the cauldron but felt he had no choice. Some advised substituting a replica, but the Qi envoy insisted that Liu Xiahui verify the authenticity of the cauldron. When the Duke of Lu asked Liu to endorse the fake, Liu refused and insisted on giving the genuine cauldron to Qi. Upon receiving the true Cauldron of Cen, the Duke of Qi, impressed by Liu's integrity, honored his word and abandoned plans to attack Lu. Thus, one single cauldron prevented a war.

强齐侵鲁索岑鼎　朝野均主伪鼎充
柳主真鼎示诚意　免除一场战乱兴

Coveting the Cauldron of Cen set Qi against its neighbour Lu,
Counterfeiting the vessel should have seen the trouble through.
Liu Xiahui ordered the real one be presented with honesty,
That won for Lu a much-needed amnesty.

三、赵氏孤儿（程婴）

程婴，是春秋时晋国赵氏的家臣。齐国的奸臣屠岸贾在晋景公面前屡进谗言，杀死赵氏满门。只有赵朔的妻子（晋景公的姐姐）在宫中不久要生育。赵朔拜托门客程婴保住遗孤。屠岸贾扬言要杀死孤儿斩草除根。程婴为了实现承诺，把自己的儿子交给好友公孙杵臼，假装藏匿孤儿，屠岸贾杀了公孙杵臼及程婴的儿后，放下了心。程婴顶着在晋国的骂名，将孤儿赵武抚养成人，并告诉他真相。屠岸贾被杀，为赵氏报了仇，实现了自己的承诺。

3. The Orphan of the Zhao Clan

Cheng Ying was a retainer of the Zhao family in the State of Jin during the Spring and Autumn Period. A treacherous minister from the State of Qi, Tu Angu,repeatedly slandered the Zhao family in front of Duke Jing of Jin, leading to the massacre of the entire Zhao clan. The only survivor was Zhao Shuo's wife (the sister of Duke Jing), who was in the palace, about to give birth. Before his death, Zhao Shuo entrusted his loyal retainer Cheng Ying with the task of preserving his bloodline. Tu Angu vowed to kill the orphan to completely wipe out the Zhao family. In order to keep his promise, Cheng Ying entrusted his own son to his friend, Gongsun Chujiu, and pretended to hide the Zhao orphan. Tu Angu, believing the child was the one to be killed, had Gongsun and Cheng Ying's son murdered. As a result, Cheng Ying was cursed by the people of Jin, who believed the Zhao child had perished. However, Cheng Ying raised Zhao Wu, the true heir, as his own son, and when Zhao Wu came of age, Cheng Ying revealed the truth. Tu Angu wsa killed. To avenge the Zhao family, Cheng Ying fulfilled his promise.

> 屠岸谗言灭赵家　程婴仗义护孤娃
> 忍辱负怨十七载　诚心可鉴中外誇

Tu Angu's lies brought Zhao's clan to fall,
Yet brave Cheng Ying protected the orphan through it all.
He bore disgrace and infamy for seventeen years,
Home and away his sincerity moved people to tears.

四、退避三舍（重耳）

春秋时期，晋献公的公子重耳在国内动乱的情势下，流亡国外。先后到过齐、曹、宋、郑、楚国。楚成王热情招待他时，在席间问重耳："将来你回到晋国执政，将怎样报答我呢？"重耳说："将来晋楚一旦交战，我退避三舍（即后退九十里）。"公元前633年，晋楚两国交战时，当了国君的重耳（晋文公）实现诺言，退了三舍。楚军骄傲地下令追击，晋军早布置好阵法，集中兵力大败楚军，取得城濮之战的胜利。晋文公成为春秋时期第二个霸主。

4. Withdrawing the Troops for Ninety Miles

During the Spring and Autumn Period, Chong'er, the son of Duke Xian of Jin, was exiled due to domestic turmoil. He sought refuge in several states, including Qi, Cao, Song, Zheng, and Chu. While in the State of Chu, King Cheng of Chu warmly hosted him and, during the banquet, asked, "How would you repay me if one day you were to return to Jin and rule the state?" Chong'er replied, "If one day our two states were to go to war, I would order my troops to retreat 90 miles (three "she")." In 633 BC, when war broke out between Jin and Chu, Chong'er, now Duke Wen of Jin, kept his promise and ordered his forces to retreat 90 miles. The Chu commander,overconfident, ordered a pursuit, but the Jin army had already set a trap. As a result, the Jin forces decisively defeated the Chu army at the Battle of Chengpu. Duke Wen of Jin thus became the second hegemon of the Spring and Autumn Period.

重耳落难苦颠连　十余年前许诺言
晋楚交战退三舍　城濮大胜霸中原

Chong'er's hardships brought him much woe,
He made a promise he was bound to keep ten years ago.
His troops retreated 90 miles when engaging the enemy,
Chengpu won for him a new hegemony.

五、葬母应约（专诸）

专诸，春秋时吴国堂邑（今南京六合）人，家里很穷，但奉母至孝。吴国公子姬光与他结交，请他对窃位骄横的吴王僚行刺，专诸答应下来，条件是老母健在不能如约。不久其母死去，专诸马上实现诺言，鱼中藏剑，刺死王僚。姬光即位，即春秋后期称霸的吴王阖闾。

5. Fulfilling a Promise After Burying One's Mother

Zhuan Zhu, from Tang Yi (modern-day? Nanjing), was a man from a poor family in the State of Wu during the Spring and Autumn Period. Despite his poverty, he was deeply filial to his mother. His close friend, Prince Ji Guang of Wu, asked him to assassinate the arrogant King Liao of Wu, who had usurped the throne. Zhuan Zhu agreed, but on the condition that he could not act while his mother was still alive. Soon after, his mother passed away, and Zhuan Zhu honored his promise. He concealed a dagger inside a fish and used it to kill King Liao. As a result, Ji Guang succeeded to the throne and became the powerful King He Lü of Wu, a hegemon during the later part of the Spring and Autumn Period.

专诸感念姬光情　奉母许诺缓履行
母逝立即承诺现　鱼剑刺僚吴国兴

For Ji Guang's trust Zhuan Zhu was grateful,
Not until his mother passed away he would kill the usurper hateful.
He fulfilled his promise after her sad demise,
Paving the way for the State of Wu to rise.

六、痛悼知音（俞伯牙）

春秋时，楚国名士俞伯牙得到一把历史上有记载、由峄阳孤桐制作的名琴。他弹琴的技巧十分高明，但一般人不解其意。有一天俞伯牙弹琴时，旁边站着一个农夫打扮叫钟子期的人在聆听。当弹到志在高山时，钟说："善哉！峨峨然若高山。"弹到流水曲调时，钟说："善哉！洋洋乎若江河。" 俞伯牙高兴地得遇知音，二人结为好友，临别时约定明年此时还在这里相会。第二年俞伯牙如约来到，但钟子期已经病逝。俞伯牙痛失知音后，摔琴绝奏，以此示信于亡友。

6. Mourning a Bosom Friend

In the Spring and Autumn Period, Yu Boya, a renowned scholar from the State of Chu, owned a famous guqin (a type of zither) crafted from the tong wood found south of Mount Yi. His playing technique was extraordinary, but few could truly appreciate the depth of his music. One day, while Yu Boya was playing, a man dressed as a farmer, named Zhong Ziqi, stood nearby and listened attentively. When Yu Boya played the melody representing "Ambition like the top of a mountain", Zhong Ziqi exclaimed, "Wonderful! It is as lofty and sublime as a mountain." When the music shifted to the "Flowing Water" theme, Zhong said, "Wonderful! It is as boundless as the rivers and streams." Yu Boya was thrilled to find someone who understood the meaning of his music, and they became close friends. When it was time to part, they promised to meet again at the same place the following year.However, when Yu Boya returned as promised, Zhong Ziqi had passed away from illness. In deep sorrow over losing his true confidant, Yu Boya smashed his guqin to express his profound grief for his departed friend.

峄阳孤桐作琴筝　优雅豪放鸾凤鸣
高山流水一曲响　伯牙子期万古情

The tong wood from Mount Yi was fit for lyres and lutes,
Such lyres would mimic a phoenix's gentle hoots.
As the running water and sublime mountain melodies intertwined,
Yu Boya and Zhong Ziqi knew they were of one mind.

七、挂剑示信（季札）

春秋后期，吴王寿梦的少子季札，才华横溢、品德高尚。当他奉命出使北方几国时，路过徐地，徐公热情接待他时，看中了他腰间的佩剑，季札也已领悟，但考虑到向北出使一些国家尤其像鲁国，是当年周公被封的礼仪之邦，无佩剑不礼。心中暗自许愿：等回来将此剑送给徐君。当他完成出使的任务又回到徐地后，徐君已经死去，他急忙到徐君墓地吊唁，并把剑挂到墓旁树上，以示守信。

7. Hanging a Sword as a Sign

In the late Spring and Autumn Period, Jizha, the youngest son of King Shoumeng of Wu, was known for his exceptional talent and noble character. During a diplomatic mission to the northern states, he passed through the State of Xu, where he was warmly received by the Duke of Xu. At the banquet, the Duke admired the sword Jizha wore, and Jizha, sensing this, quietly made a vow in his heart. Jizha was on a mission to visit several states, notably the State of Lu, which had deep ties to the Zhou dynasty and valued proper rituals. In Lu, one could not be regarded as courteous without a sword. So, Jizha promised himself that he would give the Duke of Xu his sword as a gift upon his return. However, when Jizha completed his diplomatic mission and returned to Xu, he found that the Duke had already passed away. Filled with regret, he hurried to the Duke's tomb and, as a mark of his commitment to keep his word, he hung his sword on a tree nearby.

季札奉命使列国　　佩剑光彩徐公悦
暗许挚友返程送　　悼亡挂剑示信诺

Jizha, as envoy, traveled far and wide,
The Duke of Xu admired the blade by his side..
He pledged in his heart to offer it as a gift on his return trek,
But could only hang it by Xu's graveside, the tree to bedeck.

八、文侯守信（魏文侯）

魏文侯是战国初年有名的国君，也是一位很讲信用的人。有一次，他要去打猎，安排管理禁院的人，叫他们做好准备。到了那一天，突然狂风大作，无法出门。侍从劝魏文侯不要去了，他说："我今天不去，事先没告诉他们，不能因为天气不好，就说话不算数。我如果不去，又不告诉大家，这不是失信吗？"说毕，顶着大风乘车前往，向管禁院的人说清楚以后，心里舒服了。别人对他守信的做法也从心里佩服。

8. Marquis Wen of Wei Keeps His Word

Marquis Wen of Wei was a well-known ruler during the early Warring States period, highly respected for his commitment to keeping his word. On one occasion, he planned to go hunting and had instructed those in charge of the royal gardens to prepare everything in advance. When the day arrived, a fierce wind suddenly picked up, making it impossible to go outside. His attendants urged him to postpone the hunting trip, but Marquis Wen replied, "I didn'tinform them beforehand that the plan would be canceled. If I don't go now and fail to tell them, wouldn't that be a breach of my promise? We cannot let bad weather cause us to break our word." With that, he set out into the fierce wind. Upon reaching the royal gardens, he explained the situation, and everyone was deeply impressed by his unwavering commitment to keeping his promise.

文侯狩猎日期定　狂风大作难成行
顶风前去告下属　事无巨细皆示诚

Marquis Wen of Wei set a date for hunting,
But the gale outside was howling and grunting.
He went and warned his charges about the tumult,
They were glad for his sincerity and the happy result.

九、立木守信（商鞅）

战国初年，卫国的商鞅到了秦国，秦孝公任命他为左庶长，决定用商鞅的办法变法。他们公布了发展生产、奖励军功、限制贵族权力的一些措施，对当年秦国的老传统冲击很大。商鞅怕人们不相信，就想了个办法：在国都南门外放置一根三丈长的大木头，下令谁把它扛到北门外，立即赏十金。先时没人去扛，商鞅又将赏金增加为五十金。果然有一个人扛起木头向北走，路上许多人都笑这个"傻瓜"。这人放下木头，商鞅当场赏了五十金，并当众宣布马上颁布新法，认真推行。此举在秦国取得了威信，保证了变法的成功。

9. Establishing an Example by Setting up a Log

In the early years of the Warring States period, Shang Yang, a native of the State of Wei, arrived in the State of Qin. Duke Xiao of Qin appointed him Minister of Military and Civil Affairs and decided to implement Shang Yang's reform methods. These included measures to boost production, reward military achievements, and limit the power of the nobility, all of which were a significant departure from the old customs of Qin. Fearing that the people might distrust the reforms, Shang Yang came up with an ingenious idea: He placed a 9-meter-long log outside the south gate of the capital and issued a decree that whoever could carry it to the north gate would be rewarded with ten gold coins. Initially, no one volunteered, so the reward was increased to fifty gold coins. Eventually, a man took up the challenge and began carrying the log. Onlookers laughed and mocked him as a fool. When the man successfully placed the log at the north gate, Shang Yang immediately rewarded him with fifty gold coins and publicly declared that the new laws would be enacted and strictly enforced. This dramatic act left a lasting impression on the people of Qin and helped ensure the success of the reforms.

城门立木诺言兴　移木赏金秦人惊
当众宣示言有信　保证变法能成功

The log at the gate enshrined a promise of sincerity,
The strongman's reward shocked and stirred the community.
The vow was fulfilled out in the open air,
Support for reform was won then and there.

十、焚券买义（冯谖）

战国时期齐国的孟尝君在薛的封地，好久没收上债来。门客冯谖自告奋勇到薛地收债款。他到薛地后，将所有欠债人召集起来，宣布孟尝君生性宽厚，了解大家的疾苦，接着拿出所有债券当场烧毁。回来向孟尝君复命说："我买来了你最缺的东西信和义。"孟尝君听后一时不高兴，也不好说什么。后来他在政治上失意，回到薛地，受到很多人欢迎，此时才深知信和义的价值。

10. Burning IOUs to Win People's Support

During the Warring States period, Lord Mengchang of the State of Qi owned a manor in Xue, but he had not been able to collect rents and debts for a long time. His retainer, Feng Xuan, volunteered to go to Xue to recover the debts. Upon arriving, Feng Xuan gathered all the debtors and announced that Lord Mengchang was kind-hearted and understood their hardships. He then took all the IOUs and burned them right there. When Feng Xuan returned to report to Lord Mengchang, he said, "I've bought what you lack the most—righteousness and loyalty." Upon hearing this, Lord Mengchang was initially displeased and didn't know how to respond. Later, when he faced political setbacks and returned to his manor in Xue, he was warmly welcomed by the people. It was then that he truly understood the value of righteousness and loyalty.

冯谖奉命收欠债　焚毁债券薛民快
狡兔三窟孟尝至　薛地信义早买来

Feng Xuan was tasked with rent and debt collection,
Yet burned all the IOUs and won the people's affection.
Lord Mengchang was like a sly hare with three burrows,
Winning righteousness and loyalty before he faced sorrows.

十一、千金买骨（燕昭王）

战国时期，燕昭王立志振兴，设黄金台广招贤才，一时未招到贤人。臣子郭隗说："听说有人要买千里马，三年没有买到。其手下人却用五百金买了一匹良马的骨头。"燕昭王不理解，郭隗说："此人买死马都用高价，何况活马，说明他买马有诚意。我今不才，你对我重金礼遇，何愁比我强得多的贤才不来。"燕昭王重金聘了郭隗，立招贤的黄金台，不久乐毅等贤才纷纷应聘。燕昭王重用乐毅，取得伐齐的大胜。

11. Buying a Horse's Skeleton with a Thousand Ounces of Gold

During the Warring States period, King Zhao of Yan was determined to revitalize his state, so he established a golden platform to recruit talented individuals. However, no one came. His minister, Guo Wei, then said: "I've heard of a man who sought to buy a renowned steed but spent three years searching without success. Meanwhile, one of his attendants bought the skeleton of a prized horse for five hundred ounces of gold." King Zhao of Yan was puzzled and didn'tunderstand the significance. Guo Wei explained: "If he's willing to pay such a high price for a dead horse, just imagine how much more he would offer for a living one. This shows his sincerity. Though I am but a mediocre man, Your Majesty is offering me such a generous reward. Why should you worry about attracting men of far greater talent?" King Zhao of Yan, moved by Guo Wei's reasoning, hired him at a generous price. Not long after, many other outstanding individuals, such as Yue Yi, came forward to offer their services. King Zhao appointed Yue Yi to a high position, and under his leadership, Yan secured a great victory over the State of Qi.

> 黄金台立求时贤　千金买骨远近传
> 求贤若渴示诚意　招来才俊兴北燕

The golden platform was erected to entice the able,
And buying the dead horse for gold became a well-known fable.
Sincerity proved a magnet for drawing talents,
And Northern Yan was soon awash with gallants.

十二、富商失信（富商）

　　《郁离子》里记着一个故事：一个富商过河时，船沉了，他抓住一根木头大叫："我是洛阳最大的富商，谁把我救上来，我给他一百两金子。"一个渔夫把他救上来后，他说："一个打渔的，给你十两就不少了。"渔夫不高兴，向别人说起此事。不久，此富商又掉进水里，大声呼救说救他可以给很多钱。大家都知道他是个失信的人，谁也不救他，富商就被淹死了。

12. A Wealthy Merchant Breaks his Promise

The famous text Crucible of Civility recounts the following story: A wealthy merchant was crossing a river when his boat sank. Grasping a piece of floating wood, he shouted, "I am the wealthiest merchant in Luoyang. Whoever rescues me will be rewarded with 100 taels of gold." A fisherman came to his aid, but the merchant replied, "You are just a fisherman, so 10 taels of gold will be more than enough." The fisherman, displeased by the merchant's response, told others about the incident. Not long after, the merchant found himself drowning again and once again promised a large reward for his rescue. However, by now, everyone knew he was untrustworthy. No one came to help, and he perished in the river.

世人尊重言而信　卑视说谎与骗人
富商行为背常理　无人施救害自身

Ordinary people respect a man of his word,
Liars and cheats will end up being slurred.
The merchant was a paragon of dishonesty,
And eventually paid the ultimate penalty.

十三、圯下授书（张良）

秦朝末年，韩国公子张良为反暴秦，毁家纾难，在博浪沙袭击秦始皇未成后，逃到了下邳。一日，在圯上见一老人，有意把鞋掉到桥下，令张良取上来。张良为他拾起穿好后，老人说"孺子可教"。要他明日一早来此。次日张良一早来到，老人已到，责他失信。第三天，张良再提前前去，老人又已先到。第四天，张良半夜便去桥头，见老人慢慢走来，说"孺子守信"。接着拿出一部书交给张良说："读此书可以为王者师。"张良读此《太公兵法》，帮助刘邦出谋划策，得了天下。

13. Passing on a Book under a Bridge

Toward the end of the Qin Dynasty, Zhang Liang, a nobleman from the State of Han, dedicated himself to opposing the tyranny of Qin. In the process, he lost both his fortune and his family. After a failed assassination attempt on Emperor Qin Shihuang at Bolangsha, he arrived in Xia Pi. One day, Zhang Liang encountered an old man on a bridge who appeared to drop his shoes deliberately, asking Zhang to retrieve them. After doing so and helping the man put the shoes on, the old man remarked, "This boy is teachable," and instructed him to return the following morning. The next day, Zhang Liang arrived early, only to find the old man had already arrived and reproached him for not keeping his word. On the second day, Zhang arrived early again, but the old man had already beaten him to the spot. On the fourth day, Zhang Liang came at midnight, just in time to see the old man leisurely approaching. This time, the old man said, "The boy is a man of his word." He then handed Zhang Liang a book, saying, "Anyone who reads this book can be fit to advise a monarch." Zhang Liang read the book, *The Art of War of Duke Tai*, and later shared its strategies with Liu Bang Eventually, Liu Bang rose to power and became the emperor.

流落下邳思反秦　圯桥之上遇高人
孺子守信宝书送　辅刘兴汉立殊勋

Despite wayfaring at Xia Pi, Zhang Liang remained an antagonist of Qin,
A mysterious stranger at the bridge devised tests to reel him in,
Eventually rewarding him with a book on military strategy,
Which was used to help Liu Bang found the Han Dynasty.

十四、约法三章（萧何）

秦末农民战争后，接着是刘邦、项羽之间的楚汉相争。公元前206年，刘邦率军进入咸阳，结束了暴秦的统治。为了取信于民，发展力量，申明军纪，抚恤将士，除了废除秦朝的各种苛征暴敛外，由萧何主持对咸阳的军民"约法三章"："杀人者死，伤人及盗者抵罪。" 发布后严厉执行。而项羽进入咸阳后，却大肆杀戮，放火烧了秦宫，明为诛暴秦，但在百姓面前不守信义，最终败于刘邦。

14. Promulgating Three Provisional Laws

After the peasant uprisings that marked the fall of the Qin Dynasty, the conflict between the State of Chu and the State of Han—specifically between their leaders Liu Bang and Xiang Yu—intensified. In 206 BC, Liu Bang led his army into Xianyang,the capital of the Qin Empire, effectively ending the tyrannical rule of the Qin Dynasty. To gain the trust of the people, strengthen his own power, affirm military discipline, compensate his soldiers, and abolish the harsh and exploitative taxes imposed by the Qin, Xiao He proposed "Three Provisional Laws" to the military and civilians of Xianyang: A murderer shall be put to death. Those who cause injury or theft will be punished according to their crimes. These laws were enacted and strictly enforced. In contrast, after Xiang Yu entered Xianyang, he engaged in widespread killing, looting, and burned down the Qin Palace. Although this was ostensibly to punish the tyrannical Qin, Xiang Yu failed to honor his promises to the people,leading to his eventual downfall.

秦亡楚汉战火兴　刘项二人争雌雄
约法三章示诚信　修德行仁必成功

Chu and Han waged wars after the demise of Qin,
Liu Bang and Xiang Yu competed, the leadership to win.
Xiao He's Three Provisional Laws showed sincerity,
Laying a foundation for the rise of the Han Dynasty.

十五、一诺千金（季布）

楚汉相争时，季布是项羽手下一员大将。几次打败刘邦。刘邦称帝后，到处下令捉拿他。他先在姓周的朋友家里躲藏。为了安全，朋友把他送到当时以任侠出名的朱家家里。朱家把他隐藏后，去找与刘邦关系密切的汝阴候夏侯婴。夏向刘邦说当年各为其主，不能怪他，刘邦将他赦免，并令他做了郎中。季布的同乡曹邱，当年对季布不礼，来找季布时，十分谦恭，季布也以礼相待。曹离开后，到处宣传"得黄金百金，不如季布一诺"。此后，"一诺千金"便成为赞扬人们守信的成语了。

15. One Word Can Be Worth a Thousand Ounces of Gold

During the conflict between the States of Chu and Han, Ji Bu was a distinguished general under Xiang Yu. He defeated Liu Bang several times in battle. After Liu Bang ascended to the throne, he issued a nationwide order to capture Ji Bu. Ji Bu first took refuge in the household of the Zhou family. For his safety, they then sent him to the Zhu family, known for their reputation of gallantry and chivalry. Once assured of Ji Bu's safety, the Zhu family head went to seek the help of Xiahou Ying, the Marquis of Ruyin, who was closely associated with Liu Bang. Xiahou explained to Liu Bang that Ji Bu was not at fault, as during wartime, generals fight loyally under their commanders. Ji Bu had simply been fulfilling his duty by serving Xiang Yu. After this conversation, Liu Bang pardoned Ji Bu and appointed him as a vice minister. Cao Qiu, a fellow native of Ji Bu's hometown, had once treated Ji Bu with disrespect. But when Cao came to visit Ji Bu, he showed him great courtesy, and Ji Bu reciprocated with equal respect. After leaving, Cao Qiu spread the saying: "A hundred ounces of gold is no match for Ji Bu's promise." From that time on, the phrase "one word can be worth a thousand ounces of gold" became an idiom used to praise those who are true to their word.

季布辅项功劳多　汉皇理解免罪过
曹丘感恩四处赞　千金不如季布诺

Ji Bu's deeds for Xiang Yu were grand,
Yet Emperor Liu Bang pardoned with a noble Hand.
Cao Qiu was grateful to Ji Bu and his praises widely told,
One timely word from him was worth a thousand ounces of gold.

十六、持旌牧羊（苏武）

苏武，字子卿，西汉杜陵（今陕西西安附近）人。武帝天汉初年，官至中郎将，奉命持节出使匈奴。匈奴单于诱其投降，不允，将其置于大窖中，他饮雪食毡，人以为神。又将其放逐到人迹罕见的北海，令其放羊。苏武坚守信义，手持汉节，日夜想念汉朝。过了十九年，宣帝时汉匈和好，才返回故国。苏武去世后，宣帝将其列为麒麟阁十一功臣之一，以彰显其节操。

16. Hoisting a Banner While Tending Sheep

Su Wu, styled Ziqing, was born in Duling (modern-day near Xi'an, Shaanxi) during the Western Han Dynasty. In the early years of Emperor Wu's reign, Su Wu rose to the rank of General of the Imperial Guards and was appointed as an envoy to the Xiongnu. Upon his arrival, Chanyu, the leader of the Xiongnu, tried to coax Su Wu into surrendering, but Su Wu refused. As a result, Chanyu imprisoned him in a cellar, where he was forced to drink melted snow and eat woolen carpet. The locals began to revere him as a figure of divine endurance. Later, Su Wu was exiled to Beihai, the most remote and desolate part of the empire, where he was assigned the task of tending sheep. Despite his harsh circumstances, Su Wu remained steadfast, clutching the imperial seal of the Han Dynasty and constantly longing for his homeland. After nineteen long years, when Emperor Xuan of Han finally negotiated peace with the Xiongnu, Su Wu was able to return home. Upon his death, Emperor Xuan honored him by placing him among the Eleven Great Contributors in the Qilin Pavilion, a testament to his unwavering loyalty and moral integrity.

苏武牧羊十九年　渴饮雪水饥吞毡
手持汉节永不改　心怀信义仁德全

For nineteen years Su Wu tended his flock,
Swallowing snow and carpet around the clock.
The banner of the Han was his touchstone,
He was benevolent and moral, though he suffered alone.

十七、舍子守义（齐妇）

汉朝《列女传》记：齐宣王时，有人打架斗殴被打死在路上。官吏认定兄弟二人是凶手。问到哥哥，说是自己杀的。问到弟弟，也说是自己杀的。当问到他们的母亲时，回答："是小儿子干的。" 齐相问为什么？她说："大儿子是丈夫的前妻生的，丈夫临终前嘱托自己照顾他；小的是自己生的，丈夫临终前嘱托自己照顾他，不能因私爱废除信义。"这一行为感动了齐相，报告给齐宣王，赦了他的两个儿子。

17. Discarding a Son to Remain Righteous

The Biographies of Virtuous Women, compiled during the Han Dynasty, tells the following story: During the reign of King Xuan of Qi, a man was killed in a street brawl. The authorities identified two brothers as the suspects. When questioned, the elder brother confessed to the crime. The younger brother, however, also claimed responsibility. When their mother was asked, she stated, "It was the younger son who killed him." The prime minister then inquired why she would make such an accusation. She explained, "The elder son is from my husband's first wife. Before he died, my husband entrusted me with the care of this boy. The younger son is my own child. Therefore, I cannot allow my affection for the younger one to interfere with my duty to uphold righteousness." Her unwavering commitment to justice moved the primeminister, who reported her actions to King Xuan of Qi. Impressed by her integrity, the king pardoned both of her sons.

齐义继母讲诚信　亡夫嘱托记得真
宁舍亲子全信义　关键时刻见真心

The stepmother in Qi stayed loyal and wise,
To her late husband's words, she did not compromise.
She'd give up her own son to keep her pledge tight,
In a critical moment, her true heart shone bright.

十八、鸡黍待友（范式）

东汉明帝时山阳(今山东金乡)人范式,去洛阳太学应试时,病在旅店里。与他同住一店的张劭对他精心照料,关系密切。后来双双考中,二人在太学同学三年,相互照顾,亲如兄弟。重阳节离别时,约定每年重阳时,互相去看望对方的父母。一年重阳节时,范式请母亲杀了鸡,煮好黍(黄米),以备接待张劭。等了半天还未到,范母心想:千里迢迢,张劭不一定按时来到。正午时,张劭按时骑马来到,范式家以鸡黍接待了挚友。此后,人们将他们住的范庄改名"鸡黍"。皇帝为表彰他们守信的行为,拨款在村里造了"二贤祠"。

18. Entertaining a Friend with Chicken and Millet Rice

During the reign of Emperor Ming of the Eastern Han Dynasty, Fan Shi, a native of Shanyang (modern-day Jinxiang, Shandong), fell ill on his way to Luoyang to take the imperial examination. Zhang Shao, who shared the same inn, took great care of him, and they formed a close bond. Both eventually passed the examination and spent three years at the Imperial Academy, where they continued to support each other like brothers. When they parted on the Double Ninth Festival, they made a pact to visit each other's parents every year on that same date. One year, as the festival approached, Fan Shi asked his mother to prepare a chicken and cook millet rice in anticipation of Zhang Shao's visit. After waiting for half the day, Fan Shi's mother thought to herself, "Given that Zhang Shao is traveling from far away, he might not arrive on time." But just as noon approached, Zhang Shao arrived on horseback,punctual as promised. Fan Shi's family warmly hosted him with the prepared meal of chicken and millet rice. From that day on, the village where they lived was known as "Chicken and Millet". In recognition of their unwavering commitment to keeping their word, the emperor allocated funds to build a "Twin-Shrined Temple" in the village to commemorate their sincerity.

范式张劭乐交心　重阳承诺探双亲
杀鸡蒸黍挚友至　二贤祠内赞诚信

Fan Shi and Zhang Shao, hearts intertwined,
On Double Ninth, they'd visit each other's parents, their promise aligned.
Fan Shi entertained his friend with millet rice and hen,
A "Twin-Shrined Temple" recalls the fraternity of these two men.

十九、示信亡友（朱晖）

东汉南阳宛人朱晖，有气节，讲诚信。与同县人张湛是以信义相交的好友。张的妻子怀孕不久，他身患重病，临终前拜托朱晖照顾自己的妻子及未出生的孩子，朱晖答应下来。张湛死后不久，张妻生下一个男孩取名张友。朱晖在生活上无微不至地照顾张氏母子，并教育张友读书明理。十几年后张友成为一名有为的青年。朱晖后来当上临淄太守，他的朋友推荐一官职叫他儿子去做，他为了示信于亡友，举荐张友上任。后来，张友干得很称职，朱晖为实现当年对朋友的承诺而欣慰。

19. Showing Sincerity to a Dead Friend

Zhu Hui was a man of integrity from Nanyang during the Eastern Han Dynasty, known for his sincerity and strong sense of honor. His close friend, Zhang Zhan, also from the same county, was a man of similar values. When Zhang's wife became pregnant, Zhang was struck by a severe illness. On his deathbed, he entrusted his wife and unborn child to Zhu Hui's care. Zhu Hui solemnly vowed to fulfill this responsibility. Shortly after, Zhang Zhan passed away, and his wife gave birth to a son, whom they named Zhang You. Zhu Hui took meticulous care of the mother and child, providing for their needs and ensuring that Zhang You received a proper education, instilling in him wisdom and moral values. Over the years, Zhang You grew into a capable young man. Later, Zhu Hui was appointed the governor of Linzi, and one of his friends offered him a government position for his own son. However, in order to honor his promise to his deceased friend, Zhu Hui recommended Zhang You for the post instead. Zhang You proved to be highly competent, and Zhu Hui was deeply gratified to see that he had honored his pledge to his old friend.

张湛临终托至友　朱晖受托遗愿酬
亡友妻儿勤照料　荐侄为官世少有

Zhang Zhan willed his wife and unborn baby to a bosom friend,
Zhu Hui made a promise to look after them til the end.
He oversaw the wife and son with the utmost care,
To favour this boy ahead of his own was generosity most rare.

二十、舍命护友（荀巨伯）

东汉许州人荀巨伯，到远方去看望生病的友人，正值北方的胡人攻城掠地，烧杀抢掠，全城的百姓纷纷逃跑。病友也要他快逃。他说："我来看望你的，我们是朋友，我怎能扔下你不管，只顾自己呢？"荀巨伯一直没离开病友。胡人攻破城后，见他没逃走，要杀他们。他说："为照顾病友，我不能离开。要杀先杀我，不要杀一个生病的人。"胡人被他舍命护友守信的精神感化，不但没杀他们，全城的百姓也得以幸免。

20. Safeguarding a Friend at the Cost of One's Life

Xun Jubo was from Xuzhou during the Eastem Han Dynasty. Once, he traveled a great distance to visit a sick friend at a time when northern tribes were attacking cities,looting, and burning everything in their path. The people of his friend's city, terrified, fled in all directions. Even his ill friend urged him to escape. But Xun Jubo replied, "I came to visit you, and we are friends. How could I leave you behind to save myself?" So, he remained by his friend's side. When the northern tribes breached the city walls and found the two men together, they were about to kill them. Xun Jubo said, "I cannot leave because I must care for my sick friend. Kill me first, but spare the sick man." The tribesmen, moved by his willingness to sacrifice himself for his friend,were so touched by his loyalty and integrity that they spared both men. Not only that, they refrained from harming any of the other residents of the city.

好个诚信荀巨伯　探望友人生死随
舍命护友胡人敬　赦免全城功德巍

Xun Jubo, a man of honesty rare,
He stayed by his sick friend with utmost care.
The tribesmen saw his loyalty so true,
His sacrifice spared the city, and the people too.

二十一、李善抚孤（李善）

东汉初，南阳人李善，是当地富户李元家的管家。建武年间，瘟疫流行，李元家数口人均死于瘟疫，只剩下几个月的孤儿李续。面对着李元的万贯家财，一些婢仆议论杀死孤儿，瓜分财产。李善却感念李元对自己的信任，自己也表示过忠于主人，便抱着孤儿逃到山阳瑕丘县中，含辛茹苦地赡养孤儿李续。十岁时送李续回归故里，令其读书成人。李善抚孤的事迹，被瑕丘县令钟离意上报朝廷，皇帝对其表彰，还将李善拜为太子舍人。

21. Raising an Orphan

Li Shan, from Nanyang, served as a steward for a wealthy family during the early Eastern Han Dynasty. In the Jianwu era, a devastating plague struck the region, causing the deaths of all members of the Li Yuan family except for Li Xu, an infant just a few months old. When some of the maidservants and servants suggested killing the orphan to divide up the estate, Li Shan, feeling deep gratitude for the trust Li Yuan had placed in him, remained loyal. He resolved to protect the child and, despite the challenges, took Li Xu to Xiaqiu County in Shanyang Prefecture, where he raised the orphan with great care and hardship. When Li Xu turned ten, Li Shan sent him back to his hometown and arranged for him to receive an education. The touching story of Li Shan's selflessness was brought to the attention of the Imperial Court by the magistrate of Xiaqiu County, Zhong Liyi. In recognition of Li Shan's exemplary loyalty and compassion, the Emperor praised him and appointed him as an attendant to the Crown Prince.

瘟疫夺去李元家　万贯家产乱抢拿
李善托孤守信义　朝廷表彰百姓夸

Li Yuan's whole family succumbed to an epidemic,
His fortune was coveted by the green-eyed and pathetic.
Li Shan kept his promise and raised the orphan,
And the Court and people hailed his devotion.

二十二、对童守信（郭伋）

郭伋，字细侯，东汉初期茂陵人。任并州牧时，政绩卓著。在一次巡查吏治时，几百个小孩骑着竹马欢迎他，他下马答礼。孩子们问他什么时候回来，他计算了下日程，说了个日子。此次巡查很顺利，早结束了一天，为了守信，他不进城，点起篝火在城外过了一夜，第二天进城按时和孩子们见面。此事传到宫中，光武帝说："真乃信之至也。"

22. Honouring a Promise Made to Children

Guo Ji, styled Xihou, was born in Maoling during the early Eastern Han Dynasty. As the governor of Bingzhou, he earned a reputation for his outstanding governance. On one of his official inspections, he was greeted by hundreds of children riding bamboo sticks as makeshift horses. Guo Ji dismounted and returned their salute. The children asked when he would return to visit them again. After calculating his schedule, he promised them a specific date. The inspection was completed a day ahead of schedule. However, in order to keep his promise, Guo Ji chose not to enter the city immediately. Instead, he spent the night by a campfire in the countryside and returned to the city the following day, precisely when he had promised the children. When this story reached the palace, Emperor Guangwu of Han remarked, "Here is the most faithful of men."

诚实守信是根本　不论童稚或成人
郭伋晚到示守信　信之至也诚之魂

Virtue and honesty form the core of all,
For child or adult, these virtues stand tall.
Guo Ji showed his honesty by keeping his pledge,
In faith and sincerity he took the leading edge.

二十三、葬友护子（朱震）

东汉末年，东林党人陈蕃被当权的宦官迫害致死，他的许多亲戚朋友、门生故吏均慑于宦官的淫威，不敢出面为其收尸下葬。陈蕃当年的好友朱震，时任铚县县令，听到噩耗后，马上弃官前去为陈蕃收尸埋葬，还把陈蕃的儿子保护起来。宦官将朱震捉住下狱，逼他说出陈子的下落。任凭宦官多次拷打，他绝不说出，体现出对朋友患难相助、诚实守信的高尚品格。

23. Burying a Friend and Protecting His Son

In the late Eastern Han Dynasty, Chen Fan, a member of the Donglin Party, was persecuted to death by a powerful eunuch. Many of his relatives, friends, disciples,and subordinates, fearing the eunuch's tyranny, dared not step forward to retrieve and bury his body. However, Zhu Zhen, a close friend of Chen Fan and the magistrate of Zhi County, upon hearing the tragic news, immediately abandoned his official post and went to recover Chen Fan's remains for burial. In addition, he took it upon himself to protect Chen Fan's son. The eunuch had Zhu Zhen arrested and thrown into prison, demanding that he reveal the whereabouts of Chen Fan's son. Despite being tortured repeatedly, Zhu Zhen remained silent, refusing to betray his friend. His steadfast loyalty and integrity in the face of danger, and his unshakable commitment to helping a friend in need, were a testament to his noble character.

恶宦乱政杀陈蕃　门生故吏莫敢言
好友朱震讲信义　精心育侄惧万难

The eunuch persecuted Chen Fan until he died,
His students and underlings were left tongue-tied.
Even so, his good friend Zhu Zhen's virtue prevailed,
He would not betray the victim's son even when jailed.

二十四、割发代首（曹操）

东汉末年的丞相，三国时被封为魏王的曹操，建安三年率兵征讨张秀时，正值麦熟季节。百姓们见官兵来到，扔下镰刀就跑。曹操下令全军上下都不许践踏麦田，违令者斩。大小将领、兵士们谨遵此令。突然飞来几只鸟，惊了曹操的马，此马窜入麦田，毁了一片庄稼。曹操立即叫来大家，商议如何给自己治罪。他说："按律当斩。"大家说他是主帅，不应杀头，在大家一再劝说下，曹操决定割下自己的头发、胡须，以此惩罚代替杀头之罪。

24. Cutting One's Hair to Keep One's Head

Cao Cao, the Prime Minister of the Eastern Han Dynasty and later the King of Wei during the Three Kingdoms period, led an army to subdue Zhang Xiu in the third year of the Jian'an era, which coincided with the wheat harvest. As soon as the locals saw the soldiers approaching, they dropped their sickles and fled. Cao Cao immediately issued an order forbidding his troops to tread on the wheat fields, with the penalty of beheading for anyone who violated it. The generals and soldiers obeyed the order without hesitation. However, as a few birds flew overhead, Cao Cao's horse was startled and bolted into the wheat fields, trampling a section of the crops. Cao Cao quickly called a meeting with his officers to discuss how to punish himself. He stated, "According to the law, I should be beheaded." His officers protested, saying that as the commander, he should not be subjected to such a punishment. After repeated persuasion, Cao Cao decided to cut off his own hair and beard as a substitute for the death penalty.

曹操带兵法令严　践踏麦田应问斩
飞鸟惊马已犯过　割发代首示诺言

Cao Cao governed his army with rules most strict,
Decapitation for damaging crops was one edict.
But stray birds caused his steed to bolt across the wheat field,
A trim and not a deathblow - his troops managed to make him yield.

二十五、邓攸弃子（邓攸）

晋代襄陵人邓攸，字伯道，曾任河东太守，是一位很守信用的人。晋永嘉元年羯人石勒在北方征战，邓攸的兄弟被杀前，托付他照顾自己的幼子。当他背着小侄，妻子抱着自己的儿子逃难时，乱兵追来。妻子身体纤弱，为了逃命，把儿子交给他，邓攸力气也不大，带着两个孩子也跑不动。为了不致于同归于尽，毅然抛下自己的孩子，背着侄儿跑。虽然自己的孩子死于乱兵之手，却在危难中保住兄弟的儿子，完成亡弟的重托。

25. Deng You Abandons His Own Son

Deng You, styled Bodao, was from Xiangling in the Jin Dynasty. Known for his unwavering integrity, he served as the governor of Hedong Prefecture. In the first year of the Yongjia period, Shi Le, a member of the Jie people, waged a campaign in the north. Before his death, Deng You's brother entrusted him with the care of his young son. While fleeing with his wife, who was holding their own son, Deng You carried his nephew on his back. As they were pursued by a group of rogue soldiers, his wife, frail and exhausted, handed their son to Deng You. Feeling the strain of carrying both children, Deng You realized that if they were caught together, all would perish. In a heart-wrenching decision, he abandoned his own son and continued to flee with his nephew. Though his own son was killed by the soldiers, Deng You fulfilled his brother's final request and saved the life of his nephew, proving himself worthy of the immense trust placed in him.

忠诚仁爱邓伯道　　为保孤侄亲子抛
亡弟托付守诚信　　乱世方显素质高

Deng Bodao was loyal and benevolent,
He forsook his own son to save his nephew innocent.
He kept his word and fulfilled his brother's great trust,
Troubled times will tell if a man is truly just.

二十六、乘船守信（华歆）

有一次，华歆与同伴王朗乘着一条小船逃难。船不大，又装了一些东西，走得很慢。忽然岸上有一人急切地要上他们的船逃难。华歆很为难，王朗说还装得下，叫那人上船。这样船走的更慢了。为防追兵追来，王朗叫那人下船。华歆说："既然答应他上来，不能因为危难将人家抛下。"大家努力划船，不久摆脱了追兵，也完成了信诺。

26. Taking a Boat and Keeping His Word

On one occasion, Hua Xin and his companion Wang Lang were escaping danger in a small boat. The vessel was not large and was weighed down with cargo, so it moved slowly. Suddenly, a man appeared on the shore, urgently seeking refuge on their boat. Hua Xin was troubled by the request, but Wang Lang, noting there was still space, urged the man to board. The boat's pace slowed even further. Fearing that they might be overtaken by pursuing soldiers, Wang Lang suggested that the man disembark. However, Hua Xin replied, "Since we have already agreed to let him aboard, we cannot abandon him in this moment of danger." They then rowed with all their strength, soon managing to outrun their pursuers and ultimately kept their promise.

> 乱世逃难乘小船　恻隐之心解人难
> 危急加重持原意　坚守承诺学圣贤

Fleeing in a boat at times of unrest,
Few are with compassion naturally blessed.
And yet they stuck to their original position,
Like a sage they selected a noble mission.

二十七、违约失礼（陈元方）

魏晋时期，陈太丘与一位朋友约定正午时一起出门。正午过后，等了好久，朋友还没来，陈太丘只好自己先走。过了好长时间，朋友来到，向正在门前玩耍的陈太丘的儿子陈元方询问。陈元方说："家父等了好久，您没来，他自己走了。"这位朋友气愤地说："太不像话了！约好一起走，不等我，这是人办的事吗？"小陈元方驳他说："是你失信晚来，还守着人家的儿子骂他的父亲，太无理了。"此人感到羞愧。正要再说明一下，陈元方早跑进屋里，不理他了。

27. A Breach of Etiquette Caused by Breaking a Promise

During the Wei and Jin Dynasties, Chen Taiqiu and a friend had agreed to go out together at midday. After waiting for a long time, well past noon, and seeing no sign of his friend, Chen Taiqiu decided to go ahead alone. Eventually, his friend arrived and spoke with Chen Yuanfang, Chen Taiqiu's son, who was playing in front of the door. Chen Yuanfang replied, "My father waited for you for quite a while, but since you didn't show up, he went ahead on his own." The friend, outraged, retorted, "This is outrageous! We had made a promise to go together, yet he left without me. Is this the behavior of an honorable man?" Chen Yuanfang countered, "You broke your promise, and it is impolite to insult a father in front of his son." The man, feeling ashamed, tried to defend himself but was met with silence as Chen Yuanfang ran into the house, ignoring him.

违约失信不检点　颠倒情理胡搅缠
以错为对缺诚信　稚子面前应汗颜

An adults breaking a promise is not some minor offence,
This man showed his dishonesty by feeding the child a pretence.
He asked the boy to swallow that black could be taken for white,
No wonder he ended up a pathetic, lonely sight.

二十八、守信自责（皇甫绩）

隋朝时的大臣皇甫绩，其父、祖都是北朝显宦。三岁时父亲去世，母亲带着他到外祖父家居住。外祖父对他特别疼爱，叫他与几个表兄弟一起在家塾中学习，明确规定谁不按时完成作业打二十板。有一天，几人贪玩，都没完成作业。外祖父将他几个表兄每人打了二十板。念他幼小，又是孤儿，饶了他。外祖父走后，他请表兄也打自己二十板，一再说明犯错受罚，自己不应例外。皇甫绩自小就对自己严格要求，依承诺办事，努力攻读，终于成名。

28. Being Upright and Strict with Oneself

Huangfu Ji lived during the Sui Dynasty. Both his father and grandfather had been prominent officials in the Northern Dynasties. He lost his father when he was just three years old, and his mother took him to live with his maternal grandfather. His grandfather was particularly fond of him and arranged for him to study alongside his cousins under a family tutor. The grandfather set a clear rule: anyone who failed to complete their homework on time would receive twenty strokes. One day, the cousins became distracted by play and neglected their studies. The grandfather punished the older boys, but, seeing Huangfu Ji's youth and orphaned status, he spared him.However, after the grandfather left, Huangfu Ji insisted that his cousin punish him with twenty strokes, explaining that he too was at fault and should not be exempt.From a young age, Huangfu Ji was strict with himself. Once he made a commitment, he saw it through, diligently pursued his studies, and eventually achieved great renown.

小小孩童皇甫绩　聪颖仁德爱学习
学时犯错未挨打　求补责打严律己

Huangfu Ji was clever and kind beyond his tender age,
His thirst for studying was difficult to assuage.
And yet when spared, though in the wrong,
He actively sought the rod and proved his virtue was strong.

二十九、守信归银（李勉）

李勉是唐高祖李渊的玄孙，他幼年时便努力攻读，讲究诚信，不取无义之财。有一次，他外出游学，在旅店里遇见一个准备进京赶考的学子，两人成为好友。不久，此人病倒，李勉求医买药，对他日夜照顾。此人病势日重，眼看不久人世，请他从床下找出一个小木箱，内有一百两银子，说主要用来酬谢李勉，少量交给自己的家属，李勉表示自己不能要。此人死后，李勉用这批钱给他办了丧事后，把银子全部交给死者家属。完成朋友的嘱托。

29. Returning Silver and Being Trustworthy

Li Mian was the great-grandson of Li Yuan, the founding emperor of the Tang Dynasty. From a young age, he was dedicated to his studies, emphasizing integrity and believing that wealth obtained through dishonest means was immoral. On one of his travels, he met a scholar who was preparing for the imperial examinations, and the two became close friends. Soon after, the scholar fell ill, and Li Mian, compassionate and devoted, sought doctors and purchased medicine, caring for him day and night. As the scholar's condition worsened and death seemed imminent, he called Li Mian to his bedside, where he retrieved a small wooden box containing 100 taels of silver. The scholar offered it to Li Mian as a token of gratitude, with instructions to give a small portion to his family. Li Mian refused to accept it. After the scholar passed away, Li Mian used the silver to cover the funeral expenses and returned the remaining amount to the scholar's family, honoring his friend's wishes and fulfilling his trust.

李勉助友终不弃　生医死葬示诚信
遗银不贪归遗属　方显君子坦诚心

In helping his friend Li Mian by devoted concern was led,
Buying medicine when alive and burying him when dead.
He didn't covet the money and returned it to relatives,
Showing his frankness of heart and unsullied motives.

三十、实言诚信（晏殊）

北宋时的宰相、诗人晏殊，儿时人称"神童"，年少时被推荐进京，十四岁时参加殿试，考试时沉着从容。当他看到出的题目时说："此题我以前做过，请改他题。" 宋真宗对他诚实的态度特别欣赏，考中后赐同进士出身，授其为秘书省正事。他任职时，太子东宫缺官，真宗任用晏殊，别人不理解。真宗说："一些阁臣无不去歌舞酒楼宴游，晏殊却不去。"晏殊说："我没钱，所以不去。" 真宗见他如此诚实，对他更加信任。他十九岁便当上翰林院学士左庶子。

30. Being Honest and Credible

Yan Shu was a prime minister and renowned poet during the Northern Song Dynasty. As a child prodigy, he was recommended to the capital and took the imperial examination at the age of fourteen. During the exam, he remained calm and composed. When he saw the topic, he said, "I've already answered this question before. Please provide me with a different one." Emperor Zhenzong greatly admired his honesty and, upon his success in the exam, awarded him the title of imperial scholar and appointed him to the position of archivist in the Royal Archives. When Yan Shu began his official duties, the Crown Prince's palace was short of staff, and Emperor Zhenzong appointed Yan Shu to serve in the Eastern Palace. Some people were puzzled by the Emperor's favor toward Yan Shu, so Zhenzong explained, "Most of the cabinet ministers frequent lavish restaurants and entertainment venues, but Yan Shu has never been to any of those places." Yan Shu humbly replied, "I don't have enough money to go there." The Emperor, impressed by his honesty, trusted him even more. At just nineteen years old, Yan Shu became a senior official in the Imperial Academy.

神童晏殊入殿试　考题做过请改题
爱说实话真宗喜　任命翰林左庶子

Yan Shu sat the imperial examination as a child prodigy,
And asked for a different question so as to be judged fairly.
He was admired by the Emperor Zhenzong for his honesty,
And promoted to a higher post in the Imperial Academy.

三十一、渴不食梨（许衡）

元朝人许衡，怀州河内人。他曾经在酷暑的时候路过河阳（今河南孟西县）。当时大家都很口渴，发现路边有棵梨树，许多人争先恐后地摘梨吃，只有许衡安坐树下，毫不动心。别人问他："为什么放着现成的梨不吃？"他说："不是自家的东西，没经人家主人同意，不能随便乱拿。"别人说："现在天下这么乱，这些梨树已没有主人了。"许衡回答："梨树没有主人，难道我心里也没有主人了吗？一个人在任何时候都要保持诚信的态度。"

31. Refusing to Eat a Pear When Parched

Xu Heng, a native of Henei in Huaizhou during the Yuan Dynasty, once traveled through Heyang (now located in Mengxi County, Henan) on a scorching summer day. Everyone was parched, and they happened upon a pear tree by the roadside. Many people eagerly rushed to pick and eat the pears, but Xu Heng calmly sat beneath the tree, showing no interest. When others asked him, "Why don't you eat a pear?" he replied, "We should not take what isn't ours without the owner's consent." Someone then argued, "In these troubled times, the pear trees have no owner." Xu Heng firmly responded, "Even if the pear trees have no owner, does that mean my conscience has no master? One must maintain honesty at all times, no matter the circumstances."

许衡诚信世间奇　口渴难忍不食梨
天下离乱梨无主　慎独君子严律己

An honest man like Xuheng is rare to behold,
He wouldn't steal a pear that hadn't been bestowed.
The chaos must have caused the tree's owner to flee,
But a gentleman never surrenders his integrity.

三十二、按期还书（宋濂）

明初学者宋濂，从小家里很穷，但酷爱读书。家中没有书，他到一些有书的人家借来读。好多富有人家藏书很多，怕他不还或不按时还，不愿借给他，他一再说明借书读后一定按时还。一家富户给他规定十天为限，他每次借到总是抓紧时间日夜诵读，读后按时送还。有一次下了暴雪，十天到了，他冒雪前去还书，主人很受感动，以后借给他看书的时间延长了。宋濂读了很多书，成为饱学之士，是明朝初年一位最有学问的大臣。

32. Returning Books on Time

Song Lian, a renowned scholar of the early Ming Dynasty, came from a poor family but had a deep love for reading. His household lacked books, so he often borrowed them from others. Many wealthy families had large collections, but they were hesitant to lend books for fear of them not being returned or not being returned on time. To address this concern, Song Lian repeatedly assured them that he would return the books promptly. One wealthy family set a deadline often days for him to return the books. Each time he borrowed a book, Song Lian made the most of his time, reading day and night, and always returned the books by the agreed-upon date. On one occasion, a heavy snowstorm struck just as the deadline approached. Despite the weather, Song Lian ventured out through the snow to return the book. His punctuality deeply moved the owner, who, impressed by his integrity, extended the lending period for future books. Song Lian read extensively and became a well-educated scholar, ultimately rising to become one of the most learned officials of the early Ming Dynasty.

宋濂家贫无书读　高邻家中多藏书
按时归还守诚信　明初诸贤为翘楚

Song Lian's family had no books to call their own,
He was forced to rely on neighbours who could lend and loan.
He returned the book on time to keep his pledge,
Of Ming Dynasty scholars he possessed great knowledge.

三十三、三粒种子（张老）

明朝人张老汉，一生勤劳，攒下的家业是一个饭店。三个儿子传给谁？老人想了个办法：把三个儿子叫来，拿出三粒花种，让他们各自拿回去种下，第二年检验。三人回去种后都不出芽。老大、老二便偷偷买来同样的种子种上。第二年检验时，二人喜气洋洋地夸自己种的好，唯有老三羞愧地拿着没有发芽的盆。老人说："我这三粒种子都是炒熟的，根本不能发芽。老三有实在的好品德。"日后遗产便给了老三。

33. Three Seeds

Old Zhang, a man of the Ming Dynasty, worked diligently throughout his life and eventually became the owner of a restaurant. When it came time to decide which of his three sons would inherit his business, Old Zhang devised a plan. He called his sons together and gave each of them three flower seeds, instructing them to plant them and return the following year for an inspection. When the sons planted the seeds, none of them sprouted. The first and second sons, eager to impress, secretly bought the same type of seeds and planted them. The next year, when the inspection took place, the first two sons proudly showed off their blooming flowers, boasting about how well they had cared for their plants. The youngest son, however, stood before his father holding a pot with seeds that had not germinated. Old Zhang smiled and said, "I had fried the seeds beforehand to ensure that they would never sprout. Only your youngest brother has acted with honesty and integrity." As a result, Old Zhang chose his third son as the rightful heir to his restaurant.

三粒种子验忠诚　老大老二太"聪明"
为人实在系本份　遗产理应老三承

Three seeds tested the virtues of the sons,
But the eldest two cheated, seeking new ones.
A man's nature is to be honest and sincere,
So the third son inherited, no reason he should share.

三十四、回报乡里（梁同志）

乾隆年间的梁同志，从小聪慧好学，但家里很穷，指望父亲做点小生意养家。他向父母苦苦哀求要读书，父母无钱，很为难。街坊邻居对他都很同情，纷纷伸出援助之手，给他买书供他上学。不久，又发展到全村里许多人都帮助他，他决心努力学习，日后报答乡邻。他在十七岁便中了举人，二十几岁中了状元。在朝内当官以后，未忘乡亲父老，经常给乡中办些好事，更体恤民情，人们都说他是一位恪守信义的好官。

34. Repaying One's Hometown

Liang Tongzhi lived during the reign of Emperor Qianlong in the Qing Dynasty. Though his family was poor, he was intelligent and eager to learn. His father, relying on small-scale business to support the family, was unable to afford his education. Liang pleaded with his parents to allow him to study, but they, in their financial struggle, were hesitant. The neighbors, deeply sympathetic to his situation, extended their help by purchasing books and supporting his education. Soon, many villagers joined in, offering their assistance. Determined to repay their kindness, Liang resolved to study diligently. At the age of seventeen, he passed the provincial imperial examination, and in his twenties, he became the top scholar in the imperial exams. After entering government service, he never forgot the help he received from his hometown. He frequently did good deeds for his village and showed great empathy for the people. His actions earned him a reputation as an upright official who valued integrity and kept his promises.

清代贫儿梁同志　酷爱读书学不起
邻邦乡助完夙愿　学成为官报乡里

Liang Tongzhi was poor but fond of education,
But his family could not afford his tuition.
His neighbours helped him to fulfil his dream,
Their favours he returned when he was the Court cream.

三十五、缺心警人（郑板桥）

清乾隆年间，"扬州八怪"之一郑板桥，书画均风格独特，为人也正直诚信。南昌城里有一点心店主李沙庚，做生意讲诚信，顾客盈门。但他赚了不少钱后，却掺杂使假，生意日渐冷落。他找到郑板桥，请他写几个字以招揽顾客。郑板桥挥笔写出"李沙庚点心店"。墨宝刚健有力，但人们发现"心"字缺一点，李沙庚请他补上，郑板桥说："你从前货真价实，有心，现在却不讲诚信，无心。"李沙庚重新又保证质量，恪守信誉。不久，郑板桥补上了那个点。

35. Warning a Shop Owner with a Deliberately Incomplete Chinese Character

During the reign of Emperor Qianlong of the Qing Dynasty, Zheng Banqiao, one of the Eight Eccentrics of Yangzhou, was renowned for his integrity as well as his distinctive style in both calligraphy and painting. Li Shageng, the owner of a cake shop in Nanchang, initially built his business on honesty and had a steady stream of customers. However, after making a considerable profit, he began selling inferior cakes, and his business started to decline. Seeking to revive his fortunes, he approached Zheng Banqiao and asked him to write a few words to attract customers. Zheng Banqiao wrote the inscription "Li Shageng's Hearty Cakes" in bold, vigorous script. However, upon closer inspection, people noticed that the character for "heart" (心) was missing a stroke. Li Shageng asked Zheng to complete the character, but Zheng replied, "In the past, you sold high-quality cakes with sincerity, but now you lack integrity and have no heart." Li Shageng was deeply moved and promised to restore the quality of his products. Not long after, Zheng Banqiao returned and added the final stroke to the character "heart".

货真价实客盈门　假冒伪劣少问津
板桥翰墨寓深意　重回诚信再补心

The shop thrived with customers seeking goods that were prime,
But business waned as quality fell over time.
Zheng Banqiao's calligraphy carried a moral so clear:
Restore your integrity, and the missing stroke will appear.

三十六、义葬秋瑾（徐自华）

清朝末年,女革命家秋瑾生前与挚友徐自华订有死后埋骨西湖之约。秋瑾就义后，徐自华信守当年之约，在吴芝瑛的帮助下，于 1908 年初将秋瑾葬于西湖边上西泠桥下。吴芝瑛亲自写了墓碑，徐自华为秋瑾写墓志铭，并加以印发，广泛送给亲友等人。秋瑾墓落成后，很多人前去凭吊，清政府下令毁掉。辛亥革命成功后，秋瑾墓又被迁往杭州。后建造了新墓和著名的"风雨亭"。

36. Burying Qiu Jin for the Sake of Righteousness

At the end of the Qing Dynasty, the female revolutionary Qiu Jin and her close friend Xu Zihua had made a pact that, should one of them die, the other would ensure their burial by the Xiling Bridge at West Lake. After Qiu Jin's martyrdom, Xu Zihua honored this promise. In early 1908, with the assistance of Wu Zhiying, Xu buried Qiu Jin at the agreed location. Wu Zhiying personally wrote the inscription for the tombstone, and Xu Zihua composed the epitaph, which was then printed and widely distributed to friends and supporters. After the tomb was completed, many people visited to pay their respects, but the Qing government ordered its destruction. Following the success of the 1911 Revolution, Qiu Jin's tomb was moved to Hangzhou, where it was rebuilt and named the "Wind and Rain Pavilion".

巾帼英雄生前盟　西泠桥下作坟茔
历尽艰苦还友愿　后人凭吊颂友情

When they were alive and young two heroines swore an oath,
Some day the Xiling Bridge should be the resting place for both.
Qiu Jin's wish was fulfilled after great hardship,
Later generations still come and honour her death and friendship.

第八章
清廉俭朴

Chapter Eight:

Upholding Integrity and Simplicity

一、不贪为宝（子罕）

春秋时期，有个宋国人得到一块美玉，有事要求助于当时任司城的子罕。便拿着这块玉去见子罕，说请他为自己办点事并拿出玉来说："这是一块难得的玉，是一块稀世珍宝。"子罕说："你以玉为宝，我以不贪为宝。你如果把玉送给我，我俩都失去了宝。你如果把玉拿回去，我们两人的宝都存在，何乐而不为呢？我不收你的宝，照样按规定给你办事。"子罕用这种语言拒贿，宋国人都盛赞子罕的宝：不贪。

1. Valuing Integrity Over Material Gain

During the Spring and Autumn period, a man from the State of Song came into possession of a rare piece of jade. Seeking a favor from Zi Han, the city magistrate, he brought the jade with him and said, "This is a precious jade, a priceless treasure." Zi Han responded, "You consider this jade a treasure, but I believe that refraining from greed is a far greater treasure. If you give me the jade, we will both lose our treasures. But if you keep it, both of our treasures remain intact. How about that? I will not accept your jade, but I will help you according to the rules." In this way, Zi Han rejected the bribe, and the people of Song praised him for his integrity and refusal to be swayed by material wealth.

> 不贪是宝玉是宝　宝物对人不可少
> 子罕拒宝得宝贵　留给后人识真宝

Not coveting and jade are both considered treasures,
The people use them as yardsticks and measures.
Zi Han's refusal meant his virtue stayed intact,
Later generations have learned from this fact.

二、一生节俭（季文子）

春秋时期，鲁国的执政大夫季文子，虽身居高位，吃、穿、住、行都很简朴。上朝时，孟献子见他穿粗布衣，说他小气。季文子说："一个人身居贫困，环境恶劣，知道节俭不难；身居高位知道节俭却很难。一个有道德的人，应克制自己的贪欲，才能令人信服。"一位友人到他家后，见无阔绰的家具，要送给他一套高档家具，被他婉言谢绝。他去世后，鲁君到他家看望时，见一些随葬品都是旧东西，查看他的账薄，更确认他一生节俭。

2. A Lifetime of Frugality

During the Spring and Autumn Period, Ji Wenzi, the Prime Minister of the State of Lu, led a simple life despite holding a high office. When he attended court, Meng Xianzi noticed his coarse hempen garments and mistook them for signs of stinginess. In response, Ji Wenzi said, "When a man is poor and faces difficult circumstances, frugality comes naturally. But for someone in a high position, practicing frugality is much more challenging. A virtuous person must restrain their greed to earn the respect of others." When a friend visited his home and saw the modest furnishings, he offered to buy him more luxurious furniture, but Ji Wenzi politely declined. After his death, the ruler of Lu visited his home to pay respects. There, he observed that even the items for the funeral were old, and upon inspecting Ji Wenzi's account books, he confirmed the extent of his lifelong frugality.

身居高位务节俭　何惧讥讽与闲言
勤政俭朴两相应　方显斯人仁德先

The frugal man, in high office he stood,
Unmoved by ridicule or gossip's rude.
Diligent in work, thrifty in his ways,
He showed his virtue, deserving of praise.

三、文帝俭朴（刘恒）

公元前180年，刘恒被人从代地请到京城当皇帝，是为汉文帝。他自小知民间疾苦，在母亲的教育下自奉节俭。他在位二十三年，朝内的宫室苑囿及各种饰物均未增添。臣下建议修一座楼台，他叫工匠计算了一下，要花百金。他说："这是中产人家一年的消费，还是别修了。"他规定宫内的后妃衣服不得拖地，帷帐不得饰文绣，食器不用金银。他交待自己死后葬事从简，只准戴三天孝，不要因此扰民。在他执政时，开创了"文景之治"。

3. The Thrifty Emperor Wen of the Han Dynasty

In 180 BC, Liu Heng was invited to leave Dai and ascend to the throne, becoming Emperor Wen of the Han Dynasty. From a young age, he was deeply aware of the hardships faced by the common people and, under his mother's guidance, developed a habit of frugality. He ruled for twenty-three years, during which he refrained from expanding the imperial gardens, adding lavish decorations, or commissioning extravagant works. When a court official suggested building a tower, Liu Heng had the architects calculate the cost, which amounted to one hundred pieces of gold. He remarked, "This is equivalent to the annual expenses of a middle-class family. Let's abandon this plan." He also set strict guidelines for palace life: concubines' robes were not to touch the floor, bed curtains were not to be embroidered, and no gold or silver tableware was to be used. Liu Heng decreed that his funeral should be simple, allowing only three days of official mourning to avoid causing distress to the people. During his reign, he ushered in the "Prosperity of Wenjing".

汉文古称仁德君　提倡节俭始自身
"文景之治"非虚话　勤俭致富得民心

Emperor Wen's virtue and kindness were more than ample,
He advocated thrift leading the people by example.
The "Prosperity of Wenjing" was no small feat,
His diligence and thrift won him favour complete.

四、自身裸葬（杨王孙）

汉朝城固（今陕西南郑）人杨王孙，家累千金，但反对社会上的各种奢靡行为，尤其反对当时流行的厚葬之风。在他晚年对儿孙们说："我死以后要裸葬，以恢复我的真面目。"儿孙们不理解，去请教他的好友祁侯。祁侯也表示反对，杨王孙说："厚葬花费很多钱财，在地下白白腐烂，还引来一些盗墓人掘起死者来乱翻腾，对死者有害无益。"又说，"厚葬阻碍了人与天地的关系。尧舜时并没厚葬，只是后人变了古圣先贤的规矩。"一番道理，说服了子孙与朋友。他说到做到，成为我国主张裸葬的第一人。

4. Having No Burial Objects

Yang Wangsun, a man from Chenggu (modern-day Nanzheng in Shaanxi), lived during the Han Dynasty. Despite his considerable wealth, he strongly opposed all forms of extravagance, particularly the common practice of lavish burials. In his later years, he told his children and grandchildren, "When I die, I want to be buried without any trappings, to reveal my true self." His family did not understand his reasoning, so they sought the advice of his close friend, Qi Hou. Qi Hou also disagreed with Yang Wangsun's decision, but Yang explained: "A grand burial costs a lot of money, and the items buried will decay underground, benefiting no one. It only attracts grave robbers who disturb the dead, which is harmful and pointless." He continued, "Such customs create a barrier between humans and the natural world. In the times of the ancient sages Yao and Shun, they did not engage in lavish burials. It was only later generations who changed these ancient practices."His explanation convinced both his family and friends, and after his death, they respected his wishes. Yang Wangsun thus became one of the earliest proponents of simple, unadorned burials in China.

遗言裸葬语惊人　子女好友不敢信
王孙谆谆道理讲　说到做到服众心

His request to be buried simply came as a surprise,
His children and friend could not perceive it as wise.
But Wangsun won them over by logic and reason,
His candour was authentic, true in ever season.

五、脏物弃地（钟离意）

东汉人钟离意，会稽郡山阳（今浙江绍兴）人。历任尚书、尚书仆射等职。当时交趾太守张恢犯了贪污罪，朝廷将价值千金的赃物没收后，分别赏赐给太医们。钟离意得到一些，不但不拜谢，还扔到地上。皇帝又生气又奇怪地问他为什么这样做。他说："孔子不饮盗泉之水，曾子不去胜母之宫。为了自身清白，这些东西给了我，增加了我的财富，却污了我的名声。"皇帝听后感慨地说："廉洁的尚书，太好了！"

5. Dropping Ill-gotten Gains

Zhong Liyi, a native of Shanyang (modern-day Shaoxing, Zhejiang Province), lived during the Eastern Han Dynasty. He served in several official positions, including as a Minister and Vice Minister. During his tenure, Zhang Hui, the Prefect of Jiaozhi, was found guilty of corruption. The court confiscated his ill-gotten gains, which were valued at thousands of gold pieces, and distributed them among the imperial physicians. Zhong Liyi received a portion, but instead of expressing gratitude, he threw the items onto the ground. The Emperor, both perplexed and angered, asked why he had acted in such a manner. Zhong Liyi replied: "Confucius refused to drink from the Robber's Spring, and Zeng Shen refused to visit the Palace of the Exalted Mother. They did this to preserve their personal integrity. These items may increase my wealth, but accepting them would tarnish my reputation." Upon hearing this, the Emperor sighed and said, "Ah, what an incorruptible minister!"

华丽珠宝金玉镶　贪污之财太骯髒
钟离弃之如粪土　敢效至贤步清良

Jewels and treasures may dazzle the eye,
But ill-gotten gains do not dignify.
Zhong Liyi discarded them like dirt,
His example teaches us to be ever on the alert.

六、张政民乐（张堪）

东汉时南阳（今河南南阳）人张堪，早年随刘秀军攻下成都后，被任命为蜀郡太守。那时，一些官兵每攻下一座诚池，都要抢掠珍宝，归己所用。张堪上任后，却让人清点仓库，将一些珍贵物品，一一注册，不许乱动，更不许抢掠民间之物，他自己更一点不拿，秋毫无犯。任渔阳太守时，发展生产、知民疾苦，百姓们编成歌谣赞颂他："桑无附枝，麦穗两岐。张君为政，乐不可支。"

6. Zhang Kan's Governance Pleases the People

In the Eastern Han Dynasty, Zhang Kan, a native of Nanyang (now Nanyang City in Henan Province), accompanied Liu Xiu in the conquest of Chengdu and was appointed Prefect of Shujun. At that time, it was common for officers and soldiers to loot treasures from conquered cities for their personal gain. Upon assuming office, Zhang Kan instructed his subordinates to check the inventory of the storehouses and make a detailed register of valuable items. He then issued an order prohibiting the seizure of goods and the looting of citizens' property. He took nothing for himself,ensuring that not even the smallest wrong was done to the people. Later, when he was transferred to be the Prefect of Yuyang, Zhang Kan focused on improving local production and was deeply concerned with the welfare of the people. His compassionate governance inspired a popular ballad that praised him, saying: "The mulberry tree has no crooked branches, and the wheat ears grow in pairs. Mr. Zhang's rule brings joy beyond measure."

攻城掠地多抢掠　官贼不辨积怨多
张堪主政陈规破　秋毫无犯民颂歌

Attacking cities and looting items of worth,
Soldiers seemed like bandits and the people suffered dearth.
Zhang Kan was in command and outlawed hooliganism,
Defended the people's interests, winning praise for healing schism.

七、羊车上路（孔奋）

东汉茂陵（今陕西兴平）人孔奋，光武初年被封为姑臧长、关内侯。当时的姑臧特别富裕，在此当地方官的人，很快便成为富翁。孔奋在当地任职四年，不怕别人说他"迂腐""愚蠢"，却廉洁自律，从不收受馈赠。当他被调入京城上路时，只有一辆羊车，装着简单的行李。当地的汉人、羌人、胡人感念他的恩德，自动捐钱捐物折合千万以上，追赶数百里送给他。孔奋对当地百姓的一番盛情心领神受，但所送之物一点也没收取。

7. Setting Out in a Cart Pulled by a Sheep

In the Eastern Han Dynasty, Kong Fen, a native of Maoling (now Xingping, Shaanxi Province), was appointed Magistrate of Guzang County and granted the title of Marquis of Guannei. At that time, Guzang was an affluent region, and officials who were posted there quickly became wealthy. Kong Fen served in the area for four years, during which he maintained his integrity and self-discipline, refusing to accept any gifts despite being labeled "pedantic" and "foolish" by others. When he was transferred to a new post in the capital, he departed the county in a cart pulled by a sheep, carrying only a modest amount of baggage. The local people, including Han, Qiang, and Hu ethnic groups, were deeply grateful for his fair governance. They followed him for hundreds of miles, offering donations of goods and money amounting to over ten million in total. However, Kong Fen accepted their kindness but firmly rejected all the gifts and donations.

一辆羊车上京城　清官并非富家翁
人嘲迂腐己自律　人间义重钱物轻

Riding a cart pulled by a sheep to the capital,
The clean-handed official was not wealthy at all.
People scoffed at his self-discipline and pedantry,
Yet righteousness trumps wealth in supremacy.

八、"四知"拒贿（杨震）

东汉华阴（今属陕西）人杨震，五十岁时被任命为东莱太守。向东上任时路过昌邑。当年被他举荐为茂才的王密此时为昌邑令。听说杨震来到，马上去拜见，并送上金十斤，以报答他的推荐之恩。扬震说："我认为你是个人才，才推荐的你，不必对我感谢，更不能送我礼物。"王密说："这是夜里，无人知道。"杨震说："天知、神知、我知、子知，怎么说没人知道？" 王密只得羞愧地把金收回去。

8. "Four Witnesses" Reject Bribery

In the Eastern Han Dynasty, Yang Zhen, a native of Huayin (now in Shaanxi Province), was appointed Administrator of Donglai at the age of fifty. On his way to assume his post, he passed through Changyi County, where Wang Mi, whom Yang had recommended as a "distinguished talent", was serving as the magistrate. Upon hearing of Yang Zhen's arrival, Wang Mi hurried to visit him and offered him ten catties of gold as a token of gratitude. Yang Zhen responded: "I recommended you because I believed you were capable. There is no need to thank me, and you certainly should not give me a gift." Wang Mi replied, "It's night, and no one will know." Yang Zhen retorted, "The heavens know, the gods know, I know, and you know. How can you say that no one knows?" Wang Mi, feeling ashamed, was left with no choice but to take back the gold.

行贿受贿违天理　　损德误人两坏事
杨震拒贿传佳话　　留贻后人歌"四知"

Bribery and corruption defy heaven's law,
Corrupting virtue and causing moral flaw.
Yang Zhen's refusal left a tale to tell,
The "Four Witnesses" became a legend as well.

九、合浦还珠（孟尝）

东汉时上虞（今属浙江）人孟尝，被任命为南方的合浦太守。当地不产粮食，但百姓们养蚌取珠，到交趾（今属越南）去卖，换来粮食生活。许多官员任意征发珠宝，百姓们纷纷逃离，断绝了与交趾的交易。孟尝去后，废除对珠宝的征发，百姓继续生产蚌珠，又恢复了对交趾的贸易。百姓称孟尝"神明"，从此也落了个"合浦还珠"的成语。

9. Pearls Reappear in Hepu

In the Eastern Han Dynasty, Meng Chang, from Shangyu (now part of Zhejiang Province), was appointed Prefect of Hepu in the south. The region did not produce grain, so the local people cultivated pearls, which they traded with Jiaozhi (present-day Vietnam) in exchange for food. However, many officials had imposed taxes on the pearls, leading to widespread migration and the collapse of trade with Jiaozhi. When Meng Chang took office, he abolished the levies, allowing the pearl trade to resume. The local people praised him as "divine", and this led to the origin of the idiom "pearls reappear in Hepu".

合浦地瘠难生产　养蚌取珠民命悬
孟尝废征随民愿　合浦还珠赞清官

Hepu was infertile and ill-suited to grain,
Culturing pearls brought the only monetary gain.
Meng Chang lifted levies, freeing up trade,
And won praise for the honesty he displayed.

十、张奂退马（张奂）

东汉酒泉（今属甘肃）人张奂，举贤良对策时荣获第一名，朝廷授予他安定属国都尉时，属下多为羌人。当地前任的汉人官吏多向羌人敲诈勒索，羌人不得不贿赂。张奂上任后，为官宽仁廉正，深得民心。羌人为了表示对他的感激，送给他二十匹好马，八枚金制的耳环，非叫他留下不可。他在一次羌人聚会时，全部交出来退还羌人，羌人才知道汉人中也有清正廉洁的好官。

10. Zhang Huan Returns the Horses

In the Eastern Han Dynasty, Zhang Huan, from Jiuquan (now part of Gansu Province), topped the list in the selection of able and virtuous men. He was subsequently appointed Commandant of Anding, where many of his subordinates were of the Qiang ethnicity. In the past, many Han officials had extorted money from the Qiang people, forcing them to offer bribes. However, upon Zhang Huan's appointment, he governed with integrity and kindness, gaining the deep trust and respect of the locals. In gratitude, the Qiang people presented him with twenty fine horses and eight gold earrings, insisting he accept them. At a later gathering, Zhang Huan returned all the gifts, and it was then that the Qiang people realized that there were indeed honest and upright officials among the Han.

汉人治羌多贪官　张奂与众不一般
为政宽仁退金、马　汉羌一家共怡欢

Many corrupt Han governed the Qiang minority,
But Zhang Huan was in fact a man of integrity.
His governance was lenient and he returned many a present,
So Han and Qiang enjoyed bonhomie, without anything unpleasant.

十一、悬鱼拒贿（羊续）

东汉人羊续，泰山平阳（今山东泰安市）人，曾任庐江、南阳两郡太守。他一贯反对豪绅之家的奢靡之风，更反对贪污贿赂。自己常素衣蔬食，旧车老马。一天，府丞送来几条鲜鱼，他不收，但府丞放下就走了。他却把鱼悬挂在门前。过了几天，府丞又来送鱼时，见到他门前的悬鱼已枯，知道他不接受，便不送了。他贵为朝内"三公"之一的太尉，却只有一件袍子。死前遗嘱交代不收公私馈赠，保持清廉本色。

11. Refusing Bribes by Hanging a Fish

In the Eastern Han Dynasty, Yang Xu, a native of Yangping County (now part of Tai'an in Shandong Province), served as the Prefect of Lujiang and Nanyang. He was steadfast in opposing the extravagant lifestyles of wealthy families and was particularly resolute in rejecting corruption and bribery. Leading a simple life himself, he subsisted mostly on vegetables, wore plain clothing, and traveled in a worn-out carriage. One day, his deputy brought some fresh fish as a gift and left before Yang Xu had a chance to decline. Yang Xu, however, hung the fish in front of his gate. A few days later, the deputy returned with more fish, but upon seeing the dried fish hanging at the gate, he realized that Yang Xu would not accept the gift and departed without offering it. Although Yang Xu held one of the highest positions in the court as one of the "Three Dukes", he owned only one suit of court attire. Before his death, he left a will stipulating that no mourning gifts or tributes should be accepted,demonstrating his unwavering commitment to integrity and his rejection of corruption.

羊续门前悬枯鱼　送鱼之人惊止步
羊公一生勤廉正　止贿妙法古今无

Yang Xu left the gift of fish in front of his gate,
The giver was shocked when he saw their dried state.
Yang Xu was clean and avoided all corruption,
His refusal of bribes was rare and full of instruction.

十二、河名钱清（刘宠）

东汉时牟平（今属山东）人刘宠，被任命到会稽做官后，废除了前任官员的一些苛捐杂税及各种劳役，赢得百姓一片颂声。当他被调进京城高升时，众百姓依依不舍，他们推出五六位老人，拿着一百个大钱，象征性地送给刘宠，表示对他尊敬的心愿。刘宠十分感动，一再推让，不得已收下了一枚大钱。当他离开会稽走出县境时，又把这枚钱投入河中。日后人们把这条河叫做"钱清河"。

12. A River Named Charity

During the Eastern Han Dynasty, Liu Chong, a native of Mouping (now part of Shandong Province), was appointed to an official post in Kuaiji. Upon his arrival, he abolished several excessive taxes and levies, as well as rescinding forced labor, earning widespread admiration from the local people. When Liu Chong was later promoted and called to the capital, the people of Kuaiji were reluctant to see him go. They selected five or six elders to present him with one hundred coins as a symbolic gesture of respect and gratitude. Liu Chong was deeply moved, but he repeatedly declined their offer. Finally, he accepted just a single coin. As he was leaving Kuaiji and crossing the county border, he threw the coin into a river. In the years that followed, the river came to be known as the "River of Charity".

民爱清官夹道送　清官爱民亦钟情
牟平千年留佳话　河水清沏颂钱清

The people love officials who shun all corruption,
And the official, in turn, shows deep affection.
An oft-told story is well-known in Mouping city,
How Liu Chong cast a coin into the River of Charity.

十三、去职留犊（时苗）

三国时的魏国时苗，巨鹿（今属河北平乡）人，建安中为寿春令。他上任时，乘一辆牛拉的破车，车上放一装着旧被褥的布袋，进了城入衙门时，不让人迎接。在职期间，秉公办事，深得民心。他在职时，拉车的牛生下一头牛犊，离开寿春时，对属下说："这头母牛是吃寿春的东西生下的牛犊，我走后应把他留下。"大家都不同意。时苗又说："我在寿春与百姓相处很好，留下小牛犊正是很好的纪念。"寿春一地多年盛传"去职留犊"的故事，歌颂了时苗这一清官。

13. Resigning and Leaving Behind a Calf

Shi Miao, from Julu (now in Hebei Province), served as the Magistrate of Shouchun during the Jianan era of the Three Kingdoms Period, under the Wei state. When he assumed office, he arrived in a cart drawn by a cow, with a ragged sack containing worn bedding. He refused any formal reception as he entered the government office. Throughout his tenure, he earned the trust and admiration of the people for his fair and just governance. When his cow gave birth to a calf just before his departure, he told his subordinates, "This cow has grazed the grass of Shouchun and given birth here. I should leave the calf behind when I leave." Despite objections from his subordinates, Shi Miao insisted: "I've had a good relationship with the people of Shouchun, and this calf will serve as a fitting memento." The story of "resigning and leaving behind a calf" became a well-known tale in Shouchun, commemorating Shi Miao as an upright official.

去职留犊事微小　小事已见德行超
秉公利民寿春令　官民欢乐赞时苗

Leaving a calf behind seemed rather trivial,
But it revealed the donor's spirit was convivial.
Fairness and justice were his rule of thumb,
The people and officers sang his praises with aplomb.

十四、独立使君（裴侠）

南北朝时北朝北周人裴侠，字嵩和，河东解（今山西运城西南）人，曾任河北郡守等职。此人躬履俭素，爱民敬业。当地多年有渔民向官员送鱼、猎户向官员送猎物的规矩，他到任后，明令一律废除。把当年百姓照例为官府服役的事改为叫这些人养马。日子长了，马已成群，一律归公。百姓们编成民谣赞颂他。有一次周太祖在许多官员面前说："你们这些人凡尽职清廉者，来与裴侠站到一起。" 官员们都默不作声，于是裴侠便得了个"独立使君"的美称。

14. The Upstanding Governor

During the Northern and Southern Dynasties, Pei Xia, courtesy name Songhe, hailed from Hai (now located southwest of Yuncheng, Shanxi Province) and served as the Governor of Hebei. Known for his frugality and dedication to his people, he was an official who genuinely cared for his subjects. In the past, it was customary for fishermen and hunters to present part of their catch to officials. Upon assuming office, Pei Xia abolished this practice. Instead of requiring locals to serve the government, he encouraged them to raise horses, and when the horses matured, they were made public property. The people composed a ballad in his honor. Once, Emperor Taizu of the Later Zhou Dynasty addressed a group of officials and said, "Those of you who are dutiful and free from corruption, stand alongside Pei Xia." However, the officials remained silent, and as a result, Pei Xia earned the esteemed title of "Upstanding Governor".

多年陋习民奉官　　裴侠为官已不贪
官中难得"独立君"　　清廉公正人难攀

For many years corrupt giving prevailed,
But as an official, Pei Xia was never availed.
It was rare to see one so powerful yet upstanding,
He set up standard others found too demanding.

十五、爱书卑珍（唐瑾）

南北朝时的北周唐瑾，平寿（今山东昌乐）人，累官吏部尚书。早年曾南伐江陵，功勋显著。江陵平定后，许多将领在此繁华地区大肆掠夺，一个个发了大财，唐瑾决不干这些事，他回京时带走两辆车。有人为了掩盖自己的丑行，说唐瑾带回两车珍宝。皇帝知道唐瑾的为人，不相信传言，派人去了解证实，回答是唐瑾没带回一点珍宝，两车全是别人不要的书。皇帝说："此人为官二十多年，从来不贪什么珍宝，我派人了解，正是还他个清白。"

15. Taking Books as Treasures

During the Southern and Northern Dynasties, Tang Jin, a native of Pingshou (now Changle County, Shandong Province), rose to the position of Minister of Personnel. In his early years, he participated in the campaign against Jiangling and achieved remarkable military success. After Jiangling was subdued, many generals plundered the prosperous city and amassed great wealth. However, Tang Jin refrained from such actions and instead returned to the capital with two carts. To cover up their own misdeeds, some people spread rumors that Tang Jin had brought back carts filled with looted treasures. The Emperor, knowing Tang Jin's character, did not believe the gossip and sent officials to investigate. It was confirmed that the carts contained nothing but unwanted books. The Emperor remarked, "He has served as an official for over twenty years and has never been interested in treasures. I sent people to verify this matter just to clear his name and confirm his integrity."

江陵纸醉金迷地　为官一任多中饱
诬言两车珍宝运　满载图书德智高

Jiangling was a place of luxury and dissipation,
So many officials made a fortune after choosing this location.
Rumour had it that Tang Jin piled two carts with lucre,
His only treasure was books and he embarrassed his rebuker.

十六、尚书种菜（柳元景）

南北朝时南朝宋人柳元景，河东郡解县（今山西运城）人，早年随宋文帝北伐立过战功，先后任多种官职直到尚书令，又晋升到当时朝内最高的官职：开府仪同三司。他办事公正，不谋私利，生活上一直保持着廉洁的本色。他家后面有片菜园，他叫自己的妻子、家人都吃菜园的菜，吃不了送给别人。种菜人有时将过剩的菜拉到市场上去卖，他得知后，勃然大怒，责备种菜人不该卖出，更不该廉价卖出与民争利。

16. A Minister Grows Vegetables

Liu Yuanjing, a prominent official during the Southern and Northern Dynasties, was born in Jie (now Lueyang County, Henan). In his youth, he accompanied Emperor Wen of the Song Dynasty on his northern campaigns, earning great military achievements. He later held various official positions, eventually rising to the highest rank of Minister of the Imperial Secretariat. Liu was known for his fairness and integrity, never seeking personal gain, and he maintained the lifestyle of a virtuous official throughout his career. Behind his house, there was a vegetable garden, and he instructed his wife and family to eat from it, giving away any surplus to others. However, the gardener sometimes sold the excess vegetables at the market. Upon learning this, Liu became furious, reprimanding the gardener for selling the produce. He insisted that the vegetables should never be sold, much less for a low price that could harm the livelihoods of local vendors.

帝下一人官位极　　为官淡食亦粗衣
不因官大多奢侈　　尚书种菜天下稀

He was the highest official beneath the emperor,
Yet cared not for food and comforts superior.
Despite his seniority he was never extravagant,
It's rare to see a minister tending an allotment.

十七、敢饮贪泉（吴隐之）

南北朝时南朝宋人吴隐之，鄄城（山东鄄城）人。在他所任职的广州，有许多珍宝，前任官员多贪婪成性，百姓们怨声载道。广州城南二十里处有一条小溪，由一眼泉水流成，人称"贪泉"。传说只要饮了此水，便有贪欲。吴隐之说："这是贪婪的人为自己找的理由。我今饮此水，绝对不贪！"事实证明，他饮此水后，不但不贪，还把自己的薪俸接济穷人。任满回家时没多带一点东西，皇帝赐给他的车马，也坚决不要。后来他当了度支尚书，管更多的钱财，也清廉如初，足证"贪泉"之说乃谎言。

17. Daring to Drink from the Fount of Greed

Wu Yingzhi, a prominent official during the Southern and Northern Dynasties, was born in Juancheng (now Juancheng City, Shandong Province). When he served in Guangzhou, a city known for its wealth, many of the officials before him were notorious for their greed, and the people voiced their discontent. Twenty miles south of the city, there was a creek fed by a spring known locally as the "Fount of Greed". According to legend, anyone who drank from this water would be overcome by an insatiable desire for wealth. Wu Yingzhi, however, dismissed this superstition, saying, "This is nothing but a rationalization for people's greed. I will drink from this spring today, and I will not be corrupted!" His actions proved his words true. Not only did he refrain from greed, but he also donated his salary to the poor. When his term ended, he left with little to no possessions, rejecting even the cart and horses offered by the Emperor. Later, when he was appointed Minister of the Treasury,overseeing far greater wealth, he remained as incorruptible as ever, thus proving the legend of the "Fount of Greed" to be a myth.

贪泉之说系谎言　贪官为此找根源
清官饮了贪泉水　水清如镜官照廉

The legend of the fount of greed was proved to be a lie,
A scapegoat for corruption that officials decry.
But a clean-handed official drank his fill,
And remained clean as the water still.

十八、帝俭臣效（萧道成）

南北朝时南朝齐高帝萧道成，有鉴于当年刘宋灭亡的教训，为了巩固自己的统治，也反对奢侈，提倡节俭。他常对大臣们说："皇帝不节俭，大家都会跟着学。我们吃、喝、穿、用的都是老百姓的血汗，必须珍惜。当我们大摆宴席时，要想想百姓还有吃不上饭的。当我们在深宅大院享受时，听听百姓屋中漏雨的声音。我们必须以百姓为重。" 他本人不佩戴玉饰的装饰品，座驾的华盖不镶金，还下令全国不要把金银嵌到器皿上。这些主张影响了大臣，一时出现简朴之风。

18. The Frugal Emperor Finds a Following

During the Southern and Northern Dynasties, Emperor Xiao Daocheng of the State of Qi, mindful of the lessons from the downfall of the Liu Song dynasty, sought to strengthen his own rule by promoting frugality and opposing extravagance. He often reminded his officials: "If the Emperor does not live frugally, others will follow his example. Everything we eat, drink, wear, and use comes from the blood and sweat of the people, and we must learn to cherish it. When we feast, we should remember that there are those who do not have enough to eat. When we enjoy the comfort of our mansions, we should imagine the sound of rain leaking into the homes of the poor.The welfare of the people must always come first." He himself refrained from wearing jade ornaments, and his canopy was not adorned with gold. He also issued an edict that no gold or silver should be used in the making of household items. His policies had a profound influence on his officials, and a new trend of frugality spread throughout the court.

皇帝带头倡节俭　吃穿住行民血汗
接受前朝奢亡训　节俭正为保江山

The Emperor took the lead in living frugally,
For he knew he relied on others' labour totally.
He drew a lesson from the former regime,
And made frugality his pattern and scheme.

十九、倡廉斥子（杨坚）

隋文帝杨坚，是在国内长期混战、动乱后当上的皇帝。他为保统治，厉行节俭，爱护百姓。他下令宫中所有摆设的奢侈品一律撤掉，皇帝室内帷帐的钩由白银的换成铜的。太子杨勇穿了一件华丽的衣服向他炫耀，却遭到他一顿训斥。对奢华成性的另一个儿子杨俊，文帝免了官爵予以严惩，直到他死前也不赦免。有一年，关中发生旱灾，百姓们吃糠咽菜，他也不吃肉不喝酒。其行为影响了许多大臣。

19. Advocating Uprightness and Reprimanding His Son

Emperor Wen of the Sui Dynasty ascended the throne after a long period of internal strife and turmoil. To consolidate his rule, he rigorously enforced frugality and prioritized the well-being of the people. He ordered that all luxury items be removed from the palace and replaced the silver hooks of the royal bed curtains with those made of bronze. One day, his son, Crown Prince Yang Yong, paraded before him in an extravagant robe, only to receive a sharp reprimand. The Emperor also stripped another son, Yang Jun, of his title and official position due to his extravagance, and he never pardoned him. During a year of severe drought in the Guanzhong region, when the people were reduced to eating bran and vegetables, the Emperor himself abstained from meat and wine, setting an example of self-discipline. His actions greatly influenced many of his court officials.

初建隋朝身俭约　皇室内外反豪奢
哀怜民苦频示警　痛斥孽子死不赦

In the early Sui, he lived with thrift and care,
Luxury banned within the palace, and elsewhere.
He mourned the people's hardship, gave warnings clear,
And scorned the extravagant sons, who knew no fear.

二十、"清朗""清聊"（袁聿修）

　　隋朝袁聿修，字叔德，项（今河北沈丘）人，昔日在南朝的齐国为官十年，清正廉明，一尘不染。入隋后当了十年尚书郎，除薪俸外，没要过一点分外之财，他的上级尚书邢邵对他敬佩地称作"清朗"。大业初年，他奉旨巡视各地，位高权重，从来也不收任何礼品。途经兖州，时任兖州刺史的邢邵迎送他后，送给他几尺白绸作纪念，他婉言退还。邢感慨地说几十年来他还保持清廉本色，当年的"清朗"今日成为名符其实的"清聊"了。

20. "Clean" and "Stainless"

Yuan Yuxiu, styled Shude, was a native of Xiang (present-day Shenqiu County, Hebei Province) during the Sui Dynasty. He had served as an official in the Southern Qi Dynasty for ten years, upholding integrity and remaining free of corruption. After entering the Sui Dynasty, he served as a Vice Minister for a decade, never requesting anything beyond his salary. His superior, Xing Shao, admired him deeply and bestowed upon him the epithet "Clean". In the early years of the Daye era, Yuan Yuxiu was tasked with an imperial inspection tour. Despite his high position and authority, he refused to accept any gifts. When passing through Yanzhou, the Prefect Xing Shao personally saw him off and offered a few yards of white silk as a token of respect. Yuan politely declined the gift. Xing Shao, moved by his unwavering integrity, remarked that after decades of public service, Yuan Yuxiu had not only remained "clean" but had become truly "stainless".

　　权大权小正当用　　官高官低均守正
　　京内京外不收贿　　昔为"清朗"今"清聊"

No matter the rank, high or low,
He upheld justice, letting fairness show.
Refusing bribes was in his eyes painless,
For he was not only clean, but stainless.

二十一、退金诲人（梁毗）

隋朝乌氏（今甘肃平凉）人梁毗，文帝时派往西宁新州当刺史。当地少数民族首领的帽子上常镶一些珠宝，相互攀比，甚至为此大动干戈。梁毗到后，一些首领为了巴结他，纷纷给他送金子，他多次推辞不掉。有一天，梁毗请他们赴宴，酒酣之际，放声大哭。大家问他为什么，他把金子拿出来说："这些东西饿了不能吃，冷了不能穿，你们给我落个丑名，令我像染上了瘟疫一样，你们还为它厮杀，祸害百姓。" 说后一一照单奉还。首领们取还金子，从此也煞住为此争斗的歪风。

21. Returning Gold as a Lesson to Others

Liang Pi, a native of Wushi (present-day Pingliang, Gansu Province), served during the Sui Dynasty. He was appointed as the Prefect of Xining by Emperor Wen of Sui. In this region, the local ethnic leaders often adorned their hats with jewels, competing with one another, sometimes even leading to violent clashes. When Liang Pi arrived, several chieftains, eager to gain his favor, offered him gold. Though he repeatedly declined, he could only refuse so many times. One day, he invited the chieftains to a banquet. As the revelry reached itspeak, he suddenly broke into loud, mournful cries. The guests, startled, asked him the cause of his tears. Liang Pi took out the gold and said, "These things cannot be eaten when you're hungry nor worn when you're cold. You have tarnished my reputation, as though I have contracted a plague, and yet you still fight over such things, bringing harm to the people." He then returned the gold to each of them in turn. From that moment on, the chieftains stopped fighting over gold, and the harmful practice was finally put to an end.

崇尚豪华攀比风　为示阔绰多纷争
梁毗身教加言教　退金诲人多颂声

Local tribal leaders were extravagant and flouncing,
They fought one another, charging and pouncing.
Liang Pi taught them by example and precept,
To their surprise no gold was he willing to accept.

二十二、清贫尚书（卢怀慎）

唐朝滑州（今河南滑县）人卢怀慎，玄宗开元年间任黄门监兼吏部尚书。此人官位虽高，但生活十分俭朴，从来不为自己置办财产，穿用从来不用金银、绸缎，吃饭也很简单。他妻子的一切生活与常人一样。但他却把大量薪俸送给别人，送光了也不可惜。有一次他生病，宰相宋璟到家探望，见家内一切简陋。正值下雨，漏雨的屋里用蓆遮挡。宋璟回去建议皇帝对他赏赐，他坚决不受。直到死后也一贫如洗，家无余财，人们尊他为"清贫尚书"，享誉国内。

22. The Poor Minister

Lu Huaishen, from Huazhou (present-day Huaxian County, Henan Province), served as Minister of Personnel during the Kaiyuan Era under Emperor Xuanzong of the Tang Dynasty. Despite holding a high-ranking position, he led an extraordinarily simple and frugal life. He never acquired property or used gold, silver, or silk. His meals were modest, and his wife lived in the same manner as an ordinary person. Lu Huaishen gave away much of his salary to others and felt no regret, even when he had distributed it all. On one occasion, when he fell ill, the Prime Minister, Song Jing, visited his home and was struck by its humble state. It was raining, and the family had to use a straw mat to cover the leaking roof. Song Jing returned to the Emperor and suggested granting Lu Huaishen a reward. However, Lu firmly refused. He lived in poverty until his death, with no wealth left behind, earning the title "the poor minister." His name became widely respected across the country for his integrity and selflessness.

清贫尚书卢怀慎　取之于民用于民
道高德劭甘清贫　廉正洁白光仕林

Though a minister Lu Huaishen chose a lifestyle plain,
Donating to the lowly and declining any gain.
He was willing to be poor yet in virtue excelled,
Officialdom was moved and his standards they upheld.

二十三、位尊亦俭（王旦）

宋初大名（今山东莘县）人王旦，出身仕宦之家，父亲王祐是兵部侍郎，兄长王懿任袁州知州，三弟王旭为应天知府，他是朝内一品宰相。但此人生活简朴，既不置办家产，又不贪图享受，生活如同寒士。有一次，经济上遇到困难，向自己的弟子借钱。到期以后，本息都还不上，只得把自己的马卖了还债。他三弟的儿子王质读书时，无意中翻到这张债券，十分惊讶，马上把全家的孩子叫来，以此教育子女们要保持节俭的家风。

23. Powerful Yet Frugal

Wang Dan, born in Daming (now Shen County, Shandong Province) at the start of the Song Dynasty, came from a family of prominent officials. His father, Wang You, had served as Vice Minister of the Military; his elder brother was the Prefect of Yuanzhou; his third brother was the Prefect of Yingtian; and Wang Dan himself held the position of Prime Minister. Despite his high rank, he lived a frugal life, never accumulating property or seeking luxury, choosing instead to live as a scholar of modest means. On one occasion, Wang Dan encountered financial difficulties and borrowed money from one of his disciples. When the repayment deadline arrived, he was unable to cover even the interest, so he sold his horse to settle the debt. Years later, his nephew, the son of his third brother, discovered the IOU while reading a book. Shocked, he gathered the children of the family and shared the story with them, urging them to uphold the family tradition of frugality.

富贵之家也简朴　多想尽职少享乐
忍痛卖马还旧债　子孙均照榜样学

Even a noble family lived a straitened life,
Paying attention to duty though luxury was rife.
He even sold his dear horse to pay off debts,
And his descendants followed his noble sets.

二十四、以镜为鉴（吕蒙正）

北宋初年修阳人吕蒙正，由进士升至户部尚书。宋真宗时，三度入相。此人质厚宽阔，为政持正道，举荐多贤才，宋代名相富弼、吕夷简均由他推荐。当他任中书侍郎兼尚书平章事时，位高权重，一名官员请他办事时，拿出家中多年藏的古镜送给他。说："这是件稀世珍宝，能照二里远。"吕蒙正坚决不收，诙谐地说："我的脸不到半尺，要照二里的镜子做什么？"接着说："古人以镜为鉴照形象。照一个人的品格，应以道德为镜，其中重要一项就是清廉。"

24. Taking a Mirror as a Guide

Lü Mengzheng, from Xiuyang, lived at the beginning of the Northern Song Dynasty. He rose through the ranks from scholar to the position of Minister of Revenue. During the reign of Emperor Zhenzong, he served three terms as Prime Minister. Lü was known for his broad-mindedness, generosity, and integrity in governance. He recommended many talented individuals, including the renowned statesmen Fu Bi and Lü Yijian. At one point, while serving as Vice Minister of the Military, Lü held significant power. On one occasion, an official who sought his assistance offered him an antique mirror, claiming it to be a rare treasure capable of reflecting images from a mile away. Lü Mengzheng, however, firmly declined, joking: "My face is only half a foot long—what would I do with a mirror that reflects a mile?" He then added, "Ancient people used mirrors to reflect their physical appearance. To reflect one's character, we should use morality as a mirror, and one key aspect of this is integrity."

以镜为鉴照人品　仁德之人遵古训
蒙正拒收富贵镜　正应以镜照仁人

A mirror reflects a man's heart and soul,
Virtuous ones follow the ancient goal.
Lü Mengzheng turned down a mirror so rare,
Proving his integrity beyond compare.

二十五、示廉《会约》（司马光）

北宋名臣司马光，虽位高权重，却知民疾苦，生活节俭。他鉴于当时朝内大臣、贵戚们经常花天酒地，制定了一个《洛阳耆英会约》。其中除规定各种礼仪外，又规定宴会时不用金银碗筷，桌上的菜不得超过五种，酒未喝完菜已吃完时补充菜汤，请柬不得华丽硕大……此《会约》提出后，朝内文彦博、富弼等十几名重臣一律遵守。

25. Demonstrating Frugality and Integrity

Sima Guang, a renowned minister of the Northern Song Dynasty, was known for his high rank and power. Despite his position, he led a frugal life and was deeply concerned about the welfare of the people. Disturbed by the lavish and indulgent lifestyles of court officials and nobility, he formulated a set of guidelines known as *The Rules for the Gathering of Venerable and Virtuous Individuals in Luoyang*. The rules laid out specific conduct, including prohibitions on using gold or silver tableware, limiting the number of dishes to no more than five, and substituting soup if the food was exhausted before the wine. The invitations were to be modest and not extravagant. When Sima Guang proposed these guidelines, they were embraced by many high-ranking officials, including Wen Yanbo, Fu Bi, and other prominent members of the court.

《洛阳会约》示简朴　位高更应知民苦
大臣遵守廉风起　　铺张浪费为耻辱

The Luoyang Agreement demonstrated restraint,
High officials should well know the peoples' complaint.
Court dignitaries were at the vanguard of this refulgence,
Eschewing corruption and over-indulgence.

二十六、勤俭"圣相"（李沆）

北宋初年肥乡（今河北广平）人李沆，曾任朝内最大的官同平章事（官名，是同中书门下平章事的简称）。当时国内发生旱灾，有的大臣因皇帝年幼，不愿上奏。李沆说："正因为皇帝年幼，才应叫他知道民间疾苦，远离声色狗马。"他办事勤奋、得体，人称"圣相"。他家住封丘门内，厅堂的空间只容转身，有人劝他修修，他笑之不理。庭前栏杆坏了，他也不修。他常对家人说："树上的鸟只站一枝，人的住处也不要贪多。要把精力放到国事、民事上。要向古人子荆学习，对自己的生活要知足常乐。"

26. The Frugal "Saintly Prime Minister"

Li Hang, a native of Feixiang (modern-day Guangping, Hebei Province), served during the early years of the Northern Song Dynasty. He held the highest official position of Chancellor. At the time, a severe drought was affecting the empire, but some court ministers were hesitant to report the matter to the young Emperor. Li Hang firmly stated: "Precisely because the Emperor is so young, he must be made aware of the suffering of the common people and be kept away from the distractions of indulgence and pleasure." Known for his diligence and decorum in handling state affairs, Li Hang earned the title of the "Saintly Prime Minister". He lived in a modest residence inside the Fengqiu Gate,where the central hall was barely large enough for one person to turn around. Despite othersurging him to upgrade his home, he merely smiled and dismissed their suggestions. Even when the railing outside his home fell into disrepair, he chose not to have it fixed. Li Hang often advised his family: "A bird in a tree can only rest on one branch; there's no need to seek more space for our home. Our focus should be on state matters and the well-being of the people. We should emulate the ancient sage Zijing, who lived contentedly and found joy in simplicity."

胸怀职责勤国事　生活细节不多计
力学子荆乐居室　知足常乐心欢怡

Always keep state affairs and duty at the forefront of one's mind,
Personal comforts and trivia should take their place behind.
Follow the example of the spendthrift saint Zijing,
Who knew well the contentedness a moral life would bring.

二十七、不贪遗产（安德裕）

北宋朔州（今属山西）人安德裕，父亲安重荣是五代时期后晋的成德节度使。一次用兵失败，奶妈抱着安德裕避难，被他父亲的朋友秦习收养。秦习家人人习武，安德裕却努力习文。秦习去世，他服丧三年后，恢复了安性，离开秦家前，秦家送给他很多东西，仅白金就有一万多两，安德裕婉言谢绝说："我被您家养育已感恩非浅，更不能要您家的积蓄，真正的男子汉应自己建功立业，取得富贵。"他继续努力攻读，不久中了进士甲科，当了太守。

27. Not Coveting a Legacy

An Deyu was from Shuozhou (now part of Shanxi Province) during the Northern Song Dynasty. His father, An Zhongrong, had been the Regional Commander of Chengde during the Later Jin Dynasty of the Five Dynasties period. After his father suffered a military defeat, An Deyu was carried to safety by his wet nurse and was subsequently adopted by his father's friend, Qin Xi. While the Qin family practiced martial arts, An Deyu focused diligently on his studies. After Qin Xi passed away, An Deyu observed three years of mourning before returning to his original family name. When he left the Qin household, they offered him many gifts, including more than ten thousand taels of platinum. However, An Deyu declined these offerings with gratitude, saying: "I am deeply grateful to you for raising me, but I cannot accept your savings. A true man should build his own career and earn his fortune through his own efforts." He continued his studies with determination and soon passed the imperial examinations with top honors, later becoming a prefect.

德裕幼年被收养　修德好学读华章
万两遗产不接受　男儿立身当自强

Deyu was adopted as an infant,
On study and morals he was intent.
He refused a legacy of platinum,
For fortune and status from effort should come.

二十八、夫清妻廉（杨万里）

南宋时吉水（今江西吉安）人杨万里，是一位儒学学者，也是一位清官。他在京城做国子博士，儿子是元帅。一家人循礼守法，克勤克俭，他对家人严格要求。妻子罗氏在家住着土坯盖的房子，穿戴和普通百姓一样。不论寒暑，总在天明起床自己做饭。直到八十多岁，还在菜园里种蔴，自己纺绩。他们在广东做官的儿子，把一个月丰盛的薪俸送给她，她却都分给了穷人，说："把钱用到该用的地方，心里就踏实了。"

28. AIncorruptible Couple

Yang Wanli was from Jishui (now Ji'an City, Jiangxi Province) during the Southern Song Dynasty. He was a Confucian scholar and an upright official, serving as a professor at the imperial academy. His son held the rank of marshal. Despite their status, the family adhered strictly to law and propriety, living with diligence and frugality. Yang was particularly strict with his family members. His wife, Madame Luo, lived in a simple adobe house and wore plain clothes like an ordinary person. Regardless of the season, she rose early every morning to cook for the family. Even in her eighties, she continued to grow hemp, spin the fibers, and weave them into cloth. Their son, who served as an official in Guangdong, once sent her his monthly salary. However, she gave it all away to the poor, saying: "I feel at peace when money is spent where it's truly needed."

南宋儒者杨万里　居官清廉识大义
老妻勤劳乐纺绩　助人为乐民得益

A scholar by the name of Wanli,
Fulfilled his duties with honesty.
His old wife toiled and wove,
Helping the poor she was happy to behove.

二十九、退还加薪（伯都）

元朝忙兀人伯都，延祐年间任浙江省平章政事，曾上疏陈治国之策。后来当了御史大夫。其间因生病请求辞职，皇帝允准，但仍按当年平章政事的标准发给薪俸。不久，又送给他十万缗钱。他对这些特殊照顾心中不安，多次向皇帝上疏，说不该多取，均全部退还。伯都死后，皇帝把他当年退的钱及三万五千贯丧葬费一起派人送到他家。妻子弘吉剌氏坚决照他生前的嘱咐，一概没有接受。

29. Returning the Salary Increase

Bodu, a man from Mangwu during the Yuan Dynasty, served as the Deputy Prime Minister of Zhejiang Province during the Yanyou period. He once submitted a memorial to the Emperor outlining strategies for good governance. Later, he was appointed Grand Secretary. When Bodu became ill, he requested to resign, and the Emperor granted his request. However, he continued to receive a salary equivalent to his previous post as Deputy Prime Minister. Shortly afterward, the Emperor also sent him a gift of 100,000 taels. Feeling uneasy about these special favors, Bodu repeatedly submitted memorials, explaining that he did not deserve the extra money and returning the full amount. Upon his death, the Emperor sent the money Bodu had returned, along with an additional 35,000 taels for funeral expenses, to his family.However, Bodu's wife, Madame Hong Jila, firmly refused to accept any of it, in accordance with his wishes.

伯都致仕归田园　帝赐薪俸仍如前
如数退还示歉意　妻子从夫亦清廉

Bodu retired and returned to his household,
But the Emperor wanted to reward him with gold.
He returned the money with apologies,
And his widow then emulated his qualities.

三十、捐资兴学（乌古泽孙）

　　元朝临潢（今内蒙古巴林左旗）人乌古泽孙，当年征海南时立过大功，武宗至大年间任福建廉坊使。当时朝廷有惯例：国家用于祭祀而属于卿大夫自己的用地，到秋天以后，官员可以自收粮食。乌古泽孙到任才三个月，当地农民竟按例给他五百石粮食。他心中不安，一定按照孔子"义然后取"的精神办。他令人算好自己一年的所需之外，一律捐给地方的学堂。他一生简朴，一件布袍穿好几年，妻子也朴实无华，过着和平民一样的日子。

30. Donating Money to Support Education

Wuguzesun was from Linhuang (now the Left Banner of Balin in Inner Mongolia). He had gained distinction for his military achievements during the campaign in Hainan. Later, he served as the Censor of Fujian Province during the Zhida era in the reign of Emperor Wuzong of the Yuan Dynasty. According to the court's custom, after the autumn harvest, officials were allowed to keep the grain from their land that was designated for state sacrifices. Just three months after Wuguzesun assumed office, local farmers offered him 500 piculs of grain. Feeling uneasy, he was determined to follow the Confucian principle of "Righteousness first" and only take what was rightfully his. After calculating his personal needs for the year, he donated the remainder of the grain to local schools. Wuguzesun lived a simple life, making his plain cloth gown last for many years. His wife also led an unadorned, modest life, living like an ordinary person.

乌古泽孙征海南　德及南国施政宽
退还多得身简朴　捐资兴学培时贤

Wuguzesun quested to Hainan
And pursued a virtuous plan.
He lived simply and declined a bonus,
Feeling that education should have the onus.

三十一、依法办事（廉希宪）

元朝畏兀儿人廉希宪，至元中以平章行省事在荆南当太守时，兴利除弊，办了许多善事。当时他还兼管接收从前宋朝官吏的任务。荆南有个规矩：凡是当年在宋朝做过官的人，要见太守时，必须献上珍宝，太守才能给他安排官职，否则不予接待。廉希宪上任后，却公开申明："我是代表朝廷来录用你们的，我要你们的珍宝是不义之举，你们如果从百姓那里弄来珍宝，更不义了。" 这一清廉行为感动了那些宋朝的官员，一个个任职后都很努力。

31. Acting According to the Law

Lian Xixian was a Uighur official who served as Prefect of Jingnan during the Zhiyuan era of the Yuan Dynasty. He was known for his just actions, eliminating harmful practices, and accomplishing many good deeds. In addition, he was tasked with managing the affairs of the former officials from the Song Dynasty. In Jingnan, there was a custom that required former Song officials to present valuable tributes to the Prefect in exchange for a new appointment. Upon assuming office, Lian Xixian publicly declared: "I am here to appoint you on behalf of the government. If I were to accept your tributes, it would be unjust. And if you were to take treasures from the people, that would be even more unjust." His strong stance on integrity deeply moved the former Song officials. Once appointed to their new positions, they worked diligently and conscientiously.

受命太守收官吏　秉公办事不收礼
选取贤才新朝用　一代廉风光乡里

Bound by decree, officials did their part,
But Chief Lian ruled with an impartial heart.
He sought new talents to serve the crown,
His integrity brought honor to the town.

三十二、清慎勤奋（梁寅）

明朝初年新喻（今江西清江）人梁寅，世代务农，自己艰苦学习成名。明太祖征召天下名士修订礼乐时，六十多岁的梁寅被召去。在修礼乐时，讨论精审，受到诸儒尊重，皇帝授予他金币及官爵。他年老辞归，结庐于石门山，学界称其为"梁五经"。年轻的官员问他请教为官之道时，他说："清、慎、勤，居官三字符也。"又说，"天德及王道的要领是：言忠信，行笃敬，天德也；不伤财，不害民，王道也。"依此做到为清官，否则即是庸官、贪官。

32. Diligent, Discreet and Upright

Liang Yin was from Xinyu (now Qingjiang County in Jiangxi Province) and lived during the early Ming Dynasty. His family had been engaged in farming for generations, but Liang earned fame through his own diligent study. When the founder of the Ming Dynasty, Emperor Taizu, summoned renowned scholars to revise the regulations for rites and music, the sixty-year-old Liang was called to contribute.During these deliberations, his careful reasoning earned him the respect of his fellow scholars, and the Emperor rewarded him with gold coins and a high-ranking position. As he grew older,Liang retired from public office and returned home, building a modest cottage at the foot of Mount Shimen. He was honored in the academic world and referred to as "Liang of the Five Classics" for his profound knowledge. When young officials sought his guidance on how to serve the state, he advised them:"Cleanness, caution, and diligence are the three key virtues for an official." He further explained, "The essence of heavenly morality and the kingly way is to be loyal and honest, sincere and faithful—this is heavenly morality; and not to harm the people or waste resources—this is the royal way." He emphasized that anyone who adhered to these principles would be an upright official, while those who failed would be seen as either mediocre or corrupt.

为官之道清慎勤　耄耋梁寅示后人
依此为官青史著　违此贪庸祸必临

Cleanness, caution and diligence in governance,
Were what four score Liang Yin brought to prominence.
Acting by his rule would ensure a golden name,
Defying it would open up the path to shame.

三十三、"苦行老僧"（陈瑸）

清康熙年间海康（今广东雷州市遂溪）人陈瑸，官至闽浙总督，一生清廉卓绝，远近闻名。平时布衣素食，勤于政事。早年任县令时，自己一文不取，衣食已能充足。任台湾道时，将所得三万两银子都捐出修炮台等公事用。他常说："贪取一钱，即与百钱无异。"他以自己的实际行动实现了自己的诺言。他死后只有一件棉袍，复上一个布衾。康熙在大学士面前，对他极力赞扬，称他为"苦行老僧"。

33. The "Ascetic Monk"

Chen Bin was from Haikang (now Suixi County, Leizhou City, Guangdong Province) and lived during the reign of Emperor Kangxi in the Qing Dynasty. He served as the Viceroy of Zhejiang and was widely renowned for his exceptional integrity throughout his life. Known for his frugal lifestyle, he wore plainclothes, ate a vegetarian diet, and dedicated himself to government affairs. During his early years as a county magistrate, he took no extra money from the people, and his official salary was sufficient to cover his living expenses. When he served as Governor of Taiwan, he donated his entire salary of thirty thousand taels of silver for public projects, including the construction of fortifications. He often remarked, "To covet a single coin is no different from coveting a hundred." He lived by this principle, demonstrating it through his actions. Upon his death, Chen Bin left behind only a simple cotton robe and a cloth shroud. Emperor Kangxi, in the presence of high-ranking officials, praised him highly, referring to him as the "ascetic monk" in recognition of his incorruptible and selfless character.

> 一文不取为官清　薪俸乐捐均为公
> 布衣素食勤政事　青史荣载"苦行僧"

> Clean-handed, no bonuses would he tolerate,
> And even donated his salary back to the state.
> Fastidious at work and at home austere,
> The famed "ascetic monk" of yesteryear.

三十四、廉吏第一（于成龙）

清初永宁（山西离石）人于成龙，为官清廉，勤政爱民。他六十六岁任两江总督时，经常微服私访，了解民情。平时轻车简从，天天吃糙米、青菜，请客也是青菜，人称"于青菜"。他日夜操劳、疲乏，上奏请求致仕（退休），皇帝却又叫他兼安徽巡抚。他去世后，在其箱子里发现一件袍子、一双靴子。在床头粗瓦器内发现粗米数斗、食盐数升及一些文具、书籍。他临死前交待儿子也保持清廉作风。康熙称他为"天下第一廉吏"，号召官员们向他学习。

34. The Most Honest and Upright Official

Yu Chenglong was from Yongning (now Lishi City, Shanxi Province) and lived at the beginning of the Qing Dynasty. He was known for his honesty, uprightness, and dedication to the welfare of the people. At the age of sixty-six, he was appointed Governor-General of Jiangnan and Jiangxi. Yu frequently disguised himself in civilian clothes to personally investigate the conditions of the common people. He lived a frugal life, traveling with minimal baggage and a small entourage, subsisting on coarse grains and vegetables. Even when entertaining guests, he served only simple vegetarian dishes. This humble lifestyle earned him the nickname " Vegetable Yu". Yu worked tirelessly day and night, eventually petitioning for retirement due to fatigue. However, the Emperor refused and instead appointed him as the Governor of Anhui as well. After his death, only a robe and a pair of boots were found in his belongings. Beside his bed, an earthen vessel contained coarse rice, and he had a modest supply of salt, stationery, and books. Before passing, Yu advised his son to continue the tradition of honesty and integrity. Emperor Kangxi praised him as "the most honest and upright official in the world" and urged other officials to emulate his virtuous example.

勤政为民赞老骥　粗米青菜着布衣
清廉正风康熙赞　天下廉吏数第一

Diligent and dedicated like an old steed,
Plain clothes, grain and no meat met his need.
He was praised as a model by Kangxi of Qing,
Who rated his performance as outstanding.

三十五、"三汤道台"（汤斌）

清初名臣，文学家汤斌，字孔伯，睢州人。曾任道台，江苏巡抚。为官清廉，不多取一文，每日以豆腐汤为肴，人称"三汤道台"。即：从政如豆腐汤清白，自己生活如黄连汤苦涩，对世道人心如人参汤那样滋补。他曾做到工部尚书，死时只有俸银八两，好友徐乾学助银二十两，才得殡葬。

35. The "Prefect of Three Soups"

Tang Bin, a renowned scholar and official from Sui County, was known by the courtesy name Kong Bo. He served as a Prefect and the Governor of Jiangsu during the early Qing Dynasty. An upright official, he never accepted extra money and lived simply, often having tofu soup as his main meal. This led to his nickname, the "Prefect of Three Soups." His governance was as pure as tofu soup, his personal life as bitter as goldenseal soup, and his approach to the world and the people as nourishing as ginseng soup. Despite having served as the Minister of Industry, Tang Bin passed away with only eight taels of silver to his name. It was only through a donation of twenty taels from his friend Xu Qianxue that his funeral could be held.

"三汤道台"赞汤斌　仁德清廉得民心
官至工部仍节俭　两袖清风世人钦

Tang Bin was praised through three types of broth,
His virtue and benevolence gained other's troth.
He espoused frugality as Minister of Industry,
Winning admiration for such simplicity.

三十六、《禁馈送檄》（张伯行）

清初张伯行,仪封(今河南开封)人,康熙年间进士,官做到礼部尚书。他为官二十年, 以刚正清廉著称。死后被赐太子太保。他又是一位学者,一生著述几十种, 向他学习的学生数千人。在他居官时, 为防止别人送礼, 专门写了一篇《禁止馈送檄》:"一丝一粒, 我之名节;一厘一毫,民之脂膏。宽一分, 民受赐岂止一分;取一文, 我为人不值一文。谁云交际之长, 廉耻实伤。倘非不义之财, 此物何来?"将此贴到门口, 送礼者便绝迹了。

36. *A Declaration on Refusing Bribes*

Zhang Boxing, from Yifeng (now Kaifeng, Henan Province), was a scholar and official during the reign of Emperor Kangxi in the Qing Dynasty. He was promoted to the position of Minister of Rites and served as an upright and incorruptible official for twenty years. Known for his integrity, he was posthumously honored with the title of Crown Prince's Grand Protector. In addition to his official duties, Zhang was a distinguished scholar, authoring dozens of works and teaching thousands of students. During his tenure, to prevent others from offering bribes, Zhang wrote A *Declaration on Refusing Bribes*, which he displayed at his door: "A thread and a grain represent my reputation; a tael and a tiny fraction represent the blood of the people. If I take less, the people will gain more. If I were to accept even a single extra tael, it would tarnish my virtue. I must avoid such social exchanges. If the gift is clean, where does it truly come from?" After posting this declaration, no one ever dared to offer him a gift again.

礼部尚书为官清　培育人才著作丰
门前贴示禁馈送　断绝贿赂仁德兴

The Minister of Rites had hands immaculate,
In writing and teaching a mentor accurate.
He hung his refusal of gifts on display,
Ensuring that benevolence held full sway.

第九章

卫国利民

Chapter Nine：

Defending the Nation and Benefiting the People

一、治水利民（夏禹）

禹，我国古代夏后氏部落的领袖，奉舜之命治理洪水。他手执工具，领导着青、壮、老年劳力，日夜苦干，疏通江河，兴修沟渠，导河入海。洪水平息后，人们安居乐业，农业生产得以发展。他治洪水时，劳苦奔波累得腿肚子消瘦，小腿上无毛，三过家门不入，多年来被人们歌功颂德。舜把他选为继承人。禹被奉为夏朝第一代国君。

1. Taming the Waters to Benefit the People

Yu was the leader of the ancient Xiahoushi tribe and was tasked by Emperor Shun with managing the great floods. Armed with simple tools, he led people of all ages, from the young to the elderly, working tirelessly day and night to dredge rivers, build canals, and guide water to the sea. Once the floods subsided, the people enjoyed peace and prosperity, and agricultural production flourished. During his efforts, the constant labor left his calves thin and hairless, and he passed by his own home three times without entering. For many years, his deeds were celebrated in songs and praise. Shun, recognizing his dedication, appointed him as his successor. Yu became the first ruler of the Xia Dynasty.

大禹治水盖世功　　江海疏导九州通
过门不入鞠躬瘁　　百姓安居农业兴

For generations no one could match Yu the Great,
Who caused the floodwaters to dissipate.
So single-minded he never crossed his own threshold,
The peasantry and farmers knew peace untold.

二、桑林祷雨（商汤）

商汤，古代商部族的领袖。大旱时，他在桑林向天祈祷，剪了自己的头发、指甲，即情愿自己死去，也希望上天降雨，利于百姓。他不断积累力量，陆续灭了附近的葛、夏的联盟韦及顾、昆吾等国，经十一次出征，成为当时的强国。各地百姓如大旱时望云霓一样，渴盼他来解救。在各族人民的拥戴下，一举攻灭了残暴的夏桀，建立了商朝。

2. Praying for Rain in the Mulberry Forest

Shang Tang was the leader of the ancient Shang tribe. During a severe drought, he went to the mulberry forest and prayed to the heavens for rain. In an act of profound sacrifice, he cut his hair and nails, even offering his own life in hopes that the heavens would bring rain to benefit the people. On the military front, he steadily built his power, conquering neighboring tribes and their allies—such as the Ge, Wei, Gu, and Kunwu—through eleven campaigns. As his strength grew, his people became a dominant force, and the masses from other states eagerly awaited his help, yearning for relief like people hoping for rain. With the support of various tribes,Shang Tang overthrew the tyrannical Emperor Xia Jie and established the Shang Dynasty.

桑林祷雨为黎民　　网开三面世称仁
诛灭夏桀安天下　　解救百姓如霓云

Praying for intercessory rain among the mulberries,
His benevolence won the praise of his contemporaries.
By overthrowing Xia Jie peace was won again,
And the people found liberty like timely rain.

三、吊民伐罪（姜尚）

姜尚，吕氏，姓姜名尚，字子牙。商朝末年具有雄才大略的一位贤人。周文王专程到渭水之滨请他出山时，说对他"望之久矣"，故又称吕望。他发挥自己的韬略，帮助周武王完成吊民伐罪、灭商兴周的大业。周朝建国后，被封于东方，成为齐国的开国始祖，人称姜太公。后人将他的韬略集中一起，编成《六韬》。

3. Consoling the People and Punishing the Wicked

Jiang Shang, from the Lü clan, was born with the given name Jiang and styled himself Ziya. A sage of great talent and vision, he lived during the final years of the Shang Dynasty. When King Wen of Zhou traveled to the banks of the Wei River to seek his counsel, he famously remarked, "I have longed to meet you", which led to Jiang's nickname Lü Wang ("Wang" meaning "longed for"). With his brilliant military strategy, Jiang Shang helped King Wu of Zhou overthrow the Shang Dynasty. After the founding of the Zhou Dynasty, he was granted land in the east,where he became the founding ancestor of the State of Qi, earning the title "Jiang the Grandfather". Later generations compiled his military strategies into a work titled *Six Strategies*.

文韬武略姜子牙　八十三岁始奋发
吊民伐罪大业建　始封齐国春秋霸

In military and civil matters Jiang showed facility,
And exerted himself from the age of eighty-three.
He consoled the people and punished iniquity,
Thus fortifying the ancient State of Qi.

四、爱国忠魂（屈原）

屈原，名平，战国后期楚国贵族。楚怀王时曾为三闾大夫、左司徒。他对外主张联齐抗秦，对内主张选贤任能，严明法纪，却屡遭朝内奸臣子兰、靳尚等人攻击，怀王对他逐渐疏远。怀王死，襄王即位后，被放逐江南，长期流落于沅、湘流域。楚都被秦攻陷后，投汨罗江自沉。其《离骚》等作品充满爱国热忱。后人渐以每年五月端午表达对他纪念至今。

4. Being Patriotic and Loyal

Qu Yuan, also known as Qu Ping, was an aristocrat from the State of Chu during the late Warring States Period. He served as the "Three Dukes" (Sanlü Dafu), a high-ranking official in charge of rituals and education, under King Huai of Chu. Qu Yuan advocated for strict legal reforms and the careful selection of capable officials, while also pushing for an alliance with the State of Qi to resist the growing threat of the State of Qin. However, his efforts were undermined by corrupt officials like Zi Lan and Jin Shang, leading to his gradual marginalization by King Huai. After King Huai's death, when King Xiang ascended the throne, Qu Yuan was exiled to the southern regions of the Yangtze River, where he spent years wandering through the Yuan and Xiang areas. Following the fall of Chu's capital to Qin forces, Qu Yuan,devastated by his country's downfall, drowned himself in the Miluo River. His works, such as *Li Sao* (*The Lament*), are filled with patriotic fervor. To this day, people commemorate his memory during the Dragon Boat Festival on the 5th of May according to the lunar calendar.

楚宫奸相嫉贤能　兴国大计未能行
《离骚》吟出爱国志　万民千年念屈翁

Treacherous ministers envied Qu Yuan's ability,
So his ambitions for the state ended in futility.
His Lament is a masterpiece full of national pride,
Qu Yuan is still remembered far and wide.

五、盗亦有道（盗跖）

跖，或蹠，意为足掌，人之最下部位，寓当时社会上最低层的奴隶，统治者诬称其为"盗跖"，春秋末年奴隶起义的领袖。古籍记他"休卒徒于太山之阳"，"从卒九千人，横行天下"。所到之处"大国守城、小国入保"。当时许多国家都出现跖，可知"跖"应为当时奴隶起义的代称。

5. Honour Among Outlaws

The term "Zhi" refers to the "sole" of the foot, symbolizing the lowest social class—slaves—in ancient Chinese society. Rulers slandered the famous outlaw Dao Zhi, the leader of a slave rebellion during the late Spring and Autumn Period, calling him "Dao Zhi" (meaning "the sole"). Ancient texts record that he "stationed his troops at the southern foot of Mount Tai" and "had nine thousand followers who roamed the world". Wherever he went, "great countries guarded their borders, while smaller ones paid him protection money". From this, we can infer that "Zhi" became synonymous with slave uprisings, highlighting the social upheaval of the time.

奴隶造反图生存　摆脱枷锁做完人
盗亦有道讲仁义　推翻奴制社会新

Slaves rebelled so as to escape captivity,
They broke through shackles to find liberty.
Outlaws shared a righteous code of their own,
Becoming freeman when autocracy was overthrown.

六、千古一帝（秦始皇）

秦始皇，姓嬴，名政，初为战国时秦国国君，先后兼并六国。公元前221年建立了我国历史上第一个统一的多民族的封建国家。他自称皇帝，分全国为三十六郡，统一货币、文字、度量衡，修驰道，四处巡视，北修长城，防御匈奴；南定百越，戍守五岭。推动了我国政治、经济的发展。但秦朝因严刑竣法，租役繁重，二世而亡。

6. The First Emperor

Qin Shi Huang, born Ying Zheng, was the ruler of the State of Qin during the Warring States period. He successfully annexed the other six states, and in 221 BC, he established the first unified multi-ethnic feudal empire in Chinese history. He declared himself "Emperor" and divided the country into thirty-six administrative regions. His reforms included unifying currency, writing, weights and measures, and building an extensive road system. He also conducted nationwide surveys and commissioned the construction of the Great Wall to defend against the Xiongnu. In the south, he pacified and garrisoned the regions beyond the Five Ridges. His reign spurred significant political and economic advancements for China. However, his dynasty collapsed shortly after his death, as his son, the Second Emperor, continued his father's draconian policies, enforcing harsh laws, excessive taxes, and labor burdens, which led to widespread unrest.

> 毁誉不一秦始皇　统一六国废分邦
> 政治经济促发展　严刑竣法二世亡

Qin Shihuang has a checkered reputation,
Through he unified Six States into a nation.
He revolutionised politics and the economy,
But despotism ensured the end of the Qin monarchy.

七、筑城守边（蒙恬）

蒙恬，祖籍齐，自其祖父蒙骜起，世代为秦将。秦统一六国后，为防匈奴南下骚扰，奉秦始皇命，率军三十万向北击败匈奴，收复河南地。为防匈奴再度南下，奉命修筑长城，守边多年。赵高阴谋帮胡亥即位为秦二世后，蒙恬与公子扶苏一起被冤杀。当时书写竹简用一竹棒，用线系上毛。蒙恬为书写方便，令人将毛插入竹管内，发明了毛笔。

7. Building the Great Wall and Garrisoning the Borders

Meng Tian, whose ancestral home was in the State of Qi, came from a family of military generals that had served the Qin Dynasty since his grandfather's time. After Emperor Qin Shihuang unified the six warring states, Meng Tian was ordered to lead an army of 300,000 troops to defeat the Huns and reclaim the land lost south of the Yellow River. To prevent further incursions from the Huns, he oversaw the construction of the Great Wall and garrisoned the northern borders for many years. However, after the scheming prime minister Zhao Gao helped Huhai ascend to the throne, Meng Tian and his ally, Prince Fusu, were both unjustly executed. During this time, writing was done using bamboo sticks tied with animal hair, but Meng Tian improved the process by inserting bristles into hollow bamboo, thus inventing the Chinese brush.

秦将蒙恬守北边　长城蜿蜒防狼烟
护卫万家北方靖　改进毛笔益文坛

General Meng Tian garrisoned the border regions,
And the Great Wall zigzagged to stop foreign legions.
He maintained peace and guarded the northern population,
Redesigning the writing brush was his cultural innovation.

八、首义反秦（陈胜）

陈胜，一名涉，秦末农民起义的领袖，阳城（今安徽宿县）人，雇农出身。公元前209年被秦征发戍边，天雨误期，按当时的法令误期当斩，他便与吴广等人在蕲县大泽乡联合九百戍卒反秦起义。起义军发展到几万人后，在陈（今河南淮阳）建立第一个农民政权——张楚，被推为王。一度攻破燕赵等地，后来在秦军反扑时，退至下城父（今安徽蒙城），被叛徒杀害。

8. The First Revolt Against the Qin Regime

Chen Sheng, also known as Chen She, was the leader of a peasant uprising during the late Qin Dynasty. He was from Yangcheng (present-day Su County, Anhui Province) and came from a humble farming background. In 209 BC, he was conscripted into the army to garrison the borders by the Qin Dynasty. Due to heavy rain, his unit was delayed, and under the harsh laws of the time, missing the deadline would have led to his execution. Faced with this unjust fate, he and Wu Guang rallied 900 fellow soldiers to launch a rebellion at Dazexiang in Qi County. As their forces grew to tens of thousands, they established the first peasant regime, Zhang Chu, in Chen (modern-day Huaiyang, Henan). Chen Sheng declared himself king. The rebellion initially enjoyed success, capturing territories of the former states of Yan and Zhao. However, the Qin forces retaliated, and as their army retreated to Xia Chengfu (now Mengcheng, Anhui), Chen Sheng was betrayed and assassinated by traitors.

大泽烽火戍卒燃　"张楚"势成秦丧胆
陈胜王逞鸿鹄志　虽败犹荣青史鲜

Some frontier soldiers lit the flame of the Dazexiang uprising,
The rebel regime left the Qin Empire in fear of demising.
Chen Sheng was as ambitious as a masterful swan,
His victorious defeat in legend lives on.

九、平吕兴汉（周勃）

周勃，沛（今江苏沛县）人，秦末随刘邦一起起义反秦，以军功为将军，封绛侯。汉朝建立后，又从刘邦平定韩王信、陈豨与卢绾的叛乱。吕后掌权时，任用诸吕，朝廷为诸吕把持，形势危急。他与陈平等合谋，诛杀企图夺取政权的吕产、吕禄等。平定诸吕之乱后，又到代地迎来刘邦幼子刘恒，拥立为帝（即汉文帝），后任丞相。

9. Suppressing the Lü Family and Reviving the Han Court

Zhou Bo, originally from Pei (present-day Pei County, Jiangsu Province), joined Liu Bang in the later years of the Qin Dynasty to rise up against the regime. His military achievements earned him the rank of general, and he was conferred the title of Marquis of Jiang. After the establishment of the Han Dynasty, Zhou Bo played a crucial role in helping Liu Bang quell the rebellions of Han Xin, Chen Xie, and Lu Wan. When Empress Lü assumed power, she appointed members of her clan to key positions, forming a dangerous faction that threatened the stability of the Han regime. To restore order, Zhou Bo, together with Chen Ping and others, conspired to eliminate Lü Chan and Lü Lu, the key figures behind the potential usurpation. After successfully removing the Lü faction, Zhou Bo traveled to Dai to welcome Liu Heng, the youngest son of Liu Bang, and supported his ascension to the throne as Emperor Wen of Han. Zhou Bo was subsequently rewarded with the position of Prime Minister for his loyalty and service.

> 诸吕欲把汉室篡　周勃毅然平吕乱
> 赴代迎帝续大统　中兴汉室遂民愿

The Lü family wanted to usurp the throne,
But Zhou Bo insisted it wasn't theirs to own.
A new emperor rose in Dai's embrace,
And the Han rejoiced, restoring their rightful place.

十、力挫匈奴（卫青）

卫青，字仲卿，河东平阳（今山西临汾）人，西汉名将。汉武帝的卫皇后之弟，官拜大将军，封长平侯。西汉初年，匈奴不断对北方各地骚扰，北边数郡饱受其害。汉武帝元朔二年（前127年），他奉命率军大败匈奴，控制了河套地区。元狩四年（前119年）又同霍去病一起打败匈奴主力。在汉武帝时七次击败匈奴，制止匈奴贵族的掠夺，保卫了人民的生命与财产安全。

10. Defeating the Huns

Wei Qing, styled Zhongqing, was from Pingyang (present-day Linfen, Shanxi) and was a renowned general of the Western Han Dynasty. He was the younger brother of Empress Wei, the wife of Emperor Wu of Han. Wei Qing was appointed General-in-Chief and conferred the title Marquis of Changping. During the early years of the Western Han Dynasty, the Huns repeatedly harassed the northern territories, causing significant suffering to the people. In the second year of the Yuanshuo Era (127 BC), Emperor Wu of Han instructed Wei Qing to lead the army against the Huns, achieving a decisive victory and gaining control of the Hetao region. In the fourth year of Yuanshuo (119 BC), Wei Qing, together with Huo Qubing, dealt a crushing blow to the main Han force. Over the course of Emperor Wu's reign, Wei Qing successfully defeated the Huns seven times, protecting the people from their raids and safeguarding their lives and wealth.

叱咤风云战北边　横刀立马敌胆寒
七败匈奴功盖世　边疆巩固黎民安

Wei Qing was invincible when guarding the frontier,
His martial exploits filled the enemy with fear.
He suppressed the Huns fully seven times,
Protecting the people of those northern climes.

十一、为公忘家（霍去病）

霍去病，东汉河东平阳（今山西临汾）人。奉武帝命于元狩二年（前121年）两次率部大败匈奴，控制了河西地区，打开了通往西域的道路。元狩四年（前119年）与卫青共同击败匈奴主力。他曾前后六次率军击败匈奴，保护了北方百姓的生命与财产。被封为骠骑将军、冠军侯。汉武帝要为他修建府第，他谢绝说："匈奴未灭，何以家为！"

11. Putting the State Before the Family

Huo Qubing was from Pingyang (present-day Linfen, Shaanxi) and lived during the Western Han Dynasty. In the second year of the Yuanshuo Era (121 BC), he received orders from Emperor Wu of Han and led his forces to defeat the Huns twice. He took control of the Hexi Corridor (the area to the west of the Yellow River) and opened the route to the Western Regions (the Han Dynasty's term for areas west of the Yumen Pass, including present-day Xinjiang and parts of Central Asia). In the fourth year of Yuanshuo (119 BC), Huo Qubing, alongside Wei Qing, dealt a decisive blow to the main Hun army. Over the course of his career, he led his troops to defeat the Huns six times, protecting the lives and property of the people in the northern territories. He was promoted to the rank of Chief Cavalry General and conferred the title of Champion Marquis. When Emperor Wu offered to build a grand residence for him, Huo Qubing humbly declined, saying: "The Huns are not yet destroyed—how can I think of a villa now?"

骠骑将军霍去病　屡战匈奴获全胜
匈奴未灭何为家　公而忘私大将风

Huo Qubing served as Cavalry Chief General,
Defeating the Huns made him a scourge perennial.
He refused to build a family home while the enemy was standing,
Personal affairs took a backseat to this conflict demanding.

十二、开通西域（张骞）

张骞，西汉时城固（今陕西城固）人，官至大行，封博望侯。汉武帝建元二年（前 139 年）奉命出使大月氏，约其夹攻匈奴。他越过葱岭，亲抵大月氏、大宛、康居、大夏等中亚各国。途中曾被匈奴扣押十一年，仍坚贞不屈。回国后，又于元狩四年（前 119 年）出使乌孙等地。他两次奉命出使，前后二十几年，历尽艰苦，使汉朝与中亚各国建立了联系，促进了中西经济文化的交流与发展。

12. Opening the Route to the Western Regions

Zhang Qian was from Chenggu (present-day Chenggu County in Shaanxi Province), where he held the official position of Minister of Rites and was bestowed the title of Marquis Bowang. In the Seamd year of the Jianyuan Era (139 BC), during the reign of Emperor Wu of Han, he was tasked with a diplomatic mission to the Yuezhi, with the aim of persuading them to join forces against the Huns. Zhang Qian crossed the Congling Mountains (the Pamir Range) and traveled through several Central Asian states, including the Yuezhi, Dawan, Kangju, and Daxia. During his journey, he was captured by the Huns and held in captivity for eleven years. Despite this hardship, he remained resolute and unyielding. Upon his return to China, he was again sent on a diplomatic mission in the foureh year of the Yuanshou Era (119 BC), this time to the Wusun and other regions. Zhang Qian undertook these missions twice, spending over twenty years in arduous conditions. His dedication paved the way for the Han Dynasty to establish diplomatic ties with Central Asian states, thereby fostering economic and cultural exchanges between the East and the West.

奉命出使不辱命　身陷囹圄不震惊
两赴西域伟绩建　经济交流文化兴

Fulfilling diplomatic duties seriously,
Zhang Qian remained calm even in custody.
Twice to the Western Regions he managed to quest,
Promoting exchange between East and West.

十三、扬名西域（班超）

班超，字仲升，东汉右平陵（陕西兴平）人。汉明帝永平十六年（前73年）奉命率三十六人出使西域。他毅然赶走匈奴的势力，恢复了汉朝与鄯善、于阗的关系。后来在汉朝的支援下，又击败焉耆、龟兹等国，被任命为西域都护，封为定远侯。他在西域活动达三十一年，使西域各地人民摆脱了匈奴贵族的奴役，恢复了中西交通，使汉朝国威远播四方。

13. Being Famed in the Western Regions

Ban Chao, styled Zhongsheng, was from Pingling (present-day Xingping City in Shaanxi) during the Western Han Dynasty. In the sixteenth year of the Yongping Era (73 BC) during the reign of Emperor Ming of Han, he was tasked with leading a diplomatic mission to the Western Regions with a group of thirty-six men. With firm resolve, he expelled the Hun forces and successfully restored diplomatic relations between the Han Dynasty and the states of Shanshan and Yutian. Later, with the support of the Han court, he defeated other Central Asian states such as Yanqi and Qiuci. As a result, he was appointed as the Frontier Commander of the Western Regions and was conferred the title Marquis Dingyuan. Ban Chao spent thirty-one years in the Western Regions, liberating the local populations from the oppressive rule of the Hun aristocracy. His efforts revitalized communication and trade between the East and the West, spreading the prestige of the Han Dynasty far and wide.

三十六人使西域　见机而作败匈奴
炎汉国威传播远　守边卫民大都护

Thirty-six men to the West were sent,
Seizing the moment, the Huns were bent.
The Han's great prestige spread far and wide,
Honoring the commander who guarded with pride.

十四、闻鸡起舞（祖逖）

祖逖，字士雅，东晋范阳（今河北定兴）人。少有大志，西晋末年率亲党数百家南移。常闻鸡起舞，磨炼身体与意志，准备北伐。晋元帝建兴元年（313年）任豫州刺史，奉命率部渡江北伐，他中流击楫，表示恢复中原的决心。他亲率北上的队伍，受到各族人民的响应。又进入雍丘（今河南杞县），收复黄河以南地区。但朝内矛盾重重，对他不支持，祖逖后忧郁病死。

14. Rising Early to Practise Swordsmanship When Hearing the Cock Crow

Zu Ti, styled Shiya, was from Fanyang (present-day Dingxing County in Hebei Province) during the Eastern Jin Dynasty. From a young age, he harbored great ambitions and led his clan southward during the later years of the Western Jin Dynasty. He was known for rising early at the sound of the rooster's crow to practice his swordsmanship, using the time to hone both his physical strength and willpower in preparation for a northern campaign. In the first year of the Jianxing Era (313AD) during the reign of Emperor Yuan of Jin, Zu Ti was appointed as the Prefect of Yuzhou. He was tasked with leading his troops across the Yangtze River on a northern expedition. While crossing, he struck his oar as a symbolic gesture of his determination to recover the lost territories of the central plains. His army was met with enthusiastic support from various ethnic groups. After advancing into Yongqiu (modern-day Qi County in Henan), he succeeded in reclaiming the areas south of the Yellow River. However, due to internal conflicts within the court, he received little support. Overcome by illness and despair, he eventually passed away.

闻鸡起舞赞祖逖　誓收失地中流楫
军进河南万民颂　宏愿未达空嘘唏

Zu Ti was praised for practising at the cock's crow,
Reclaiming lost territory was in his marrow.
In Henan, the people sang his name,
But sorrow fell when he failed to claim his aim.

十五、汉化交融（拓跋宏）

拓跋宏（元宏），即北魏孝文帝，公元471—499年在位。他自小在祖母冯太后的教育下，学习汉族进步文化。五岁即位。在冯太后临朝时，曾改革吏治，实行三长制、均田制。他亲政后，又进一步汉化改革。太和十八年（494年）从平城迁都洛阳，改鲜卑姓为汉姓，改革鲜卑人落后的风俗、习惯及服制、语言，奖励鲜卑人与汉人通婚，改革官制、朝仪等。加速了北方各族汉化的过程，促进了中华民族大融合。

15. Sinicisation

Tuo Bahong (Yuanhong), better known as Emperor Xiaowen of the Northern Wei Dynasty, reigned from 471 to 499 AD. Under the guidance of his grandmother, Empress Feng, he was introduced to the advanced culture of the Han people from an early age. He ascended to the throne at the age of five. During the regency of Empress Dowager Feng, significant reforms were made, including the establishment of the Three-Level System (where five families form a neighborhood, five neighborhoods form a village, and five villages form a town) and the Equal-Field System. When Emperor Xiaowen came of age and assumed full control, he further intensified the Sinicisation reforms. In the eighteenth year of the Taihe Era (494 AD), he moved the capital from Pingcheng (modern-day Datong) to Luoyang, implemented a policy of changing Xianbei family names to Han surnames, and sought to reform the backward customs, habits, attire, and language of the Xianbei people. He also encouraged intermarriage between the Xianbei and the Han and reformed both the official system and court rituals. These measures accelerated the process of Sinicisation and played a crucial role in promoting the integration of China's diverse ethnic groups, fostering a stronger sense of national unity.

好个北魏孝文帝　决心改革顺民意
多次诏令促汉化　民族融合现百利

Emperor Xiaowen was unquestionably great,
Launching reform in line with popular mandate.
With countless edicts, he urged the change,
And unity brought benefits within his range.

十六、巾帼女杰（冼夫人）

冼夫人，南朝及隋朝时的少数民族领袖。高凉（今广东阳江）人。她仁德爱民，能团结各族人民，海南等地归附者千余人。嫁给高凉太守冯宝。冯死后，继续帮助陈国统一岭南，击败谋反的广州刺史欧阳纥。陈武帝永定二年（558年），遣其子率百越首领朝见陈武帝。陈亡后隋将韦洸入广州时，又击败王仲宣的叛乱。后被隋文帝封为"谯国夫人"。百姓们对她感恩，尊为"岭南圣母"。

16. A Heroine

LadyXian was a leader of minority groups during the Southern Dynasties and the Sui Dynasty. She hailed from Gaoliang (modern-day Yangjiang, Guangdong). Known for her benevolence and compassion, she had the remarkable ability to unite various ethnic groups, and as a result, thousands of people rallied to her cause. She married Feng Bao, the Prefect of Gaoliang. After his death, she continued to support the State of Chen in its efforts to unify the Lingnan region, defeating Ouyang He, the rebellious Prefect of Guangzhou. In the Seamd year of the Yongding Era (558 AD) under Emperor Wu of Chen, Lady Xian sent her son, along with the tribal leaders of the Lingnan region, to pay tribute to the Emperor. Following the fall of the Chen Dynasty, when General Wei Guang of the Sui Dynasty entered Guangzhou, she helped crush the rebellion led by Wang Zhongxuan, earning the title "Lady Who Safeguards the State" from the Sui Dynasty. The common people were deeply grateful to her and revered her as the "of Lingnan Sage Mother".

巾帼女杰冼夫人　团结各族爱黎民
维护统一屡平叛　民间乐颂比作神

Lady Xian was a heroine of repute,
Allying ethnic groups and pacifying dispute.
Time and again rebellions she put down,
Among ordinary folk she had a godlike renown.

十七、贞观之治（李世民）

唐太宗李世民，陇西成纪（今甘肃秦安）人，唐高祖李渊和窦皇后的次子，初封秦王，任尚书令。陆续战败农民军及各地割据势力后继李渊称帝，贞观二年（628年）统一全国。在位期间，吸取隋亡的教训，推行均田制、租庸调法、三省制，虚心纳谏、重用贤才，加强对地方官的考核，经济得以发展。又派兵击败东突厥的骚扰，与周边各族友好交流，促进与各族各国的文化交流，史称"贞观之治"。

17. The Benign Administration of the Zhenguan Era

Li Shimin, better known as Emperor Taizong of the Tang Dynasty, was born in Chengji, Longxi (modern-day Qin'an County, Gansu Province). He was the second son of Emperor Gaozu (Li Yuan) and Empress Dou. Initially granted the titles of Marquis of Qin and Prime Minister, Li Shimin followed in his father's footsteps. After years of quelling peasant uprisings and defeating various warlords, he ascended to the throne, unifying the country in the second year of the Zhenguan Era (628 AD). During his reign, Li Shimin learned valuable lessons from the fall of the Sui Dynasty. He implemented the Equal-field System, a new taxation and conscription policy, and the Three Departments system of governance. Renowned for his openness to advice, he actively sought counsel and appointed capable officials. He also reformed the assessment of local officials, which helped stimulate regional economic growth. Additionally, Li Shimin suppressed raids by the Eastern Turkic Khaganate (Tujue) and established friendly relations with neighboring ethnic groups, fostering cultural exchanges across the borders of the Tang Empire. This period of stability and prosperity became known as the "Benign Administration of the Zhenguan Era", a model of effective governance in Chinese history.

屡平群雄秦王功　"贞观之治"盛唐兴
纳谏爱民行仁政　史载盛唐誉寰瀛

The Marquis of Qin eliminated local agitation,
Shaping the Tang into a benign administration.
His cornerstones were counsel and benevolence,
The Great Tang Dynasty was widely praised hence.

十八、守边为民（李勣）

李勣，即徐懋功，名世勣，因功赐姓李，为避唐太宗讳，名李勣，离狐（今山东菏泽）人。初从翟让反隋，参加瓦岗寨起义，以战功封东海郡公。归唐后，任右武侯大将军，封曹国公。唐太宗贞观三年（629年）与李靖联合出击东突厥，因功封吴国公。他曾奉命镇守并州，防御突厥南下达十六年，保护了北方各地人民的生命财产。

18. Guarding the Border for the People

Li Ji, originally named Xu Maogong, was granted the family name Li by Emperor Taizong of Tang in recognition of his service. To avoid confusion with the emperor, he shortened his name from Shiji to Ji. He hailed from Lihu (modern-day Heze, Shandong Province). Initially, he followed Zhai Rang in the revolt against the Sui Dynasty and participated in the Wagangzhai uprising, earning the title Duke of East Sea for his military achievements. After pledging allegiance to the Tang Dynasty, Li Ji was appointed Grand General of Youwuhou and conferred the title Duke of the State of Cao. In the third year of the Zhenguan Era (629 AD), he joined forces with Li Jing in a military campaign against the Eastern Turkic Khaganate,earning the title Duke of the State of Wu for his contributions. Li Ji was then assigned to guard Bingzhou for sixteen years, defending against the southward incursions of the Tujue. His efforts protected the lives and property of the northern people, securing peace in the region.

李勣本是徐懋功　反隋兴唐赐李姓
防卫突厥十六载　万民称赞曹国公

Xu was Li Ji's original surname,
But was altered in recognition of his fame.
Defending foreign troops for sixteen years,
The Duke of Cao was glorified by commoners and peers.

十九、平叛惠民（郭子仪）

郭子仪，唐代郑县（今陕西渭南）人。初中武举，官至北都护府史。安禄山、史思明叛乱时，受命任朔方节度使，在河北击败叛军。唐肃宗即位后，任副元帅，配合回纥兵收复长安、洛阳，因功升中书令。唐代宗广德元年（763年）仆固怀恩叛乱，纠合回纥、吐蕃对唐朝西北各地骚扰时，他说服回纥酋长，与唐朝恢复友好关系，保持了西北的安宁。

19. Crushing Rebellions for the Benefit of the People

Guo Ziyi was from Zheng County (now Weinan City, Shaanxi Province). He began his career as a provincial martial arts candidate and was later appointed to an official position in the Northern Frontier Command. When An Lushan and Shi Siming led their rebellion, Guo was appointed as the Prefect of Shuofang and successfully defeated the rebel forces. After Emperor Suzong ascended the throne,Guo was promoted to Vice Marshal and worked alongside the Huihe troops to recapture Chang'an and Luoyang, earning him the position of Head of the Secretariat. In the first year of the Guangde Era (763 AD) during Emperor Daizong's reign, when Pugu Huai'en led an insurrection and allied with the Huihe and Tubo tribes to raid the northwest of the Tang Empire, Guo Ziyi successfully persuaded the Huihe leaders to restore friendly relations with the Tang Dynasty. His diplomatic efforts played a key role in maintaining peace in the northwest.

安史之乱祸盛唐　玄宗避难走仓忙
幸有名将郭子仪　兴唐安民大任当

An Lushan unsettled the rich Tang Dynasty,
And compelled the Emperor Xuanzong to flee.
But Guo Ziyi, a general true and grand,
Brought peace and order back to the land.

二十、为国殉难（颜杲卿）

颜杲卿，字昕，唐朝临沂（今山东临沂）人，初任范阳户曹参军，曾被安禄山提升为常山太守。安史叛乱后，他为了维护国家统一，毅然设计杀死安禄山的部将李钦凑，生擒安的部将高邈、何千年后，押送京师。因功升卫尉兼御史中丞。接着与其弟颜真卿一起继续抗击安、史。次年，史思明破常山，他被擒押往安禄山处，誓不屈服，被肢解殉难。

20. Sacrifice on Behalf of the Country

Yan Gaoqing, who styled himself Xin, was from Linyi (now Linyi City, Shandong Province). He initially served as a staff officer in Fanyang Prefecture and was later promoted to Prefect by An Lushan. When An Lushan launched his rebellion, Yan devised a plan to eliminate An's forces. He killed General Li Qingcou and captured two of An Lushan's key followers, Gao Miao and He Qiannian, whom he escorted to the capital. For his heroic actions, Yan was promoted to Chief of the Praetorian Guard. Together with his younger brother, Yan Zhenqing, he continued to fight against the forces of An Lushan and Shi Siming. However, in the following year, Shi Siming's forces captured the city of Changshan, and Yan was taken prisoner to An Lushan's headquarters. Refusing to surrender, Yan was tortured and dismembered, ultimately sacrificing his life for the country.

> 常山太守颜杲卿　忠奸是非辨识明
> 禄山提拔反禄山　视死如归气如虹

Yan Gaoqing was the head of Changshan,
He stood up against rebels as a righteous man.
And broke with An Lushan, his one-time patron,
Smiling though he faced execution.

二十一、满门忠烈（杨业）

杨业，即杨继业，世为麟州（陕西神木）地方势力的领袖。初为北汉刘崇的将领，任建雄军节度使，守卫北方边境，号"杨无敌"。归宋后，任代州刺史。宋太宗雍熙三年（986年）率军北伐攻辽时，曾收复云、应、寰、朔四州。不久因宋军在河北战败，奉命撤退。在孤军无援的情况下，陷于陈家谷口（今山西朔州南）重伤被俘，绝食而死。其子孙亦继续抗辽，后世有很多杨家将忠烈抗敌的故事。

21. The Loyal and Heroic Family

Yang Ye, also known as Yang Jiye, was the leader of local forces in Linzhou (now Shenmu, Shaanxi Province). His family had held leadership in the region for generations. Initially, he served as a general under Liu Chong of the Northern Han Dynasty, where he was appointed Prefect of the Jianxiong Army, responsible for defending the northern borders. He earned the title "Yang the Invincible" for his military prowess. After pledging allegiance to the Song Dynasty, Yang was appointed as Prefect of Dai State. In the Third year of the Yongxi Era (986 AD) during the reign of Emperor Taizong of Song, he led an army to campaign against the Liao Dynasty, successfully recovering the states of Yun, Ying, Huan, and Shuo. However, following a defeat of Song forces in Hebei, he was ordered to retreat. Isolated and without support, Yang was trapped at the mouth of Chenjiagu Pass (now in southern Shuozhou, Shanxi Province), where he was mortally wounded and ultimately died from starvation. Despite his death, Yang's descendants carried on the fight against the Liao Dynasty. The heroic exploits of the Yang family, famed for their loyalty and valor, have been passed down through many stories of steadfast resistance against the enemy.

契丹惧怕"杨无敌"　守卫北疆战火熄
满门忠烈杨家将　惊天动地鬼神泣

Armies of rival states feared "Yang the Invincible",
Who defended the northern frontier on principle.
The Yang family bred warriors for generations,
The heavens, earth and spirits admired their dedication.

二十二、守卫汴京（李纲）

李纲，字伯纪，邵武（今福建邵武）人，宋徽宗时进士，北宋末任太常少卿。宋钦宗靖康元年（1126 年）金兵初围汴京（开封）时，阻止钦宗南迁，以尚书右丞相任亲征行营使，团结军民击退金兵，保卫汴京。不久被投降派排斥。次年，高宗在临安（杭州）即位，李纲为丞相，主张北向收复失地。多次上疏陈述抗金大计，虽未被采纳，但一直被百姓称颂。

22. Safeguarding the Capital City of Bianjing

LiGang, from Shaowu (now Shaowu County in Fujian Province), styled himself Boji. He became a top scholar during the reign of Emperor Huizong of Song and, at the end of the Northern Song Dynasty, served as the Shaoqing Minor Minister in the Ministry of Rites. In the first year of the Jingkang Era (1126 AD), when the Jin army first laid siege to Bianjing (Kaifeng), Li Gang played a crucial role in preventing Emperor Qinzong from retreating south. Appointed as Prime Minister and given the title of "Head of the Front Command", he led the defense, uniting both the military and civilians to resist the Jin invaders and protect the capital city. However, soon after, he was sidelined by those who favored surrender. The following year, when Emperor Gaozong ascended to the throne in Lin'an (Hangzhou), Li Gang was reinstated as Prime Minister. He continued to advocate for military action to recover the lost territories to the north, repeatedly submitting memorials with his strategic proposals to counter the Jin Dynasty. Although his ideas were never adopted, his loyalty and resolve were remembered and praised by the people.

金兵南下汴京危　力拙降派坚守卫
功业未就虽遗憾　民间称颂好口碑

The capital of Song was in deep jeopardy,
But Li Gang withstood resistance to guard the city.
Although his dreams were left in tatters,
People felt his vision was what really matters.

二十三、力抗金兵（宗泽）

宗泽，字汝霖。义乌（今浙江义乌）人。宋哲宗时进士。钦宗靖康元年（1126年）知磁州，招募义勇抗金兵。次年任东京留守，招集王善、杨进等义军，联络两河八字军等部，用岳飞为将，屡败金兵。南宋初年他多次上书，力请高宗北上返回汴京，收复失地，都被投降派阻拦，以致忧愤成疾。临终连呼三声"过河"而死。

23. Determined Resistance Against the Army of the Jin Dynasty

Zong Ze, courtesy name Rulin, was from Yiwu (now Yiwu City in Zhejiang Province). He passed the imperial examinations during the reign of Emperor Zhezong of the Song Dynasty. In the first year of the Jingkang Era (1126 AD), during the reign of Emperor Qinzong of Song, Zong Ze was appointed as the Prefect of Cizhou. He immediately recruited volunteer forces to resist the Jin army. The following year, he was promoted to Guardian General of Dongjing, where he rallied additional volunteer forces led by Wang Shan and Yang Jin. He also coordinated with other military factions and appointed Yue Fei as General in Command. Under their leadership, the Jin army suffered repeated defeats. In the early years of the Southern Song Dynasty, Zong Ze submitted multiple petitions to Emperor Gaozong, urging a northern campaign to recover Bianjing and reclaim lost territories. However, his proposals were consistently blocked by defeatist factions within the court. Deeply disheartened, Zong Ze succumbed to illness. On his deathbed, he cried out "Cross the Yellow River" three times before passing away.

老将抗金多致胜　降派掣肘功未成
虽殁未损报国志　"家祭勿忘告乃翁"

An old general resisted the Jin army on many occasions,
But naysayers were immune to his powerful persuasion.
He would serve the country to the point of death,
And remembered his majesty in his final breath.

二十四、丹心汗青（文天祥）

文天祥，字履善，号文山，庐陵（今江西吉安）人，宋理宗时进士第一名。蒙古军攻鄂州时，上书反对迁都，未被采纳。宋度宗德祐元年（1275 年）蒙古军南下，在赣州组织义军抵抗。次年任右丞相，被派往元军议和，遭扣留。在镇江脱险后，沿海北上，与张世杰、陆秀夫联合抗元。被俘后押往大都（北京）。多次威胁利诱，终不屈服。就义前吟诗："人生自古谁无死，留取丹心照汗青。"

24. A Loyalist's Name

Wen Tianxiang, courtesy name Lü Shan and styled Wenshan, was a native of Luling (now Ji'an City in Jiangxi Province). He topped the imperial examinations during the reign of Emperor Lizong of the Song Dynasty. When the Mongol army attacked Ezhou (modern-day Ezhou, Hubei), Wen Tianxiang petitioned the Emperor, opposing the idea of relocating the capital. However, his petition was not accepted. In the first year of the Deyou Era (1275 AD) during the reign of Emperor Duzong, when the Mongol forces advanced southward, Wen organized a volunteer army in Ganzhou to resist the invaders. The following year, Wen was appointed as Deputy Prime Minister and sent to negotiate with the Yuan army. However, he was captured during the negotiations. He narrowly escaped danger in Zhenjiang, then joined forces with Zhang Shijie and LuXiufu in the coastal resistance against the Yuan. Eventually, he was captured again and brought to the Yuan capital, Dadu (modern-day Beijing). Despite repeated threats and offers of rewards, Wen Tianxiang remained steadfast and refused to surrender. Before his execution, he composed the famous lines: "Since ancient times, who has not died? I shall leave behind a loyalist's name in history."

自动抗元聚义兵　故邦扣押铁骨铮
屡拙屡起勇战斗　"留取丹心照汗青"

Wen rose against the Yuan with forces of his own,
Though captured by foes, his resolve had only grown.
Time and again he fought with courage, unbowed,
"Let my steadfast heart illuminate the ages, proud."

二十五、蒙古崛起（成吉思汗）

成吉思汗，即铁木真。出生于蒙古部孛儿只斤族。12 世纪被推举为首领。1206 年被拥戴为成吉思汗，建蒙古汗国。即位后，创蒙古文字，建司法制度。1214 年向金、宋进攻，占领中都（北京），后被尊为元太祖。进入中原后，成吉思汗得到大量人力、物力和中原的先进武器及军事技术。后来又大举西进，建立了横跨欧、亚的蒙古大汗国。

25. The Rise of the Mongols

Genghis Khan, born as Temujin, was a member of the Borjigin clan of the Mongol people. In the 12th century, he was elected as the leader of the Mongols. In 1206, he was formally proclaimed Genghis Khan, marking the foundation of the Mongol Empire. After ascending to the throne, Genghis Khan introduced the Mongolian script and established a judicial system. In 1214, he launched successful campaigns—one against the Jin Dynasty and the other against the Song Dynasty. He captured Zhongdu (modern-day Beijing) and laid the foundation for the, earning the title of "Founder of the Yuan". Upon entering the Central Plains, Genghis Khan gained significant resources, including manpower, military technology, and advanced weaponry. later, he initiated a large-scale westward campaign, ultimately establishing the vast Mongol Empire that spanned both Europe and Asia.

蒙古崛起在北疆　成吉思汗统各邦
灭金败宋元朝建　横跨欧亚霸东方

The Mongols rose from the northern skies,
Genghis united the tribes, their power to rise.
He crushed Jin and Song to found the Yuan,
His empire stretched from Europe to Asia's span.

二十六、灭元建明（朱元璋）

朱元璋，字国瑞，濠州钟离（今安徽凤阳）人。出身贫农，少时为僧。元朝末年参加郭子兴领导的红巾军。在元末群雄逐鹿中，战胜一个个对手，1368年建立明朝，年号洪武。同年攻下大都，推翻元朝统治。即位后普查户口，丈量土地，均平赋税，兴修水利，建立学校及科举制度，使元末社会经济残破的现象得以恢复与发展。

26. Destroying the Yuan Dynasty and Establishing the Ming Dynasty

Zhu Yuanzhang, courtesy name Guorui, was from Zhongli in Haozhou (present-day Fengyang County, Anhui Province). Born into a poor peasant family, he became a monk in his youth. In the later years of the Yuan Dynasty, he joined the Red Turban Army led by Guo Zixing in their resistance against the Yuan rulers. Amid the chaotic struggle for power during the decline of the Yuan Dynasty, Zhu Yuanzhang emerged victorious over his rivals and established the Ming Dynasty in 1368, adopting the era name Hongwu. In the same year, he captured the Yuan capital, Dadu (now Beijing), effectively overthrowing Yuan rule. Upon ascending to the throne, Zhu conducted a nationwide census, surveyed the land, standardized taxes, launched major water conservancy projects, and established schools along with an imperial examination system. These reforms helped restore and develop the severely damaged economy that had plagued the Yuan Dynasty's final years.

逐鹿获胜朱元璋　推翻元蒙乐梓桑
恢复生产多改进　大明王朝立东方

Zhu Yuanzhang wrested the throne from feudal lords,
Saving the people from the Yuan Dynasty hordes.
He resumed production with energy increased,
So the Great Ming stood proud in the East.

二十七、捍卫北京（于谦）

于谦，字廷益，明代浙江钱塘人，进士出身。任山西巡抚时，平反冤狱，为民称颂。明英宗正统十四年（1449年）土木堡之变，英宗被蒙古人也先截获后，任兵部尚书。在瓦剌接着南下时，力反迁都，调集重兵，亲率石亨等将领，修理城堡、训练军队，加强长城一线的防御，保住了北京。次年，也先见无隙可乘，遂释放了英宗。

27. Defending Beijing

Yu Qian, courtesy name Tingyi, was from Qiantang (modern-day Hangzhou, Zhejiang Province) and was a graduate of the imperial examination. During his tenure as Governor of Shanxi, he rectified wrongful convictions, earning widespread praise from the people. In the fourteenth year of the Zhengtong Era (1449), during the Battle of Tumu Fortress, Emperor Yingzong was captured by the Mongol leader Yexian. Subsequently, Yu Qian was appointed Minister of War. As the Oirat Mongols advanced southward, Yu strongly opposed the plan to relocate the capital. Instead, he mustered forces and, leading generals such as Shi Heng, oversaw the repair of fortresses, trained troops, and strengthened the defenses along the Great Wall. His efforts successfully preserved Beijing. The following year, realizing his mission had failed, Yexian released Emperor Yingzong.

力阻南迁调重兵　排除干扰保北京
修城聚将勤守卫　也先无耐放英宗

Yu Qian did his utmost to resist relocation,
He thought Beijing the best capital for the nation.
He raised troops and made fortifications strong,
So Yexian had to release the captive Yingzong.

二十八、抗倭名将（戚继光）

戚继光，字元敬，明朝东牟（今山东莱芜）人，将门出身。初任登州卫指挥佥事，后调浙江任参将、抵抗倭寇。他见旧军素质不良，遂至义乌招募农民、矿工，训练新军，即戚家军。戚家军军纪严整，战斗力强，倭寇闻风丧胆，成为抗倭主力。在台州曾获抗倭大胜。次年援闽，捣破倭寇在横屿的大本营。后又与俞大猷联手，剿平广东的倭寇，解除东南倭患。

28. A Famous General Resisting the Japanese Pirates

Qi Jiguang, courtesy name Yuanjing, was from Dongmou (modern-day Laiwu, Shandong Province) and hailed from a military family. Initially, he served as a military officer in Dengzhou, but later was promoted to Military Commissioner in Zhejiang, where he was tasked with defending against Japanese pirates. Observing the poor martial quality of the soldiers, Qi traveled to Yiwu to recruit peasants and miners, training them into a professional fighting force, known as the "Qi Family Army". The army became a key force in resisting the Japanese pirates, with its strict discipline and formidable combat skills instilling fear in the invaders. The Qi Family Army won a decisive victory against the pirates in Taizhou. The following year, they moved to Fujian, where they destroyed the Japanese pirates' main base on Hengyu Island. Later, Qi Jiguang teamed up with Yu Dayou to eliminate the pirate threat in Guangdong, effectively rooting out the danger from the southeastern coast.

倭寇为患年复年　万千百姓苦难言
戚家军兴灭倭寇　东南沿海百姓安

The Japanese brutes were a perpetual menace,
To the ordinary Chinese a scourge horrendous.
The Qi Family Army in defence rose,
Saving the coast from enemy blows.

二十九、东北新秀（努尔哈赤）

努尔哈赤，姓爱新觉罗，东北建州女真人。其先世曾被明朝封为建州卫指挥使。明英宗时迁到赫图阿拉（今辽宁新宾）。他少时常到抚顺互市，接触汉族文化。1583年起兵，用十年统一了建州各部。他制定满文，建立军政合一的八旗制度。1616年建元天命，表示继承女真族先世的帝业。他在东北经营四十多年，团结分散的女真各部，吸取汉族的文化与技术，为日后清军入关和建立清朝做下大量准备工作。

29. Arising Star in Northeast China

Nurhachi, whose clan name was Aisin Gioro, was a member of the Jurchen tribe from Jianzhou in northeast China. His ancestors had served as Military Commissioner of Jianzhou. During the reign of Emperor Yingzong of the Ming Dynasty, the clan moved to Hetuala (modern-day Xinbin County, Liaoning Province). As a young man, Nurhaci frequently visited the market fairs in Fushun, where he was exposed to Han culture. In 1583–1593, he began his campaign to unite the various Jurchen tribes of Jianzhou. He formalized the Manchu script and established the Eight Banners system, which integrated both military and civil governance. In 1616, he declared the founding of the Jianyuan Era, signaling his intent to carry on the legacy of his ancestors. For more than forty years, Nurhaci managed the region, uniting the Jurchen tribes, incorporating advanced Han culture and technology, and laying the groundwork for the eventual conquest of the Shanhai Pass and the founding of the Qing Dynasty.

建州女真起东北　努尔哈赤功绩巍
八旗铁骑闯天下　入关汉化民心归

The Jurchen of Jianzhou emerged in the Northeast,
Nurhachi's feats were praised the most.
The Eight Banners Cavalry overran the whole land,
Defeating the Ming and gaining the upper hand.

三十、驱洋卫台（郑成功）

郑成功，本名森，字大木。明朝南安（今福建南安）人，曾受明隆武帝赐姓朱，人称国姓爷。永历时为延平郡王。1646年清军入关后，1646年，郑成功反对其父郑芝龙降清，毅然起兵反清。以厦门、金门为根据地，活动于闽、粤、江、浙一带，曾北进入长江沿岸各地。1661年，应台湾人民要求，率舰队渡台湾海峡，驱逐侵占我国领土的荷兰殖民主义者。次年收复全岛，建立政府，制定法律，使汉人与高山族人民共同开发宝岛台湾。

30. Driving Out Foreign Invaders and Defending Taiwan

Zheng Chenggong, originally named Zheng Sen with the courtesy name Damu, was from Nan'an (modern-day Nan'an, Fujian Province) in the Ming Dynasty. The Emperor Longwu bestowed upon him the family name Zhu, the same as the imperial family, earning him the title "Guoxingye" (Lord of the National Surname). During the Yongli era, he was proclaimed the King of Yanping. In 1646, Zheng Chenggong opposed his father, Zheng Zhilong's decision to surrender to the Qing. He resolutely took up arms in resistance.Using Xiamen and Jinmen as his base of operations, he conducted military campaigns across the provinces of Fujian, Guangdong, Guangxi, Jiangsu, and Zhejiang, even advancing along the Yangtze River. In 1662, at the request of the people of Taiwan, he led his fleet across the Taiwan Strait to drive out the Dutch colonizers who had occupied the island. The following year, he successfully recaptured the entire island, established a government, and enacted laws. His leadership fostered cooperation between the Han Chinese and the indigenous Gaoshan people in developing the island.

民族英雄郑成功　渡海驱逐荷兰兵
中华男儿志气显　筑城垦荒宝岛兴

Zheng Chenggong, a hero of the land,
Drove out the Dutch with a mighty hand.
A son of China with ambitions grand,
He built and farmed the treasured island's land.

三十一、吴淞抗英（陈化成）

陈化成，字业章，号莲峰，福建同安人，鸦片战争中的爱国将领。历任总兵、提督。1840年7月曾率福建水师打退英军进攻。同年调任江南提督，反对投降派牛鉴求和，在吴淞口积极备战。他率众与英军开战时，击伤英舰八艘。因牛鉴溃逃，使他在西炮台孤军奋战，与所属官兵八十余人壮烈牺牲。

31. Resisting the British at the Wusong Estuary in Shanghai

Chen Huacheng, courtesy name Yezhang and styled Lianfeng, was from Tong'an in Fujian Province. A patriotic general during the Opium War, he held various military positions, including brigade general and governor-general. In July 1840, he led the Fujian naval forces to successfully repel the advancing British fleet. Later that year, he was appointed Governor-General of Jiangnan. Opposing the defeatist stance of Niujian, who advocated for peace, Chen Huacheng prepared for further battle. He once again led his forces against the British fleet, damaging eight British warships in the process. However, after Niujian's retreat, Chen found himself left to defend the position alone. In the end, he and over eighty of his soldiers heroically sacrificed their lives in defense of their country.

江南提督陈化成　爱国佑民勇抗英
孤军奋战吴淞口　百姓建祠颂英雄

Chen Huacheng was Captain General of Jiangnan,
Who patriotically fought the British to a man.
Single-handedly he defended the Wusong Estuary,
And the people built a shrine to his noble memory.

三十二、勇销鸦片（林则徐）

清朝中期，西方资本主义侵略者在中国大肆贩卖鸦片，毒害中国人，并攫取中国大量白银。在江苏治河有功、在湖南禁绝鸦片有成的林则徐临危受命，被任为广东总督、钦差大臣，赴广东查禁鸦片。他冲破重重阻力，查获鸦片二百三十七万多斤，在虎门当众销毁，并积极筹备防务，倡办义勇，多次打退英国侵略军的武装挑衅。

32. Destroying Opium Without Reservation

In the mid-Qing Dynasty, Western capitalist invaders aggressively smuggled opium into China, poisoning its people and draining the country of vast amounts of silver. Lin Zexu, who had successfully managed river dredging and flood control in Jiangsu, as well as enforcing the opium ban in Hunan, was appointed at a critical moment to serve as Viceroy of Guangdong and Guangxi, as well as Imperial Commissioner with the responsibility of eradicating opium in Guangdong. Despite facing significant resistance, Lin Zexu seized more than 2,370,000 catties of opium and publicly destroyed it at Humen Beach. He also took proactive measures to strengthen military defenses and organized volunteer forces to repel repeated British military provocations.

临危受命显刚才　　虎门销烟英夷呆
备战御敌靠民志　　近代劲史林公开

At a critical moment he displayed talent and mettle,
Knowing that spoilt opium would the British unsettle.
He readied the people for an all-out war,
Winning praise from historians for evermore.

三十三、抗法卫台（刘永福）

刘永福，字渊亭，广西上思人，雇工出身。早年参加天地会农民起义军，后组黑旗军在中越边界活动。曾协助越南人民保卫河内，击毙法国海军大佐李威利，收复河内。后去台湾，参加台湾人民反对清政府割台的斗争，在台南屡败日军。因在台孤立无援，退回广东。1915 年袁世凯与日本签订"二十一条"后，又组织义勇军北上抵抗。遗愿未竟而死。

33. Resisting the French and Defending Taiwan

Liu Yongfu, courtesy name Yuanting, was from Shangsi in Guangxi Province. Born into a peasant family, he joined the Heaven and Earth Society, a militia dedicated to popular uprisings, in his youth. Later, he raised an army known as the Black Flag Army, which operated along the China-Vietnam border. He assisted the Vietnamese in defending Hanoi, where he killed French naval captain Henri Rivière and drove the invaders from the city. Afterward, he traveled to Taiwan and joined the local resistance against the Qing government's decision to cede the island. Although he achieved victories over Japanese forces in southern Taiwan, he was eventually isolated and forced to retreat to Guangdong Province. In 1915, after Yuan Shikai signed the "Twenty-One Demands" with Japan, Liu organized a volunteer army to march north in resistance. However, he passed away before he could see his mission fulfilled.

出身微末报国勤　抗法援越护近邻
英勇卫台万民敬　青史荣载黑旗军

He served the country well despite being of humble stock,
In Vietnam's defence the French hordes he did block.
He won acclaim for protecting Taiwan gallantly,
His Black Flag Army has been fabled through history.

三十四、黄海忠魂（邓世昌）

邓世昌，字正卿，广东番禺人，福建水师学堂第一届毕业生，历任海东云、振威、镇北、扬威各舰管带（舰长）。1887年赴英接受致远号巡洋舰，任总兵兼致远号管带。1894年9月在黄海大东沟与日本舰队作战时，见定远舰指挥旗落下，立即悬旗督战，掩护主舰。因炮弹用尽，决定加快速度撞击敌人的吉野舰，不幸被鱼雷炸毁，全舰官兵二百五十余人壮烈牺牲。

34. The Loyal Spirit in the Yellow Sea

Deng Shichang, courtesy name Zhengqing, was from Panyu in Guangdong Province. He was a graduate of the first class of the Fujian Naval Academy and served as the captain of several ships, including the Haidongyun, Zhenwei, Zhenbei, and Yangwei. In 1887, he went to England to take command of the cruiser Zhiyuan, serving both as garrison commander and acting battalion commander. In September 1894, during the Battle of Dadonggou in the Yellow Sea, when he saw the flag of the Dingyuan ship fall, he immediately ordered his crew to raise the flag and continue the fight, providing cover for the main vessel. As their ammunition ran low, he made the bold decision to accelerate his ship and ram the enemy vessel, the Yoshino. Tragically, the ship was struck by a torpedo, and all 250 crew members perished, sacrificing their lives for their country.

日寇侵略祸东邻　甲午海战起风云
千古讴歌致远舰　邓公壮举海军魂

Japan's aggression brought woe to the land,
In 1894, war took a fierce stand.
The Zhiyuan cruiser's fame endures,
Though sunk at sea, Deng's spirit ensures.

三十五、变法就义（谭嗣同）

谭嗣同，字复生，号壮飞，湖南浏阳人。1895 年中日战争失败后，在浏阳倡"复学社"，到各处游历，吸取新知识。不久，又办"时务学堂""南学会"，办《湘报》，提倡新政，进京任四品卿衔军机章京，与康有为、林旭、杨锐等参与变法，因欲争取新建陆军，被袁世凯出卖，为变法英勇献身。死后被人将其倡变法、倡新政的作品编成《谭嗣同全集》。

35. Sacrificing Himself for Political Reform

Tan Sitong, courtesy name Fusheng, styled Zhuangfei, was from Liuyang in Hunan Province. In 1895, after China's defeat in the First Sino-Japanese War, Tan initiated the Fuxue Society in Liuyang and traveled extensively to acquire new knowledge. Soon after, he established the School of Current Affairs and the Southern Society, and began publishing the *Xiang bao*. He was a strong advocate for political reform and, in pursuit of these ideas, went to Beijing where he served as a Fourth-Rank Official. Tan became involved in the reform movement alongside figures such as Kang Youwei, Lin Xu, and Yang Rui. His efforts to secure support for military reform, particularly in the creation of a new army, led to his betrayal by Yuan Shikai. Tan Sitong ultimately gave his life for the cause of political reform. After his death, his writings on reform and political renewal were compiled posthumously into *The Complete Works of Tan Sitong*.

清廷腐朽国势下　立志救国倡变法
壮哉戊戌六君子　身教激起辛亥花

The Qing Dynasty was corrupt and its power declined,
So Tan Sitong advocated reforms well-designed.
How gallantly the six martyred gentlemen died,
Their deaths would a lasting inspiration provide.

第十章

改革创新

Chapter Ten:

Reform and Innovation

一、伏羲画卦（伏羲氏）

伏羲也写作庖牺、宓羲，古时传说"三皇"之一，即我国远古传说的东方夷族首领太昊。传说他与女娲结婚生人，被尊为"人文始祖"。他教民结网捕鱼，教民狩猎畜牧，象征着我国原始社会渔猎经济的开始。他又"仰观于天，俯察于地，观鸟兽之文与地之宜，近取诸身，远取诸物"，画八卦，日后演成六十四卦的《周易》，在我国及世界文化史上做出突出贡献。

1. Fuxi Draws the Trigrams

Fuxi, also known as Paoxi or Mixi, was one of the Three Sovereigns in ancient Chinese mythology. He is said to have been Taihao, the leader of the Eastern Yi people. According to legend, he married, Nüwa, and is revered as the "First Ancestor" of humanity. Fuxi taught the people how to weave nets for fishing, hunt, and raise livestock, marking the beginning of China's primitive hunting and fishing economy. He then "looked up at the heavens, looked down at the earth, observed the markings of birds and beasts, and considered both nearby and distant phenomena", Fuxi is credited with creating the Eight Trigrams, which later evolved into the sixty-four hexagrams of *The I Ching* (*The Book of Changes*), making a profound contribution to both Chinese and world cultural history.

> 人文始祖人崇敬　始作网罟渔猎丰
> 仰天俯地画八卦　惠及全球科技兴

People pay homage to the ancestor of humanity,
The creator of fishing nets, the first hunter in history.
He observed the heavens and earth to draw the Eight Trigrams,
Benefiting the entire world through his wisdom.

二、神农务农（神农氏）

古时传说"三皇"之一，其部落以火德王，故又称炎帝。起于烈山，又称烈山氏。相传远古人民过着渔猎采集生活，他用木作耒耜，教民耕作，象征着我国原始社会由采集及渔猎经济进步到农耕社会。他又遍尝百草，发明医药，给人治病。他还"立市廛以为货财"，即建立了原始商业活动。他还作五弦之琴，使人娱及身心。

2. Shennong Tills the Land

Shennong, one of the Three Sovereigns in ancient Chinese mythology, was also known as the "Flame Emperor" due to his tribe's mastery of fire. He hailed from Mount Lieshan, which is why he is sometimes referred to as Lieshan. According to legend, the people of primeval society lived by fishing and gathering. Shennong then crafted wooden plows and taught them how to cultivate the land, marking the transition from a fishing and gathering economy to an agrarian society. In addition,Shennong sampled a wide variety of herbs, classifying them and inventing medicines to heal the people. He also "established markets for trade", representing an early form of commercial activity. Furthermore, he invented the five-stringed zither, which served as entertainment for the people and helped enrich their lives.

> 神农烈山倡务农　远古生产始农耕
> 遍尝百草治百病　市廛始立商兴隆

> Shennong from Lieshan led the people to till,
> Founding agriculture and rousing a new will.
> He tasted every herb to determine their use,
> And founded markets to trade in produce.

三、助齐首霸（管仲）

管仲，名夷吾，春秋初年颍上（今属安徽）人。初辅齐国公子纠，战败后，由鲍叔牙推荐给齐桓公，释却前仇、备受重用。他在齐国进行改革，建立乡村组织，分全国为十五士乡和工商六乡，以士乡的乡里组织为军事单位，寓兵于农。又制订人才选拔制度、官营盐铁、发展铸造业、调剂物价等。改革后，使齐国成为春秋首霸。后人依其经济思想等集为《管子》八十六篇。

3. Helping Qi to Become the First Hegemony

Guan Zhong, born Yiwu, was from Yingshang (now in Anhui Province) and lived during the early Spring and Autumn Period. Initially, he served as an advisor to Prince Gongzijiu of the State of Qi. After their defeat, he was recommended by Bao Shuya to Duke Huan of Qi, who set aside past grievances and appointed Guan Zhong to a prominent position. Guan Zhong then introduced political reforms in the State of Qi. He established village-level organizations, dividing the entire state into fifteen military villages (for knights) and six administrative districts (for workers and merchants), creating a system that integrated military and agricultural units. He also devised a talent selection system, established state-run salt and iron industries, formalized the foundry sector, and regulated commodity prices. These reforms helped Qi become the dominant power, or hegemony, of the Spring and Autumn Period. Later generations compiled his economic ideas and policies into an eighty-six-chapter work titled *The Works of Master Guan*.

管仲战败沦阶囚　桓公重才释前仇
改革创新齐国治　春秋首霸青史留

Guan Zhong was defeated and put into prison,
Duke Huan forgave him with just reason.
His reform and innovation made the state prosperous,
And the earliest hegemon became historically famous.

四、"科圣"墨翟（墨翟）

墨子名翟，春秋末年鲁国人，他在当时是代表下层人民的思想家，也是一位发明家。在《墨经》中有许多光学、力学、数学、逻辑学等方面的内容。他为了制止战争，发明了守城的吊桥，攻城的云梯；用土瓮放在井中，可听到远方的声音。依据杠杆原理发明了秤。依据墨子提出的光学"小孔成像"的原理，人们发明了照相机。他始造"飞鸢"，成为日后飞机的雏形。

4. Modi, the Sage of Technology

Mozi, whose given name was Di, was from the State of Lu and lived at the end of the Spring and Autumn Period. He was both a philosopher who represented the lower classes and an inventor. In his work *The Mohist Canons*, there are numerous discussions on subjects such as optics, mechanics, mathematics, and logic. In his efforts to stop warfare, Mozi invented the drawbridge for city defense and scaling ladders for attacking fortresses. He also placed an earthen jar in a well, which allowed him to hear distant sounds. Drawing on the principle of leverage, he designed the Chinese steelyard (a type of balance scale). Based on his principle of "pinhole imaging", people later invented the camera. Mozi is also credited with inventing the "flying kite", which later became the precursor to modern airplanes.

摩顶放踵为黎民　墨学大师更创新
光力逻辑多创意　飞鸢腾空世绝伦

Mozi feared no hardships when assisting the ordinary,
He was both an inventor and philosopher extraordinary.
His pinhole image principle proved innovative,
And the "flying kite" supremely creative.

五、"工圣"鲁班（鲁班）

鲁班本姓公输，名般（班），鲁国（今山东曲阜）人，春秋末年著名的建筑工匠。他善于动脑，勤于发明创造。在手工业方面发明了铇、锯、划线的"班母"；刨木料的"班妻"；生活方面发明了磨、碾、碨等。军事方面发明了战船、钩强、云梯等。在土木建筑上的发明更多。他在建筑前绘制图形，计划用料，然后施工。屋顶上的斗拱，相互穿插、联系，既符合力学原理，又有很高的观赏价值。后世被尊为木匠、铁匠、泥瓦匠的祖师爷。世称"工圣"。

5. Lu Ban, the Sage of Carpentry

Lu Ban, whose original family name was Gongshu and given name was Ban, was from the State of Lu (now Qufu, Shandong Province). He was a renowned carpenter at the end of the Spring and Autumn Period. Known for his creativity and diligence in invention, Lu Ban made significant contributions to various fields. In handicrafts, he invented the plane, saw, and ink marker; in daily life, he developed tools such as mills, grinding stones, and stone rollers. In military technology, he invented warships, wall-climbing hooks, and scaling ladders. His innovations in engineering construction were even more numerous. He would first design blueprints, calculate the necessary materials, and then carry out the construction work. The Dougong brackets in wooden roofs, for example, were designed not only for their structural function but also for their aesthetic appeal. Later generations revered him as the ancestor of carpenters, blacksmiths, and masons, honoring him with the title"Sage Worker".

工圣鲁班历代颂　勤钻苦研多发明
建筑工程壮且美　工农器具惠民生

The Sage carpenter Lu Ban is known to each generation,
For the devices he produced through diligence and hard creation.
His constructions stood grand, both sturdy and fair,
And his farming tools were practical, beyond compare.

六、医祖扁鹊（秦越人）

扁鹊姓秦，名越人。春秋时期齐国渤海郡人。早年向长桑君学习医术，经过十几年的刻苦钻研，成为医术高明、勇于创新的一代名医。他精通妇、儿、五官科，对内科也有很大成就。在总结前人经验的基础上，他归纳出望、闻、问、切四种诊病方法，掌握了许多秘方，医治过十多年的疑难病症，他还主张没病前先防病，不要等病情严重、发展后再治疗。民间流传很多他救死扶伤的故事。

6. Bian Que, the Forefather of Medicine

Bian Que, whose family name was Qin and given name Yueren, hailed from Bohai Prefecture in the State of Qi during the Spring and Autumn Period. He studied medicine under Changsang Jun in his youth and, through years of rigorous dedication, became a renowned and innovative physician. Bian Que excelled in gynecology,pediatrics, ENT, and internal medicine. Building on the knowledge of his predecessors, he developed the four diagnostic methods: observation, listening,questioning, and pulse examination. He mastered numerous secret remedies and successfully treated many complex and chronic illnesses, some persisting for over a decade. Moreover, he advocated for preventive care, emphasizing the importance of addressing health issues before they worsened. Many folk tales celebrate his life-saving deeds and contributions to healing.

医术高明多创新　救死扶伤惠万民
望闻问切诊难症　民间竞夸秦越人

Bian Que was a doctor of excellence and skill,
Healing the wounded and saving the mortally ill.
He diagnosed rare diseases through listening and observation,
Feeling the pulse won the praise of the entire nation.

七、首撰《法经》（李悝）

战国初年的法家代表人物李悝，在任魏文侯相时，主持变法。在经济上推行"尽地力之教"。将耕地分作九等，分别等次收税。鼓励精耕细作，增加产量。国家丰年时以平价购余粮，荒年时平价卖出。政治上实行法治，废除归贵族的世卿世禄制，奖励立军功的人。使魏国成为战国初年最早的强国。他著的《法经》是我国最早最完整的一部法典。

7. The First Book of Law

Li Kui, a prominent figure of the Legalist school in the early Warring States Period, served as Chancellor to Marquis Wen of Wei and spearheaded significant political reforms. In economics, he implemented the principle of "making full use of the land", dividing farmland into nine categories and levying taxes based on each classification. This policy encouraged intensive farming and increased agricultural productivity. During years of surplus harvest, the state purchased excess grain at stable prices and sold it during times of scarcity to stabilize the economy. Politically, Li Kui advocated for the rule of law, abolished the hereditary privileges and stipends of the nobility, and rewarded individuals for military achievements. These reforms positioned Wei as the earliest dominant power of the Warring States Period. Li Kui's *Book of Law* was the first and most comprehensive legal code in China's history.

改革明令尽地力　平籴精耕民受益
战国初霸魏作首　《法经》书成法肇基

Li Kui conducted reforms to fully utilise the land,
Intensive cultivation meant supply could meet demand.
The State of Wei became the first hegemon of its era,
His *Book of Law* made the legal field far more clearer.

八、修都江堰（李冰）

战国时期的水利家李冰，被秦昭王任命为蜀郡太守。他和他的儿子征发民工在岷江流域兴办了许多水利工程。都江堰采取中流作堰的办法，在宝瓶口上游的岷江中心，筑一道分水闸，使江水流到这里分洪，分别灌溉两边的良田。他还在今宜宾、乐山境开凿滩险，疏通航道，又修建白木江、洛水等灌溉和航运工程，使蜀地农业丰饶，成为"天府之国"。

8. Building Dujiangyan

Li Bing, a renowned hydraulic engineer during the Warring States Period, was appointed Prefect of Shu by King Zhao of Qin. He and his son mobilized labor to construct numerous water management projects along the Minjiang River Valley, the most famous being the Dujiangyan irrigation system. At Dujiangyan, he implemented an innovative midstream dam technique by building a diversion weir at the center of the Minjiang River upstream of the Bottle-Neck Channel. This structure redirected floodwaters and allowed for controlled irrigation of the fertile fields on both banks. Li Bing also excavated hazardous rapids and dredged waterways in the area of present-day Leshan and Yibin, improving navigation. Additionally, he developed irrigation and navigation systems on the Baimu and Luoshui Rivers. These projects transformed the Shu region (modern-day Sichuan Province and Chongqing) into the "Land of Abundance", renowned for its agricultural prosperity.

都江堰成万民悦　江水分流灌溉多
惠民工程传万代　造就巴蜀天府国

People were in awe of the Dujiangyan Project,
Irrigation achieved by a simple bisect.
The programme has shown enduring resilience,
Turning Sichuan into the "Land of Abundance".

九、制豪富国（桑弘羊）

西汉初年的桑弘羊，洛阳人，出身商人家庭，汉武帝时任治粟都尉兼大司农。为了发展经济，他加强了朝廷平准、均输等机构，用以控制全国的产品。政府主持贱买贵卖、平抑物价，使富商大贾不能获取暴利。这些措施都增加了西汉政府的收入，打击了豪强地主和大商人的势力，为汉武帝时国力富强、外抗匈奴奠定下经济基础。

9. Suppressing Strongmen and Strengthening the Nation

Sang Hongyang, born into a merchant family in Luoyang during the early Western Han Dynasty, served as Minister of Finance and Agriculture under Emperor Wu of Han. To strengthen the economy, he enhanced the central government's control over production and distribution through the "Price Equalization" and "Transport Equalization" systems. These mechanisms allowed the government to buy goods at low prices and sell them at higher prices, stabilizing market prices and curbing the excessive profits of wealthy merchants. These policies increased state revenue,weakened the power of large landlords and wealthy merchants, and provided the economic foundation for a prosperous nation. This economic strength supported Emperor Wu's efforts to resist the Xiongnu and expand the empire's influence.

汉初司农桑弘羊　主管经济多主张
限制豪强国得利　财力丰厚国富强

Sang Hongyang administered finance in the early Han Dynasty,
He took measures to improve the economy with industry.
The government became prosperous by curbing the strong,
The country grew powerful with wealth all along.

十、天仪测天（张衡）

张衡，字平子，东汉时期南阳西鄂（今河南南阳石桥镇）人，是一位具有多项成就的古代科学家。他制作浑天仪，形象地阐明了天与地的关系。他指出朔望现象取决于太阳和月亮的相对位置，日蚀的原因是地遮蔽了月光。他还测出日、月的视直径数值，与当今所测相差不远。他制作"候风地动仪"，是测地震的一种发明。

10. Inventing the Celestial Globe for Astronomical Observation

Zhang Heng, courtesy name Pingzi, was a renowned scientist from the Eastern Han Dynasty, born in Xi'e, Nanyang (now Shiqiao Town in Nanyang, Henan Province). He was a man of many accomplishments. He invented the celestial globe, which vividly illustrated the relationship between the Earth and the heavens. Zhang Heng explained that the syzygy phenomenon (the alignment of the sun, moon, and Earth) is determined by the relative positions of the sun and the moon, and that solar eclipses occur when the Earth blocks the moon's light. He also measured the apparent diameters of the sun and moon, with results that closely align with modern-day measurements. In addition, Zhang Heng invented the "Houfeng Seismograph", an instrument used to detect and record earthquake activity.

> "浑天仪"成天地通　朔望变化解读清
> 日月视角测试准　　"地动仪"成地震明

The celestial globe revealed the heavens' lore,
Tracking the moon's phases and much more.
Zhang Heng's insights on sun and moon were precise,
His seismograph helped measure earthquakes with advice.

十一、蔡伦造纸（蔡伦）

蔡伦，字敬仲，东汉时桂阳（今湖南郴州）人。和帝时为中常侍，曾任主管制造御用器物的尚方令，后封龙亭侯。他总结两汉以来用麻质纤维造纸的经验，改进造纸技术。利用树皮、碎布、旧渔网等粉碎后造纸，原料廉价，工艺完备。和帝元兴元年（105 年）奏报朝廷后，被称作"蔡侯纸"。在1990年国际造纸历史协会上，与会专家一致肯定了蔡伦的业绩。

11. Cai Lun Invents Paper

Cai Lun, courtesy name Jingzhong, was from Guiyang (now Chenzhou, Hunan Province) in the Eastern Han Dynasty. He served as a Regular Palace Attendant and later as the official in charge of manufacturing the emperor's instruments and weapons. He was eventually ennobled as Marquis Longting. Cai Lun built upon the paper-making techniques using hemp fibers that had been practiced in the Western and Eastern Han periods, and he improved the process. He developed a method of making paper using inexpensive raw materials such as tree bark, old cloth, and fishing nets. The result was both cost-effective and efficient. In the first year of the Yuanxing Era (105 AD) during the reign of Emperor He of Han, Cai Lun reported his innovation to the court, and the paper became known as the "Paper of Marquis Cai". In 1990, the International Association of Paper Historians officially recognized Cai Lun's contribution.

古时书写多艰难　新法造纸破难关
蔡伦改进造纸术　"蔡侯纸"名遍宇寰

In ancient times writing materials were scant,
Before Cai Lun's discovery most important.
He improved the technology for paper-making,
The "Paper of Marquis Cai" won fame breathtaking.

十二、发明算盘（刘洪）

刘洪，字元卓，东汉时期泰山郡蒙阴（今山东蒙阴）人。他通过多年对天象的观察，编修了《乾象历》，是我国第一个考虑到月球不均匀的历法。他精于计算，曾任过"上计椽"的职务，专管对地方上上报的户数、人数、地方粮食等汇集成册后，层层上报。为便于计算，他在以前筹码计算的基础上改进并发明算盘。他的学生徐岳著《术数记遗》一书中对此有详细记载。近世在沂南汉墓中发现公元193年的算盘，便是明证。

12. The Invention of the Abacus

Liu Hong, also known by his style name Yuanzhuo, hailed from Mengyin in the Prefecture of Mount Tai (modern-day Mengyin in Shandong Province). After years of meticulous observation of celestial phenomena, he compiled *The Calendar of Heavenly Phenomena*, the first calendar in China to account for the irregular movements of the moon. Renowned for his exceptional calculation skills, Liu Hong held the position of "Shangji Yuan", overseeing the compilation and reporting of data such as household numbers, population statistics, and local grain production. To enhance efficiency in calculations, Liu Hong improved upon the traditional method of counting with loose chips, developing the abacus with strung beads. This innovation is vividly described in *Anecdotes on Divination and Mathematics*, a work by his student Xu Yue. In modern times, an abacus dating back to 193 AD was unearthed in a Han Dynasty tomb in Yinan, providing tangible evidence of Liu Hong's groundbreaking contribution to computational tools.

精于历法益农桑　　计算精确管钱粮
《术数记遗》多创意　历代乒乓算盘响

Skilled at farming technology and calendar-design,
It fell to Liu Hong the abacus to refine.
His Anecdotes reveals where applied maths succeeds,
Chinese history resounds with the clack of abacus beads.

十三、千古"医圣"（张仲景）

张仲景，本名张机，东汉末年南阳涅阳（今河南邓州）人。他一生行医，系统地总结了汉代以前对伤寒及各种杂病治疗的经验，著《伤寒杂病论》16 卷。他在诊断辨明症状时，用"八纲"（阴、阳、表、里、虚、实、寒、热）、"四诊"（望、闻、问、切）等方式，包括内科、外科、妇科，还介绍了针灸、温熨、按摩、浸足及人工呼吸等治疗方法，被后世尊为"医圣"。

13. The Eternal "Sage of Medicine"

Zhang Zhongjing, originally named Zhang Ji, was born in Nieyang (present-day Dengzhou in Henan Province) during the late Eastern Han Dynasty. Devoting his entire life to medicine, he systematically consolidated the knowledge and experience of treating typhoid fever and various other diseases accumulated prior to his time. His monumental work, Treatise on Febrile Diseases, spanned sixteen volumes and became a cornerstone of traditional Chinese medicine. Zhang Zhongjing employed diagnostic methods grounded in the "Eight Principles" (Yin, Yang, external, internal, deficiency, excess, cold, and heat) and the "Four Examinations" (observation,listening, questioning, and pulse-taking). His contributions extended across internal medicine, surgery, and gynecology, and he also introduced a range of therapeutic practices, including acupuncture, warming and ironing therapy, massage, foot baths, and even artificial respiration. For his extraordinary contributions, later generations honored him as the "Sage of Medicine".

伤寒杂病研究细　　"八纲""四诊"勤创意
多方治疗解民苦　　"医圣"美称青史记

He examined carefully typhoid and various ailments,
Describing the "Eight Principles" and "Four Measurements".
He relieved the pain of many on his medical trips,
Praise for the "Saint Physician" was on many people's lips.

十四、"脉圣"叔和（王叔和）

东汉时的名医王熙，字叔和，山东高平（今邹城、微山一带）人。他出身寒微，见百姓疾病缠身，立志学医。曾任曹魏时的太医令，主持朝内医政。他整理当时张仲景散失的《伤寒论》，人称"仲景、叔和，医之圣也"。王叔和最大的贡献为著十万余言的《脉经》，是对历代脉学的继承和发展，明确提出"三部"（寸部、尺部、关部）九候（每部各以轻、中、重的指力相应分为浮、中、沉三候，共为九候），使诊脉既简化，又准确，被后世尊为"脉祖"。

14. "The Pulse Sage"

Wang Xi, also known by his style name Shuhe, was a distinguished physician of the Eastern Han Dynasty, hailing from Gaoping (modern-day Zoucheng and Weishan Counties in Shandong Province). Born into a humble family, Wang Xi was moved by the suffering of the sick and resolved to pursue medicine. During the Cao Wei Dynasty, he served as the Head Imperial Physician, overseeing court medical affairs. He also undertook the meticulous task of compiling the scattered fragments of Zhang Zhongjing's *Treatise on Febrile Diseases*, earning the accolade: "Zhang Zhongjing and Wang Shuhe, the saint physicians." Wang Shuhe's most significant contribution to medicine is his seminal work, *The Pulse Classic* (Maijing), a comprehensive text of over 100,000 characters that advanced the study of pulse diagnosis. In this work, he proposed the "Three Sections" (Cun, Chi, and Guan) and the "Nine Indicators" (each section being assessed at superficial, intermediate, and deep levels), thus simplifying and standardizing pulse-taking techniques. This groundbreaking approach made pulse diagnosis both more accessible and precise. For this achievement, later generations honored him as the "Founder of Pulse Diagnosis".

立志学医解民困　　　　细心阐释《伤寒论》
"三部""九候"诊断准　　"脉圣"功高益万民

Wang Shuhe was determined to relieve people's pain,
Zhang Zhongjing's Treatise did he carefully explain.
His "Three Parts and Nine Pulse-taking" was groundbreaking,
And celebrated was he the "Founder of Pulse-taking".

十五、神医华佗（华佗）

华佗，字元化，三国时期沛国谯（今安徽亳州）人，他勤奋好学，刻苦钻研，精通医术。在继承前人医学遗产的基础上，总结出许多医疗实践经验。在内科、外科、妇科、小儿科等方面均有造诣，尤其精通外科手术。他不贪功名，不恋钱财，到过很多地方为穷苦百姓治病。他还发明了可健身的"五禽戏"。可惜他被曹操冤杀，其著作没传留下来，但民间却传诵他的很多故事。

15. The Divine Physician

Hua Tuo, known by his style name Yuanhua, was a legendary physician from Qiao County in Peiguo (modern-day Bozhou, Anhui Province) during the Three Kingdoms period. Gifted with intelligence and a love for learning, he dedicated himself to the study of medicine and became highly proficient in the field. Building upon the medical knowledge of his predecessors, Hua Tuo contributed significantly to practical medicine, excelling in internal medicine, surgery, gynecology, and pediatrics, with a particular expertise in surgical procedures. Renowned for his compassion and humility, Hua Tuo shunned fame and wealth, traveling extensively to treat the illnesses of impoverished people. He also developed the "Five-Animal Exercise", a form of therapeutic gymnastics designed to promote physical health. Tragically, Hua Tuo was falsely accused and executed by Cao Cao, leading to the loss of his written works. Despite this, countless stories about his medical brilliance and humanity have been passed down through folklore.

精通医术利万民　外科手术视为神
五禽戏作健体魄　名医盛名医者魂

A medical expert and pioneer,
To many Hua Tuo's surgery made him a seer.
He created "Five-Animal Boxing" for exercise,
Becoming the image of a physician so very wise.

十六、绘图规范（裴秀）

西晋地理学家裴秀，河东闻喜（今属山西）人。一生从事地理及绘制地图，他总结历史上的经验，提出了绘制地图的六项原则：一分率（即比例尺）、二准望（即方向）、三道里（即人行路径）、四高下（及高低）、五方邪（即方取邪）、六迂直（即迂取直）。依这六种原则，绘制出的地图准确、详细、奠定了中国地图学的理论基础。

16. The Conventions of Mapping

Pei Xiu, a renowned geographer of the Western Jin Dynasty, hailed from Wenxi in Hedong Prefecture (modern-day Shanxi Province). He dedicated his life to the study of geography and the art of cartography. Building on the accumulated knowledge of his predecessors, Pei Xiu formulated six essential principles for map-making: 1. Proportional Scale–ensuring accurate representation of distances; 2. Orientation–maintaining precise directions; 3. Transport Routes–clearly depicting pathways and roads; 4. Elevation–accounting for differences in terrain height; 5. Contour Accuracy–accurately outlining irregular landforms; 6. Direct Line Measurement–converting winding paths into straight-line distances. By adhering to these principles, Pei Xiu created highly accurate and detailed maps that established the theoretical foundation for Chinese cartography.

地学发展绘图本　比例准方描绘真
高下方邪正误现　利于国家益于民

Peixiu advanced the art of mapping design,
With proportional scales both accurate and fine.
With height and straight lines, mistakes were undone,
His work served the people and the state as one.

十七、《齐民要术》（贾思勰）

北魏益都（今山东青州市）人贾思勰，任高阳太守时就很重视农业生产，他经多年实地考察和检阅大量资料，写成著名的农学著作《齐民要术》。该书九十二篇，十卷。系统全面地总结了当时北方劳动人民的经验。对谷物蔬菜瓜果的种植法、种树法、养家畜家禽法、养鱼法、酿造等方面都有详细的记述，是我国古代一部最优秀的农业百科全书，也是世界农学史上珍贵的作品。

17. Important Arts for the People's Welfare

Jia Sixie, a native of Yidu (modern-day Qingzhou City in Shandong Province), was a dedicated advocate for agricultural development during his tenure as Prefect of Gaoyang. Through years of field research and extensive review of existing documentation, he authored the renowned agricultural treatise *Important Arts for the People's Welfare*. This comprehensive work comprises 92 chapters across ten volumes, systematically summarizing the accumulated knowledge and practices of farmers and artisans in Northern China. It provides detailed accounts of methods for cultivating cereal grains, vegetables, and fruits; techniques for tree planting; guidelines for raising livestock and poultry; fish farming; and brewing. As a result, the treatise stands as one of the most exceptional agricultural encyclopedias in ancient China and a treasured contribution to the global history of agriculture.

贾公为官重农耕　　广收博采记录丰
《齐民要术》十万字　世人获利农副兴

Mr. Jia took agriculture seriously as an official,
And his book compiled data most beneficial.
Important Arts ran to 100,000 characters in length,
And infused agriculture and farmers with unprecedented strength.

十八、精注《水经》（郦道元）

北魏范阳（今北京大兴）人郦道元，字善长，延昌年间为荆州刺史，后为关右大使。他生平好学，多阅奇书，善游历，作《水经注》。当年汉朝人桑钦作的《水经》，过于简略，用词多不准确。郦道元在此基础上经过实地考察，对全国地理情况作了详细记载。《水经注》不仅博采前人著作，作者还亲自考察。把各地的名胜、古迹、异产、人物史迹等都采入书中。语言精妙，注文远远超过正文，是我国古代研究地学的一部名著。

18. Annotations on the Classic of Waterways

Li Daoyuan, styled Shanchang, was a native of Fanyang (modern-day Daxing District in Beijing) during the Northern Wei Dynasty. A scholar and explorer, he served as a Prefect during the Yanchang era and later held a key official post. Known for his passion for learning, he read extensively and traveled widely, which culminated in his seminal work, Annotations on *the Classic of Waterways*. The original *Classic of Waterways*, authored by Sang Qin during the Han Dynasty, was overly concise and imprecise in its language. Building on this foundation, Li Daoyuan conducted extensive field investigations and meticulously recorded the geographical features of the entire country. His Annotations not only integrated insights from earlier texts but also enriched them with his firsthand observations. This monumental work goes beyond geography, including descriptions of historical landmarks, cultural relics, distinctive local products, and accounts of notable figures and events. Written with remarkable precision and eloquence, Li's annotations far exceeded the original text in both detail and depth, earning it recognition as a landmark achievement in ancient Chinese geography.

古时《水经》多舛错　亲履实测方确切
《水经注》成四十卷　存史资政益地学

The ancient *Classic of Waterways* had errors profound,
Li Daoyuan's fieldwork turned it around.
His Annotations, in forty volumes compiled,
Enriched geography, history, and governance reconciled.

十九、算圆周率（祖冲之）

祖冲之，字文远，南北朝南朝范阳逎（今河北涞水）人，是一位有突出贡献的天文学家、数学家。在数学上，他用前人刘徽的割圆术，推算出圆周率在 3.1415926—3.1415927 之间，并以 22/7 作为疏率表现，355/113 作为密率表现。他还和儿子祖暅一起修订了《大明历》、合撰《缀术》。他们的成就与西方同类的进展相比，早几百年乃至千余年。

19. The Calculation of Pi

Zu Chongzhi, styled Wenyuan, was a renowned astronomer and mathematician from Fanyang (modern-day Laishui, Hebei Province) during the Southern and Northern Dynasties. His contributions to mathematics were groundbreaking. Building upon the work of his predecessor Liu Hui, he employed the method of inscribed polygons to calculate the value of pi to an astounding precision of 3.1415926 to 3.1415927. He also used 22/7 as an approximate value and 355/113 as a more accurate fraction. In addition to his mathematical achievements, Zu Chongzhi, along with his son Zu Geng, revised the *Da Ming Calendar* and co-authored *the Method of Interpolation*. Their discoveries predated similar advances in the West by several centuries—indeed, their work was ahead of its time by as much as a thousand years.

献身科学创新多　疏率密率多精确
父子同修《大明历》　亲历推行促农作

Devoted to science and bold exploration,
Zu's rough and fine ratios sparked innovation.
Father and son shaped the *Da Ming Calendar's* course,
Aiding agriculture, its guiding force.

二十、建赵州桥（李春）

隋朝工匠李春，曾于开皇、大业年间在洨河上设计并建成了一座安济桥（赵州桥），此桥为单孔，全长 50.82 米，桥面宽约 10 米，跨径 37.02 米，拱圆矢高 7.23 米，弧形平缓，拱圆由 28 根并列的石条组成，上设 4 个小拱。这样既减轻了桥的重量，节省材料，又便于排洪，还很美观。此法为后世广泛采用，赵州桥是我国公元 6 世纪的重要创新。

20. Building the Zhaozhou Bridge

Li Chun, a renowned artisan of the Sui Dynasty, designed and constructed the Anji Bridge (also known as the Zhaozhou Bridge) across the Xiao River during the Kaihuang and Daye Eras. The bridge spans 50.82 meters in length and 9.6 meters in width, with a main span of 37.37 meters. It features a single arch composed of 28 closely arranged stone segments, with four smaller arches positioned above. The rise of each arch reaches 7.23 meters, and the arch has a gentle, sweeping curve. This innovative design not only reduced the overall weight of the bridge, saving on materials, but also improved its ability to manage floodwaters and enhanced its aesthetic appeal. The design principles used in the Zhaozhou Bridge were widely adopted by future generations. Completed in the 6th century, the Zhaozhou Bridge stands as a remarkable engineering achievement in ancient China.

赵州桥传鲁班留　实为工匠李春修
巧思实用兼优美　世界桥史占鳌头

Legend has it that Zhaozhou was built by Lu Ban,
When in fact it was the work of Li Chun, an artisan.
Practical yet splendid, its design stands tall,
A milestone in bridge-building, admired by all.

二十一、僧解天文（僧一行）

僧一行，俗名张遂，唐初巨鹿（今河北巨鹿）人，唐初邹国公张公瑾之孙。他不应武三思之聘，却出家为僧，为佛教密宗之祖。在科技上贡献很大。他制造出"黄道游仪"，可以观察日月星的位置和运动情况，还发现了恒星。他制作了"水运浑象"，为近代钟表之祖。他设计了"覆矩图"，是第一次对地球子午线进行的实测。他通过几处丈量，得出的数据比《周髀算经》的结论又进了一步。

21. Seng Yixing Studies Astronomy

Seng Yixing, born Zhang Sui, was a native of Julu (now Julu County in Hebei Province) during the early Tang Dynasty. He was the grandson of Zhang Gongjin, the Duke of Zou. Despite being offered an official position by Prime Minister Wu Sansi, Seng Yixing chose instead to become a monk, ultimately founding the Tantric Buddhist school. Seng Yixing made significant contributions to science and technology. He invented the Ecliptic Instrument, which allowed for the observation of the positions and movements of the sun, moon, and fixed stars. He also created the Water-rotating Celestial Globe, a precursor to modern clocks. Additionally, he designed the Fujutu, an angle-measuring device, and conducted the first field measurements of the Earth's meridian. His findings advanced the conclusions presented in *the Zhoubi Suanjing*, surpassing earlier astronomical calculations.

一行和尚密宗首　科技殿堂勤运筹
天文历法多创造　献身科学佳话留

Master Seng, a Tantric pioneer so wise,
Made scientific pursuits his ultimate prize.
Advancing calendars and astronomy's lore,
His devotion to science is remembered evermore..

二十二、"药王"思邈（孙思邈）

孙思邈，唐朝京兆华原人，隋文帝召他为博士不就，唐太宗授给他谏议大夫，仍不就，却致力于医学研究。他博采古代各家之长，经数十年辛勤劳动，从病理、治疗、药物、方剂等基础理论，以及内、外、妇、儿、针灸等科全面总结，他认为"人命至重，有贵千金"，书写成后，名《备急千金要方》一称《千金方》。在医疗学上、药物学上、急救、食疗等方面都有一些创见。他还作《丹经》，系统地说明了火药的制法。

22. The King of Traditional Chinese Medicine

Sun Simiao, a native of Huayuan, Jingzhao (modern-day Xi'an) in the Tang Dynasty, was highly esteemed as one of China's greatest physicians. Although Emperor Wen of the Sui Dynasty invited him to serve as a physician, he declined, and similarly, when Emperor Taizong of the Tang Dynasty offered him a position as a supervisory officer, he also refused. Instead, he dedicated himself entirely to the study and practice of medicine. Drawing on the wisdom of earlier physicians, Sun Simiao spent decades of diligent study to comprehensively summarize medical knowledge. His work covered foundational theories such as pathology, treatment, pharmaceuticals, and prescriptions, as well as specialized fields like pediatrics, surgery, gynecology, and acupuncture. He believed that "a person's life is more precious than gold", and his most famous work, *For Urgent Use* (also known as *Qianjin Fang*), reflected this conviction. In addition to his contributions to medical theory, Sun Simiao also made innovative advancements in areas like emergency medicine, pharmacology, and food therapy. He authored *The Classic of Alchemy*, a work that systematically described the method for manufacturing gunpowder.

大哉"药王"孙思邈　辞去官职学医道
实践理论融一体　《千金方》成乐熙皋

The "King of Traditional Medicine" Sun Simiao,
Resigned his post to perfect his medical know-how.
He merged practice with theory so grand,
For Urgent Use brought joy to the land.

二十三、刘晏理财（刘晏）

刘晏，字士安，唐朝南华（今山东东明）人，理财家。历任东都河南江淮，转运租庸盐铁常平使等职。安史之乱时，社会经济凋敝、紊乱，户口亡十之八九，州县多为藩镇割据，朝廷府库耗竭，关中粮食奇缺。他用分段转运方法，使江淮的粮食顺利运往关中，岁运十万斛，使安史之乱后朝内外经济紊乱的状态得以恢复。

23. Liu Yan Manages Financial Affairs

Liu Yan, whose style name was Shi'an, was born in Nanhua (now Dongming County in Shandong Province) and became a renowned financial expert during the Tang Dynasty. He held various positions, including transport commissioner, rent control commissioner, and salt and iron commissioner in regions such as Dongdu, Henan, and Jianghuai. During the Anshi Rebellion, the economy was in shambles, with widespread social disorder causing the population to dwindle by nearly 90%. Many localities were controlled by separatist warlords, the central treasury was depleted, and food supplies in the Guanzhong area were critically low. To address this, Liu Yan implemented a segmented transportation system, coordinating the transfer of grain from the Yangtze and Huai Rivers to Guanzhong. He managed to move a total of one million dou of grain, effectively stabilizing the economy and restoring order in the aftermath of the rebellion.

安史之乱祸黎民　藩镇割据失国魂
刘晏理财残唐救　关中输粮得人心

The Anshi Rebellion harmed the civilian population,
Weakening the authority of the Tang administration.
Liu Yan restored hope with his financial art,
His grain caravans won the people's heart.

二十四、宋改革家（王安石）

被列宁称作"中国十一世纪的改革家"的王安石，字介甫，宋初临川（今江西临川）人。宋仁宗时进士，官至宰相。他鉴于当时社会上的积弊，坚持对天、人、权威三不畏，主张改革。积极推行青苗、均输、市易、免役、农田水利法，这些措施打击了大官僚地主及豪绅的特权，以期富国强兵。后来虽在保守派的攻击下被罢相，但在当时影响很大。其诗文也很有特色，被后世誉为"唐宋八大家"之一。

24. The Reformer of the Song Dynasty

Praised by Lenin as "a reformer of 11th-century China", Wang Anshi, styled Jiefu, was a native of Linchuan (modern-day Linchuan District in Jiangxi Province). He achieved success in the imperial examinations and rose to the position of Prime Minister during the reign of Emperor Renzong of the Song Dynasty. Recognizing the deep-seated issues plaguing society, Wang Anshi boldly advocated for reform, undeterred by opposition from heaven, the people, or powerful elites. Wang implemented transformative policies such as the Green Sprouts Program, the Equal Tax and Transport Law, the Market Regulation Law, the Abolition of Corvée Labor, and the Agricultural Irrigation and Water Conservancy Law. These measures aimed to curtail the privileges of bureaucratic landlords and the gentry while strengthening the nation's economy and military. Although his tenure as Prime Minister ended under attacks from conservative factions, his reforms left a lasting impact. In addition to his political legacy, Wang Anshi was an accomplished writer, renowned for his distinctive poetry and essays. He is celebrated as one of the "Eight Masters of Prose of the Tang and Song Dynasties".

北宋一大改革家　敢于破旧变新法
富国强兵固国本　天人权威三不怕

Wang Anshi, a reformer of the Song so bold,
Challenged the old to usher in the new mold.
He strengthened the state with wealth and might,
Fearing neither heaven, man, nor power'sheight.

二十五、《梦溪笔谈》（沈括）

沈括，字存中，宋朝杭州钱塘县人。他一生除从事政治活动外，又不断进行科学研究。他对天文、数学、历法、历史、地理、生物、医药，乃至文学、史学、音乐都有研究和成就。一生著作颇丰，尤以晚年《梦溪笔谈》著名。此书分故事、辩证、乐律、象数、机智、技艺、器用、药议等十七目，内容均达到当时自然科学的最高水平，被英国科技专家李约瑟教授称作"中国科学史上的座标"。

25. Dream Pool Essays

Shen Kuo, styled Cunzhong, was a native of Qiantang County (modern-day Hangzhou) during the Song Dynasty. In addition to his political career, he dedicated himself to scientific research, making significant contributions across a wide range of disciplines, including astronomy, mathematics, calendrical science, history, geography, biology, medicine, literature, and music. A prolific writer, Shen Kuo is best known for his *Dream Pool Essays*, a work completed in his later years. The book is organized into seventeen categories, covering topics such as stories, dialectics, musical temperament, mathematical image-number theory, ingenuity, craftsmanship, and medicine. Its comprehensive scope and depth represented the pinnacle of natural science during that era. Joseph Needham, the renowned British historian of science, described *Dream Pool Essays* as "a coordinate in China's history of science".

> 精研科技薄利禄　《梦溪笔谈》脱颖出
> 诸多技艺均展现　惠及后人光史书

Placing research above wealth or fame,
Shen Kuo's *Dream Pool Essays* earned lasting acclaim.
Showcasing skills in a wide array of arts,
His legacy shines bright in history's charts.

二十六、活字印刷（毕昇）

北宋庆历年间布衣毕昇，在雕版印刷的基础上，创活字印刷。先用胶泥刻一字一印，火烧后其变坚。依照要求，放进一个铁框内，将字排好后，浇以松脂、蜡等，用火烧令其凝固，成为一体。上用平板压平后，即可印刷。此后又有木活字、金属活字等。元代又发明转轮字架，使印刷术日益完善，大大促进了文化事业的发展。

26. Movable Type Printing

Bi Sheng, a commoner during the Qingli Era of the Northern Song Dynasty, revolutionized printing by inventing movable type, building upon the existing block printing technique. He began by engraving individual characters onto pieces of clay, which were then fired to harden. The hardened characters were arranged into iron frames according to the desired layout, and a mixture of pine resin and wax was poured over them. This was heated to fix the characters securely in place. Once leveled using a flat slab, the frame was ready for printing. Subsequent innovations introduced wooden and metal movable type printing. During the Yuan Dynasty, the invention of the rotating character wheel further advanced printing technology,significantly improving its efficiency and precision. These developments greatly accelerated cultural dissemination and the progress of knowledge.

改革创新民为本　毕昇承印实践勤
活字印刷创新技　推广文化惠世人

Reform and innovation should serve the people best,
So Bi Sheng pursued printing with tireless zest.
He invented movable type, a groundbreaking feat,
Spreading culture widely, his legacy complete.

二十七、燕肃研海（燕肃）

燕肃，字穆之，北宋时青州（今山东青州）人，曾任礼部侍郎，但他却热衷于精心观察和分析海潮的变化，写成《海潮论》，绘制了《海潮图》。他首先提出潮汐是随着日月的运行而变化的观点，还精确推算出每天潮汐涨落的时间，为航海及渔业提供了宝贵的资料。他还研制出一种新式的刻漏计时器莲花漏，还依据文献多次实验，复制了早已失传的指南车和计里鼓车。

27. Yan Su Studies the Sea

Yan Su, styled Muzhi, was a native of Qingzhou (modern-day Qingzhou City, Shandong Province) during the Northern Song Dynasty. Though he once served as Assistant Minister at the Ministry of Rites, he was deeply dedicated to the precise observation and analysis of tidal patterns. His work culminated in the treatise *On Sea Tides* and the accompanying *Sea Tides Chart*. Yan Su was the first to propose that tidal changes were governed by the movements of the sun and moon. He also accurately calculated the specific times of daily tidal rises and falls, providing invaluable data for navigation and fishing industries. In addition to his contributions to oceanography, Yan Su invented the Lotus Water Clock, a novel timekeeping device. He also conducted extensive experiments based on historical texts to recreate two long-lost inventions: the compass carriage and the range-finder drum carriage.

茫茫大海望无垠　　潮汐变化规律循
《海潮论》成又实用　航海方便乐渔民

The waters of the sea are boundless and wide,
But Yan Su tried to discover the laws of the tide.
His treatise was a priceless investigation,
To both fishermen and those in navigation.

二十八、黄婆纺织（黄道婆）

黄道婆，又称黄婆，元代女纺织技术家。松江乌泥泾镇（今上海华泾镇）人，少时出身贫苦，受封建家庭压迫，流落到崖州（今海南省三亚市），从黎族人民那里学到纺织技术。元成宗元贞年间还乡，着手改革纺织生产工具。传授有关轧花车、弹棉推弓、纺车和织机等技术，使松江一带的纺织业繁荣发展，对当时的植棉业也有一定的推动。上海在当年的港口镇曾建有"黄母祠"。

28. Huang Daopo and Textile Innovations

Huang Daopo, also known as Grandma Huang, was a prominent textile innovator during the Yuan Dynasty. She was born in Wunijing Town, Songjiang (modern-day Huajing Town in Shanghai), into a poor family and endured harsh treatment from her relatives. Seeking refuge, she traveled to Yazhou (now Sanya City in Hainan Province), where she learned advanced textile techniques from the Li ethnic group. Upon returning home during the Yuanzhen era of Emperor Chengzong's reign, Huang Daopo revolutionized textile production by improving tools and processes. She introduced innovations in the use of cotton gins, cotton arches, spinning wheels, and weaving looms, teaching these methods to others. Her efforts led to a thriving textile industry in the Songjiang region and significantly boosted cotton farming during that period. In recognition of her contributions, a "Mother Huang Temple" once stood in Gangkou Town, Shanghai, honoring her enduring legacy.

流落崖州生计惨　虚心学习本领添
还乡推广纺织技　历代尊崇享香烟

Grandma Huang endured hardship in Hainan,
A humble and diligent, skillful woman.
She brought textile crafts back to her land,
Revered through the ages by countless hands.

二十九、王祯《农书》（王祯）

王祯，字伯善，山东东平人。元代农学家及活字印刷术的改进家。他在旌德、永丰做县尹时，提倡种植桑、棉、麻等经济作物和改良农具。他认为农业是"天下之大本"。他所撰的《农书》，由《农桑通诀》《百谷谱》和《农器图谱》三部分组成，是我国第一部从全国范围对农业做系统论述的著作。其《造活字印书法》附于《农书》之后，是最早叙述活字印刷的文献。

29. Wang Zhen and the Book of Agriculture

Wang Zhen, styled Bo Shan, was a native of Dongping County in Shandong Province. A prominent agriculturalist and innovator of movable type printing during the Yuan Dynasty, he made significant contributions to both fields. While serving as the county magistrate in Jingde and Yongfeng, Wang Zhen promoted the cultivation of commercial crops such as mulberries, cotton, and ramie. He also introduced improvements to farming tools, driven by his belief that agriculture was "the foundation of the nation". His seminal work, *the Book of Agriculture*, is divided into three parts: *Know-How on Agriculture and Ramie, A Guide to Grains,* and *Illustrations of Farming Tools*. This comprehensive treatise was the first systematic study of agriculture on a national scale in China. Attached to the *Book of Agriculture* is *Movable Character Printing*, the earliest known document describing the technique, cementing Wang Zhen's dual legacy in agricultural science and printing innovation.

县尹提倡种粟桑　　关心农事多改良
一部《农书》喜呈观　促进生产农为纲

The County Magistrate advocated planting mulberry and grains,
Eager that technology would yield handsome gains.
His *Book of Agriculture* was widely disseminated,
Farming became the bedrock on which society was created.

三十、守敬多技（郭守敬）

郭守敬，字若思，元代天文学家、水利学家、数学家。顺德邢台（今河北邢台）人。曾任都水监兼提调通惠河漕运事，主持修治过很多河渠。与王恂、许衡等人共同编制了比以前精确的《授时历》。他通过实践创造改进了简仪、仰仪、高表、候极仪、景符和窥几等十余种观测天文的仪器，以及玲珑仪、灵台水浑等表演天象的仪器。他在全国设立了二十七个观测站，进行规模巨大的大地测量工作，重新观测了二十八宿及其他一些恒星的方位，均达到较高的精确度。

30. The Polymath Guo Shoujing

Guo Shoujing, styled Ruosi, was a distinguished astronomer, hydraulic engineer, and mathematician of the Yuan Dynasty. He was born in Xingtai, Shunde Prefecture (modern-day Xingtai City, Hebei Province). Guo served as the Capital Water Affairs Supervisor and Director of the Tonghui River, where he oversaw the repair and management of numerous rivers and canals. Alongside Wang Xun and Xu Heng, he co-authored *the Shoushi Calendar*, which was significantly more accurate than its predecessors. Guo Shoujing's ingenuity led to the creation and refinement of over a dozen astronomical instruments, including the abridged armilla, the projection semi-sphere, the gnomon, the pole-observing instrument, the solar observation tool, the Kuiji, the Linglong instrument, and the armillary sphere. He also pioneered large-scale geodetic and celestial surveys by establishing 27 observatories across China. His meticulous work redefined the positions of the 28 lunar mansions and other stars with unprecedented precision.

> 修渠治水利民生　发明创造均实用
> 精研天文多发现　科坛荣记郭守敬

Guo Shoujing dug canals and tamed the raging torrent,
His inventions and ideas were worthy of warrant.
A master of astronomy, his insights were vast,
In the halls of science, his name will ever last.

三十一、白英治水（白英）

明朝初年的民间水利专家白英，山东汶上人。明朝初年，因黄河决口，运河北段的会通河完全淤塞，不能通航。明成祖命工部尚书宋礼征发三十万人疏浚会通河，但水引不到北方去。宋礼到民间去访白英。白英主张在汶河的戴村修堤，引汶河水至水脊南旺，再分水流向南北。依此做法，使汶水急流奔腾至堤下鱼嘴处，被一劈为二，河水六分北流，四分南流，彻底解决了北段断流及水不足的问题，使朝廷每年向北可运送漕粮三四百万石。

31. Bai Ying Tames the Waters

Bai Ying, a self-taught water management expert from Wenshang, Shandong Province, rose to prominence during the early years of the Ming Dynasty. At the time, breaches in the Yellow River had caused severe siltation of the Huitong Canal, a northern section of the Grand Canal, rendering it unnavigable. Emperor Chengzu tasked Song Li, the Minister of Works, with mobilizing 300,000 workers to dredge the canal, but the effort failed to direct water northward. In search of a solution, Song Li sought advice from Bai Ying. Bai Ying proposed constructing a dam along the Wen River near Dai Village and diverting its waters to Nanwang, a high point on the watershed, where the flow could then be split northward and southward. His ingenious design funneled the Wen River's powerful currents to a forked outlet shaped like a fish's mouth beneath the dam. At this juncture, 60% of the water flowed north and 40% flowed south, effectively resolving the water shortage in the northern section of the Grand Canal. This innovation enabled the transport of 3 to 4 million dan of grain annually, ensuring the smooth operation of the canal and securing a vital lifeline for the Ming Dynasty.

实干方能显英雄　修堤分水运河通
千里良骥伯乐荐　躬请白英宋礼功

Only practical deeds make a hero eminent,
To this Bai Ying's dam is living testament.
A champion thoroughbred is a rare commodity,
Hence the Emperor rewarded Bai's patron Song Li.

三十二、《本草纲目》（李时珍）

李时珍，字东璧，明朝湖广蕲州（今湖北蕲春）人，著名的药物学家。他出身于一个历代行医的家庭里。年少时经常背着篓筐，随父兄到山中采药，成年后四处行医。他有感于前人对药物的记载不确、不全，便到处采药与古籍对照，纠正以前的错误，提出新的主张，著《本草纲目》五十二卷，190 多万字，成为对前人药物学总结的一部大书，此书的创新精神与内容已传遍全世界。

32. The Compendium of Materia Medica

Li Shizhen, styled Dongbi, was a renowned pharmacist of the Ming Dynasty, Huguang from Qizhou (modern-day Qichun County, Hubei Province). Born into a family with a long tradition of practicing medicine, he was immersed in the study of herbal remedies from a young age. As a child, he would carry a basket and accompany his father and brothers into the mountains to gather medicinal herbs. As an adult, he traveled extensively to practice medicine. Dissatisfied with the inaccuracies and omissions in earlier medical texts, Li Shizhen undertook the task of collecting herbs and cross-referencing his findings with ancient records. Through meticulous research and innovative thinking, he corrected past errors and introduced new concepts. His life's work culminated in the compilation of *The Compendium of Materia Medica*, a monumental 52-volume text comprising over 1.9 million characters. This masterpiece not only summarized centuries of pharmacological knowledge but also introduced groundbreaking ideas, earning widespread acclaim and recognition around the world.

自小采药满山爬　长大立志辨真假
《本草》二百多万字　成就世界药学家

From a young age, Li Shizhen roamed the hills to find,
Gathering herbs with a discerning mind.
Two million words filled his book so grand,
Making him a legendary pharmacist, known across the land.

三十三、霞客《游记》（徐霞客）

徐霞客，原名徐弘祖，明朝常州府江阴县人。小时家庭富裕，能博览群书。许多古今史籍、舆地志、山海图等过目不忘。青年时应试不得志，决心走出书斋，投入大自然怀抱，实地考察，取得实际知识。几十年来，他的足迹遍于国内十九个省市，其作品《徐霞客游记》不只记下各地山岭、江河、溶洞，以及对它们的勘察、辨讹，还有对各种种植的比较和鉴别，砂石开采等，是一部难得的地理学著作。

33. *The Travel Diaries of Xu Xiake*

Xu Xiake, originally named Xu Hongzu, was a native of Jiangyin County in Changzhou Prefecture during the Ming Dynasty. Born into a wealthy family, he had access to extensive education and developed a prodigious memory, effortlessly retaining knowledge from numerous historical texts, geographical records, and maps. After failing the imperial examinations in his youth, Xu resolved to leave the confines of scholarly study and immerse himself in nature, acquiring practical knowledge through firsthand exploration. Over several decades, Xu Xiake traveled extensively, leaving his footprints in 19 provinces across China. His magnum opus, *The Travel Diaries of Xu Xiake*, is far more than a travelogue. It meticulously documents mountains, rivers, and karst caves, offering precise observations and correcting earlier geographical inaccuracies. The book also provides insights into agriculture, plant identification, and mineral extraction, making it an invaluable contribution to the field of geography.

> 地学切忌纸谈兵　亲履方能辨识清
> 霞客立志行万里　一部《游记》舆地明

Armchair theorists can't define the land's true face,
Only through travel can one grasp its trace.
Xu Xiake journeyed ten thousand miles far,
His Travel Notes illuminated the map like a guiding star.

三十四、《天工开物》（宋应星）

明朝人宋应星，字长庚，江西奉新县人，曾任亳州知府等官职。但他却致力于科学研究，著成百科全书式的《天工开物》十八卷。涉及粮食、油料等农产品，手工业品的各种制造，金属冶炼、铸造、矿物开采等人类衣食住行所涉及的各种物质生产。宋应星对这些内容不但作了详细的记述、总结，还用了许多数据，实事求是地记述，是我国乃至世界上一部重要的科技作品。

34. The Exploitation of the Works of Nature

Song Yingxing, styled Changgeng, was a native of Fengxin County in Jiangxi Province during the Ming Dynasty. Although he served as a magistrate in Bozhou Prefecture, his true passion lay in scientific research. He authored the encyclopedic masterpiece *The Exploitation of the Works of Nature*, an 18-volume work that remains a landmark in the history of science. The book systematically explored various aspects of production, including agriculture (covering crops such as grains and oilseeds), handicrafts, metal smelting, forging, mineral mining, and other industries related to the essential needs of daily life——food, clothing, housing, and transportation. Song Yingxing's work not only provided detailed descriptions and summaries but also incorporated extensive data, offering an accurate and empirical account of the technologies of his time. This comprehensive and practical approach made *The Exploitation of the Works of Nature* a seminal contribution to science,earning recognition not only in China but also globally as a pivotal work in technological history.

身为知府重科技　　发明创新讲道理
《天工开物》多涵盖　三十六行均辨析

Song Yingxing valued science while being a magistrate,
Intent on the rule of reason and the need to innovate.
His *Exploration of the Works of Nature* covered wide,
With insights on all trades, it's a guide to abide.

三十五、《农政全书》（徐光启）

明末人徐光启，字子先，上海人。少时家道中落，从小参加劳动，获取了一些实际知识。中年考中进士，晚年升为内阁大学士。他虽居高官，却不多过问政事，而是致力于科学研究。他不只介绍了西洋的科学知识，修订了历书，还编写了《农政全书》。用科学方法总结了中国传统的农业知识和生产经验，宣传"人定胜天"的思想。《农政全书》还吸收了西方的科学技术，成为一部"总结农家诸书"的农业科学巨著。

35. The Complete Book of Agriculture

Xu Guangqi, styled Zixian, was from Shanghai in the late Ming Dynasty. Raised in a family that experienced a decline in fortune, he worked from an early age, gaining practical knowledge through manual labor. In middle age, he passed the imperial examinations and was eventually promoted to the position of Grand Secretary of the Cabinet. Despite his high-ranking official position, he was not deeply involved in political affairs, instead dedicating himself to scientific research. Xu was instrumental in introducing Western scientific knowledge to China, revising the imperial almanac, and compiling *The Complete Book of Agriculture*. This work applied scientific methods to summarize China's traditional agricultural knowledge and production practices, and it championed the philosophy that "Man can conquer nature". By incorporating Western technological advancements, Xu's book became a monumental work in agricultural science, often regarded as a comprehensive compilation of earlier agricultural texts.

内阁学士徐光启　　专心钻研新科技
《农政全书》倡农学　中西合璧多创意

Xu Guangqi was a cabinet secretary,
Who chose to concentrate on new technology.
His masterwork prioritises agricultural production,
Eastern and Western knowledge combined in its construction.

三十六、中西会通（梅文鼎）

梅文鼎，字定九，明末清初宣城（今安徽宣城）人。他接受西方传来的科学知识，著书 88 种。他在数学方面的《平三角举要》，系统阐述了三角的定义、定理、三角形的解法及在测量中的应用。他创造了球面三角形的图解法。他用勾股定理证明了《几何原理》中的许多命题，在多面体研究中纠正了西方学者的错误。

36. Having a Thorough Knowledge of both West and East

Mei Wending, who had the style name Dingjiu, was from Xuancheng (now Xuancheng City in Anhui Province), living during the late Ming and early Qing Dynasties. He absorbed scientific knowledge from the West and went on to compile eighty-eight books. His mathematical work, *Essentials of the Plane Triangle*, systematically expounded on trigonometry, covering its definitions, theorems, and applications in measurement. He also developed a diagrammatic method for spherical triangles. By *applying the Pythagorean theorem*, he was able to prove many propositions from Euclid's Elements and correct errors made by Western scholars in the study of polyhedra.

清初梅公善创新　冲破旧俗学洋人
精研三角供实用　勾股定理发新蕴

Mr. Mei was a creative scholar in the early years of Qing,
He broke down old customs, gleaning knowledge foreign.
Trigonometry he applied for practical purpose,
And revived the principles of Pythagoras.

后　记

　　《中华传统美德》中英文对照版历经 3 年多无数次的修订，终于面世。

　　从最先开始出版的中文版、英译版、汉语拼音版到现在的中英文对照版，可能后续还有其他的版本，《中华传统美德》多个版本的面世，前后历经近 10 年时间。这期间，除了我本人之外，各版本的作者、译者以及编者、出版机构等都付出了巨大的辛劳。耗费如此人力、物力投入出版，其实自始至终我只有一个目的：以通俗易懂、短小精悍的故事，彰显中华民族五千年优秀文明，历数中国古代优秀名人典故，树立仍可作为现代人参考的做人标杆，作为我们道德言行的规范尺度。

　　古往今来，社会的文明道德危机，大都来自于遗忘、舍弃乃至背弃自身的优秀传统文化。期待《中华传统美德》中英文版犹如一面历史之镜，所有人都可以看懂：正面是真善美，可以正衣冠，鉴言行；背面自然是假恶丑，是我们应该警惕反省的，是我们要竭力防微杜渐的。

　　本着这样的目的，我和一帮志同道合的老师朋友开始策划编撰一部可以得到传播的作品，用言简意赅、通俗易懂的方式讲好中国古代故事，最终我们将书名定为《中华传统美德》。为此，我特地邀请了山东曲阜师范大学孔子文化学院副院长骆老先生帮忙编撰。在英文翻译方面，特地延请西京学院外国语学院院长胡宗锋教授、西京学院外国语学院英语系副教授罗宾·吉尔班克及其团队人员做英文翻译。骆老在传统文化建设和传播方面做出过重要的贡献并多次获奖，胡院长及其团队精通中英文化，我期待以这样的作者团队打磨好书稿。我们一起商榷体例，最终拟定：以中华民族五千年文明史为时间轴，以史料和少数可靠传说典故为线索，按照十大美德选择典型代表人物，拟定 360 个典型人物及故事。每个人物故事中文部分不超过 500 字，每一个人物都用一首诗来总结其历史功绩，歌颂其美德，并对照翻译为英文。

我想，如果每天读懂并学习一个中国历史优秀人物，一年按 360 天计算，那我们读一本书的收获会非常大。

读书，本是一件快乐的事情。在书中我们可以找到：喜欢热爱的东西，能带来无限的快乐；找到心中疑难问题与长期困惑我们的答案；了解本行业杰出人物的观点方法与思想；见证感受历史人物与当代智者的思言行，与他们同呼吸共命运；能让我们了解自己先人的历史，掌握传统文化与社会常识；知道科学与社会发展的基本规律，拥有认知事物差异性的能力；拥有认识世界与辨别事物的能力，辨别真善美与假丑恶的能力。

人的生命是有限的，但人通过创造价值可以无限拉伸有限的生命价值。如果每个人把人生的每一件产品都做合格，甚至精益求精打造为艺术品，那么这样的人生应该是无限美好的。期待读书、读好书可以成为人生生产的重要营养机器。很多优秀的民族因为热爱读书学习，诞生了许多大师级的人物、工匠，他们成为民族与国家发展的栋梁。

2018 年以来，《中华传统美德》已经出版印刷几万册，其中向社会各界捐赠了 12000 册。希望通过这种宣传推广，可以让更多的人遵守国家法律，传承传统道德规范，老老实实做人，踏踏实实做事，做一个对社会有用的人。

作为一个喜欢并愿意以一己之力去终身践行中华传统美德的人，我期待让身边的人多学习了解几个传统美德故事，多传递几个人，让我们更多的下一代，在接受优秀传统文化的过程中，提高国民道德的自觉性，在心灵与行为上，有所改变与进步。我更期待通过接力传播中华优秀传统美德，产生更多的民族脊梁，让我们中华民族的伟大复兴早日实现。

同时，作为中英文对照的图书，我也期待这本书成为一座桥梁，让喜欢中国历史文化的外国人，对中国多一个了解的途径。

中国需要世界，世界更需要中国。

在《中华传统美德》中英文版这部书稿的出版过程中，特别感谢我的老师李裕民教授与裴效维先生的指导，神木职业技术学院与艾国院长的支持。在书稿的修订方面，感谢中央财经大学外语学院赵淑洁老师对英文稿件的专业审读、润色，感谢群言出版社责编老师提出的审读意见，更感谢李满意先生对书稿诸多历史细节错误提出的宝贵修改意见，从始至终对图书出版的支持帮助。

蔡向升

2025 年 3 月 20 日于（中国陕西）神木希文书院